ELGAR AND HIS PUBLISHERS

Elgar and his Publishers

Letters of a Creative Life

VOLUME 2
1904–1934

BY

JERROLD NORTHROP MOORE

CLARENDON PRESS · OXFORD
1987

Oxford University Press, Walton Street, Oxford OX2 6DP

Oxford New York Toronto
Delhi Bombay Calcutta Madras Karachi
Petaling Jaya Singapore Hong Kong Tokyo
Nairobi Dar es Salaam Cape Town
Melbourne Auckland
and associated companies in
Beirut Berlin Ibadan Nicosia

Oxford is a trade mark of Oxford University Press

Published in the United States
by Oxford University Press, New York

British Library Cataloguing in Publication Data
Elgar, Edward
Elgar and his publishers: letters of a creative life.
1. Elgar, Edward   2. Composers—England
I. Title   II. Moore, Jerrold Northrop
780'.92'4   ML410.E41
ISBN 0–19–315446–3

Library of Congress Cataloging-in-Publication Data
Moore, Jerrold Northrop.
Elgar and his publishers.
Bibliography: p.
Includes index.
Contents: v. 2   1904–1934.
1. Elgar, Edward, 1857–1934—Correspondence.
2. Composers—England—Correspondence.   I. Title.
ML410.E41A4   1987   780'.92'4   87–5557
ISBN 0–19–315446–3

Photoset by Latimer Trend & Company Ltd, Plymouth
Printed in Great Britain at the Alden Press, Oxford

CONTENTS

ILLUSTRATIONS

Volume 2 (*between pp. 666 and 667*)

Jaeger's response was clearly a letter of deep depression. He had been told his contributions would no longer be required for *The Musical Times*, and wondered whether he could earn money by coaching such singers as Clara Butt and Louise Kirkby Lunn. On top of all he suspected that others were supplanting him in Elgar's confidence.

V.S.Giov: Alassio
Jan 3 1904

Oh! most colossal & peculiar Mosshead!
Dear old chap:

I am very angry with you for writing such rot: I can't think why you think I've written to other people & not to you. I sent a line to Jos Bennett asking him (so as to save my poor pocket pounds sterling—really—of postages) to say what address wd. find me—which he *didn't* say I believe & I've sent cards to Pitt & Kalisch [who were writing programme notes for the Elgar Festival at Covent Garden].

Private

Now: there's nobody in my precious confidence more than you: this visit has been, is, artistically a complete *failure* & I can do nothing: we have been *perished* with cold, rain & gales—five fine days have we had & three of those were perforce spent in the train. The Symphony will not be written in this sunny(?) land. You must understand that when a wind *does* come—& it is apparently *always* on—it is no bearable, kindly east wind of England—but a tearing, piercing, lacerating *devil* of a wind: one step outside the door & I am cut in two, numbed & speechless: I have never regretted anything more than this horribly disappointing journey: wasting time, money & temper. Our house *is* comfortable & there is a decent English library here: Carice is here— Miss Burley brought her—& we are all happy together & only want weather!

I am trying to finish a Concert overture for Covent Garden instead of the Sym but am writing definitely *tomorrow* to the authorities so don't say a word yet.

I really get no news at all—even of the things which concern me: people at home are so curious about writing—a *p.c.* wd. tell what one wants to know: but most folk will not start writing abroad until they think they can see time to write a long letter: then they write a lot of envy of sunny skies (which we haven't got) warm weather (which we never feel—or seldom) &c.&c.—& then the[y] put 1ᵈ stamp on it & I have to pay 75c. Joking apart the amt. of excess postage I have pd wd. pay the rent: almost every post brings lyrics, libretti with *1.50* to pay on each!!

Cuss! I'm not stingy I trust but this awful waste of money is wretched. P.S. YOUR *letters are all right*!

Glad to hear about Köln &c &c. You will be there of course. *must* be there.

I've no Violin music, I'm sorry to say, at all worthy of your wife's attention—would I had—I don't think I shall ever write any now—in fact this cold air has completely withered any brains I ever possessed: but it *is* lovely when fine. & the local wine, at 3ᵈ a bottle is A I. but 'poor Tom's a-cold' frozen, & it will take months of sunshiny England to unfreeze me.

I had no idea 'Apostles' was to be done in N.York.

Don't be *down* about the M.T.—the actual *joy* of writing I think was not much to you—I know you ought to make some money by coaching people—Lunn & Butt for instance now. Do not bother about anybody's oratorio unless they *pay* you to look thro' it. It is not fair at all & you have been badly treated by too many.

Now good-bye & buck up old man & be a little lively & don't fret. If you were in the midst of this icy land you might feel *blue* but not in London

> Our kindest rgrds—no
> love to you all.
> Yours ever
> (with a frozen circulation[)]
> Edward.[1]

A few days later he announced the abandonment of the symphony to Alfred Littleton:

V. S Giovanni   Alassio
7/1/04

My dear Littleton:

One hurried line to say that I am greatly disappointed to find that it is impossible to complete the Symphony: the weather has been too awful to think of anything except keeping oneself warm. Now it is better but the winds are very trying.

I hope—for the Festival—to complete in time an Overture 'In the South' or some such title: I am working at it now & it is brilliant & cheerful—I will say definitely in one week if I can finish the score in time.

I hope this will in some sense make up for the non-appearance of the Symphony—I need not say how much I regret disappointing *you*

In greatest haste

> Yours ever
> Ed: Elgar

I am hoping to write to you about the kind business proposal in a day or two[2]

Two days later he was deep in the composition of the Overture.

His next communication was a postcard to Jaeger.

---

[1] HWRO 705:445:8676.   [2] Elgar Birthplace parcel 372 (photocopy).

Alassio
[*postmark*] 18 1 04

Thanks for the sc: *Lux Xti* which will come anytime during the next 3 weeks

So glad a score of Ap[ostles] has gone to N[ew] Yk. Richter will want one also I suppose.

I wish my friends wd. not gossip about me: Ettling wrote from *Weingartner* asking for first German perf[orman]ce of Sym. promising Munich Berlin &c. So I wrote to *W*. saying it wd. not be ready for him this season &c.&c. then apparently Ettling writes off to Pitt! Bless us all!

Weather better. E.E. d?

> Love to you all.
> Edwd.[3]

Bad weather returned. And when on 21 January an invitation arrived for Elgar to dine with King Edward VII on 3 February and conduct *Pomp and Circumstance* March No. 1 at a 'Smoking Concert' afterwards, they made their plans for returning to England. Elgar sent a card to Jaeger.

[*postmark*] Alassio
Sunday. 24 1 04

In with chill, cold, *rheumatism* &c.&c. East winds for a week enough to scarify the D——l!

I *think* I return this day week & hope to bring most of the new score for you to go on with: we shall be in good time only your people will have to look alive *as usual*. I return all the Ap. sc. proofs as they come &, as I hear no complaints from you, I conclude they reach you safely. Oh! this weather— what a delusion the world is.

> Much love dearest Moss
> Yrs ever
> Edward

I have, *at last*, started an eyeshade & find the benefit[,] thanks to your Nimrodic preaching.[4]

Alfred Littleton had written to remind Elgar that he had made no reply to the firm's proposal of an exclusive publishing contract. He also sent news that the concluding concert of the Covent Garden Elgar Festival would include the trio for the three soloists in Scene I of *Caractacus*.

---

[3] HWRO 705:445:8674.   [4] HWRO 705:445:8675.

V.San Giov: Alassio
Jany 24 04

My dear Littleton:

Very many thanks for your letter of the 16th.

I am hoping to start for England next Saturday & shd hope to bring most of the score of the new overture '*In the South*' (I am open to receive suggestions for a better title) so that as much hurry in preparing the parts can be saved your people as possible.

I have concurred in the suggestion that the Trio from Caractacus shall be given; this is a very fair specimen of my work.

I am very sorry I have not definitely replied to your kind suggestion: my first impulse was to accept offhand & only my *indefinite* entanglements with other publishers make me hesitate: I must talk these over with you as I don't feel entirely free in the matter: I need not repeat here my thanks to you & your firm for their splendid offer & it is only the want of *exact* knowledge of how much is expected of me in other quarters that makes me hesitate.

It is *fine* here now but a *bitter*, BITTER wind & I'm quite prostrate with cold (catarrh) rheumatism & all the things we left England to avoid, & I am under the doctor's hands: so much for my one attempt at real relaxation!

> Kindest regards
> Yours v sinc'y
> Edward Elgar

1 February found the Elgars back in London, staying with Frank Schuster. Next day Elgar wrote to Littleton of the engagement to conduct the Royal Amateur Orchestra before the King.

at 22 Old Queen st[,] Westminster
Tuesday [2 Feb. 1904]

My dear Littleton:

One line to say we are safely back in old England.

My rheumatism requires care & I have to rehearse tngt & conduct tomorrow night—R.A.Orch & [*illegible*]

The King expresses a wish that I should do this & the P[rince] of W[ales] has invited me to dine Marlboro' House to meet H.M. & accompany them to the Concert

This I must do!

But I shall try to get to Berners st to see you before I fly home to work

> Kindest regards
> Yours very sincy
> Edward Elgar

at 22 Old Queen st[,] Westminster
Tuesday [2 Feb. 1904]

My dear Jaggs:

One line to greet you—we arrived last night. My rheumatism must be cared for but I will try to come up. I can do any work here however.

In haste, with love

Yours ever
Edward[5]

On 3 February, the day of the Royal Concert, Alice Elgar noted in her diary: '... The Mosshead & Mr.Pointer came to see E. & brought some of the Score of the Apostles for him to see. The Moss stayed to lunch ...' And two days later: 'E. into town to Berners St. & Boosey. E. saw some of his Overture copied already.'

He had begun the scoring in Italy, and had handed the first section to Jaeger the day after his return. Through the following weeks of finishing the composition Jaeger and his men had to work flat out to get the score and parts of *In the South* ready in time for the première performance at the final concert of the Covent Garden Elgar Festival on 16 March.

Yet with all the care and attention he could receive, old hurts still rankled in a man of Elgar's insecure temperament. Apparently during his meetings with Jaeger, Elgar complained of his treatment fifteen years earlier, when he was a new man as far as London publishers were concerned—and when in truth he had little to offer them. Jaeger sent a reply to follow him home to Malvern.

1, Berners Street, London, W.
Feb 5 1904

Dear Eddward

I have just wired to you the Contents of the enclosed mad message. Being addressed to *Elgar Jaeger* I thought it was some 'joke' at *my* Expense. So I opened it. Hope you dont mind.

As for enclosed page [of *The Apostles* in German], Kindly settle which version of 'It is I' You prefer! Buths has written *both* in his copy & left it to us to choose. *Brause* chose; whether to *your* liking I know not. Kindly Return quickly

I say, what about the firm's offer? I thought you would come & discuss things *freely, friendlily & openly* with A.H.L. with whom you would get on *splendidly* if only you would be natural & say *exactly* what you *wish & dont wish*. He cant guess your thoughts. If anything in his propositions don't please You, just *say nay*; that's what he wants; not any beating about the bush. He is a fine fellow, is A.H.L.[,] and a gentleman with plenty of Brains of a very useful sort.

You would like him very dearly if you only Knew him. But you dont yet! Nor he knows *you*.

But there, what's the use to talking? only I'm awfully sorry that you two

5 HWRO 705:445:unnumbered.

always flit past each other like the Boy & Girl minding the Geese, in Andersen's fairy-Tale.

That we didnt do EVERYthing for you *15 years ago* is nothing.

Did any *other* firm in the world do *one tenth* as much? NO; they 'came in' after we had spent thousands making your name Known. You mustnt be ungracious & ungrateful for such help as the firm could *dare to* give You 'fifteen years ago'.

I say, it seems that Baughan did get the news about *no* Symphony from *me*, NOT from Kalisch. I am sorry, but we were talking about the disappointment in store & I said more than necessary, I dare say, & though I said that You [']*don't wish the news made public*' YET, B. abused the Confidence. I thought that perhaps Kalisch & he had agreed to publish the news simultaneously, but Kalisch does not seem to have been guilty of that.

My trop de zèle, as usual! Really, a Journalist has no soul & no conscience. I am very sorry for my misdeed

Ever yours
AJJgr[6]

Littleton had written again about the firm's proposition, inviting Elgar to join him for a short holiday, as they had not met during Elgar's days in London.

Malvern
Feb 8.1904

My dear Littleton:

I was indeed very sorry to miss you: I sent a message by Jäger, thanking you for your very kind invitation to Clacton—but I had too much to do & really cannot 'work' away from home.

I hope you are having good weather still—here it is dreary but I can shut myself up with my score &, above all, my *books*! (not account books)

I sent the first part of the Score (Overture) to Berners st—(I shd. say Jäger took it) & am sending more, & the remainder soon.

I will not say anything now about your proposition—as I said the only thing which makes me hesitate is my engagement with other publishers—which must in honour be fulfilled—however we will let it wait until we meet

Kindest regards
Yours v.sincy.
Edward Elgar

1, Berners Street, London, W.
Feb 11 1904

My dear Elgar.

Mr Clayton asks me to send you this Booklet with Swan Sonnenschein's letter. We wonder whether any of the poems may tempt you to set 'em for a partsong? Say page 13.

[6] HWRO 705:445:8711. The enclosure is missing.

Please send along more 'South' Score. Geidel is engraving the String-parts as far as we have them, but the Engravers can't do much till they see the *continuation*; the 'laying out' is affected thereby.

I hope you & yours are well in this 'Sunshiny' England.

If you want a GOOD quartet part for your [Malvern Concert] Club concerts, try the WESSELY quartet. They are *excellent*; I never want to hear better quartet playing. And let them do McEwen's quartet. I have heard it 5 times now & it is really fine & *musical*. Except you, no living composer would write a finer quartet. Let [Adolf] Brodsky [and his string quartet] do it. Mac is the most modest man in creation, a dear fellow. I'm delighted he has at last had a real success. This quartet is being done *again* (6th time) this or next week at Leighton House, and a P.F. Sonata now in hand (here) is quite big & fine, especially a large, and very impressive Funeral march. I 'discovered' him (as regards this firm) & am proud of him.

> Much love to you
> Ever yours
> AJJaeger[7]

The following evening Elgar posted to Novello pages 45–72 of *In the South* full score, and three days later pages 73–92.

As the Covent Garden Festival programme included the *Froissart* Overture, Novello wanted to have a piano arrangement in print. They had asked Otto Singer.

1, Berners Street, London, W.
Feb 16 1904

My dear Elgar,

Thanks for Score 'From the South'. The Copyist (Dodd) is hard at it, but the Engravers (Geidel) cannot do much until they see *more 'copy'*. So kindly let us have the Remainder as fast as you can, there's a good man. I suppose there is no possible chance of getting a *P.F. arrangement* out before the Festival? We ought to have something to sell to the audience, but I fear that is utterly impossible under the circumstances? Or have you a P.F. Score perchance? Geidel would engrave it in *a day* if necessary

Singer could not, alas! do the 'Froissart' overture (P.F.) in time (He is so full up with Strauss &c). So we were compelled to ask West to do it[.] He is very proud to undertake it & will do his *best*. You will see proofs soon & I hope you will *not* be disgusted with it.

There are no 'arrangers' in England it seems to me. But W. is no fool & he will do something decent.

You will get the Score of 'The Snow' in a day or two. Wood has already asked me for the Scores, So we must buck up. We are *overwhelmed* with work. The 'Apostles' Score & parts give us awful 'beans', & to supply the needs of the various conductors turns my hair grey. I am *bewildered*. For your next *big* work we must really arrange a 'close' time, say 6 months, in which to get out (in peace & order) all the Parts & Score. The way Pointer

[7] HWRO 705:445:8712.

checks everything takes a FEARFUL time. And the continual interruptions (sending the parts to various Rehearsals) upsets all our calculations & delays Engravers, printers, proofreaders &c &c.

I dropped into Queen's Hall for 20 minutes last night (after working here till 10). A *magnificent* House [for a performance of *Gerontius* by the new London Choral Society under Arthur Fagge], every seat taken; uninspiring performance I thought, though the Choir sang 'nicely'. [Marie] Brema rubatoed dreadfully & threw poor Conductor Fagge & orchestra out eventually. [Ffrançon] Davies with his 'mission' was dull I thought. He may 'feel' a lot but doesn't convey his 'feeling' to others.

Poor Pitt's songs last Saturday fell *dreadfully flat*, I grieve to say. Poor Percy!

We sold 100 Scores & 750 Analysis [of *Gerontius*] last night. I wish to goodness I had a 1d royalty on my stuff!

Yours ever
A.J.Jaeger[8]

1, Berners Street, London, W.
Feb 17 1904

My dear Elgarlein

I send you to-day the M.S. score of '*Fly Singing Bird*'[.] It seems that You have left out an *arco* either on page 14 or 16. We cannot decide which place may be the right one to place that mystic word upon.

N B! Kindly *wire* tomorrow morning '14' or '16' & we shall know what to do. Also Return the Score. Wood wants the parts by *Saturday*. Heaven knows why, for *I know* that his rehearsal is not till Saturday *week*

Anyhow, we have to do as he requests, & unless we get your decision about that 'arco' *at once* we cannot get the Cello & Bass parts ready. So I hope you wont mind the worry. Moral: Don't leave out important directions.

*N.B.*2! *more 'In the South' please*!

We are now reading the Vocal Parts (German) of the Apostles, but cant put 'Sitzen' & 'Stehen' in, 'cos Mr Wilson [the Birmingham Festival Chorus master, now preparing Richter's Hallé performance] (Manchester) evidently wont part with his vocal score even for a day. I wrote him a friendly letter weeks ago, c/o [the Manchester concert manager] Forsyth. He has never replied. I suppose you couldn't press him?

Shouldnt you also read the complete proofs of the German Vocal Score before we print? We are now approaching printing time & you haven't been worried with proofs yet (Boosey's wouldn't let You off so easily I know!) You needn't read every note, but, I fancy, You should put your imprimatur on the thing, Don't you think so? Please tell me.

I say, I dont see how Pitt & Kalisch [who were to write programme notes for the Covent Garden Festival] Ltd can have the Score of 'In the South' for

their Analysis. Dodd really cannot spare it a minute, unless over *Sunday*, (*if*
Dodd *doesn't* work on Sundays).

I fancy you will have to send them your themes, all nicely copied out for
'em. Lucky Beggars, they'll write a few pages & then charge everybody £1.1.0
for the use of their stuff & become millionaires. Talking of dear P.P. wasnt
the D[aily] T[elegraph] *beastly* about his *fine*, though ineffective (in the
popular sense) songs?

Ever yours
A.J.Jgr

Tell me. Do You wish to see the Full Score of Apostles again before we print?
We *ought* to get it out for the [Covent Garden] Festival—What about
preliminary notes, as regards orchestra (compare Gerontius) Anything
Special?

Lots of questions, you see. I wonder how many you will *answer*?[9]

[*postmark*] Malvern
[18 Feb. 1904]
Dearest Mosshead.

I wired as you said & return the M.S.Score of Singing Bird.
By this post pp.93–118 incl: 'In the South'.*
I am not well [—] chill [—] but will write fully tonight

Yours ever
Edwd.

*The *Schluss folgt*[10]

In the event Elgar was unable to answer Jaeger's questions until four days later, when
he sent a letter to accompany the final portion of *In the South* manuscript full score.

M'vern
22 ii 04
My dear Jaggs:

Please address the enclosed—I have mislaid the direction

By this post copy [of *The Apostles*] with *Rise & sit*; I think it's all right—
please return it.

Now. I send the end of the Overture—Buck up! Can the parts be ready by
this day week? Ha! Ha! ???

Yes: I ought to see the final proofs of anything—German &c. I'll just
glance over them.

Yes: there should be a preliminary page in the full sc. Apostles, similar to
Gerontius.

I've been 'liver-chilled' & not well & I shd. have written a fortnight ago, my *eyes* have been troublesome—but I dare not say so 'cos it gets into the 'pipers' & I have to write 120 letters to tell everybody & explain! Hence my silence. I may be in town soon & will of course let you know.

Tomorrow I am wanted at Manchester[.] They *seem* to be doing my things in several places.

I am writing to Pitt & Kalisch about the Overture:—I think you will like it—especially the *Romans*! (episode)

Goodbye, old Moss.

Yours ever
Ed:

Jaeger was horrified at Elgar's suggesting that the orchestral parts for *In the South* could be drawn out, printed, and returned within a week, and telegraphed to that effect.

[*WPS stationery*]
Feb 23.04

Dear Jaggs:

I was only choking (as Ettling wd. say) when I suggested Monday for the parts but be as quick as you can. I want particularly to have time to *play* through all the wind so as to have no mistakes in case rehearsing time is short.

Let me know when Mr.Dodd can see his way through to the end & I *must* have the score to check the parts with because, as usual, I have only a scrawl of a sketch which I can't read

The weather is better now & I took my bike out 100 yards to try it—it felt good

How is yours getting on? You should be a bounding terror on Muswell Hill by this time.

Atkins did Olaf a week ago: it *is* jolly to hear.

Much love
Yours ever
Edwardo.

1, Berners Street, London, W:
Feb 24 1904

My dear E.E.

You *shouldn't* frighten us thus! Poor Dodd is at Collapse's door & I had to wire him this morning that you had been 'joking'. Poor Dodd! He is doing his very best, & will finish as quickly as ever he can, but next Monday is too early a date, I fear. Geidel is going it prestissimo, but he has been delayed through receiving the M.S. *piecemeal*

—Here Mr Schuster came in to buy a Full Score Apostles, which he cant have yet—. Also: Dont frighten us again for noddings. It's bad for our nerves & livers. I'm grieved to hear Your eyes have been bad again & your liver too.

Oh dear! our livers! I have been & am still full of Rheumatism in back & arm (its painful to write even.)

You shall see Proofs of Parts of 'Snow' & 'Bird', & Revises of Scores in due course. I have sent you Apostles Score proofs to Settle queries & a batch (Second proofs) of German Vocal Scores. Also a Gerontius 'Directions' (re orchestra &c) page; which Kindly alter to suit Apostles Score. I fear you must do the finishing touches, much as I would like to save You trouble.

Thanks for Vokkel Score Apostles with 'Sits & stands', of which we shall make proper use. We will Return it anon.

Why the Divel have you a *silent Bar* in your Coda (Overture)? You WILL play pranks with Your Kodas. Foolish boy!, unsagacious neophite! Weber, Beethoven Wagner Knew better. It's never too late to do the wrong thing, however. But that there overture looks Dem fine allee Samee.

We will see to the E^b chord at End of Caractacus Trio. Shall ask West to Score that chord, & Rivers will get the parts in order for Covent Garden. I wont try it, thanks ofly.

I say, IF the C.G. people give you any tickets which you *cant* do with remember poor 'Nim'. I really can't afford to pay & I *should* like to hear at least the *overture*. You have no poorer friend now than

Yours ever
Moss.

oh! havent the New York critics gone for the Apostles!? The poor dears.[11]

Next day came a letter from Novello's editor E. J. Pointer—one of the very few to Elgar to survive.

1, Berners Street, London, W:
Feb.25th.1904
Dear Dr.Elgar

Will you kindly look at the enclosed (p.131 of [*The Apostles*] German vocal score)[.] You will see that Professor Buths does not consider the footnote necessary in the German score as the voices enter after a rest. He also objects to a pause over the quaver rest. The difficulty with us is that the Full Score— which does not contain the German text, but which will have to be used for German performances—contains the footnote. Would it not therefore be better to put it also in the German V.S. and make it agree with the full score? Otherwise I am afraid it will be rather confusing. Possibly Professor Buths has mistaken the meaning of the word 'sometime'. Please let me know your wishes as soon as possible.

Yrs.sincerely
John Pointer

---

[11] HWRO 705:445:8714.

By the bye is there any chance of your being able to provide me with tickets for the Festival? I hate to trouble you, but I should like to know as early as possible, as in the event of your *not* being able to do so, I must try & get a couple somehow.[12]

Elgar's reply to Pointer has not been traced, but he replied in a general way over *The Apostles* in his next letter to Jaeger.

Malvern
Feb 28.1904

My dear Jaeger: (the hunter)

I think you can go on with the full score Apostles—of course with English words only.

Now: the rehearsal of the new overture is in Manchester Wedy March 9th in the morning: so on Tuesday the parts corrected must be there.

Richter will be *here* on Friday—can I have the score back by that time? I *must*!!

Mr.Dodd could send me all the wind & score here by Wednesday morning *next* & I could correct them & the remainder of the strings as they come in.

I think it looks smoothe enough to work it so, nicht wahr? Wire me tomorrow (*Monday*) if the score & parts (wind & any strings ready) can be *here* on Wednesday because I must arrange with Mr Austin to come & help me as usual. don't put it off till Thursday if you can help it 'cos it cuts it so fine.

I think that's all.

By the way the bar's rest is practically ½ a bar: why quote Beethoven if you don't know the 2nd or 5th Symphonies for instance?

Yours ever
Jaeg*ee* (the hunted)

Oh! Title
Concert-Overture—'In the South' (Alassio)
    Edward E. Op.50.
(drop the *fantasia*)

In the South had originally been described as a 'Fantasia Overture', perhaps in homage to the example of Tchaikovsky.

During Elgar's absence in Italy, *The Musical Times* had published an article entitled 'Round About Soho' with references to Thomas Arne. Elgar heard of this, and in a few days of comparative leisure between finishing *In the South* and beginning proof correction he asked the editor about it.

    [12] HWRO 705:445:7638.

Malvern
Feb 29. 1904

My dear Edwards:

How are you? I hope well.

I gather that you had an article on Arne sometime ago—it must have *'happened'* when I was away & all my papers have evaded me. I should like to see the Arne notice: could you cause one to be found & sent here, I *might* write you something as an Appendix.

If this is any trouble don't proceed

Kindest regards
Yours sincly
Edward Elgar[13]

Unfortunately Elgar's 'Appendix' was never written, for he was overtaken by events in the preparation of *In the South*. First came an agonized response from Jaeger over the availability of the single manuscript score:

1, Berners Street, London, W:
Feb 29 1904

My dear Elgar

Your letter has taken my breath away! I wired at once to Dodd, & here is his reply. Moreover I consulted Oppenheimer who had this morning a letter from Leipzig saying that the completion of the proofs of the String parts would be dispatched tomorrow, Tuesday [1 Mar.]. This means that they won't reach us till Thursday [3 Mar.], which means that they *can't* be read, returned to Leipzig, corrected & printed & dispatched to reach Manchester on the 8<u>th</u>! [the day before the first rehearsal] so after much calculating & pondering we have come to the conclusion that the *only* thing to be done is to print *copies* for the Band from the *un*corrected plates; Supposing they dispatch these parts (sufficiently for the Hallé orchestra) on Wednesday [2 Mar.], they would reach us on Friday, when all our Readers & copyists (available) would devote themselves to checking the parts with the Score & copying the corrections into the *duplicate* String parts. You will not have to see them at all; there is no time, if they have to be with Richter on Tuesday [8 Mar.] or Wednesday. You really waited too long with your Coda. (I *don't* mean to suggest of course that You could have been any quicker!) Things have been driven so close, that it is *physically impossible* to do your behests. Even if I took away the Score from Dodd & asked another copyist to do the latter part of the Wind parts, things wouldn't be improved because the Engravers cant be quicker than they have been, & are. You see, an Engraver must see the *End* of a work to enable him to *lay out* sensibly. Otherwise he might run into a cul de sac; he might find himself at the End with a line or 2 lines de trop for the last page. How would you like that? no better than we

---

[13] BL Egerton MS 3090 fo. 81. 'Round About Soho' by 'Dotted Crotchet' appeared in *The Musical Times*, 1 Feb. 1904, pp. 81–7.

should! If Dodd is as careful as usual, I fancy you can dispense with the usual 'playing over', especially as Hans Richter is a genius at detecting errors quickly & you will be there too, to help. Anyhow, I am awfully sorry, but try as we will, we *cannot* do any better; So nothing remains to be done but play the oriental philosopher & say 'Kismet'.

As regards the Apostles we are in quite as dreadful a fit, but I won't worry you with that now.

I fear you must put Richter off on Friday, alas!, unless You interrupt Dodd in his work. We are in a fix allround, but the delay in receiving the M.S. is the only cause. We haven't lost a minute & have put everything else aside that could wait.

I have just telegraphed to you. Please thank Mrs Elgar for her Kind letter. I bow & am mute but not convinced. However, thats my furrin ignorance.

Yours, ever & this time very much disturbed over things

AJJgr[14]

Next day Jaeger wrote again, enclosing a note addressed to the firm by the copyist:

13 Bushwood Rd. Kew. S.W.
Mar.1/04

Gentlemen/

I am sorry Dr. Elgar wants the parts so soon—I have been trying to make a good job of them as regards 'cues'—and separate parts means nearly double work—I shall be able to send him a good batch of Score & parts in a couple of days to go on with—and I can finish it all off this week—but I hope I can finish it myself,

I am, Gentlemen
Yours very truly
William Dodd.

1, Berners Street (W.)
March 1 1904

Dear Doctor

Read Enclosed please. But isn't it more important that *we* should have the Score *here* to check the 8.8.6.6.4 Sets of Strings with, before we send *them* to Manchester next Tuesday? Since Dodd wrote this letter, I have written to him about the grave position of affairs & he has Returned the Coda (from 53) so that *another* copyist can work at that. That copyist started this morning. NB Kindly WIRE tomorrow whether the Score is to go (in bits) as per Dodds letter) to *you* or to *us*, as suggested above. Surely, Richter only needs a word or two from you on the Podium (Rostrum) before the Rehearsal to grasp your main idea, Eh? Anyhow, try as we will, with every Copyist 'going', &

[14] HWRO 705:445:8715.

being badgered[,] we can't do more than we *are* doing to get this thing finished in time for your Rehearsal on the 9th. Forsyth Bros write *Monday* the 9th[:] I hope to Buddha they don't mean Monday the 7$\underline{th}$.?

Yours,
AJJgr[15]

One other frantic note, undated, was sent about this time:

1, Berners Street (W.)

Dearie E.E.

I am still in my senses, but that there Festival & the other Apostles performances are driving me cracked. I am arranging for copyists galore[,] telegraphing wildly all over London & Suburbs, interviewing R Newman (Re Leeds performance) C.Garden Librarian, writing & wiring to Forsyth, Embleton[,] Schulz Curtius, Neil Forsyth, holding conferences with A H.L, Pointer, Brause, Copyists &c &c

Oh my *poor* head.

Ever yrs
AJJgr

To night I see 'Little Mary' for a change.[16]

Jaeger had been working such hours that his little daughter was in bed before he returned home and not yet awake in the morning before he left the house.

On 2 March Elgar telegraphed to Jaeger: 'Send everything here as soon as possible'.

1, Berners Street, London, W.

2/3.1904

Dear E.E.

Your telegram says 'Send EVERYTHING here & as soon as possible.'

Does that mean you do *not* wish *us* to read the String parts & copy all & any mistakes into the Duplicates. These latter (Enough for Richter's Band) will arrive, properly printed for performance, but *un*corrected, to-morrow, I hope, as already explained. Do *you* want to undertake to put the whole batch (8.8.6 6 4 or something like that) in order for the Rehearsal. If so we shall be delighted, but I guess you dont mean it. Only Your *Everything* means a lot.

So Kindly send a *wire* in the morning & explain [—] say *Wind only* & I know what you mean.

Hastissimo
Yours everissimo
AJJaeger[17]

[15] HWRO 705:445:8716.   [16] HWRO 705:445:8642.   [17] HWRO 705:445:8717.

Malvern
Mar 2:04

Dear Jaeger:

I think you had best send Score & pts here (as I wired)

I shall have Mr.Austin here all day on Sunday & we can then look thro' everything necy & if I have anything earlier I can prepare the way: strings had best come here also

Dr.Richter said rehearsal at 9.30 (or 10 I forget) on *Wednesday, 9th Mar.* So I leave here on Tuesday so as to be in time.

Don't worry—all will be well—I really can't help the Apostles printing!— could I now?

re overture again! I can do, & get done, checking of strings here & take 'em with me. but I hope they will be with me early.

Cold & more snow. Thank your stars you are in a nice snug office

Yours ever
Ed E.   PTO

The small score is lovely!

Next morning he telegraphed again:

Please send complete strings when corrected here Malvern Wells Station or by post[.] Wind as already arranged[.] I will take all to Manchester.   Elgar

1, Berners Street, London, W.
4/3 1904

My dear E.

Now listen:

By letter post *registered*, comes the Score, (In the South), all but 30pp or so, which Dodd can't spare yet. I have had these 130pp or so stitched loosely together. Mrs Elgar or Carice can easily unstitch them again to slip into their place the Dodd pages which in any case ought to reach you on Sunday morning. I send also in another parcel to Malvern Wells Station all the String parts (and *1 over* of each in case of accidents) corrected partly with the Score, partly with Dodd's copied parts only. These are the best we & Geidel could do, & I fancy it is a very creditable 'best' under such circs. I also send in this parcel the whole of the remaining Wind parts except those Corresponding with Dodd's portion of the Score; this Remainder as already stated, Dodd will let me have in Time (I hope) so that we can let you [have] them on Sunday morning. So You & Mr Austin will have a fine time of it. I wish I could be there to help you! (I play the jews' Harp & tooth comb)

There was absolutely no time to *duplicate* all the Woodwind. You must explain that to Richter. We have SEVEN(!) copyists busy up to their necks in duplicating Apostles parts for the Leeds Rehearsal at St Andrews Hall *here* on Tuesday next. Others have been on this In the South job. The continual

interruptions in the *Engraving* of the Parts (due to Rehearsals & performances here there & everywhere) delays & worries us *frightfully*. I shall insist
on a *close time* for Your next work, in which to produce all, Score & parts in
peace instead of in pieces. This present method is Bedlam, to be sure!

> Much love
> Ever yours
> AJJgr

I hope you have only *4* Horns at the Festival[.] We can get no reply from
Schulz Curtius. Forsyths say: 'the usual Double Wind', but I guess they mean
Wood wind. The Richter Concerts Bandlist gives only <u>4</u> Horns![18]

1, Berners Street, London, W.
5 March 1904
My dear E.E.

I have just wired to say that the Bulk of Score & parts of 'In the South with
E.E.' was sent last night by Pass[enger] Train to M.*Wells* Station, and
according to the R[ailwa]y people's story should be delivered to you *this*
morning. The Remainder will reach you this afternoon or Evening by
Registered LETTER *post*. Dodd has to duplicate the Harp part which he will do
to-morrow. I have asked him to send it straight to you to reach you *Monday*,
as I was afraid, if he sent it here first, we might not Reach you till after you
have left for Manchester.

So I hope everything is in good order & the stitching together of parts &
Score will be the worst evil you have to combat now. I think those printed
parts are marvellously correct, seeing that they were never Read before they
were printed!

Dodd wishes me to 'Remind' You about the Tympani part *not* being quite
playable (*muta*ble) in places

Well: Good luck to the new work! I wish I could be at the Rehearsal!

I enclose 3 pages of Dodd's M.S. containing suggestions[.] Kindly consider
them & destroy the sheet.

I hope everything is in order. I have done my best anyhow

> Ever yours
> A.J.Jgr.

I am glad you like West's arrangement of the overture Froissart. Please
thank Mrs.Elgar for her letter.[19]

[18] HWRO 705:445:8718.   [19] HWRO 705:445:8719.

Craeg Lea
Sunday [6 Mar. 1904]

Dear Mr Jaeger

A flying line to tell you from E. that he has recd. all safely, & has been very hard at work, dreadfully disappointed as Mr.Austin is rather ill & cannot come—E. is so much obliged at all the sending &c & is so glad to have it.

Best Grüssen
Yrs sicy
C.A.E.

As Elgar sat in his study correcting *In the South* parts on the very day he was to leave for Manchester and the rehearsal, Jaeger wrote again.

1, Berners Street, London, W.
March 8th 1904

My dear Elgar,

If possible please let us have the Score of 'In the South['] Back for a day or two so that we may bind it in a somewhat more substantial cover. But *if you dont think it necessary* (it will have to be *un*-bound again when the work is Engraved) never mind.

I had quite a *long* talk to Richter yesterday. Well, I heard amazing things.

I saw Hugh Blair also, who came specially to ask me whether one 'dresses' for 'Receptions' commencing at 10.p.m! For all the world as if I were a Society pusson, 'which is absurd', as Dear old Euclid has it.

You *will* have festive times next week! Don't let 'em spoil you, you 'dear, innocent guileless Child,' as dear old Hans calls you in his fatherly, loving way. Ta ta!

Your loving uncle
Nimrod

Oh! I have been asked by an *outside* firm to write a *Book* on Your music. 6^{d} Royalty[.] Tempting, but I fear I haven't the time.[20]

Grand Hotel, Manchester.
March 9: 1904

Dear Mr. Jaeger:

The time has now come when I think all familiarity between us should cease: the position I now hold—greatly owing to your exertions & friendship—warrants me in throwing you over.

Yours truly

Now, you old moss, read the other side.

---

[20] HWRO 705:445:8720.

[*verso*]

Dearie Moss:

What an old frump you are!—whenever anything of mine is to be done you beg me not to be conceited & not to forget my old friends &c.

I hope the letter on the other side, if you only had the luck to read it first, gave you a very proper & deserved fit.

You are an old *PIG* & deserve some such letter as the unfinished one on the other side [—] anyhow you always seem to be *expecting* it: be assured you wont receive anything of the kind from me. There is no fear that I shall forget anyone.

That overture is *good* & the Roman section absolutely *knocking over*. They read it like angels & the thing *goes* with tremendous energy & life.

Fanny Moglio [a musical figure humorously identified for Elgar's daughter] figures largely all through to Carice's intense amusement.

I am *not* bringing the Score as Richter wants it: it can be bound later—I don't want to alter a note except one or two false ones.

Don't bother me about conceit again—I haven't any except that I always resent any familiarity from outsiders & I *do* stand up for the *dignity* of our art—not profession.

> Ever deary Moss
> with love
> Yrs
> Edward[21]

The Elgar Festival at Covent Garden, attended by King Edward VII and Queen Alexandra, was an enormous success—with *Gerontius*, *The Apostles*, and on the final night, 16 March, a miscellaneous concert with *In the South* at the centre of it. The Elgars asked Jaeger to arrange to bind Canon Gorton's 'Interpretation' of *The Apostles* libretto for presentation to Queen Alexandra.

1, Berners Street, London, W.
18/3 1904

Dear Mrs Elgar

first of all: Congratulations, thousands of them from the bottom of my heart, upon the magnificent success of this memorable week. I called (in the M.T.) that Richter Concert years ago when the Variations were first done an '*Historical* concert'. I may call this week's doings with even more truth an Historical *week*. I guess there were few really more *gratified* men (or proud men) in the audience there than myself who have had faith for many years in E. & have spoken up when things looked desperate here. I was sorely tempted to rush into Your Box at C.G. & pour out my congratulations there, but 'Ehrfurcht hielt mich fern' as Poor Tristan says.

Well, it's over, and now for more works, better & gloriouser (that's lovely!) than ever.

---

[21] Elgar Birthplace parcel 343.

I saw Rivière's the Binders to-day & they'll do something nice & good by Tuesday. To bind in Vellum or silk would have taken *ten days to a fortnight*. They know the Queen's wishes & likes, & so they are binding C Gorton's Book accordingly

I'm half dead with a cold & want to go Home *at once* & to bed.

> With kindest regards
> & love to dear EE
> Yours sincerely
> AJJaeger[22]

And four days later:

1, Berners Street, London, W.
March 22nd 1904

My dear Mrs Elgar

By same post, carefully packed, we send the Gorton Book for Her Majesty. Rivières, the Binder, assure us that the 'white Levant' Binding & the monogram with crown are *exactly* what the Queen likes. They have quite recently bound a lot of Reference Books (a present from her Household on the High Lady's birthday) in this style, so, they say, its 'quite correct'

Mr Littleton hopes you'll like it. He is not very *greatly* in love with it, though in such matters we generally give 'carte blanche' to the Binders.

I hope you are well after the Exciting Festival Times. It *was* good of that dear Edward to come & see us last Saturday & I appreciate it greatly.

I wrote a LONG account of the Festival for the M[usical] T[imes], but friend Edwards has 'cut' me again quite furiously[.] He *is* an erratic. I daresay it *was too* long, but then—we haven't had many such Festivals!

In greatest Haste

> Yours, sincerely
> AJJaeger[23]

The special binding met with approval at Craeg Lea, and Alice Elgar wrote to ask where to send payment. Jaeger replied:

1, Berners Street, London, W.
March 25 1904

Dear Mrs Elgar

I am glad You like the binding of Canon Gorton's Booklet. We enclose Rivières' invoice & have charged E.E's account with the amount (£1.5.0) Kindly Return Rivières' account to us, as we shall pass it through *our* account, so that you need not bother to communicate with them. If you consider the amount high I must explain that these special Bindings are always charged at fancy price & this 25/- is the *Trade* price, to us[.] Rivières' told me personally that the price to you would have been about 35/-!

---

[22] HWRO 705:445:8795.   [23] HWRO 705:445:8794.

Kindly ask Edward to Return us the Full Score of the Overture as quickly as possible so that we may proceed with the Engraving & the arranging of a P.F. version.

Things seem stale & flat after the Festival. I shall look forward to Cologne now, though I *fear* they won't send me this time.

> With Kindest Regards
> Yours sincerely
> A.J.Jaeger

P.[S.] I *was* surprised to see the interview in what E.E. called 'that Rag'— alias 'the Daily news'—this morning. My love to him & congratulations upon having surmounted a prejudice against an excellent newssheet of high principles.[24]

The *Daily News* interview with Edward Baughan was one of many given by Elgar at the time of the Covent Garden Festival. The Baughan interview had taken place on 18 March, the day on which Elgar met the Prime Minister Arthur Balfour. The possibility of a knighthood was broached, 'but matters were not in train for a definite announcement'.

Another part of the Baughan interview concerned the question of musical copyright. A parliamentary bill, long needed, was just then in process of being watered down, as Elgar said to his interviewer:

'While the world of fashion, as well as the middle classes—the real supporters of music—were honouring the art at Covent Garden, at the other end of the town our legislators were heaping indignities on it by whittling down the Musical Copyright Bill by inserting clauses which will make it quite inoperative.

'Why, of all the arts, should music be supposed to have no rights?' asked the composer, knocking out his pipe with savage emphasis. '. . . A pirate may photographically reduce the score of an important work which has taken perhaps a couple of years to write and sell it at an absurd price, and there is no practical remedy . . .'

He had also discussed the matter with the Prime Minister, and one fragment from that discussion survives in a later report of Elgar's conversation with a friend:

Told Arthur Balfour (among others) that he dared not raise the question of music in 'the House' as he would not be taken seriously. A.B. agreed.[25]

One man who took it very seriously indeed was William Boosey (1864–1933), a cousin of Arthur and George Boosey, and now a principal in the firm of Chappell and Co., who specialized in light opera and ballads and were thus easy prey for the pirates. He was forming a Musical Defence League, and wrote to Elgar on the day the Baughan interview appeared:

[24] HWRO 705:445:8793.
[25] Conversation of 2 June 1914 with Elgar's old friend Hubert Leicester, recorded by Leicester's son Philip immediately afterwards. (MS).

Chappell & Co., Ltd.
50, New Bond Street, London, W.
March 25th, 1904.

Dear Dr.Elgar,

Permit me to congratulate you upon being the first of the representative English musicians to express your opinion with regard to musical piracies, and the indifference of the attitude of the House of Commons towards the big art and industry of music. Although, naturally, more serious music does not sell in the same quantities as do ephemeral publications, the principle involved is equally vital to composers like yourself and the composers who write the lightest form of music.

I may add also that it has been a subject of frequent comment in the House of Commons, both during the second reading of the Bill and the proceedings in committee, that apparently the whole of the representative composers of this country appear to be absolutely indifferent as to whether we succeed in our present fight for the protection of musical copyright or not, since not one of them has put in an appearance at the house nor made any communication to the press.

Mr.Geo.Boosey indicated to me yesterday that you had suggested giving expression to your views in the papers, and I told him I considered it would be of the utmost benefit if you did so. You will quite understand that composers of your weight and position exert immense influence, both amongst Members of the House of Commons and the public generally, and, as a matter of fact, the present battle has been fought entirely by Messrs.Boosey, Messrs.Francis & Day, and ourselves, not even the composers of the lighter music, which has been pirated over and over again, having come forward to take a prominent part in the necessary agitation for the promotion of the Bill.

While I am writing to you, Capt.Basil Hood, oddly enough, called on me to-day to ask whether you would care to entertain the idea of writing an opera, not necessarily a grand opera, but something perhaps more in the style of the opera comique in Paris. Would you care to meet him and have a chat with him? If so, I could arrange that we might meet at lunch, and discuss the subject.

Yours very truly,
William Boosey.[26]

Basil Hood was a leading writer of light opera libretti, having collaborated with Sir Arthur Sullivan and Edward German. But this was not Elgar's interest, and there was still the question of an exclusive contract with Novello. (In April there was an approach from the Italian publisher Tito Ricordi, which also came to nothing.[27]) Elgar did agree to appear at a large protest meeting over musical copyright which Boosey was organizing at Queen's Hall in July.

Another of the interviewers who visited Elgar before the Covent Garden Festival was Rudolph de Cordova for *The Strand Magazine*. He had asked pointedly about

[26] HWRO 705:445:2914.   [27] HWRO 705:445:8190–1.

Elgar's plans for continuing *The Apostles* trilogy. The magazine interview was not to appear until May. Alfred Littleton asked to know just what Elgar had said. From Frank Schuster's house on the last day of his stay in London, as he was about to go to Leeds to arrange further performances there, Elgar replied.

Westminster
Mar:22 1904

My dear Littleton:

I see the *Note* at the beginning of the Apostles is *nearly* all right—I think if (in the second par) we say 'the *sequel*' instead of 'second part' that wd. be sufficient alteration—this I think is required for the full score & possible reprint of the 8vo. score.

As to the announcement concerning the completion I have told the Strand that I am reverting to my *original plan* & there will be three oratorios: each complete in itself but connected with each other. The second will deal with the 'Mission' of the Apostles & the establishment of the Church among the Gentiles (as mentioned in the Note)[,] the third part will shew the 'fruition' of the whole—Antichrist[,] Judgement & the final reward.

That is about what I said.

I'm just starting to Leeds.

Kindest regards
Yours ever
Edwd.Elgar

And two days later, from home:

Craeg Lea, Wells Road, Malvern.
Mar 24 04

My dear Littleton:

I arrived home last night & find a weary pile of —— begging letters, libretti & M.S.S. of young composers for my kind revision!!

I find amongst these the enclosed papers: I think they are out of date & we have settled what is to be done—but you may want them for reference.

In haste
Yours v sincy
Ed:Elgar

Private. I have been to Leeds & think all is now smoothed [in regard to promises Elgar had made to produce a Symphony at the Leeds Festival of 1904 which he could not now fulfil]. Also the Philharmonic [Society in London] propose Gerontius next March & the [Leeds] Choral Union Apostles (again) and Gerontius on *two successive nights*!!!

Craeg Lea, Wells Road, Malvern.
March 25. 04

My dear Jaeger:

Thanks for your note concerning the pts &c of 'In the South' which I daresay will reach me during the day: you shall hear, bless you, if they don't.

I wrote to Mr Alfred yesterday & will you bring to his notice the possibility of German performances of the Overture.

I received several letters more or less chiding & angry because somebody suggested that the future Symphony might be produced at *Essen*!

Weingartner sent word through his friend Ettling that *he* wd. gladly produce it—if he had the first performance, in Berlin & Munich—I understand he would do this with the Overture. Anyhow he (and Ettling) will be in London soon & you can settle that:—I suppose no introduction *cd.* be better possibly. So don't go suggesting it in Deutschland to other folk until Weingartner has been to London.

As to the Essen Concert before I can say anything about going & leaving all terms out of the question for the moment, can you tell me what time in the year they want me—what orchestra &c. they place at my disposal & what rehearsals.

In great haste,
Yours ever
Edward E.

Steinbach *may* want the Overture first[28]

1, Berners Street, London, W.
March 26th 1904

My dear Edward E.

Thanks for letter. I'll write to Hehemann & let you know his reply re Essen Concert. However that Rumour come about *I* certainly *never* suggested such a thing, because I know the importance of Weingartners position. At the same time *if* you wanted to give a special éclat to Your Essen concert & *draw German conductors to it* I see no reason why *You* shouldnt give the first *German* performance[.] Even Weingartner couldnt grumble at *that*, See? Anyhow, you might reserve for *your*self the first performance in the populous & artistic *Rhinelands*, in other words the West of Germany. Of Course if Steinbach should want it for the Cologne Festival, *nobody should say him nay* for that would be *very* a [sic] important event.

But let's have everything back so that we can start Engraving at once

We get lots of Enquiries for PF. Solo Arrangement. Who shall do it? Singer, Schmid, West? the *quickest* chap should have a look in[:] Schmid says he could devote Easter week to it

28 HWRO 705:445:8678.

I sent You yesterday MacEwen's things just to show You that this quiet, modest fellow is capable of doing better Work than those Anthems which he wrote for us under protest more or less.

> Great Haste
> Ever yours,
> AJJgr[29]

Craeg Lea, Wells Road, Malvern.
Mar 31 190[4].

My dear Jaeger (Moss).

On p.179 please put f instead of B. (Ger. voc. sc. *Apostels*) Buths put the B as the note was *tied* in the original.

This 'bogen' of 16pp was stuck in at the end of my advance copy accidentally.

By post I send full sc: of '*In the South*'. I cannot suggest anything about arrangements for P.F.   Simrock used to do piano solo
> piano duet
> 2 pianos

at once & one thing advertised the other: I have craved (for other people who write to me 1000 times) for Variations P.F. duet but it's not done.

As to 'preface' in German by all means leave it out except about the Augener's tune.

The 3 stave sketch of the overture is of no use to anyone & there are only a few bars here & there readable.

Some wretched paper has announced that I am in Bournemouth—haven't been & am not going—but I am inundated with begging letters from there!

Life is not all joy!

> Much love
> Yours ever
> Ed: Elgar[30]

1, Berners Street, London, W.
March 31st 1904

My dear Elgar

Thanks for Letter & Score received this morning; we shall lose no time to get the P.F. arrangement & Score out. P.F. Duet no doubt later on, when Score is *engraved*. Also Variations, I'm *sure*[.] Have a *little* more patience [—] I Know you have had *much* already.

I want to drown all people worrying you with letters & things

You ought to be left alone with your work: you have enough in hand for 10 years! When will You do it if these fools & Rogues & snobs worry you so? I

---

[29] HWRO 705:445:8721.
[30] HWRO 705:445:8679. Elgar dated the letter '1903', but the contents make clear that it was written in 1904.

am jealous for your work's sake. I'll promise to worry you as little as ever possible, but to work hard & get things out quicklissimo possibile.

Hehemann (Essen) writes they would like you on *October 29* for their next Season's first concert. He of course wants the *Symphony* if possible, & wonders whether an orchestra of about 70 players. He mentions nothing of Terms yet but 'wants to Know[,] dont you know'. I daresay we could easily get a larger orchestra; these things are cheaply managed over there, & it strikes me that N[ovello] & C. might engage a few extra 'Strings', Eh?

In any case I take it he couldn't get the Symphony, as you refused to let Leeds have it?

No time for more just now.

Cheer up in this nice cold weather & Keep warm!

> much love
> Yours ever
> AJJaeger[31]

Throughout these years Elgar received a constantly increasing volume of enquiries from conductors proposing to perform his works. Now the subject was once again the notorious change of note-values in *The Banner of St George* which had already occasioned correspondence with McNaught in March 1900.

Craeg Lea, Wells Road, Malvern.
Ap 1: 04
My dear Moss:

I am sending all the parts of 'in the South' (& should like to send this pen also out of my sight—it has just gone wrong!) You are a pig of many kinds—I thought I cd. keep all the stuff for a month or two!

Good boy! come and drown, burn & scarify everybody—I truly *am* worried by letters out of all belief. Oh! that letter U in Banner of St.George.—cannot something be done? it's as clear (to me) as daylight but a Lady writes (PROFESSIONALLY) 'I am preparing an orch: to take (somewhere) & the conductor wishes to take at letter U the minims—dotted—as in the previous bars: I think, & *have rehearsed the orchestra*(!!!!) to play at U the dotted minims in the time of the preceding* crotchets(!)'
                    Think of that.
Ask West about it

*as the dotted minim goes at about M.M.84 you see the minims at letter U will come out (according to this lady) at MM $\underline{\underline{252}}$. I shd. like to see that orchestra after playing it at that speed. I wd. set up an undertaker's business in the locality.

I cannot say anything about Essen: I am *not* keen to go: the Symphony cannot be done there anyhow.

---

[31] HWRO 705:445:8722.

I am up to my eyes in work & a shrimp has had a baby in my tank & between times I have to nurse them in a teaspoon! It all takes time.

Yours ever
Ed Elgar

P.S. Proof of Ger: libretto goes to 1 Berners st.
I hope you are at home (your pretty home—so glad I've seen it) having a rest.[32]

Craeg Lea, Wells Road, Malvern.
Ap 6 04
My dear Jaggs:

Very sorry to hear of the children & hope it will soon be better—these things *will* come & generally at the most inopportune times.

Proofs enclosed—I think Mr Alfred knows all about the continuation of the *Apostles* [trilogy]

Just going out—tired of life.

Yours ever
Ed:[33]

Next day Elgar went to London, principally to attend rehearsals for a performance of *Gerontius* to be conducted by Felix Weingartner at Queen's Hall on 9 April. On the morning of the performance Elgar called in to Novello's offices to offer tickets to Jaeger.

1, Berners Street, London, W.
Ap 9/ 4
My dear Jaguar:

I have my two tickets for the circle—they are waiting for *you* at Langham Hotel: please use them.*

I am unhappy.

Yours ever
Edward

* this is a brute of a pen.[34]

Jaeger took his wife, and after the fine performance they had tea with Elgar and Alfred Kalisch at the Langham Hotel.[35]

While Elgar was in London, Alfred Littleton had pressed him again about the exclusive publishing contract. Returning home to Malvern, Elgar sent this response:

[32] HWRO 705:445:8680.
[33] HWRO 705:445:8681.
[34] HWRO 705:445:8682.
[35] The performance is described in a letter of 10 Apr. 1904 from Mrs Jaeger to Alice Elgar (HWRO 705:445:8812).

Craeg Lea, Wells Road, Malvern.

Ap 13 1904

My dear Littleton:

Referring to our conversation last Thursday night please do not think me very absurd or fickle, but on talking over the rough idea of your kind proposal with my friends they strongly dissuade me from accepting it: I have, naturally, not gone into minute particulars with even those whose advice I sometimes seek, but the general principle does not appeal to them & I must ask for further time to consider.

Mr.Embleton is bringing his chorus to London for Mdlle Ravogli on June 3 & would place the chorus at my disposal for a performance of the Apostles—he first suggested a 'philanthropic motive' might arise & he wd. place the chorus at the disposal of a concert giver. He *now* is anxious for his people to be heard in my work on June 4. I don't want to conduct as I am tired, but if you think anything of the idea—the chorus wd. cost nothing— you might let me & Mr.Embleton know: one's thoughts naturally run to Wood & his orch.

> Kindest regards
> Yours sincy
> Edward Elgar

The orchl. rehearsal [for the Royal Choral Society *Apostles*] is very satisfactory at the A[lbert] Hall.

Next day Littleton wrote to Elgar—not a reply to Elgar's doubting letter, but written as if he had not received it (which perhaps he had not yet).

1, Berners Street, W: *Copy*

April 14,1904

My Dear Elgar

In reference to our various conversations and my letter addressed to you at Alassio about terms for publishing your works I understand that you agree to all my suggestions—with certain exceptions—and it will now be an advantage perhaps if we exchange letters & so confirm the arrangement.

The understanding is that you will offer us all future works of yours which you wish published and we undertake to publish all the works you so offer to us.

In the case of choral works we agree to pay you a royalty of 25% on the marked price on all copies on which we have been in the habit of paying you a royalty. On Orchestral works we agree to pay you the same royalty on the orchestral Score and on any pianoforte or similar arrangements which may be published.

The question of a payment down before royalties become due must I am afraid be left for arrangement in each individual case—but as we have now several precedents to go on I do not think this can cause any difficulty. It is understood that this arrangement leaves you free to publish with Messrs. Boosey your four Military Marches, a second Overture in connection with your Cockaigne Overture already published by them—an Opera in case Messrs.Boosey should provide you with a libretto by Mr.A.C.Benson which you agree to accept—and a Cycle of Songs to be written for Mr.Plunkett Green [*sic*] With regard to this last we might try & persuade Mr.Plunkett Green to allow us to publish the Cycle of songs—but of course the decisions to be left to him.

I think I have mentioned all important points and shall be glad to hear that I have stated things as they are already in your mind.

> Yours very sincerely
> Alfred H. Littleton.

In case either of us should at any time wish to discontinue the arrangement— the best plan perhaps would be that the agreement should last for five years certain—each of us having the right to give 12 months notice of our wish to cancel it at the end of five years or any future date. This would suit us all right & I hope you will find it good also.

On 25 April (a day Elgar was in London for a further visit), Littleton noted:

Elgar Agreement
April 25.1904

Saw Dr.Elgar about 12.30 when he promised to write accepting my propositions contained in letter dated April 14/1904

But once again Littleton had to wait.

The correspondence with Jaeger continued steadily from Jaeger's acknowledgment of his pleasure in hearing *Gerontius*.

1, Berners Street, London, W.
April 13 1904

My dear Elgar

You might just look over enclosed proofs, the LAST I hope. If nothing amiss (I shall have those 2 missing s's corrected) you will kindly tear them up. We don't want 'em back.

I say, You have woke 'em up last Saturday!!!! We talk of nothing else wherever we go. Here is MacEwen writing to me: 'I think there is a d— lot of big stuff in it & it is all very fine & *musical* & much of it is as strong as it is beautiful. Altogether the biggest thing that has been done in England, or for that matter on the Continent of latter years'; which is what some of us said four years ago, Eh?

I Saw Weingartner this morning[.] We have promised him the first performance of the overture in *Munich & Berlin*. The parts are already in Leipzig. The Score [*In the South*] will be sent directly Schmid brings the first installment with his [piano] arrangement. Weingartner is clamouring for that there E.E. *Symphony*:

I hope your Baby Shrimps & Tadpoles are happy & well.

Young Wendt just come back from Buenos Ayres. He has been *Cattle Ranching* there at £2 a month. He looks splendid, bronzed & strong[.] Now he wants to start music again, poor Chap.

> Much love
> Ever yrs
> AJJgr[36]

The water creatures, in which Elgar took a lifelong interest, were cultivated partly for his thirteen-year-old daughter Carice.

On the question of arranging *In the South* for piano, Elgar had been approached by Emil Kreuz (1867–1932), a German-born viola player with the Hallé Orchestra who was also a composer.

Craeg Lea, Wells Road, Malvern.
Ap: 14: 04.

My dear Jaeger:

The orchl. rehearsal was very good & only one error in the score which is also very good considering the complications.

Mr Kreuz (Emil) who you know is a first rate musician, asks me if I am settled with an arranger for P.F.—of course *I* am not & I think if there's anything to do he might have a chance: anyhow I should be sure to like his work if the firm (I am telling him to apply to the firm) wd. like him to do anything.

I was going to write to West only he's away, thus:—Dr Sinclair points out that a passage like this [in *The Apostles*]

is confusing on acct of the pause for 2nd.Clar coming where it is: I think so too & the 2nd.Clar. rest shd. be omitted & the passage printed I°. & stems down.—I have not copied it exactly but this is the sort of thing he means. Tell Mr Pointer for future scores of the ~~Brit~~ English school!

Sinclair wants to keep the score he is using today for a space with a view to suggesting some organ arrangements—may that be?

> Yours ever
> Ed:Elgar:*

*Wisdom approacheth.
ΑΘΗΝΑΙΟΝ[37]

[36] HWRO 705:445:8723.   [37] HWRO 705:445:8683.

For Elgar had just been elected to The Athenaeum under its rule providing for special invitation to 'persons of distinguished eminence in science, literature or the arts, or for their public service . . .'. He had been proposed by Parry and seconded by Stanford.

1, Berners Street, London, W.
April 15 1904
My dear Elgar
 'Athenian'!

I congratulate You *sincerely* on the Honour which has just been thrust upon ye. It *is* an honour more precious, it seems to me, than a Dr degree or a Knighthood. Well done You, I mean the A. Club. You *are* getting on. What more *do* you want? I am delighted that the Athenaeum fogies have honoured themselves by electing You. You will take an interest in *owls* now, Eh?

We'll bear Kreuz in mind. He called the other day. Pointer has arranged a lot of the Variations for *2 P.F.*'s; may he send You some of it for your condemnation?

Pointer & West have *noted* what You say about *Pauses* in Scores. Selah!

Let Sinclair keep the Score by all means, *but* if you expect *him* to make the arrangement, You will wait till *Doomsday*. He is the most procrastinating Beggar over Business matters that I *ever* saw. Perhaps *you* can stir him into activity

       Ever yours
       A.J.Nimrod
       (Foolishness retireth)

Oh, I say, poor Hehemann [who was to write a Guide for the coming German production of *The Apostles* at the Lower Rhine Festival] is quite upset because he can't trace in the Full Score of the 'Apostles' the *Passion* motif of which I speak in the Analysis[.] He means at 20 (see Vocal Score page 15). You will remember that you told me to put a B♯ into the Chord

to show the theme . But alas! & Woe is me, in the Full Score the Clarinet has the Angel theme right enough, but that B♯ to complete the Passion (suggestion) appears only in the *lower octave* in the Bassoon. I thought you would have given that B♯ to the Second Clarinet or an oboe or something else thats *nice* & *Elgarish* (synonymous terms, you Know!) Wont You, before the parts are *finally printed*? Please drop me a card that I may put Hehemann out of his agony of suspense. He has nearly finished his Apostel 'Führer'.

           A.I.I.[38]

[38] HWRO 705:445:8724.

Craeg Lea, Wells Road, Malvern.

Ap 16 1904

Dear Jaguar:

No I can't alter the bit at 20. Quite unnecessary—the *harmony* suggests the passion theme coming in quite enough & your quotation (I haven't a copy!) will shew what it arrives at: it's all right & intended & conformable!

So tell dear Mr Hehemann to go on with his *Führer* & not be *furious*

Yours ever
Edwd.

The Apostles was a fine performance at Birmingham [on 14 Apr. with Sinclair's Birmingham Festival Choral Society.][39]

Jaeger sent a proof of the introductory note for the German edition of *The Apostles*. Elgar returned it corrected to Alfred Littleton:

The Athenaeum

Ap 22 1904

My dear Littleton:

Only time for a line to accompany the paragraph. I wd. have written it long ago but I thought it was for the M[usical] T[imes] & not for the 8vo sc[ore] &c.

However the enclosed as amended will do very well

In greatest haste
Yours sny
Edward Elgar

The Athenaeum

Ap 22 1904.

My dear Jaguar:

Thanks for your letter with the par[agraph]: I have revised it & returned it to Mr.A.H.L.

No time for more[.] I strenuously tried to get Macpherson's Ps[alm 137] in the Leeds Choral Union Gerontius programme—tell me if you hear if it *is* included. I hope so.

Curiously, I have had a letter from C[harles] M[acpherson] just while I was talking his Ps. into people.

Yours ever
Edward[40]

At the end of April the Elgars went again to Canon Gorton's Morecambe Festival, where the *Greek Anthology* part-songs were performed with great satisfaction. Meanwhile Jaeger, busy preparing *Apostles* material for its German production, fell foul of Alice Elgar by hinting that the new oratorio was not perhaps quite comparable to *The Dream of Gerontius*.

[39] HWRO 705:445:8684.   [40] HWRO 705:445:8685.

1, Berners Street, London, W.
2/5 1904

My dear Elgar,

Kindly mark on enclosed proofs *what* drumsticks (timpani, Gran cassa or tamburo piccolo) you require to beat the unoffending Piatti with. I'll do the German translation if one is necessary.

I feel quite 'hurt' because dear Mrs.Elgar charges me with 'not following the development of Your Genius'! I cry with Marke: '*Nix* das! Tristan; Dein, Tristan, *mir*'!? Tant de bruit pour une omelette? I thought I 'followed' the Apostles pretty well. Has any critically reliable person appreciated it more & said so in more honest words? (I dont count hysterical sentimentalists who would Rave in similar terms over Perosi if he came along again, dressed in priest's garb.)

I count those part songs a *very* small 'omelette' by the side of 'The Apostles'. Verb.sap. I say, Prof Schwickerath of Aachen (do you Remember meeting him at that jolly lunch at Mrs. von Weise's?) is making inquiries about the Material for the Apostles. I hope he will do the work at *Aachen*!

F Steinbach asks me whether you are not coming to Cologne. In fact he says 'Surely Dr E *is* coming'. We have referred him to *you*, as I fancy You told me You would *not*.

I have not yet been asked to go & 'Report'. I am not anxious & dont think they'll send me.

Dear Dorabella is in town once more enjoying her sprightly self.

Yours ever
AJJgr[41]

1, Berners Street, London, W.
May 10 1904

My dear Elgar

Have you by any chance the Glockenspiel-Side Drum-Triangle *part* of 'In the South' by you at Craeg lea.

It has mysteriously disappeared & we cannot imagine where it can be, unless it was *not* Returned by the C.Garden people (& Rivers did not check the Returned parts carefully,) or You Retained it to 'prepare for Engravers'. Kindly have a look round your study & drop me a postcard 'yes' or 'no'. In the latter case we must have another part copied out by Dodd before next Wednesday's rehearsal. There's plenty of time, thank goodness.

Is Muriel Foster singing at Cöln? I see she is singing in Gerontius at Cincinnati on the 13th inst. How she will get back from there & to Cologne by the 21st Heaven only knows. Anyhow, it's a close shave & if she should catch another cold on the journey, who else will sing her part?

[41] HWRO 705:445:8725.

I have just decided *not* to write that book about you, & have written to the Editor of the Series accordingly.

> Ever yours
> A.J.Jaeger.

I suppose you havent the *proof* of the Full Score of 'The Snow'? That also is lost, strange to say & West is reading another proof.[42]

Langham Hotel, London.
Wedy night [11 May 1904]

My dear J.

I came up unexpectedly last night & have been busy all day or I would have come in—I am hoping to call at No 1 [Berners Street] about 12 o'c tomorrow.

I *don't* remember anything of Glock: &c. *or* the proof of '*Snow*': my wife has read your letter & will reply to it (she has just sent it on here).

I don't know *anything* about Köln—except that they've asked me to go: I am quite tired of being supposed to 'Bless' performances of my things which are not 'coached' by me or my advice is asked when it is too late to make any change: but if I *must* go I must—only I don't want to go at all.

> In great haste
> Yours ever
> Edward

My teeth are the cause of my unhappy visit![43]

Elgar's behaviour over going to attend this great German tribute to himself and his music was typical of his nervousness over exposure. He lingered in London as the time for departure drew closer. On 16 April Alice came to join him. Next day: 'E. very unsettled about going. A. to Berners St. Mr.A.Littleton urged going.' So they went to Cologne on 19 April. There he attended Steinbach's rehearsals and the performance on the 22nd. Elgar wrote from his hotel:

Dom-Hotel, Domplatz, Köln
May 26.1904

My dear Littleton:

I had hoped to have written to you long ago, that is to say, on Monday but I have been seized upon & could not find a moment: now I am in bed with a chill and *must* scribble a line to say that it was a splendid performance of Sunday & was rapturously received. Steinbach was splendid, the orchestra the same, chorus very good & the soloists were not bad. Steinbach wanted to talk to Jaeger but there was never any opportunity what with rehearsals & *feasts* & concerts so I persuaded Jäger, with much difficulty, to stay yesterday. S. wants to conduct the work in London with *his* orchestra & I

---

[42] HWRO 705:445:8726.   [43] HWRO 705:445:8686.

think it might be done with Mr.Embleton's assistance. We have had a glorious time but this is rather a sad wind up. I hope to see you in London

Kindest regards
Yours ever
Edward Elgar

(*In bed*).

Returning home at the beginning of June, Elgar sent a new direction for the confusing cue in *The Banner of St George*:

Craeg Lea, Wells Road, Malvern.
June 3. 04
My dear Jagpot:

I shd. think the enclosed ought to definitely settle the point: I shd have preferred $\rnode{}{}\ \cdot = \rnode{}{}\ \cdot$ of preceding bar. but anything that is understanded will do.

We arrived home last night & I am in a whirlwind of epistolary tomfoolery which will take me a month to clear. If a lucid moment comes I'll try & write some sense.

I've made a sweet looking blister on my face! tried Menthol for the pain (toothache) &, as that did not work, made a compress of eau de cologne which has persuaded the skin to come off in reams. Will you make an offer for it to bind the Apostles in?

Yrs ever
Edward[44]

Then at last he signalled his acceptance of the Novello exclusive contract.

Craeg Lea, Wells Road, Malvern.
June 7:1904
My dear Littleton:

In reference to your very kind letters of April 14th & the propositions contained in them I write now to accept your offer. That is to say in future for five years certain & after that time so long as we may wish—the engagement, that is, to be terminated by six months notice on either side, I send you everything I write (except the things already promised to Messrs.Boosey which I enumerate below) & you pay me a royalty of one fourth of the marked price & a sum 'down' for new works such as you have been in the habit of paying for in addition to royalties, or on account of royalties.

The exceptions are the following works:—
remainder of the Pomp & Circumstance Marches.
the pendant to Cockaigne
the Cycle for Mr.Plunkett Greene

---

[44] HWRO 705:445:8687.

an Opera *if* Mr. A C Benson finds the libretto
and a possible addition to a Song they have for Soprano making it a portion
of a cycle. These are the things I mentioned to you.

I am sorry for the delay but I have had some trouble to find your letters
which were left here on our departure for Köln.

> With kindest regds
> Believe me
> Yrs v sincerely
> Edward Elgar

Plas Gywn, Hereford [*deleted*]
June 10 1904
My dear Littleton:

I forgot to say that the [Covent Garden] Syndicate sent me a cheque for 50
gns—for 'the first performance of the Overture'—as this is a reasonable fee &
sent in the usual 'festival' way I had much pleasure in accepting it

> Ever yours
> Edward Elgar

By now Elgar had decided to leave Malvern altogether and go to live in Hereford,
some twenty miles westward. There they had found a larger house called Plas Gwyn
on the edge of the city.

Craeg Lea, Wells Road, Malvern.
Monday [13 June 1904]
Dearie Jag:

Don't forget I want to see parts & Score & PF. [arrangement] of 'in the
South' & shall just have time to revise 'em before moving—we have been very
busy making arrangements & shall flit soon.

At the Mount [Miss Rosa Burley's school] (bei Carice) they have German
measles so we may miss our jog while this slight ailment is in progress.

Love to you—you old sinner: when do you take holiday?

Frank Damrosch [the New York choral conductor who produced *Gerontius* there] came here to see me & it was a great pleasure to see him

> Yours ever
> E.[45]

1, Berners Street, London, W.
14/6 1904
My dear E.

I hope to send you the whole pack of proofs (Score & parts) *to-morrow*.
J.E.W[est] has been worrying through them these last 6 weeks! I hear from
Mr A.H.L. that you are going to spend some days at [Littleton's home in]

[45] HWRO 705:445:8688.

Barnet. That will give You a nice chance of reading everything quietly in pleasant surroundings, far from the madding crowd of autograph hunters & interviewers.

I say; I never told you, that '*Pfingsten* WAR' is quite correct after all. It's unusual to say the least. I think it stands for '*war gekommen*', as one always says '*es* ist Pfingsten' '*es* war Weihnacht', &c; & thus, by transposing the *order* of the words: 'Es war Pfingsten' should be turned into 'Pfingsten war *es*', or war's, See?

I had a dreadful fall off my (your) Bike last Saturday; nearly broke my collar bone! Took the nerve out of me pro Tem.

We take *no* Holiday this year. Shall stay at no.37 & play with the dear, amusing bairns & *work*.

Have even refused to spend a week at Wimbledon with Kind friends. (Holdings)

A.Schmid has been ill with a slight attack of Diphtheria[.] Hence delay over P.F. *Duet*. Received it Yesterday. Will send it you tomorrow.

> Much love!
> Ever yours
> Nim.

I hope *Carice* hasnt German measles? If yes, I trust she will soon be well again.[46]

Elgar did not in the end visit Alfred Littleton. When the proofs of *In the South* were ready, Jaeger sent them to Malvern.

1, Berners Street, London, W.
June 15 1904

Dear Eddward,

I send you the whole pack of proofs & M.S.S. 'In the South' by Rail to-day: *Score, Parts*[,] *P.F.Solo* & *P.F.Duet*, as they all want your Kind & honourable attention. It will be a stiff job for you, but then I know you likes it! Saw dear old Hans Richter this morning. Kindly thank Mrs Elgar for her letter & 'Zeitschrift', of which I'll try to make some use.

> Yours ever
> AJJgr

Are you doing the 'Dreamers' now or the Symphony?[47]

'Dreamers' referred to a setting of Arthur O'Shaughnessy's Ode beginning 'We are the music makers, And we are the dreamers of dreams', which had been announced as Elgar's next project in the *Daily News* interview in March.

In point of fact, he was working at neither project, but travelling at that moment to Durham to receive an honorary degree. Meanwhile Jaeger sent a request for information of a different kind. He referred to a small portrait medal of Elgar in profile, by the sculptor Percival Hedley.

[46] HWRO 705:445:8728.   [47] HWRO 705:445:8727.

1, Berners Street, London, W.
June 21 1904
My dear E.E.

Here is a funny request: the Editor of a paper called 'The Troubadour' came & asked me what *decoration you wore in your coat* on that Saturday afternoon when Weingartner conducted the 'Gerontius['] at Queen's Hall!! I said You had no decoration, as far as I know except Your great works & Your friends' love, but he said he *saw it himself* when you were *'called'* & a correspondent has now written to them to 'know, dont you know'. So I suggested Hedley's Medal which I showed him. Anyhow, *they want to Know.* Could You drop me a Card by Thursday morning? I daresay you will say 'let him go to the D——l'[.] Anyhow I promised to write to the Johnny on Thursday. Perhaps You have got the Garter or the Star of India after all! one never knows. It would be just like an original cuss like You to wear the garter as Your chest protector

How are you. I have the Hump badly.

> Ever thine
> AJJgr.[48]

Craeg Lea, Wells Road, Malvern.
June 22 1904
My dear Moss:

Don't be a fool! I wore *no* decoration at Queen's Hall or any other time. Just back from Durham.

> Much love
> Yrs ever
> Edward

I mean I wore *nothing* except my clothes. I never do[49]

Yet this was disingenuous, for that very day he had received and accepted the offer of a knighthood. Two days later the news was published with the Birthday Honours. Amongst the hundreds of congratulations received were letters and telegrams from Charles Volkert of Schott's,[50] George Boosey,[51] Boosey's engraver Leighton,[52] F. G. Edwards of *The Musical Times*,[53] W. G. McNaught,[54] Alfred Littleton and his wife,[55] Novello's copyist William Dodd,[56] and two from Jaeger—one from himself:

Happy and delighted beyond words thousands congratulations upon honour most nobly earned   Moss Nimrod Jagpot August[57]

and one from his family:

Sincerest congratulations to our dear meister best truest friend and sturdiest helpmate   Hoch sollt Ihr Leben   Dacapo dreimal hoch   Nimrod family[58]

[48] HWRO 705:445:8729.
[49] HWRO 705:445:8689.
[50] HWRO 705:445:5130.
[51] HWRO 705:445:5311.
[52] HWRO 705:445:5352.
[53] HWRO 705:445:5358 and 8230.
[54] HWRO 705:445:5188.
[55] HWRO 705:445:5338.
[56] HWRO 705:445:5229.
[57] HWRO 705:445:5360.
[58] HWRO 705:445:5361.

Craeg Lea[,] Wells Rd[,] Malvern
24 June 1904

My dear Mr. Jaeger

I must send one line at once to one of the very warmest & best of friends & his Frau Gemahlin to thank you both for yr. kind, warm words & congratulations. I am so thankfully happy at my dear E. being appreciated & honoured & it gives us both the keenest pleasure. I shall feel really quite 'fluffed' up if you say such nice things to me! Over 50 telegrams already, our hearts are very full at so much affection & kind thoughts of friends.

E. is gone to the Golf Club but will write soon

Yr. friend of you both
C.A.Elgar[59]

1, Berners Street, London, W.
June 28 1904

My dear Lady Elgar,

It was very kind of you to write me a Card after my Telegram. I know how *fearfully* busy You must have been & must be still, to reply to your many friends. I have spared you & Edward—Beg Pardon *Sir* Edward (that sounds good, *Sir Edward Elgar*!) another *letter* of Congratulation. You know how happy I am to see one honoured by his King & Country, in whose gifts & great qualities of head & heart I have believed for so many years. May you both live long, happy years to enjoy the honour. Nobody that ever Received a similar honour can have deserved it more thoroughly, for no one can have lived a life more earnestly devoted to the highest & best & purest in life & in art

We were all *jubilant* when I opened my paper on the morning & read out *the* news. I jumped up from my chair, & leaving my breakfast in the lurch, rushed to the Piano & played *the* Tune in 'Pomp & C. No. 1 in D'. The Bairns marched around the Table, the grown-ups sang, & my neighbours, who had read *their* paper, Knocked on the wall in Rhythmical approval & sympathy. *Such* Doings!

Well, I write now, not to worry you with these petty details, but because a certain Mr Glover, the Director of the Cincinnati Festival Chorus[,] has asked me to write & learn whether he may take the liberty of calling upon Sir Edward (at his, Sir E's) pleasure. You will remember that at the Cincinnati Festival they did *Gerontius, Variations, Grania & Diarmid, Sea Pictures* & the *Marches*. Almost an Elgar Festival! Mr Glover trained the Choir, & is now on a visit in England.

Could E.E. *possibly* see him? He would not take up much of his time. He would bring greetings from Th[eodore] Thomas, Elgar's chief champion in the States & from many admirers. He seems a nice young fellow & not too much Yankee. Try & persuade Edward to let the young man pay his respects. It will do him (E) no harm & will hardly bore him.

Now I must go home.

With my kindest regards to the new Knight* & his Lady

Yours sincerely

AJJaeger

*I hope he wont look a '*Black* Knight' when he hears of my worrying request![60]

A few days later Elgar sent a postcard photograph of himself and his eighty-one-year-old father, taken by his niece May Grafton (1880–1963):

[*postmark*] Hereford

[1 July 1904]

I rode over to tell father the news June 23:04[.] He is at Stoke. One of my nieces made this.

We are at Plas Gwyn Hereford now, henceforth & for ever

E.E.[61]

Another congratulation had come from the head of the Boosey firm, Arthur. But it went on to deal with the big protest meeting over musical copyright:

[60] Elgar Birthplace.   [61] HWRO 705:445:8690.

295, Regent Street, London, W.
June 24 1904
My dear Elgar

First let me offer you my hearty congratulations on the Birthday honour conferred upon you—an honour that will please the whole musical world & may you live long to enjoy it with more Honours to follow.

The Great Public Meeting of the Musical Defence League is to be held at The Queen's Hall on Monday Ev: July 4 at 8 o'ck.

The Duke of Argyll has kindly consented to take the Chair and we have formed a Committee of the following Gentlemen—I ventured to add your name & we can have an informal meeting on the Monday afternoon to tell you what will take place—There is to be a Committee Meeting at The Royal Academy next *Tuesday* evening at 5.30 but I told my cousin [William Boosey] I did not think you would be able to come.

The Committee is made up as follows
Sir Hubert Parry
Sir A.C.Mackenzie
Sir Edward Elgar
Sir Charles Stanford
Mr.F.Cowen
Mr Stephen Adams
Mr.McMann
Signor Tosti
Mr.E.German
Mr.Lionel Monckton
M.Messager
Mr.Sidney Jones
Mr John Murray
Mr.Scutton K.C.   ?Sculton
Mr.Fenwick [Musicians Co.]
Mr [David] Day
Mr.L.Stewart [Leslie Stuart]
Mr.Clayton [of Novello]
Mr A.Boosey
Mr W.Boosey

We hope you as the leading composer will make a speech—Let us know if you will kindly do so.

Are we to have the pleasure of seeing you & Mrs.Elgar next Saturday to Monday at The Cedars—We shall be proud & pleased if you can come.

Yrs. very sincerely
Arthur Boosey[62]

Elgar did not accept Arthur Boosey's hospitality, but he did appear at the Queen's Hall meeting on 4 July. It was the eve of his investiture, and he met a vociferous reception. In response, he made a short speech:

[62] HWRO 705:445:5133.

'My life, ladies and gentlemen, has, as you know, been a self-made one. London called me from my country home, and *you* have made me what I am. But you call other composers from their homes to you, and you allow the law to deprive them of their livelihood. That is all I have to say'—and he retired quietly to his chair.[63]

Next day, after the ceremony, he wrote to Alfred Littleton.

Langham Hotel, London.
July 5.1904
My dear Littleton:

I am so very sorry to have missed you yesterday a.m. & again today.

I found I *could* not leave my wife to struggle with the moving alone so I stayed near the scene of wreckage.

We are getting into the new house shortly but it seems to be very comfortable: at present all ideas of music are very distant I fear.

Kindest regards & best thanks for your kind congratulations on the recent event

Yrs v. sny
Edward Elgar

[*typewritten*]
Plas Gwyn, Hereford.
July 11th 1904
My dear Jaggs:--

I have at length found time to look through all the stuff & send it back with my blessing; observe the following words of weight.

1.) One harp part will do with the addition of the marks 'a 2.'—'I° 8va' etc. it shd be however 'I^{ma}' I suppose & not 'I^{mo}', eh? All the tempi marks want to be added to the parts as they now appear in the skoughrre.

As to the pinoa, that shd have been P I A N O arrgts the solo will do if one or two little things I have marked are put right: as to the duet, I tried it thro' with Atkins & find it too full in the heavy parts, a great deal of the quiet parts come out very well but it's not piano music by any means fo [*sic*] for which, Praises be! albeit I & the Publishers will starve over in consequence.

We are far from settled yet but it is very lovely here & thi[s] weather magnificent, you must come soon.

Our love to you in which Troyte, who is heey [*sic*] joins mildly.

Yours ever,
Edward.[64]

Invited to dine at Marlborough House with the Prince and Princess of Wales on 14 July, Elgar made plans to visit his London tailor for final alterations to his court suit.

[63] *The Pall Mall Gazette*, 5 July 1904.   [64] HWRO 705:445:8691.

Plas Gwyn, Hereford.
Wednesday [13 July 1904]

My dear Littleton:

I have come up to London this evening & shall be in town over Thursday: I am bidden to a party at Marlborough House & have sundry sartorial eccentricities to try on: should you be disengaged on Thursday morning I would gladly call say at 12. or so.

I shall be at the Langham tonight & tomorrow night

> In great haste
> Yours ever
> Edwd.Elgar

Only a few records of Elgar's royalty payments from other publishers survive, but two of them came close together just as the exclusive Novello contract began to operate.

54 Great Marlborough Street, London W.
July 11th 1904

Sir,

At the request of our Leipzig firm we beg to hand you herewith statements of the sales of your compositions, together with cheque value £4/19/8.

Trusting you will find the same quite in order,
We are, Dear Sir,

> Yours faithfully,
> for Breitkopf & Haertel
> Otto Kling[65]

Plas Gwyn, Hereford.
July 20 1904

My dear Boosey:

Many thanks for the cheque on account which safely arrived a few days ago.(50£)

As to 'Land of Hope' in the Lancers I think your judgement is good & leave you to decide: the [Coronation] ode is naturally dead & I shd. think the Song won't go much farther.

I am only just home & find, as usual, nothing but letters

> Ever yours
> Edward Elgar

P.S. I have not forgotten your kind offer of the Blind for my Study—only I have five windows & cant settle which one shd. have the choice! the three together in the bay don't want a blind I think so I shall have to decide which of the two others is to be honoured.[66]

---

[65] HWRO 705:445:2916.   [66] Boosey & Hawkes archives.

As Novello published most of his major works, however, Elgar's correspondence
with them increased over proposals for performance, now coming in very quickly in
the wake of his knighthood. Several of the proposals involved appearances in the
United States where Elgar was very reluctant to go. He asked Littleton and Clayton
to 'manage' these enquiries.

Hereford
July 26 1904
Dear Jaggs:

I hear via Ettling that Weingartner will do *Alassio* in Berlin & Munich.
I hope the 'stuff' will soon now be thro' the press.
I sent back the M.S. Duet arrgt and the proof of Solo.
Oh! the weariness of these arrgts.

Your ever
very dismal
Edward

*Spur.

a knight.   67

A month into his residence in the new house and place, Elgar was feeling the effects
of dislocation.

Plas Gwyn, Hereford.
July 30. 04

My dear Jagpot!

I send back the title [for *In the South*] in anr. cover.

I haven't written because everything is dull & goes on slowly: & I am tried very much liverwise & am wofully short of money. I really think I must take some Violin pupils again: only, as I have not touched it for so long, I should have to begin once more with elementary ones! Such is life & I hate, loathe & detest it.

Write & tell us how you all are & where you go for your holiday.

Don't forget Steinbach has the Overture down early for Köln—I wish you wd. write to him about it & tell him the 'stuff' will be ready soon.

Yours ever
Edward[68]

Without any creative project before him just then, Elgar fitted the so-called 'Canto popolare' (actually his own tune) from *In the South* to Shelley's verses *In Moonlight*.

Plas Gwyn, Hereford.
Augt 2:1904

My dear Littleton:

Here is an adaptation of the melody which people liked so much from the Overture. The words just suit the mood & are, of course (?) non copyright. I wish you wd. get it out quickly as I think it should be quite popular: it wd. be necessary to issue several keys at first.

I am also arranging, quite easily, the same air for Violin, Cello, Viola &c. Let me know what you think of them

Kindest regards
Yours ever
Edward Elgar

Plas Gwyn, Hereford.
Augt 5:1904

My dear Littleton:

Many thanks for yours: I'm glad you like the look of the little song: it's a pity for the tune to be 'wasted' in the Overture & there is no reason—if it takes—that the thing should not be as popular as 'Salut d'amour'.

I therefore send arrgts for 1 Violin & piano
                              2 Cello & piano (same accpt.[)]
                              3 Viola & piano (in C)
and a sketch of an arrgt for *piano solo* in E^b: this last is always the difficulty. I think the Violin & piano arrgt. shd be done for small orch also: & this I will

[68] HWRO 705:445:8693.

do if you say yes: but the first thing to decide is whether *that* v. & p. arrgt. will *do*.

All these differ from the Song necessarily[.] As to the Song I don't see who is to sing it at Leeds—*anyone might* & I could orchestrate it in a suitable way in a short time.

I have written to Mr.Chester as you suggest & will let you hear the result.

Yours ever
Edward Elgar.

The great thing in a case like this 'Canto popolare' is to have several arrgts out at once—one 'helps' the other so much: I got quite worldly & commercial over 'Salut d'amour' which alas! belongs not to me at all, or to you!!

Plas Gwyn, Hereford.
Augt 6 1904

Dear Jagernaut:

I could not write yesterday—was away.

You will perhaps be seeing some arrgts of the *Canto popolare* which ought to be of some use: the keys chosen are more suitable I think than the original: the piano solo is always the trouble & I'm not sure if my arrgt will do—it *looks* better, & there is more in it than Schmid's—see pp 16–18 of his arrgt. piano solo [of the entire *In the South*].

It's all very well to talk to me about doing Sextetts & Symphonies & all the things I *want* to do, but tell me what & who is going to keep a roof over our heads? nobody thinks of that.

Yrs ever
Edwd.

I note all you say about U.S.A. & wait to hear more from the fountainhead—I have talked to Mr A.H.L. about it [—] by pen I mean.[69]

Plas Gwyn, Hereford.
Augt 7: 1904

My dear Jaeger:

Here's the proof for which thanks: but let me see another please.

Yes: go on with the Vio. & p[iano] arrgt. & send me *two* proofs—*one to keep* for *orchestrat".* & I will send a score in no time.

The piano arrangemt. troubles me—see how it goes.

If it does not 'go' I could use Schmid p 16–18 as a *basis* but it's rather bald.

In great haste
Ever yours
Edward the Elgar[70]

---

[69] HWRO 705:445:8694.   [70] HWRO 705:445:8695.

1, Berners Street, London, W.
Aug. 9th 1904
My dear Elgar

Many thanks for your letter. I fear me that Symphony will never be published! Oh dear! what a disappointment. If I had money I'd buy it of you at a good price. Perhaps some artloving Millionaire will come along & give you a fat commission & pay cash down. Who Knows? Anyhow, I am awfully sorry to hear that you of all composers living should even now be troubled with money difficulties. It's too damnable for words.

That P.F. arrangement seems O.K. & sounds allright. Pointer suggests a few trifling alterations. See enclosed. Kindly express Your views, after which I will give it to Brause to go on with at once. All the other things are in hand.

Revise of Full Score of 'In the South' & of parts are now being Read. Will reach you shortly.

Dear old Sanford is in town as nice as ever. He has a *wonderful* upright Steinway piano for you. Do *him the Kindness* to *accept* it

He admires you *tremendously* & is an awfully good sort. Ask him to bring it to 'Plas Gwyn' himself. You will never regret it, especially if you go to America. You know that his old Father died some months ago & left him (so I'm told) about *7 million Dollars*. He chucks his money about now in his generosity. He Gave me (*much against my will*), a *beautiful* stick, Chinese carved ivory handle gold mounted, Teak wood &c *much* too 'swell' for *me*. But one can't please him more than by allowing him to please one!

I have played on that Steinway & he has played to me. It *is a marvellous* instrument.

Dont Rub him the wrong way. He is a good fellow at Heart & means you well. Would do *anything* for you, in fact. .

Please thank ~~Mrs~~ Elgar
              Lady (I forgot!!) for her Kind Card the other day.

                                        Best regards to you both
                                        Ever yours,
                                        Nimrod.[71]

Plas Gwyn, Hereford.
Augt 10: 1904
My dear Jaeger:

Here's the M.S.—Pointer's suggestions are all thankfully adopted.

Don't worry about me, cos after all my troubles are not really my own. The sickening part of it all is that to make anything (tangible) I have still to do all the work: when you think that the Variations have brought me in about eight pounds(!) you will see how easy & beautiful it is to sit down &

[71] HWRO 705:445:8730.

write great & glorious works for old mossheads. I have quite the artistic feeling I hope, but I have no ambition & no conceit (yet) & there is, apart from these last, absolutely *no* inducement to write out & air the big stuff.

I hope to see Prof:Sanford before he leaves England. Give him my kind regards. I wrote to him (Paris address) a few weeks ago: his letter came during our scramble & waited for some time.

Glad to hear of your stick which must be a sight to see.

Mr Wilson (Pittsburgh) and a Mr Hamilton were here yesterday *en route* for N.York.

I should come & see you but I can't afford it!

Yours ever
E.E.[72]

Plas Gwyn, Hereford.
Augt 11:1904

My dear Jaybird:

I return the revises with all questions answered like a good boy.

I have heard from Prof:Sanford—a delightful letter about tobacco & *the* piano: I hope I may see him & have telegraphed this a.m.—I am terrified at accepting the piano.

In great haste
Yrs ever
Edd.[73]

Next day Jaeger sent a draft analysis of *In the South* which he had been commissioned to write for the Gloucester Festival in September.

1, Berners Street, London, W.
12/ 8 1904

My dear E.E.

Kindly do me the Kindness to look through the enclosed nice M.S. (my wife's) [of Jaeger's analysis of *In the South*] & strike out anything that does *not* represent your views. That *Battle Scene* (I'm sure it's a Battle scene) gave me 'beans'. I couldnt get the 'Hang' of it (the '*meaning*' I mean). I daresay I have gone wrong. If so, cut out what is wrong. Dont mind my feelings—I havent any, *except a desire not to misrepresent Your meaning*. The form also puzzled me greatly at first. Oh these Amateurs who would be critics or analysts! Please, if at all possible, let me have the wretched stuff back by Monday 'cos the Gloucester people want it. Any Examples that you would wish set out more *orchestrally* than in the P.F.Score You might, if not too great a trouble, scribble out for me, otherwise I will take the majority from the P F Score, for the Amateur. I hope You wont *dis*like the stuff. I consider the work a real Beauty & *most* poetic & suggestive.

Bravo you

Completion of Score proof sent same Post. Kindly Return it by *Monday morning*, as we must get copies printed by the Rehearsal week.

Thanks for letters. I saw Sanford last night & he told me he had written to you & that you had wired. He was so sorry He couldnt go down to Your place.

> Ever yours
> AJJgr[74]

Plas Gwyn, Hereford.
Augt 13 04
My dear A.J.J.

Many, many thanks. I return remainder of full skowre.

Also titles &c of the song [*In Moonlight*, setting words by Shelley to the 'Canto popolare' from *In the South*].

Also—your admirable analysis of the Overture. I think it's all right: I knocked out the *Sirs* & an adjective.

Perhaps the Ex: shd. come from the P.F. copy as being more understood, but please yourself.

I do not think I should put that about Strauss at the beginning—not necessary—S. puts music in a very low position when he suggests it must hang on some commonplace absurdity for it's [*sic*] very life. More of this some other time

The Battle Scene is all right, only it's very short & not worthy of so much description

All thanks to Madame for the lovely writing—oh! if we could scrawl *fast* like unto that.

I have found some lovely nooks here. You will have to walk.

> Much love
> Yrs ever
> Edward.[75]

During the summer of 1904 a new firm of publishers contacted Elgar. It had been founded in the previous year by William Wolfe Alexander Elkin (1863–1937) to concentrate on lighter repertory. But the timing of this approach, in the first year of Elgar's exclusive contact with Novello, was unfortunate.

[74] HWRO 705:445:8731.   [75] HWRO 705:445:8698.

8 & 10, Beak Street, Regent Street, London, W.
8th August, 1904.
Private

Dear Sir,

We wrote you on the 17th June, but have not had any reply to our letter.

Mr. Elkin would like to have seen you to have asked whether you would feel inclined to write a short song or piece to be published at a considerably lower price than that usually adopted.

It is perhaps hardly necessary to point out that this question of price has really nothing whatever to do with the infringement of copyright from which we have all been suffering. In our opinion there is a large demand to be expected for good new copyright music issued at a low price, and we hope shortly to be making the experiment with one of the large publishing houses which has not yet issued music. The scheme does not permit of a royalty to the composer, but we should be happy to offer you a substantial sum down.

We should be extremely glad to add your name to the list of those who are supporting the scheme, and shall be happy to give you any further information that you may require.

Begging the favour of an early reply,

Yours faithfully,
W.W.A.Elkin[76]

Elgar sent this on to Alfred Littleton at Novello with a note:

Plas Gwyn, Hereford.
Augt 15. 1904

My dear Littleton:

I hope you are having a pleasant change: I send the enclosed on at once for fear I may forget it later. I have of course said *no* to this extremely silly offer.

Yours ever
Edward Elgar

Littleton sent two requests—one to consider an enquiry to conduct in America, the other to lengthen the various instrumental arrangements of the 'Canto popolare' from *In the South*.

Plas Gwyn, Hereford.
Augt 18. 1904

My dear Littleton:

Many thanks for your two letters:

I will see if I can make the arrgts of the Canto popolare longer—but it wd. be difficult as it means adding extraneous matter; in other wds., another theme.

[76] HWRO 705:445:2917.

I have heard nothing from Mr Chester & I do not think much will come of it: they all want either *first* or *only* appearance and a new work thrown in apparently. These U.S.A's amuse me: after talking 'big' for four hours & boring me to distraction they make the poorest suggestion I have ever heard of.

We have still the cook who can't cook & can't get any other & I have been very ill.

> Yrs ever
> Edward Elgar

Jaeger's next letter raised the oft-considered question of assigning *The Dream of Gerontius* to one of the recognized categories:

1, Berners Street, W:
22/8/4
My dear Sir Knight!

Lookee here! Do you mind our placing your Gerontius amongst your *Oratorios*? See Mr A.H.L.'s note on enclosed proof. I fancy it would be better; but we leave it to *you*.

I have just given out the Parts & Score of your '*Spanish Serenade*' to be engraved. I suppose you dont wish to do any alteration in the Scoring, do you? Now's your 'chance'[.] If you wish to glance over the Score, kindly let me know *at once*, before Brause lays it out.

I'm Coming to the Gloucester Festival after all & bring my Frau too! She has never been to a Fest & she *will* enjoy it, if only the weather will be fair. I cant somehow Keep away & go to a dull Seaside place *instead* of Gloucester. That overture, of which I have been trying to write an analysis, has done the trick for me.

I'm off to Germany for a week with Holding on Thursday or Friday.

> Much love.
> Ever yours
> AJJaeger

I hope you & Lady Elgar are well!
Oh! *many* thanks for recommending my analysis of the overture to Spark [secretary of the Leeds Festival]. The Leeds people can afford to *pay* a guinea cant they?[77]

Leeds had been very annoyed indeed when, having been told that Elgar could not write the symphony he had promised for their 1904 Festival, the première of *In the South* had been given at Covent Garden. Some of the Festival authorities had wanted to cut Elgar's name out altogether, but their conductor, Stanford, had successfully pleaded for the inclusion of *In the South*.

[77] HWRO 705:445:8732.

Plas Gwyn, Hereford.
Augt 23. 04
Augustus darling:

Only a hurried line.
by all means, put Gerontius in the Oratorio list.—there's no word invented yet to describe it.

Yes—Leeds shd. pay a guinea altho' they are mean enough to get it for nix—but don't be had:

No I don't want to see Spanish Serenade—the scoring is all right; if young England could turn out as *neat* a piece of work as that—there wd. be some hope for it!

So glad you are coming to Glo'ster[—]my wife is writing
Glad the overture works into your innards: I *love* it: it's alive!
I am better but jolly down.

Yrs ever
in haste
Ed Elgar[78]

At the end of the month Elgar was in London for Gloucester Festival orchestral rehearsals. There he saw Professor Sanford, and accepted the gift of the piano. Calling at Novello on the 27th, he found Alfred Littleton on holiday. Clayton showed him some correspondence with the new London Symphony Orchestra. Their plan had now changed, and in place of *Gerontius* they proposed that Elgar conduct them in a miscellaneous orchestral concert. Novello were prepared to act as Elgar's concert agents, even though the concert might not be made up entirely of works they published. Littleton had drafted a reply for Elgar's approval.

Plas Gwyn, Hereford.
Sep 3.1904
My dear Littleton:

I am quite sorry to trouble you with business while you are away from home.

I saw Mr.Clayton two days ago & he told me—or rather read me your letter concerning the Sympy Orch: Concert: it is too bad of them to advertise my name when there is everything except the orch: to be considered: may I still consider the matter to be in your hands: perhaps you will enquire & let me know the result sometime.

Mr.Schuster, who is in Venice, thinks the Canto popolare wd do well with *Italian* words: if such an edition were prepared wd. it be possible to issue it *in*

<hr>

[78] HWRO 705:445:8699.

Italy through an Italian publisher as agent? I only thought of this possible course, because Mr.Clayton suggested a French publisher as sort of 'issuing agent' in the case of a French edition of Gerontius: German & French words will also be wanted some day for this trifle!

The Meistersingers, I am told, announce that they make a special feature, or something, of my part songs. I am glad of this because the things want to be *understood* & when people have heard them properly done they like them—not before. (I wish you cd. have heard some of the choirs singing—impromptu—in the moonlight on the sands at Morecambe 'Feasting I watch'.) Do you know these Meistersingers because if it could be arranged without causing affront or misunderstanding I would gladly go through the things with them. Some of your people wd. be sure to know some of them & a word might put it *en train*.

Forgive a long letter

Hope you are having a nice time

Yours sincy
Edward Elgar

At the Gloucester Festival Elgar conducted the Prelude and Angel's Farewell from *Gerontius* (as the Dean of Gloucester forbade the entire work being sung there), *In the South*, and *The Apostles*. Yet he needed money, and after the Festival asked Alfred Littleton whether something of the £500 due on the sale of 10,000 copies of *The Apostles* vocal score could be paid now, as the work was selling well.

Plas Gwyn, Hereford.
Sep 20 1904
My dear Littleton:

Would it be possible, I mean agreeable, to your firm to send me before the evil quarter day *something on account of royalties* OR on acct. of the next possible payment on a/c of Apostles? If usual I wd. of course pay any interest or any business way shd be followed. I want 100£ or £150 whichever is possible.

I have heard nothing from N.Y or Mr Chester.

Kindest rgds
Yrs ever
Ed:Elgar

The firm sent £150, which Elgar acknowledged on 23 September.

It fell to Jaeger to announce the first big benefit of Elgar's exclusive publishing contract with Novello:

1, Berners Street, London, W.
Sept 24 1904

My dear Sir Knight
yclept Edward ye wizard of Plas Gwyn

I'm sure it will give you *some* little pleasure (—tho' forsooth, there be little enough left, I fear me, to bring a thrill of pleasure to *your* pampered soul[)] (pampered Soul is good!)—that we are now *Engraving* the *full* Scores of

Caractacus
King Olaf
Banner
Light of Life
Black Knight.

'The Complete works of The Master' will soon be an accomplished FACK! Anything that yet remains will also be done. Geidel are doing the Car. Olaf & Black Knight, & Brause the remaining. Proofs of Car. will commence to reach us next week I hope & they have undertaken to Engrave 1000 pages of Elgar Score in 4 weeks! *Don't Know anything about this*, if Mr Alfred should himself write about the matter. (perhaps he has written already?) maybe he wants to 'prise you (as my little girl says) with the news. If I have forestalled him I am sorry. But I feel almost sure he has written already.

Brewer [organist of Gloucester Cathedral and conductor of the Gloucester Festival] was here. He asked me whether Barrett Cooke [Festival secretary] had sent me a cheque for £3.3.0 for those analyses. I said 'no, he aint'. It seems I am *supposed* to get that, *though* I saw that the accounts were closed. So if I *do* get that cheque I shall be better off than I imagined.

I offered that analysis (Overture) to Mr Alfred for the M.T. October. [The editor] Edwards prints instead Grove's analysis of *Mendelssohn's Scotch symphony*! Hurrah!

The Gran Ban of the Midlands [Granville Bantock, whose choral rhapsody *The Time Spirit* had been performed at the Gloucester Festival] writes me thumping letters about my depraved taste in music. Ye Gods! He is certainly welcome to his Camel bells & the Tom Tomming of the Keepers. The mighty Gran Ban (long may he wave, dear old fellow!) seems to want only one kind of muscular, Billposter music. I told him I like Gerontius some, THOUGH the In the South (a *very* different kind of music) lifted me out of my seat.

He (The Gran Ban) told Brewer that he & Br. & Atk[ins] & Sincl[air] 'have the music in the Midlands in their hands & *must do something for it*.' I said to Brewer: 'a Simple matter; of course you will perform each other's music.' Br. blushed & smiled & this *morning came in & begged* copies of *the Gran Ban's* male voice *partsongs*! I thought that funny & roared pp ma dolce e con gran espressione like your Trombones.

Ever yours, with kindest regards to Lady Elgar & yourself

Ever yours
AJJgr[79]

[79] HWRO 705:445:8733.

Jaeger sent proofs of instrumental arrangements of the 'Canto popolare' from *In the South*, together with news of his own acquaintance with the redoubtable Archibald Ramsden, President of the 'U.B.Quiet' Club.

1, Berners Street, London, W.
27/9 1904
Dear Edward,

There seem to be some discrepancies between the texts of these various arrangements. Will you Kindly make them 'uniformed' (Brause's English) if they *should* be so?

Mr Ramsden came in this mg & inquired after you. He has asked my wife & me to dine with him on Thursday!!!!

Dear Buths acknowledges receipt of (Gratis) Full Score *In the South* which he will study forthwith. He cannot do it this season, as he is full up, & all programmes settled long ago. He says he has not forgotten 'Apostles', but his committee refused to do it *directly after the* (RIVAL) *Cologne*. He says: 'another year.' He also writes that the 'Apostles' will be done by a colleague (Musikdirektor P. Müller) at *St Gallen* Switzerland. Orchestra & Chorus both large & competent. Müller (whose card he encloses) proposes Palm Sunday next year for the date.

> Hastissimo.
> Ever yours
> Nimrod

Buths inquires after you & says he has heard nothing for a long time from you.[80]

Plas Gwyn, Hereford.
Sep 28.1904
My dear Jagpotte.

Just home from [Leeds Festival rehearsals at the Royal College of Music in] *London*: I went to G[reat] W[estern] Hotel & only had a few mins: in town: rehearsal [of *In the South*] this a.m. at ten & then fled!

I say WHAT a row we made! Gosh! The real Romans were not in it!

Glad to hear all your news—Apostles at *Norwich fest* [in 1905]—Also glad you are going to Ramsden[.] He is a brick though a very odd one *sometimes* to *some* people—not to people he believes in bless him.

Proofs shall be retd vy quick

> Yrs ever
> Edwd[81]

80 HWRO 705:445:8734.   81 HWRO 705:445:8700.

Plas Gwyn, Hereford.
Sep 28 1904.

My dear Littleton:

I fled up to town for the Leeds rehearsal & back at once.

I used an overcoat which I had not worn since Gloucester & stuffed into the pockets were letters given me in the Cathedral & *never opened*—People always give one things just as one is going to conduct the Apostles!

One of the letters is from you & I fear you may have thought me a pig.

As to the Symphy Orchl.Concert—if they have a vocalist & cd. get Muriel Foster for the Sea pictures perhaps it wd. be well to go on with the engagement: to save a bother: I leave it to you as I said.

I see that Gerontius is announced for Brussels—does that mean a French translation?

The score of 'In the South' looks lovely: I *should* like you to hear it with that superb Leeds orchestra

Yours v sincy
Edward Elgar

Dealing with the instrumental arrangements of 'Canto popolare', Elgar decided to ask the advice of Mrs. Jaeger in editing the violin arrangement. He wrote to Jaeger on the typewriter:

Plas Gwyn, Hereford.
29/9/1904.

Dear Aged & Gray:– –

In grt haste I send back the prfs of the Canter popolare.

Note that ye slight variations fr ye origal are intentional for private purposes.

Note that I have phrased ye clart prat[*sic*].

Note well that I have NOT done the Violin & Cello: I have indicated, in the vio part the bowing as it is in the score; NOW would your dear wife complete it and make it nice for people to play? Do ask her; she knows how I want it to sound and I shd be very grateful. Supposing she will graciously do this, the bowing must go in for cello also and– – mark ye– – into the accompt likewise.

I think all is clear now except that Mrs Jaeger make [*sic*] take revenge on me for my many grievous insults to the capering Moss (Which is Orgustus) and refuse to touch the mercenary page.

Well, if so, tell me.

You shd have been at the R.C.M. to hear the Alassio— — you cd not only hear but fe

      feel also; it's a jolly fine orchestra.

              Yours ever,
              Pospectively,
              Edward the "$() - ; *' : \% / - \frac{1}{4}!\frac{1}{2} + \frac{3}{4} = £$

[*handwritten*] Those exercises have done me no end of good.

Why not ask Atkins to make an easy *organ* arrgt. now[82]

1, Berners Street, London, W.
Oct 6 1904

My dear Elgar,

I send to-day the first instalment of 'the master's collected works in full Score.' More will follow quickly & the *whole* of Caractacus will reach *us* from Leipzig this week. How long the 'reading' will take us, Heaven only knows.

I also send the final proofs of the Canto popolare V^n, Cello & Clarinet. My Frau has fingered the Violin part very carefully & thoroughly, as she takes it that you intend the piece chiefly for amateurs. If any of her phrasing or Fingering is not as you like it, kindly just Run Your pencil through it & I'll have it taken out of the plates.

My wife, not being a Cellist, cannot put any fingering into the *Cello* part. I daresay you will get one of your many Cellist friends to do it, though I guess You Know as much about it as they./

Granville Bantock is *very* wroth with me, because in reply to a 'cracked' letter full of orientalisms he axed me to send him a full Score of 'Alassio' & we *charged* him for it (to get you your fat Royalty!) thinking that it was part of the *Liverpool* order. But he Reminds me (what I had clean forgotten) that you asked me at Gloucester to send him a Score, and that you would write in it later. As I said, I *quite forgot* that (though I Remember your promise & request *now*) So I take it that we may give that Score to the Gran Ban & charge Your Royalty account with it, so that you get not that fat percentage on that Score. I wish you would just drop me a card to say that this is in accordance with your wishes, (i.e. *present* G.B. with one)

I see they (N & C) have only sent you *one* copy. If you would like more you can *of course* have them, but don't forget that each time you give away your Royalty. But shouldn't dear old *Hans* receive one from *you*? Tell me that, & I'll send you one. If you think he has procured one already (we have ALREADY disposed of about *30*!) dont send another, of course.

I wish I could have heard the thing with the Leeds orchestra.

I was at Leeds Saturday to hear [Walford] Davies [*Everyman*] & J.Holbrooke [*Queen Mab*]. Expensive Enthusiasm!

As regards the Canto popolare for *organ* I had already suggested it to *Brewer* for HIS Series. His arrangements of Chanson de M[atin] & de N[uit]

&c have sold very well. I promised him a proof as soon as finally passed. If Atkins does it (who is quite welcome as far as *I* am concerned) the piece must go into J.E.West's Series & your things get scattered about some. Atkins might'nt like appearing under the protecting Editorial wings of friend J.E.W. Write me a line re Ban &c.

> Yours ever
> AJJgr

I am so glad you will have [Charles] Tree as Caractacus at Worcester [Festival Choral Society concert on 9 Nov.]. You will *like him*. Voice & style are alike admirable to my mind.
There is talk of sending Rosenkranz & me to Paris & France generally (?also Switzerland) on a tour of *Elgar Propaganda*! *MUM*!![83]

Charles Tree (1868–1940) had a lengthy career as a singer of oratorios, ballads, and folk-songs.

Plas Gwyn, Hereford.
Saty [8 Oct. 1904]
My dear Jaggs.

   Just home & hasten to send some of the accumulated rubbish.
   Thanks very many to yr. dear wife: the '*editing*' is *excellent*: look only at p.3 Vn.pt.—you are already in III pos[ition] & the figures seem redundant or one may have been omitted which wd. take us back to I pos.—otherwise all is most clear & good.
   You had better put 'Edited by Isabella Jaeger' on the Violin part. *Do* ask Mr A.H.L. for this. If you like I would ask Squire to do the Cello & Hobday the Viola & Draper the Clarinet: but let me know what you think—anyhow I return all the stuff now.
   Thanks for your letter which I will reply to later. I am awfully busy. I can't stop to talk of Leeds. Walford Davies [*Everyman*] was good

> Yours ever
> Ed Elgar

P.T.O.
Of course *give* Gran-Ban-the-Sheikh the Score & charge to me.[84]

Alfred Hobday (1870–1942), William Henry Squire (1871–1963), and Charles Draper (1869–1952) were all leading instrumental players of their day, well known to Elgar in the orchestras he conducted.
   Elgar's next letter extended the scope of giving full scores to choral conductors and organists who helped his work in the north. These were Herbert Austin Fricker (1868–1943), the City Organist of Leeds; Alfred Benton, chorus-master of the Leeds Festival; and Thomas Tertius Noble (1867–1953), organist of York Minster.

---

[83] HWRO 705:445:8735.   [84] HWRO 705:445:8702.

Plas Gwyn, Hereford.
Oct 10. 1904

Private somewhat

My dear Jaeger:

Many thanks for your note with the proofs. Yes: I wanted Bantock to have the Score 'In the South' costing *him* nothing. Richter should have one too.

I procured from Mr.Smith (your agent at Leeds during the festival) a copy for *Mr.Fricker* who is preparing Gerontius: I gave it to him.

Would you ask the firm to let me have a *full score of Gerontius* as reasonably as they can because I want to give it to Mr.Benton who has prepared so many of my things including York Minster performance & is doing (Leeds Choral Union) Geron. & The Apostles.

Also, in view of the work done by Mr.Noble of York in clearing the way for the performance & perhaps future deeds in the Minster I think he should have a score also from me—or from the firm. If further music on a large scale is given in York it will largely depend on Mr.N. Will you bring this before Mr A.H.L.—I think he's away.

Yrs ever
Ed:Elgar

I have not said anything except to you about the organ arrgt. (Canto popolare) so go ahead as you please[85]

Jaeger replied next day, but his letter seems not to have been preserved. Elgar responded with another excursion on his typewriter.

Plas Gwyn, Hereford.
13/ 10/ 1904.

My dear Jaeger:——

Your letter, dated 11th, received this a.m. and for it thanks. I am in a wild hurry and so take this odd means of writing!

As to the fingering, or rathir phrasig [*sic*] of the cello, viola & clarinet arrgts, I think the artists wd. probably do the little required for nothing if I may say to them that you will put 'edited by Blank' on the copies: this is what I asked you I think; anyhow it's what I want to know; I should not propose any 'fee'.

Now, as to the proposed presentation scores: never mind the royalty, you commercial old moss, but send them to me and I will forward them; I wanted to know if Mr Alfred approved of the idea: I gathir [*sic*] from your lette[r] that he does: Benton should have Gerontius & Richter 'In the South': I said 'a' score for Mr Noble because I dont know what he has or has not. This I will find out if the firm approves as aforesaid: I only wanted to suggest that a

[85] HWRO 705:445:8703.

man who had done so much and is understood to be trying all he can for the future might be pleased at some little recognition*: do you see?

> Good-bye,
> Yours in hste
> E.E.

[handwritten] *& I don't like to give away scores to anybody without the firm's appro[val] I mean
  Oh! dear how difficult it is to write[86]

Meanwhile the engraving of full scores of Elgar's early choral works was in full spate at Novello.

1, Berners Street, London, W.
Oct 14 1904

My dear Elgar

You will receive a big bunch of proofs to-day—I mean to-morrow. As for Caractacus, *only answer Mr Pointer's queries*; He has another Set of proofs with the *mistakes* corrected also. So you need not worry with reading every note &c. J.P. is, as you Know, *quite* reliable & you may be spared all *rough* reading. All 'Caractacus' is already in proof (309 pp) & Pointer will get on fast now. 'Olaf' will turn up next week I guess. 'The Banner' is also getting on fast.

Don't forget to let me Know your decision about those 'In the South' *or* Gerontius, *or* Apostles Scores which you wish to present to friends. (Richter, Benton, Noble.) Return the *P.F Duet* quickly, please. I want to rush that out

> Ever yours
> A.J.Jgr[87]

Plas Gwyn, Hereford.
Oct 15.1904

My dear Littleton:

I have been thrilled by receiving proofs of various full scores of my things & I understand that many of them are coming out: I send you an especial word of thanks for this which I think you know gratifies my artistic sense &, I begin to think, my vanity too—I only trust that the things will pay for themselves: I can't help saying this although I know you do not think of this side of it.

Sinclair has just left me & expresses a hope that the 'very useful first page' of directions for the Conductor, as given in Gerontius & The Apostles[,] may be also given in Caractacus &c. I do not know which of your men drew up those pages, but I daresay someone will do so & let me see it before printing.

I forget if I told you I saw Mr.Beale of Birmingham: if the new oratorio is ready *they expect it*—they will give two performances, preceded by the

Apostles—_3_ performances, I mean programmes [in the 1906 Birmingham Festival], to me alone! enough to satisfy a moderate ambition. I am working away at the oratorio but have nothing to shew you yet, & I sometimes feel overweighted

> Kindest regards
> Yours ever sincerely
> Edward Elgar:

37 Curzon Road[,] N
17/x/4
My dear Elgar,

On going through multitudinous unanswered letters in my breastpocket I came across yours of the 13th & now hasten to say that Mr Alfred _quite agrees_ to your giving those Scores to Richter[,] Benton & Noble. So Kindly say what Noble is to have & I'll send all in one bundle, see?

Well, Mr Alfred is also quite ready for Hobday[,] Squire & Draper to 'Edit' your 'Canto'. Shall I therefore send you proofs of the piece three times over, with corresponding Parts? I will do that during the next day or so unless I hear from you to the contrary.

I'm sorry I forgot to reply, but all day I am doing _Junior Clerk work_ at No.1 & I am getting sick of it, I can tell you. I can't get any assistance & I had thought I had proved myself capable of doing better work for the firm. But only _one man's_ advice is ever sought & followed at No.1 & that is the jokist of the M.T. [F. G. Edwards], ye Gods!

> Ever yours
> AJJgr

I have proposed to the said jokist to print my Analysis of the Overture [_In the South_] in the M.T., as a sort of 'Review' of the Full Score[.] I know his answer beforehand, but did it as a joke.[88]

The instrumentalists who had been asked to edit the arrangements of the 'Canto popolare' sent in their results. First came the clarinettist Draper.

Bohemia[,] Allfarthing Lane[,] Wandsworth
Oct 20th 1904
Dear Sir Edward

It seems quite strange that this beautiful tune which has almost haunted me should have come to me in this way, however if my suggestion will be of any value I shall be more than delighted.

I feel that the best thing would be to write it all for the A Clarinet. I suppose there would be time to change? From letter B it is infinitely better on the A Clarinet and the first part and also last part will suffer little or nothing, in fact I think the whole thing will be more sympathetic on the A Clarinet. I

---

[88] HWRO 705:445:8783.

do not think that I can alter anything to make it more effective than it already is. I should feel very proud for my name to be connected with this, but feel that I have not done sufficient to entitle myself to such an honour.

With many thanks for your kind remarks about my playing, and coming from you, I value it most highly

> I beg to remain
> Yours very truly
> Chas Draper

Plas Gwyn, Hereford.
Oct 20.1904

Dear Sirs:

Enclosed I send the Clart. arrgt. of the Canto popolare. You will see what Mr Draper says & it will be necessary, I am sorry to say, to reengrave these two pages again in A^b.

I will send on the other two arrangements soon

> Yrs v try
> Edward Elgar

24, Gunterstone Road, West Kensington, W.
Oct 21:04

Dear Sir Edward.

I have put a few finger marks in the Canto popolare which you sent me & I trust they will meet with your approval. I take it as a compliment & I consider it a great honour to have been asked to do this by you—it was very kind of you to think of me. My wife & I are most likely giving a recital during the winter & I shall certainly include this charming piece, which is so effective for the viola.

When are you going to give us a string quartet? I am most eagerly looking forward to one! Kindly note my 'new' address now 3 years old!

> Kindest regards
> Yours sincerely
> Alfred Hobday.

Plas Gwyn, Hereford.
Oct 23.1904

My dear Littleton:

I enclose Mr.Hobday's note which accompanied the Viola pt of the Canto. Mr Squire will send the Cello part in a day or two.

Would you make a note that these four 'editors' shd. receive a few copies each when ready: I think that would be nice.

I have to-day heard from Mr.Noble & he wd. like the full Sc: of *Gerontius* So that if two cd. be sent to me (one for Mr Benton) I would write in them & send them on to these two pioneers.

Yours ever
Ed.Elgar

Travelled *in the night* from Liverpool & nearly dead to-day.

In Liverpool with the Orchestral Society (founded by Rodewald and now regularly conducted by Bantock), Elgar had conducted the *'Enigma' Variations*. This enabled him to answer a query from Novello's music editor J. E. West.

Plas Gwyn, Hereford.
Oct 23.1904
My dear West:

Many thanks for your letter re 2nd bar p.100 of the Variations: yes, it is an error undoubtedly, but on looking at it I *thought* it must be one of those things which *sound* all right owing to the *timbre* of the insts. I waited until yesterday when I was conducting rehearsal & concert in L'pool & listened to the bar. Do you know it *sounds* all right to me—sort of inverted (perverted) pedal & I don't think we'll alter it. If you hear the Vars: again listen & tell me what you think.

Kind regards
Yours ever
Edward Elgar[89]

Then came the cellist Squire's observations on the 'Canto popolare' arrangement for his instrument:

11, Tavistock Road, Westbourne Park, W.
Oct 24th/04
Dear Sir Edward,

I am returning the proofs you sent me and I have gone through the 'Canto Popolare' very carefully. I think the marks I have added will help any amateur to some extent—but the piece is deceptive, inasmuch as it is more difficult to play than it looks!

I trust you won't mind my taking out one of your slurs!

Also forgive me, please, for adding a ⟶ which I have found by experience conveys more than the written 'dim'.

I have been only too pleased to overlook this part & beg of you to make any further use of me should opportunity occur.

With kindest regards

Yours very sincerely
W.H.Squire.

[89] MS in possession of Raymond Monk.

All these arrangements appeared in due course, under the 25 per cent royalty agreement.

There was further correspondence over the proposed concert with the London Symphony Orchestra. The question of a programme had been the subject of a letter from Jaeger:

1, Berners Street, London, W.
Oct 18 1904
My dear E.E.

I'm sorry, but I find I must write You another letter! I don't 'preach' *this* time.

It's about your Symphony orchestra concert. Mr A.H.L. asked me about your proposed programme & invited suggestions[.] So I said; if Sir E. can't write a *new* work for the occasion, I would recommend something out of the 'Black Knight' being done.

That fine little work is quite unknown to London. Can we not play the '*Banquet & Dance music*' or '*Dance & Banquet Music*' as an orchestral piece? If you approve & will mark in enclosed copy what Selection we might arrange, we might get some clever youngster to Knock the thing together *orchestrally* & issue it. You need not have much trouble in the matter

There are such jolly Tunes & catchy Rhythms in that music, it's a 1000 pities the work is ignored here in London & the other *big* towns. Think on it—

Of course if you'd Rather not have it done, then just say so & there is an end to the business.

In haste
Ever yours
AJJgr[90]

Meanwhile Alfred Littleton had been drafting a possible programme. Elgar responded:

Plas Gwyn, Hereford.
Oct 21:1904
My dear Littleton:

Many thanks for the sketch programme: it does not look very well I fear—all the old things being done again! But do they want to announce it yet? It is quite possible that some new thing might turn up before March but I cannot possibly say definitely.

You have been so good with advice that I venture to ask you to look at the enclosed letter about stamping royalty things. Do you think I shd. get somebody to stamp the things; if so *who*—I know nothing of these matters:

---

[90] HWRO 705:445:8737.

Boosey long ago suggested something of the kind but I like to trust a man utterly or—not at all.

Still if it is better from a business point of view I would get somebody to go to Williams & Boosey: can you recommend me anyone? one of your own men—oh! but he couldn't do it after hours[:] I forgot that.

Kindest regards
Yrs ever
Edward Elgar

Neither Littleton's reply nor any correspondence with the other firms seems to survive on the question of mechanically numbering individual copies sold as a check on royalty payments. One letter from the Joseph Williams firm alluded to it.[91]

Novello had commissioned a new French translation of *Gerontius* by J. d'Offoël, in view of a performance in Brussels to take place early in 1905. Jaeger wrote:

1, Berners Street, London, W.
Oct 26 1904

My dear E.E.

Here is the Frenchy's first installment, also his letter (which Kindly return.) His veiled sneer at Buths is unkind. Buths *did* preserve the *rhymes* which make one's work of *treble* difficulty. In fact, the Rhymes in adapting to music are the greatest difficulty[.] Ask Lady Elgar! I suppose the Frenchman *may* drop them? What thinks Plas Gwyn?

Another matter.

I have been pressing Mr Alfred to have everything in the way of *Extra* 'Extras' in your Scores; Gongs, antique Cymbals [in *The Apostles*] &c &c *made for* us, and in the House to hire out to customers[.] We can't be dependent on [the London Symphony percussionist] Mr.Schröder's pleasure & favour, what say you? So I went to [the instrument maker] Hawkes to order 'antique cymbals', but they didn't know what Exactly You require. Is the sound not required to be *silver & bright*? I suggested something *quite Small* that will vibrate well & freely? Silver seems to be the metal required. Something like the lids of Biscuit bowls (or glasses). At least I have something at Home in the way of a lid of that kind which seems to make just the sort of noise.

Can *you* help Hawkes & us?

In frantic Haste

Yours ever
AJJgr

'Variations' I see at *Bremen* this Season.[92]

---

[91] HWRO 705:445:8209.   [92] HWRO 705:445:8738.

Plas Gwyn, Hereford.
Oct 27: 1904

My dear Jäger:

I have had a chill & find a heap to do—four letters from you unanswered among other crimes of omission.

1.) full sc. Apostles. p 99 Bar 3 Bassoon notes *are correct*. (*a nice buzz*:)

2). Dr Sinclair wd. like to do some small thing [with his orchestra] at his choral Concert: so I asked about the parts of 'Canto popolare'. Now wd. the firm allow it to be done: he wd. want Strings 4.4.3.4. & one each wind, &c. I enclose the firm's letter—if he could have these parts or rather if *I* cd. have them in a fortnight it wd. do: but yes or no please by return on acct of printing programme.

3). I don't think the Black Knight arrgt. will do—at least not for the [London] Symph Orch

4). I had no idea a french traduction was afoot! Who is M.d'Öffel or whatever name he bears: we will look it thro' & return it very soon: for the present I will only say I wish I had as good an opinion of myself as he has of his own Ego. He must drop the rhymes in French: assonances in that vile & beastly *conversational* language limit the literary beast much.

[5]) Antique cymbals: Schroeder [the London Symphony Orchestra percussionist] gets the noise I want by placing a bell

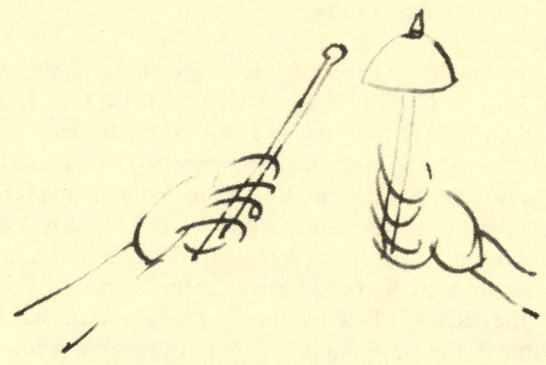

on the end of a stick & hitting it with another stick: I fear if a *pair* of cymbals is employed—which wd. be correct—the ordinary player wd not be able to make them 'ring' in time.

(Harking back—is there any hurry about that French translation? the one person *I* shd. like to see it is Mrs Edward Speyer & she is in Italy for a long time—I will of course *mark* a selection in B[lack] K[night] for possible future use.)

Steinbach told me 'In the South' was down for *Dec 6*. but I am enquiring if any new arrgt has been made. Sorry to hear of your flu & hope you are better.

In greatest haste
Yours ever
Edward Elgar.[93]

1, Berners Street, London, W.
Oct 28 1904

My dear E.E

Thanks for your letter. By all means announce
1 Canto in Sinclair's programme. You *shall have* the parts within a fortnight, I'll promise.
2 *D'Offoël* is a real Swell amongst translators. He has done all Wagner's works & his translation is supposed the best by far, *though* Cosima is bound to Wilder's (or what is his name) version by contract or something. Everybody recommended d'Offoël, incl. Volckert [*sic*]. It seem [*sic*] to me well done, & I guessed that in French Rhymes wont work in 'musical' Translations like this Gerontius. He has certainly kept to your notes remarkably well. He is waiting to hear whether we approve (& *you*) of Part I before he does Part II. That's part of our Contract with him. And as there's a performance at Bruxelles on March 30 (I believe) & we have to get Vocal Score & parts done with all the mass of other work in Hand there is not much time to be lost. Don't you Know Mrs Speyers whereabouts? We might wait for a week or 2, but scarcely for her Return to London. Percy Pitt has a very good idea of French poetry. He is *always reading* it & might help *you* (if not *us*!)
3 I'll see Hawkes again Re Cymbals.
I'll hope You can write the [London] Symphony orchestra a short new work. Why not a *brilliant* quick *String* Scherzo, or something for those fine strings *only*? a real bring down the House *torrent* of a thing such as Bach could write (Remember that *Cologne* Brandenburger Concerto!) a five minutes work would do it! It wouldn't take you away from your *big* work for long. You might even write a MODERN FUGUE for Strings, or *Strings & Organ*!
That would Sell like Cakes.

Awful Haste
Ever yours
AJJgr[94]

This suggestion for a string piece might have joined with Alfred Hobday's request for a string quartet a week earlier. But nothing immediately emerged.

[93] HWRO 705:445:8705. In place of '5' in the body of the letter, Elgar repeated '4'.
[94] HWRO 705:445:8739.

Plas Gwyn, Hereford.
Nov 3. 1904
My dear Jaggs:

In greatest haste

I saw Sinclair's arrangement, he played it to me, of prelude pt II Apostles & I think it excellent & it sounds well.

I send back all proofs, only keeping *first proofs Viola & C[ello] & B[ass]* of small orch ['Canto popolare']—the 2nd. proofs were not in the parcel, but I suppose they'll come on.

Thanks for your note re novelty for the [London] Sym. Concert—I cannot settle on any idea! The weather is too lovely! warm & lunch out of doors last Saturday in the hot sun!
What a climate.

Your exercise cure has done *wonders*: I take *no* physic now—a most xtrordy thing! Atkins & I are going to give you a testimonial

I am to conduct Carac: for him at Worcester next week[.] I suppose the [printed] score will not be ready in any rough form—but if he has a Dodd [manuscript copy] score I shall manage—How well it looks in print.

I feel that those Editors' names [on 'Canto popolare'] shd. be in the same type as the instruments they edit. see my note on the Viola part: it wd. look all right larger—dont you think?

Yours ever
Edward Elgar

I wrote to Pitt some days ago & have not heard. I conclude he's away. I am sending the French 'Gerontius' to Mr Schuster & you will receive it, with 'notes', in a day or two.[95]

1, Berners Street, London, W.
Nov 5. 1904
My dear EE.

Many thanks for your letter. Oh! Isabellas & Alfred [Hobday]'s names are *quite big enough* enough [sic] really, & I wont alter them again. Sinclair's 'arrangement' now being considered. Must go in *West's* new Series of arrangements, no doubt. How does the Mus Dr Cantuar like appearing under the Editorship of J.E.W.?

Atkins has the *Dodd* Score of Caractacus. We cannot yet spare the *proofs* of the Score [—] Dodd ought to suffice unto ye.

I say the Viola & Cello-Bass Parts of the 'Canto' must have been Returned to you by mistake *uncorrected*. Kindly Return them to me at once & I'll send you Revises on Monday. The plates are *un*corrected at present! Very sorry.

Lucky man to have a chance of *enjoying* this lovely weather—Lunch out of doors in *November*! It suggests a joke, coming out of England. My bairns

[95] HWRO 705:445:8706.

enjoy the weather to the full, out all day in the Streets with their Hoops! Sunday mornings to Highgate Woods to Romp with 'papa' amongst the dry leaves carpeting the ground everywhere. We *do* have fun! I'm so glad the exercises do you good. I stick to them religiously *every morning*, & I can honestly say I feel another man & much fitter for work. So persevere, and if you do feel a bit 'stiff' one morning, that's the very time when you need them most.

D'Offoël is worrying to know whether he may proceed with *Geron*. So kindly dont keep him long. I saw Pitt about 14 days ago. He said nothing about going away then.

> Ever your
> AJJaeger[96]

When nothing had been heard from Elgar for a week, Alfred Littleton wrote again about the *Gerontius* translation. He also enclosed a copy of Shelley's poems. Remembering Elgar's use of *In Moonlight* set to the 'Canto popolare', he wondered whether other poems might inspire Elgar. It would be interesting to know whether Littleton's suggestions included the *Ode to the West Wind*, from which Elgar was to make a part-song three years later, or the poem beginning 'Rarely, rarely comest Thou, Spirit of Delight!' which became the epigraph for the Second Symphony in 1911.

Plas Gwyn, Hereford.
Nov 14 1904
My dear Littleton:

Many thanks for your letter about the French 'Gerontius': I am sure the best has been done to find a 'man' & I think, if he had not been so exact in retaining the actual crotchets & quavers[,] he might have escaped criticism. I do not understand French well enough to say much & possibly, *probably* I mean[,] my friends are too *exigeant* but I am sure all will come out right.

Many thanks also for the Shelley: I will think over the poems you name but I fear they are too lyrical for a scene painter like me but I would do anything to please you & will try anyhow.

We have settled down to life here & find it most comfortable & quiet: I hope someday we may persuade Mrs.Littleton & yourself to pay us a little visit: we would do our best to make you happy here.

> Kindest regards
> Yrs v. sincerely
> Edward Elgar

Percy Pitt was visiting the Elgars, and Jaeger made this the occasion of another appeal for a final decision about d'Offoël's translation:

[96] HWRO 705:445:8740.

1, Berners Street, London, W.
Nov 16 1904

My dear E.E.

I heard last night that P.Pitt is staying at 'Plas Gwyn'. So I thought that that was a splendid opportunity of your asking him his view of the d'Offoël translation of Gerontius. It seems to me that only a person either a literary Frenchman or a foreigner who like P.P. knows French *'intimately'* & is *steeped* in FRENCH POETRY & at the same time appreciates the *difficulties* of a fellow translating *for music* can sit in judgement on a man who, like d'Offoël is thought good enough, *in Paris*, to prepare a new translation of a masterpiece like Tristan, which translation has been officially adopted by the Grand Opera (So I understand) for the performances in the new year, *in place of Wieder's* (or whatever the other Johnny's name is)

Already there are in the enclosed copy alterations, suggestions, & remarks by E.E., Mr L.F.S[chuster,] Mr Edwards, Mr Shedlock & I believe Mr A.H.L. I guess that d'Offoël will smile if he doesn't cuss. Mr Shedlock was asked because he is supposed (by *Mr F.G.E[dwards]*) to know French well! Well, So do 25,000 English School mistresses! He makes a few suggestions on the piece of paper enclosed.

One thing is plain, d'Offoel had Retained your musical Text ADMIRABLY, and, after all, that is something—a *great* deal—to his credit. To get *everything* even to those finest shades of Newman's meaning is evidently impossible in a translation *for music. Buths hasn't that! It can't be done*!

Mr Littleton says dont hesitate to mark the copy with suggestions & observations. He has no doubt he can get d'Offoël to agree to your wishes. *I have* doubts, but I don't count. I have myself adapted—translated—words to music & Know the difficulties, though I dont pretend to be clever, Heaven forbid. D'Offoël *is* evidently a gifted man for this kind of work.

Query: how far can one dictate to him?

Anyhow do what you think wise & Mr A.H.L. will see the thing through. Retain your music where you can! We are losing precious time, meanwhile.

                                        Ever yours
                                        AJJgr.

Kind regards to P.P. Tell him why the D—— does he play *rot* like Wolf?[97]

Elgar's reaction to pressure in an area where his knowledge was less than perfect was finally unhelpful.

Plas Gwyn, Hereford
Friday [18 Nov. 1904]

My dear Jäger

You are a funny dawg. You send me a translation to look at; I send *one* set of suggestions & ask a well-read French friend to look at it. You then write

---

[97] HWRO 705:445:8741.

me today that it has been shewn to *4* more people & then say *I* must not expect too much & want all their ideas incorporated.

Dear boy: *I* don't want any.

When Mr. Alfred is satisfied so am I.

The few suggestions in type made here seem, after all, to be the main points & may or may not be 'alterable'.

Percy Pitt says 'it' is good on the whole with a few weak spots: anyone with an ear can see e.g. that Marie cannot take the place of vierge &c. &c.

So go along.

I return the sheaf of suggestions.

I am not well.

> Yours ever,
> Ed. Elgar[98]

He was in fact coming to value Alfred Littleton's advice over many things. He was being pressed urgently to accept a professorship of music in the new University of Birmingham. He had refused several similar offers, but this time Granville Bantock was closely involved, and many other friends and acquaintances (mostly from the Birmingham Festival) were implicated. On 21 November Elgar went to London especially to consult Littleton over this question. (He took the occasion to drop into Boosey the new score of a third *Pomp and Circumstance* March—one of the few items excluded from the Novello contract. The terms were £50 plus a royalty on all arrangements.)

Littleton advised acceptance of the professorship, but with an added provision that Elgar might resign after three years. Returning home, Elgar sent this note:

Plas Gwyn, Hereford.
Nov 22: 1904 6 p.m.

My dear Littleton:

I arrived all safe [—] very cold!

Many thanks for your good advice which I have acted upon.

I am reconsidering the Mainz trip [to hear Fritz Volbach conduct *The Apostles* on 30 Nov.] as Steinbach is doing 'In the South' in Cologne on the 6th [December]. I have long promised to go: also I think Mr.Schuster will go with me so I shd have an admirable *Compagnon de Voyage*.

We send kindest regards

> Yrs ever
> Ed.Elgar.

I have just heard them [Sinclair's orchestra] rehearsing the new small orch. version of Canto popolare. It *sounds* charming & quite easy.

Another area in which Elgar sought Littleton's advice was over various proposals to visit the United States. These had begun with Professor Sanford's offer of an honorary degree from Yale University in June 1905. An expression of interest from

[98] HWRO 705:445:8298.

the Worcester (Massachusetts) Festival came in a card from William H. Pendleton, whose wife, the soprano Lillian Blauvelt, had recently appeared at Covent Garden. Elgar wrote:

Plas Gwyn, Hereford.
Nov 22: 1904

My dear Littleton:

I found the enclosed card here.

Mr P. (who you may remember is Mad:Blauvelt's husband) wrote to me sometime ago & I put him off vaguely.

I don't think he is at all the sort of man for me—but I may do him wrong.

The point which I hesitate over is this—he says 'a new work for our biggest festival'[.] Is this the old Worcester thing which I refused or is it something else? Can you do anything with it? If you do not care to mix it up with the other U.S. things I shall just say 'no'—only I shd. like to know what I am saying 'no' to.

> Yours ever
> Ed:Elgar

Littleton's reply is missing, but he probably advised against the proposal as Elgar never produced a work at the American Worcester Festival or attended it.

His ten days on the continent included the performance of *The Apostles* at Mainz on 30 November, another at Rotterdam on 1 December, and *In the South* conducted by Steinbach on 6 December. Next day Elgar paid a visit to Julius Buths in Düsseldorf. Back in Cologne for his last day in Germany, he wrote to Jaeger.

Dom Hotel, Köln Domplatz.
Dec 8. 1904

My dear Jaeger:

I must send you one line from the Rhine: we have talked of you much & wished you were here & in Düsseldorf: we were paying a short visit to Buths yesterday: much rain.

I will tell you of the performances when we meet. At Mainz the *real* effect of the shepherds [in *The Apostles*]

outside was beautiful & quite justifies my 'stage direction' ['remote']. The Judas at Rotterdam [Van Post] was the best we have yet had—in fact I could scarcely wish for anything better!

> Love to you all
> Yrs ever
> Ed E

Just starting for Bruxelles [on the way home]
P.T.O.
P.S. I fear I forgot to tell you that [Charles] Tree in Caractacus [at Worcester on 9 Nov.] was really *fine*—I think very highly of him[99]

Back in London, Elgar and Frank Schuster plunged into activity. Volbach came to London to conduct his *Raffael* at the Royal College of Music on 13 December. Two nights later Steinbach conducted the London Symphony Orchestra in Bach, Beethoven, and Brahms. From Schuster's house Elgar wrote to Jaeger, who was ill again. He had tuberculosis, and was to be sent to Switzerland for the winter.

22 Old Queen st[,] S.W.
Dec 16 1904
My dear Moss:

I cannot tell you how grieved we are to hear of the illnesses in your house, we can only hope you are improving & will soon be all right again.

I was looking forward to much talk with you over past schemes, present schemes, &, above all, *future* ideas.

Well this must wait until we meet.

Dear old Volbach & Steinbach, auch, send all sorts of messages to you— Volbach, whose ideas of the size of London are very vague, about 5.30 one evening expressed a desire to pay you a little visit: I had reluctantly to tell him it was not possible to get to you [at Muswell Hill], & back to Westminster to dress, dine, & be at the R.C.M. at eight.

Now my love to you all & send word how you are going on.

Yours ever
Edward

The [Steinbach] concert yesterday was divine.[100]

In preparing *The Banner of St George* for printing in full score, West found discrepancies between the manuscript score and parts which had been in use, and wrote to ask about these.

Plas Gwyn, Hereford.
Dec 23 1904
My dear West:

Many thanks for your letter about the Scores & Parts.

The discrepancies arose in this way: I sent the score—in the old days—to the firm & never had it back to correct or compare the parts; it could not be spared as the M.S. Wind pts were being prepared from the score while the string pts were going through the press (proof copies for performance): I corrected the Strg pts only by comparing them with Dodd's copies & by playing them thro'[.] I always imagined the Scores had been made to correspond with the Parts: probably even the phrasing of the string passages differs because (very probably) I never had 1st & 2nd Viol:, for instance, at the same time & I don't think I have seen any *original* full score since 1897!

I am sorry for all the trouble you have had & send many thanks; I will carefully go through the whole lot. If there remains anything else of mine to engrave in score it wd. be best to roughly collate everything before beginning work.

Kindest regards & best wishes for Christmas

Yours sncly
Edward Elgar[101]

Two days after Christmas Elgar had what his wife described as 'an odious letter from Stanford'. There had been friction of temperaments almost since the two composers became acquainted, and this was a final parting. The Stanford letter does not appear to survive, and the only known clue to its contents is contained in Elgar's next letter to Alfred Littleton.

Plas Gwyn, Hereford.
Dec 29:1904

My dear Littleton:

It is very near the end of the year & I must send you all good wishes for the New One & add thanks, very many, for all your kindness during not only the past year but in many before that. I do not write the same thing to the firm, but I am sure the members of it are very human (although I don't know them all!) & I shall be very much obliged if you will be so good as to let them know how grateful I am for all they have done & are doing & how satisfied I am with our present arrangements.

I have been overwhelmed with accumulations of letters & have had no time to work &, also, many *disagreeables* arise from a certain quarter over my new appointment [at the University of Birmingham] which seems to have caused bitter irritation; no more of that now. This is a time of peace & goodwill but it does not always come to the top somehow. We are all fairly well & I am recovering from the effects of many German banquets & suppers—I hope your son made an earlier return to the paths of healthy digestion; perhaps his youth saved him from dyspepsia, but in my old age—alas!

My wife joins me in kindest regards to you & Mrs.Littleton

Always very sincerely yours
Edward Elgar

There was a last flurry of correspondence with Jaeger before his departure for Switzerland.

---

[101] MS in possession of Stanley West.

Plas Gwyn, Hereford.
Dec 28. 1904

My dear Moss:

I am glad you are about again & mercifully the weather here looks better &
it is warmer. May these improvements reach you.

No: this cymbal is of no use [in *The Apostles*]: I thought we settled all this
once before! Schroeder uses a little Bell in C, perched on a stick, thus,

and strikes it with a little drum stick (wood)—this gives a clear note & 'mixes
up' with the other percussion & *suggests* the right sort of sound: ask him. It
really is not of much importance.

Yes: it is dreary about poor [Arthur] Johnstone [the *Manchester Guardian*
critic who had just died at the age of 43], one of the best fellows & *the* best
critic we had.

No time for more now: I am up to my eyes in work—not music, alas!

Yrs ever
Edward

Please send 'In Moonlight' [(] in F. I shd. think) to Mr. Cary Elwes: I haven't
his address.[102]

Gervase Cary Elwes (1866–1921) was beginning to make his name as a memorable
interpreter of Gerontius.

[102] HWRO 705:445:8709.

1905

Plas Gwyn, Hereford.
Jan 1:1905
My dear Littleton:

1.) On looking through my memoranda I find I scored the two Ladies' voice trios [*The Snow* and *Fly, Singing Bird*] for orchestra last Jany. I promised to do these for Henry Wood's Concert. I don't know if they are any good in this form & I don't remember settling with you anything about the scores. I leave it *entirely to you* & if the firm understood that I was doing the scores to oblige Wood I do not expect anything.

2.) I am sadly needing 100£ now to clear off the remainder of our moving, can you let me have that [from the royalty account]? After this I think all will be clear.

I do not repeat good wishes as you will have recd. my letter.

Yours ever
Edward Elgar

Littleton proposed 25 guineas for the two Trio orchestrations, and sent the £100 from the royalty account, which Elgar accepted on 5 January.

Jaeger, as his departure came closer, was apprehensive for the future. He wrote a letter to Elgar (now missing), and Elgar responded:

Plas Gwyn, Hereford.
Jan 3. 190[5]
My dear Jaeger:

I—we [—] are truly distressed to receive your sad-toned letter & trust things are shaping to make your peremptory journey *possible* &, as far as may be, comfortable. I feel sure the firm will do all possible for you. This is no comfort &, indeed, it is impossible to say anything under the circumstances that does not appear foolish or at least jejune.

I have no doubt Pure air out of London will set you up: Elsie Buths is at Davos & our friends the Jebb-Scotts in Egypt on the same errand.

My love to you old boy, & send me word what is going on.

Our kindest regards to Mrs. Jaeger

Yours ever
in frantic haste
Edward Elgar[1]

[1] HWRO 705:445:8743. Elgar dated the letter '1904' in error.

37 Curzon Road, Muswell Hill
8/ 1/ 5
My dear Edward,

I hope to be able to leave on Wednesday [11 Jan.]—shall be away for *months*. So I just scribble a line (I am *fearfully* busy clearing up affairs & getting ready) to say Goodbye & Auf Wiedersehen under Happier circumstances. I am relieved to say that the firm are behaving liberally to me, though in *any* case this is a great worry & trouble, I need not say. I worry over your *muse*, for I fear greatly we shall get less & less out of you. This is the danger of success artistic & social! (especially social, of course). I grieve over it, & so do all those who most sincerely love & admire you. We know you *must live*, but England *Ruins* all ARTISTS

With kindest regards to Lady Elgar

much devoted love
Ever yours
A.J.Jaeger[2]

37 Curzon Road[,] Muswell Hill
9/1/5
My dear Edward,

Pray excuse a short scribble[.] I am *fearfully* busy getting ready to start on Wednesday & *quite exhausted* with the work at No.1 & here. But I *must* write a line to thank you from my heart for your kind letter & the really VERY welcome gift from our dear old President [of the 'U.B.Quiet' Club, Archibald Ramsden], *through you*!! I have had such *heavy* expenses getting ready, that only this morning in Bed I worried how to pay for the things I *must* have *without disturbing the little 'deposit' account* at the Bank. Imagine then how *grateful* I was (& am) for the splendid gift which relieved me of genuine worrying anxiety. I thank you & A.R. *very* warmly.

Send me your 'theme' to shorten the journey! Do! I hope to leave Wednesday morning or afternoon & WISH I were there! I dread the whole business.

And now goodbye & 'Auf Wiedersehen' & Bless You!

Kindest regards to Lady Elgar & much love to you

Ever yours
AJJaeger

Dear J.B.MacEwen sent me £15 directly he heard I had to go away. I returned it of course, because he only emerged from absolute *poverty* a few years ago. But I was *much* pleased with the kind thought that prompted his action[.] He is a brick.[3]

² HWRO 705:445:8751.   ³ HWRO 705:445:8752.

Plas Gwyn, Hereford.
Jan 11:1905
My dear Littleton:

We have been very much distressed to hear of Jaeger's illness & his enforced absence abroad for a time. It has brought to mind a proposition I intended making some time ago & if you think well of it, it might give him something more or less interesting to do at odd times & he might feel he was not quite out of things. The proposition is to let him make analyses of some of the old things which have never been adequately done. 'King Olaf' was done by Joseph Bennett in a great hurry & many themes are left out. 'Caractacus' I don't remember but I think Thompson did it more or less sketchily.

I don't know if the shorter things 'The Light of Life' & the 'Banner' are important enough, but I don't think they have been analysed at all.

I have said no word of this to anyone.

Yrs ever
Edward Elgar

Unfortunately the scheme came to nothing, as Jaeger's first letter from Switzerland showed all too clearly.

Hotel Buol[,] Davos-Platz
19/ 1/ 5
My dear Edward

I ought to have written to you before what I now mean to write, but I havent felt sufficiently settled down in this Godforsaken, lonely [*altered to lovely*] Hole in the —— the d—— Alps. The Hole & the Alps are allright & 'pretty' (as the English miss said of the 'Appassionata' of Beethoven) but I prefer Muswell Hill & wife & family, or Berners Street & *work*! Well, here I am & I mean to try & bear the *boredom* & the Homesickness.

Now then: When I was staying at Plas Gwyn last Sept. I suggested your writing something *specially* for Buths' Lower Rhine Festival in May. You then said he (B) 'would want nothing'. I said 'D—— nonsense'. Now I have been to see Buths & while he was away conducting a Rehearsal I had a long talk with Mrs.B. She told me that 'The Apostles' being impossible *after* Cöln (*B.* ALSO *said that*) they must do without you, but, when I asked whether an orchestral work *especially written would be welcome*, Mrs. B. said she felt *quite sure* B & the Committee would *jump at it*: But it must be a *Ur*-aufführung, see? First production *any*where. Now seeing what B has done for Your fame, I think you ought to see whether you cant do something. But it must be of your *Best* entre nous, because You will be matched with Mahler whose 3rd Symphony with chorus will form an important part of the Fest. most likely (this is a secret *at present*.) Of course you may have nothing Ready. In that case never mind! I feel sure you wont mind my suggesting such a thing.

Life here is boredom in excelsis so far, & *fearfully* expensive; Everything costs '*extra*', until one doesnt Know what one may do, eat—drink & breathe 'free'.

Send me a card when you have [a] moment & say how you are & Lady Elgar & Carice

The Morning's Post is the only bright spot of our Existence, for I may not indulge in any sport & am only allowed to walk a *little, slowly*. The rarified atmosphere makes breathing difficult *at present*. I shall get used to it. I dream horribly every night (last night that A.C.Mackenzie was dead!) another effect of the air.

> Much love,
> Ever your
> AJJgr[4]

[*postcard*]
Plas Gwyn, Hereford.
Jan 21: 1905

My dear Moss:

Very glad to receive your address: don't worry about the doctors' reports, here or there, but just roll round & get fat & well. I cannot write a letter at this moment because I am full of *business* (alas!). Here we are in the depth of winter, ground covered with frozen snow; fog abounding & frost very severe: my balcony is alive with countless birds of all sorts. Carice & my niece feed them too well perhaps. I have no news, musical or otherwise. We all send our love & hope to write soon with accounts of anything interesting—if anything interesting ever turns up again, which I doubt.

> Much love.
> Yours ever affectly—
> Edward Elgar

Thanks also for the view.[5]

Five days later Elgar was implementing Jaeger's suggestion of a scherzo for strings, to be ready for his London Symphony Orchestra concert in March.

[*postcard*]
Plas Gwyn, Hereford.
26/ 1/ 05

Dear Moss: I'm doing that string thing in time for the Sym: orch: concert. Intro: & Allegro—no working out part but a devil of a fugue instead. G major & the sd. divvel in G minor

---

[4] HWRO 705:445:8753.   [5] HWRO 705:445:8742.

with all sorts of japes & counterpoint. I will write soon.

Yours ever affectly
Edward[6]

But with Jaeger far away, Elgar's correspondence with Novello turned more and more to Alfred Littleton. He and his staff gave generously of their time and experience in the cause of promoting Elgar as a concert artist—despite the fact that not all the works performed were Novello publications. In the London Symphony concert, Elgar proposed to the Orchestra's secretary Thomas Busby to include the première of *Pomp and Circumstance* March No. 3 (published by Boosey) side by side with that of the *Introduction and Allegro*—the first important work appearing under the virtually exclusive Novello contract.

Plas Gwyn, Hereford.
Jan 24: 1905
My dear Littleton:

I have sent a sketch programme (Copy with this) to Mr.Busby to-day: I have the new March ready (score in print) so they may as well do that.

The new String Orchestra thing I will send to you as soon as possible—it will be rather a rush to get the parts out but I will send the score in 'pieces' commencing in a few days I *hope*

The enclosed* things may interest you: I fear there must be a considerable cessation of music in Poland & Russia just now—It is really too horrible.

Yours sincerely
Edward Elgar

*my wife wd. like them back sometime

Revolutions in the East seemed far away as Elgar finished most of the *Introduction and Allegro* and posted it to Novello.

---

[6] Elgar Birthplace parcel 343.

Plas Gwyn, Hereford.
Feb 6.1905

Dear Sirs:

By this post regd I send pp 1–90 incl. full score op 47 for the Sym Orch Concert.

There will be about 20 pages more which will reach you this week: please get on with the parts as soon as possible

Yrs v fa[ithfu]lly
Edward Elgar

Two days later Elgar conducted the London Symphony Orchestra for the first time—at Oxford, where the *'Enigma' Variations* figured in a concert to celebrate a degree ceremony in which Elgar was given an honorary doctorate. He returned to finish the *Introduction and Allegro*.

Plas Gwyn, Hereford.
Feb 13 1905

My dear Littleton:

I have been very busy with my Op 47 & very busy with *liver* also—alas! Better now.

I send today the remainder of this work which I hope you will like—it is not for amateurs but I think as there are two good tunes in it, it may be boiled down for small String Orch.

By the way they want me to conduct the London Symphy orch: on *Sunday* (Concert Society) Q's Hall on March 19th. I suppose you will allow us to do this new piece—it will not be advertised they say until *after* March 8.

Barings have written again about U.S.A. & I have asked them to write to you.

I saw [the LSO manager] Mr.Sharpe & Mr Busby at Oxford & said I wd. go to the North [on a tour] with the orch. but have heard nothing since.

Hope you well

Kindest regards
Yours ever
Edward Elgar:

Two minutes for post.

Composing finished for the moment, he could turn to other matters. One was John E. West's piano arrangement of *Froissart*.

Plas Gwyn, Hereford.
Feb 16 1905.

My dear West:

Many thanks for your letter: I quite agree with you as to avoiding pianistic squeakiness but occasionally one has to throw a passage up an octave & avoid confusion and it doesn't sound bad I think in a piano, i.e. soft, passage.

Enclosed I send a suggestion for the 'thick' bars which clears the passage up somewhat daringly but the effect is all right.

I think the rest is excellent.

> Kind regards
> Yours sincerely
> Edward Elgar

And a letter written the same day to Jaeger contained the confirmation that Professor Sanford had arranged an honorary degree at Yale University as the central event of Elgar's first visit to America in the coming summer.

Plas Gwyn, Hereford.
Feb 16 1905

My dear Jagpot:

At last I feel I can write a few lines: I hope you are much better & feel that resignation to a monotonous existence for a time is doing you a world of good.

Now: I wrote to S.S.Sanford & I hear from him—a most kind & affectionately worded letter—& you must let him do all he wishes to do—in case, that is[,] that he wishes to do more. This I beg you for all our sakes: I did not offer to send you anything because I think you know that anything I have is yours!

I have finished the string thing & its all right; of course it will take you sometime to get used to it, but it will sound really wholesome — bring out much tone from the Strings. There are all sorts of wild ideas afloat as to my conducting [the première] but at present all is sub rosa. ·

The weather has been better lately & makes it possible to get out between work but I miss my golf sadly—the Links here are too far away.

We had a nice time at Oxford when the degree was conferred[.] Parry was in great form—there was a dinner & a Concert. The London Symphy orchestra played the Variations better than ever; it is a jolly fine orchestra.

Steinbach has been again in London: I think you wd enjoy his readings—so strong & so *tender*. The critics made fools of themselves as usual: he played the boisterous Brandenburg String Concerto [No. 3]: some of em said Bach requires more *delicate* treatment; so he does in delicate movements. How is [it] that they always try to say the *idiotic* thing?

I make my inaugural address in Birmingham on March 16th, but cannot say much to the point: but in time I shall be able to speak out on many points.

Do you do much reading? if so what? If you did not see it, you might try
'The Forerunner' by Merejowski—fine but long—
Send a p.c. sometimes [—] never mind a long letter.
I must now conclude as I have long business letters to write & light wanes.

Your [*sic*] ever
Edwd.

I dedicate the String thing to Sanford, bless him![7]

Elgar's tour of northern cities with the London Symphony Orchestra was fixed for November 1905. One of its sponsors was the Birmingham agent Percy Harrison, described by Henry Wood as

. . . the real old type of concert manager. He would run three or four tours a season, losing heavily on the swings but occasionally making a good thing out of the roundabouts. I must say he did the thing handsomely and I never heard an artist murmur a word against him. He was a fresh-looking, dapper little fellow of uncertain age.[8]

Another partner (a silent one) in the venture was Frank Schuster, for Alice Elgar's diary for 20 February 1905 contains the line: 'E. settling with Frank about conducting the Concerts.'

Plas Gwyn, Hereford.
Feb 20 1905
My dear Littleton:

Yes: I agreed to the terms 26 gui[nea]s a day and Rly expenses (not Hotel) if the whole tour is gone through: at least that is what I understood. Thanks for all your information: I was very decided (with Mr.Sharpe) that I wd. have nothing to do with any 'infant prodigies' or vocalists of whom I don't approve. Harrison is 'sound' on these points but Barings [of Cheltenham] may want looking after.

As to U.S.A.—I have no idea what Barings have in their minds: I think I have sent you every letter from the other side also. The idea of a visit—professionally—to the States seems to be talked about. & Professor Sanford in a letter in which he invites me to pay him a private visit thro June says 'it might be the way to crystallise the various schemes for your conducting'. I think my wife & myself *may* go for a month at the end of May, but I leave all the conducting things with you.

It is awfully cold here with N.E. wind & snow
A thousand thanks for all you are doing.

Yrs sincy
Edward Elgar.

---

[7] HWRO 705:445:8744.   [8] *My Life of Music*, p. 189.

Over the preparation of his new music, however, Elgar was missing the help of Jaeger. Through formal notes to the firm, he had arranged for score and parts of the *Introduction and Allegro* to arrive in time to go through them with John Austin on 24 February.

Hereford
Feb 24 1905
Dear Sirs:

By this post I return the proofs of the *Tutti parts* corrected & the M.S.Score

I *keep* the *Solo*-Quartet copies (M.S.) which I will distribute to the players *unless* I hear from you by return that you must have them during next week for engraving: the Soloists will no doubt be glad to see them but I will keep them here until Monday night.

Never mind the heading for the present[.] I will talk to Mr.Alfred Littleton when I am in town.

as to the Score: the Quartet should go at the *top*—I only wrote it in its present position for convenience.

Could you have the score *stitched* before Sunday.

Please note that the rehearsal is on Sunday morning so the librarian should have the custody of the parts on Saturday. Will you make sure of this.

Yours v try
Edward Elgar

The Jaeger correspondence now devolved upon Alice Elgar.

Plas Gwyn, Hereford.
1 March 1905.
My dear Mr.Jaeger

I must send you a few lines as E. has been so *very* rushed with proofs & letters endless, business &c.

First we do hope you are feeling *much* better & perhaps able for more out of doors wh. wd. be some little help to passing the time less wearily.

We have had a long phase of cold stormy weather wh. quite stopped E's [bicycle] rides, & as it is his only recreation here, he has missed it very much— Before that we had some lovely days & this dear country looked delightful & Springlike.

On Friday, all being well, we are to go to London & E has rehearsals of his new String Op. & new [*Pomp and Circumstance*] March [No. 3]—Both are so delightful. I am longing to hear the full effect with Orch—I will try & let you hear as I know you will be longing to learn & to be there to hear too.

It promises, all being well, to be a very busy month, as besides E.'s Inaugural Lecture at Birmingham, he is to conduct 'Gerontius' at Leeds, & the 'Apostles' at Hanley. & on Sunday aftn. in London his String Serenade at the New Concert Club Concert.

Did I tell you about our Oxford Visit? We had a really very nice time. We were staying in New College at the Wardens, & Carice & our niece [May Grafton] who is with us now, with some other friends. Sir Hubert [Parry] made a good Latin oration & E. looked very nice in the Robes & as for the performance of the Varns. I never heard any like it, it was gorgeous—

We have all sorts of things coming up in the garden & are hoping to see them quite in blossom in 2 or 3 weeks.

Did I tell you about E.'s portrait? Mr. Talbot Hughes came down & stayed here & painted it. I think it will really be *very* nice; he wants another sitting or two. The pose is so easy & nice & it is so good to have so many of his own intimate surroundings as it was painted here—I suppose it will be in the Academy & then I do not know what its fate is to be. We missed it so much—it fired E. with a great desire to paint & he has bought a box of oil colours, & paints strange symbolical pictures à la Böcklin, & Segantini & Blake! He certainly has a power of representing a scene from his imagination. & one that he has done of a river with sombre trees & a boat crossing is very suggestive. We will explain the symbolism some day I hope to you—

I do hope you have good accounts from home & will be restored there strong & well—You shall have all the news I can send you, best remembrances[.] E. is out or wd. send his love,

Yrs sincerely
C.A.Elgar[9]

On 3 March the Elgars left for London, to stay with Frank Schuster in Old Queen Street. There on the following morning Elgar rehearsed the solo quartet parts with the London Symphony first desk men—Arthur Payne, W. H. Eayres, Alfred Hobday, and Bertie Patterson Parker (1871–1930). Their preliminary practice and two full rehearsals with the Orchestra failed to secure a brilliant performance of the new work. Elgar conducted in some bad health—brought on in all probability by the approaching inaugural lecture as Professor of Music at the University of Birmingham on 16 March.

The lecture attracted much attention—a good deal of it hostile, as Elgar was very outspoken in finding fault with the practice of music in England. Alice sent a summary to Jaeger:

Plas Gwyn, Hereford.
28 March 1905.

Dear Mr. Jaeger

You will be quite vexed & disappointed at not having heard for so long, & I am very sorry—but I have really had no time & since we returned home have been so tired out, that one letter more, having *so much* to write for E., seemed just too much—It seemed so sad not to see you at the Rehearsals & Concerts especially. Several people said they were going to write to you & send you papers, I seemed never to be able to get any papers—The Concert on the 8th was really splendid. E. conducted superbly & the Orch. is gorgeous

[9] HWRO 705:445:8841.

& play splendidly for E. *Grania* was more than beautiful & poetic, the Variations delightful & the new String piece quite fascinating. Many people think it the finest thing he has written, the 4^t. comes in with so beautiful an effect, the peroration towards the end *is* fine. The new March is *thrilling*[:] the most pacific friends were ready to fight! The critics, some of them, of course were frightened at it, but happily the Audiences judge for themselves—The Sunday Concert too was a great success—

My dear E. was unwell all the time we were away [—] the weather had been bad for some time before & he cd. not get out enough & the day after we reached London he had to have a Dr. & to be kept up just to get through his work, one day better, another day *so* bad—On the Sunday, he went from bed to the Concert & back to it, just managed to get through it—Next day the Dr. sent us home but he was quite unable to go to Leeds, wh. was of course very unfortunate. He is really better I hope & trust, & been out for a walk today, & we are trying to get him well enough for Hanley on the 30th. He dined at Buckingham Palace one Evening, it was so unfortunate the King was laid up with a cold so the Prince entertained them. E. enjoyed the Evening.

Now we do *hope* you are really better, has Spring begun at Davos yet? I do hope you are able for more outings wh. will make it less tedious for you—I was so sorry not to see Mrs.Jaeger but with E. to help & the Birmn. expedition & having a severe cold myself & many social functions, I had no moment—E. spoke splendidly at Birm. & looked very nice in gown & hood—Had a great reception—Carice & the dear niece who is with us do great things in the garden & all is helping to look nice. Forgive pencil but I am sitting by the fire. Edward's love & hopes that you are better

> Best of greetings
> Yrs. Sincy
> C.A.E.[10]

A few days later Elgar sent a postcard to Jaeger with news of the Birmingham lecture:

Plas Gwyn, Hereford.

3/ 4/ 05

My dear Jaggs:

    Thanks for yours:

I have been very unwell but am better now: glad to hear of your progress & shall write soon. It really makes one disgusted with English musical life to see the way everybody (except Kalisch who heard me speak) misquotes me! I set a high ideal for the younger men & said incidentally that three of them [Bantock, Walford Davies, and Holbrooke] had tried to uphold *serious* art in this country at the festivals: I did not say a word as to the *value* of the music

---

[10] HWRO 705:445:8839.

neither did I put them *above* any other men who did not have a festival chance last year.

Love to you
Edwd.[11]

By now several proposals were in the air for Elgar to conduct in the United States. He had written to Alfred Littleton on 27 March: 'I will not go for less than Weingartner who has £2,500 (not dollars) for sixteen concerts: they can either take me or leave me.' At Hanley three days later to conduct *The Apostles*, he talked with Muriel Foster, who had sung widely in the United States. She brought a semi-official request for Elgar to conduct at the Cincinnati May Festival in 1906.

North Stafford Hotel, Stoke-on-Trent.
Mar 31. 1905
My dear Littleton:

We had a gorgeous performance of the Apostles last night

I had a long talk with Miss Muriel Foster last night referring to *U.S.A.*: she brought all sorts of messages; nothing absolutely definite but regarding the Cincin*natt*i Festival (spe[l]t it wrong!)—they want to make it more or less of an Elgar Festival—two whole programmes[.] Now, this wd. be very nice *if* they will make it worth my while to go: she says they *will* do so.

I mention this now because as things progress & shape you might be able to divert things to Cincinatti [*sic*] if you think it worth while.

I *may* ask a young man here who is very clever to send an account of last night to the M.T.—if he does it, it shall go straight to you.

Yrs ever
Ed Elgar

I am not well

The young man was Havergal Brian (1877–1972), who asked Elgar for advice about his own compositions. Brian did send an article on the Hanley *Apostles* to *The Musical Times*—only to have it returned by the editor.

At Novello they had proofs of *The Black Knight* newly printed in full score. A letter was sent from the firm to Elgar:

---

[11] HWRO 705:445:8745.

1, Berners Street, London, W.
April 13th 1905
Dear Sir/

In correcting the proofs of The Black Knight full score, we notice that the passage beginning at [cue] X in Scene IV (p.65 of vocal score) is marked (in the full score) 'Four voices only to each part', and 'Tutti' seven bars later. These directions do not appear in the vocal score—should they be added?

Awaiting the favour of your reply,

> We are, Dear Sir,
> Yours faithfully
> Novello & Co.Ltd.
> H.L.B[rooke]

Plas Gwyn, Hereford.
16/ 4/ 05
Dear Sirs:

Black Knight
(I enclose your letter to save time.)

The words *did* appear in the first issue of the voc.score but were subsequently withdrawn & should not be printed in the full sc.

> Yrs v try
> Ed:Elgar

As for Jaeger, he was to have another operation—so serious that his wife and children went out to be with him. Alice Elgar wrote in late spring:

Plas Gwyn[,] Hereford
29 May 1905.
Dear Mr/ Jaeger

We have been wondering *where* we could think of you & Mrs.Jaeger & much wanting news. Now E. has yr. card from Glion this morning—I am *so* sorry you have had bad weather, now Summer has come to England[.] So I hope you may at last have it too—I do trust & hope you are much stronger & better & Mrs.Jaeger & the babies well, I know you must be revelling in being together again.

We are *very* busy preparing for the departure [to the United States], all being well, next week—& I trust it will do E. an immense amount of good. He is looking much better I am thankful to say. We are, D.V. to be away between 5 & 6 weeks, & shall hope to see you again on our return *very* much restored, & strong. We are to go in the 'Deutschland' from Dover on the 9th. & shall hope to write & tell you about the new country & experiences & our kindest of hosts above all—

We had a nice time at Morecambe, the Fest. was more wonderful than ever, & the singing more truly *unimaginably* beautiful. It is of no use trying to describe it, it must be heard. It wd. have done you good to have heard 'King Olaf' with *such* a chorus

Plas Gwyn is looking very sweet & nice, flowering shrubs all out & all so green & today sunny—The garden is full of young birds who give E. much anxiety, & he tries to assist the parents in saving them from dangers.

Carice has been looking so well & *very* much grown, She is very devoted to the garden here, & some dear bunny rabbits & doves—

E. will want to add a note & with my love to Mrs. Jaeger & every hope & good wish to you both

Yrs. very siny
C.A.Elgar

[note added by Elgar:]

My dear Jaeger: I am so sorry not to write fully but I have really nothing to *tell* you: I wish you all good & a very happy return home. We shall meet on our return from the good S.S.S[anford].

Yours ever
E E[12]

Hereford
June 6. 1905

My dear Jaeger:

Thanks a many for your letters: I'm so glad you are having your nasal business thoroughly done & wish you the best of things. I will deliver all your messages to S.S.S. & he will be delighted to hear of you. Let us hear how you get on; *his* address will be ours until July 11. (about).

What an extraordinary professor your doctor must be—he is rightly called Mahmoud but I hope he really does know what he is talking about. but we must not be too hard on doctors it seems: Jebb-Scott has been suffering for years & has undergone many operations, but *this* year they have suddenly discovered that they have been at the wrong place all along & have *now* attacked the root of the evil—he's doing finely but it was a much more severe business than yours—such comfort you'll say.

I don't hear anything of music now or rather of *music* I hear much, of musicians, little: they are always quarrelling.

Saw Pitt the other day & he's all right. Brewer is now a Canterbury doctor & all the others angry & he delighted: but you will hear all when you return. I

[12] HWRO 705:445:8838.

have no news of myself as I have for ever lost interest in that Person—he ceased to exist on a certain day when his friends interfered & insisted on his ——

It is very sad.

Good luck to you.
Yours ever
Edward Elgar

Morecambe was a real joy: such singing & such real *art* feeling.[13]

Just as they were sailing, the Elgars heard that Jaeger had come through the operation. Alice wrote a card from the ship:

Hamburg-Amerika Linie 'Deutschland'
9 June 1905

Just had Mrs. Jaeger's card & thankful to hear opn. over. We trust & pray you will now speedily recover. It must have been a great trial to you *both*. We started at noon today rather rainy but quite smooth. E. has a headache but will soon I trust be set up by sea air—

Best wishes & love from E. to both

Ys sicy
C.A.E.[14]

Almost as soon as they arrived in America she wrote again, from Professor Sanford's house.[15] At the Yale University graduation ceremony on 28 June, Elgar received the honorary doctorate. The following day found them awaiting a visit from the President of the Cincinnati Festival, Lawrence Maxwell Jr. After considerable correspondence with Novello, it was agreed to fix Elgar's Cincinnati fee at £1500.

Fifty-two Hillhouse Avenue[,] New Haven, Conn.
June 29:1905

My dear Littleton:

This climate is too much for me & I have been knocked over *twice* by the heat & had the doctor.

Sanford is more than kind & we have been to the Sea which was refreshing. The degree business went off well & was an imposing sight.

I really have no brains left. & have only felt well *one* day: it's very sad.

Mr Maxwell of Cincinnati is coming to see me on Friday & we may settle something—my *feelings* are dead against coming here again but my pocket gapes aloud.

Kindest rgds
Yours ever sincy
Edward Elgar

We sail on July 11.

---

[13] HWRO 705:445:8746.   [14] HWRO 705:445:8837.   [15] HWRO 705:445:8860.

Maxwell arrived next day, and they settled the matter.

A smooth return voyage, accompanied by Professor Sanford, brought the Elgars home on 17 July. By now Jaeger and his family were back in England.

· Hereford
Tuesday [18 July 1905]

My dear Moss:

One line to say we arrived safely yesterday & are both well: this is to bring you all our love & good wishes: send a p.c. to say how you are & what sort of a journey you had: I was laid up with the heat [—] too much to be pleasant but our kindest of hosts made everything lovely

Yours always
Ed:[16]

[*postmark*] Hereford
Sunday night [23 July 1905]

Dear Jaggs:

Many thanks for your letter: so glad to hear all about you. I have no moment to spare to say anything coherent. There is a *trunk* full of letters accumulated during the six weeks we were away. I will write soon

Yrs ever
Ed Elgar[17]

Jaeger reminded Elgar that there was now not much more than a year's time before the next Birmingham Festival, at which the second oratorio of the *Apostles* triology was expected. He asked for a copy of the new *Pomp and Circumstance* March No. 3, and suggested the possibility of a song cycle to poems by Henry Kirke White (1785–1806).

Plas Gwyn, Hereford.
Augt 6. 1905

My dear Moss:

Kirke White isn't much of a poet but the idea is good [—] I have the poems somewhere in the house, an old book of my dear mother's (as usual)[.] I don't think I can do anything with it—the two last lines in your copy had better be omitted.

I send you an old proof of No.III P.&C.; if it's not what you want tell me.

I know nothing about Apostles pt.2. or any analysis: if it is ever finished I imagined you might take on the analysis *if* properly recompensed: my life now is one incessant answering of letters & music is fading away.

Love to you all
Yrs ever
Edwd.[18]

The *Introduction and Allegro* was to be played at the Worcester Festival in September, and copies of the new piano duet arrangement would be wanted for sale then. Before the end of August Jaeger sent the first instalment of proofs.

1, Berners Street, London, W.
August 23rd. 1905
My dear Elgar,

Here is the completion of your (& S.S.S's) String piece, P.F. Duet. Kindly send the proofs back prestissimo possibile, as I want to get the plates corrected & then some advance copies pulled *at once*, to secure the American copyright before the Worcester Festival for which event I want to get the *sale* copies ready. While the advance copies are on the way to Washington, we can complete & [*sic*] the proof Reading (sending second proofs to Singer) & printing, See?

Dear J. Buths has just written to me that he will do the 'Apostles' at his 8th subscription concert on April 5/ 1906, & he asks me to tell you. He enquires about the Soloists you had at Mainz & Rotterdam & I am giving him all the information I can, from the short notices in the January *M.T.* But they don't give the names of the soloists at the Dutch port, except that of the Judas, Herr van Post. Perhaps Lady Elgar, or your Secretary will Kindly write a line to the dear little Professor. Doubtless Lady Elgar has kept the R'dam programme?

I saw my Dr (Schofield) last night; He says I have done *splendidly* at Davos, but that the left lung is not yet quite right, & I ought to return to D. next November. Dr Buol at Davos told me the same thing, but the Professor Demiéville (Lung Specialist) at *Lausanne* said I was quite fit to return to England to work. Needless to say I am fearfully depressed over Dr S's (a *very* capable & honest *friend*) finding & yet I know that to get ever *quite* well & safe from that terrible disease, that 'damnèd spot' (between the 3rd–4th Rib) *must* be healed up.

I haven't dared to tell anybody here yet.

Ever yours,
AJJgr

Siloti is doing the String piece in St Petersburg[19]

---

[19] HWRO 705:445:8755.

Alexander Siloti (1863–1945) was one of the most distinguished Russian musicians of his generation. He was a piano pupil of Liszt and, as conductor of the St Petersburg concerts, was Elgar's most important advocate in Russia.[20]

Plas Gwyn, Hereford.
Augt 24:05
My dear Moss:

Glad to hear from you: keep up your spirits, you old dear, & all will be well. Thanks for telling me about yourself

Look here: Can't you come to Worcester [Festival] for a day or two—they are going to give me the 'freedom of the city' on Wedy [actually Tuesday 12 Sept.]—then there's the String piece & Apostles &c.&c. We can find you a bed. & the fare won't cost you anything I'll see.

You will receive—the firm will—a new part-song—my best bit of landscape so far in that line[.] You won't make anything of it on the PF.—Morecambe is the place to hear it.

Much love
Yours ever
Ed E[21]

The new part-song was a setting of a poem by Coventry Patmore. Eventually it was entitled *Evening Scene* and dedicated to the memory of the Morecambe Festival conductor R. G. Howson.

37 Curzon Road, Muswell Hill[,] N
25/8/5
My dear Elgar,

Many thanks! It is awfully nice of you to invite me down to the Worcester Festival, & needless to say I should LOVE to come. But consider! How Can I ask the firm to give me 2 more days Holiday after having been absent from No.1 for *6 months*? I wouldn't have the impertinence to say a word about it, especially in view of the fact that very likely I *must* ask for another 'Swiss

---

[20] An undatable note (perhaps referring to *Cockaigne*) shows something of Siloti's interest.

Grand Hotel[,] Birmingham
Saturday

My dear Jaeger:

Read the enclosed & *if you can* do send for me the analysis of the Philharmonic Concert.

I *have* written to Siloti telling him it will reach him: also telling him its very long but that he may gather a par: or two from it.

If any *deadly* trouble never mind—because he might gather the idea—if that is all that is required [—] from my letter [—] See?

Love
Edward

(HWRO 705:445:unnumbered; filed with 1904).

[21] HWRO 705:445:8750.

Holiday' by the End of October. I feel that I *must* get away then by Hook or Crook, for as long as my left lung is not *quite* healed I am not safe from fresh outbreaks. So you see I can't very well ask for a 'Festival' Holiday as well. But look here: Mr Alfred would *refuse you nothing* now, and if you told him (what may be a polite fib, viz:) that *you would like me* to be present &c. &c. &c. I fancy he would say 'Allright.' But *if* you write to him in that sense you might *make him understand that I refused* your invitation for *the Reasons stated above.* I could, I fancy, easily be spared, because we are not likely to be fearfully busy. There will be only Parry's String parts of the (very jolly) '[Pied] Piper' to worry my Department then, & they are not really wanted till middle of October. However, if you are too shy to ask Mr A., never mind, though I feel sure he won't say 'nay' to you.

I say, You *are* being 'honoured' past all belief & beyond all precedent. I suppose there never has been a case of a composer receiving the Freedom of his native city? May you live long to enjoy the privileges (whatever they may be) which it (or 'She' with a big S) is supposed to grant you.

We (at No.1) are now in communication with Leipzig re a performance of the 'Apostles' there, & with Crefeld re 'Gerontius' (the Crefeld conductor, Prof Müller-Reuter is said to be A 1) Siloti wants us to promise him the first performance of your apocryphal Symphony, but I had to explain that we cannot promise anything for a country whose laws do not protect our *Performing Rights.* Anyone who would be clever enough to obtain Score & parts (say through Leipzig) *before* Siloti could forestall him without our being able to prevent him. But what of that Symphony? I daresay it is *still* in the Clouds, or in your Brainbox. I wish I could lift the veil surrounding that much talked of & long expected Symphony.

I havent yet seen that new Partsong. Have you sent it? Right you are, I'll *hear* it at Morecambe, if I'm alive.

I have seen a great deal of J. Holbrooke lately. He comes to my House frequently (*uninvited*) & we play Beethoven Symphonies (P.F.Duet) together. He is actually coming round to the extraordinary view that there's something in B's Diatonic Harmony & modulations. He is now anxious to write a Symphony *in Form.* There is hope for the young Bounder yet. For he is a *Bounder* in many ways, & lately I have had occasion to write him two such letters (quite dignified, without any abuse) as he quite humbly(!) confesses he has never received before. Mr A.H.L. & A[ugustus] J[ames] L[ittleton] & Mr. H.R.C[layton] *can't bear him*, and I have had a *very* heavy job getting some of his things accepted. And then, when N & C won't do exactly as he likes, he writes *me* a rude letter in which he insults the Firm. By Jove, I gave him 'what for', and told him some truths about his lack of manners *generally* (He *insults* all who cross his path, publishers, critics[,] musicians &c). He wants a lot of Educating yet before decent people put up with him & his cockney vulgar-isms & 'ganuin' impertinences. He is a brilliant fellow in many ways, but his character is that of a money-grabbing, *greedy*, objectionably loquacious *Jew* (I believe he *is* of Jewish descent) He is now writing *for money*, he confesses,

& the Norwich (or is it Bristol) 'Bohemian Song' contain stuff which is distinctly written to please the gallery. (There is one *poem*—the *words* I mean—by himself, all about a Drum, which becomes dumb rummin' tea-tum!) And the 'Jugendsünden', some of them *quite* unworthy of his present reputation, which he now brings forward to make money prove him the reverse of a true artist. I advise him to burn or drown them like first puppies, but he wont, & so I spend hours pointing out utterly false accentuations in his texts &c.&c And oh! how *slovenly* he is in every way!

And now, through your help, he will get a commission for B'ham[—] Lucky Dog! I am going to help Bell all *I* can. Poor, splendid young fellow! He is a man of *sterling, manly* qualities & producing beautiful stuff now, after his experiences of previous efforts.

Ever yours
AJJgr[22]

37 Curzon Road
29/8/5

My dear Elgar,

I took a proof of the 'Evening Scene' home to study & have been much moved by the thing: a most poetic conception fully charged with an exquisitely peaceful 'Abend-Stimmung'. More Harmony than Melody, and yet of the very essence of *music*. I am reminded of Schubert (Der Leier-mann),—I suppose because of the opening fifths,—or Hermann Goetz, though why of the latter I dont know. But I mean to suggest no 'reminis-cences'. It's the peace & poetry about the thing which brought the composer of that lovely F major Symphony into my mind, I daresay.

The use of Drone-Bass fifths & progressions in Sixths & octaves suggests to me a *wide expanse of* country for the 'Scene', such as fills the soul with a sweet melancholy—at Eventide, & prompts the mind to indulge in reveries. Those passages of octaves in Soprano & Tenor moving against octaves in Contralto & Bass will sound wondrously mysterious & 'far-away'. Alto-gether a perfect gem of a 'picture'.

But it will require marvellous singing to bring out all the poetry that is in the piece. A rough performance will utterly ruin it & the average concert going ass 'wont see anything in it'. Anyhow, I congratulate you on the lovely creation & the Morecambe people on the chances they will have of hearing it properly performed.

Tomorrow Holbrooke is again coming to my House when I want to point out a lot of absurdities in one of his partsongs. He doesnt know what to do with the *Chords* in a partsong; omits noun, verb & everything in some of the

[22] HWRO 705:445:8754.

parts, so that they sing *nonsense*. To him words are only means for making a *musical* effect. never mind whether he mauls them about in some of the parts & makes nonsense out of them.

Ever yours
A.J.Jaeger

Don't waste time to reply![23]

Alfred Littleton's house-hunting had found its answer in a house named Hatteral in Hereford, within walking distance of Plas Gwyn.

Plas Gwyn, Hereford.
Augt 20. 1905
My dear Littleton:

No cottage for your gardener yet!

This is only to say that I have recd a letter from Görlitz about some American scheme wh. sounds *colossal*: there seems to be a chance of my seeing him on his tour so I thought it best to fit in with this plan: I have always turned things of the sort over to you & if this should get so far as to require terms to be arranged, I will do so again. but at present the thing is vague: so we will talk it over & if you are in the mind to be bothered I will refer G. to you: don't trouble to answer this: it is only to let you know what is happening.

Kindest regards
Yours ever
Edward Elgar:

Next day Elgar went to Chester to meet Hugo Görlitz, and reported:

Plas Gwyn, Hereford.
Augt 26. 1905
My dear Littleton:

I saw Görlitz & his scheme is a revived form of the affair Mr.Chester wrote about Wanamaker's Hall opening: Görlitz says it is in his hands now. They wanted the affair in January or some such time, but my agreement with the Cincinatti [*sic*] people prevents this: he is cabling this & suggesting November in next year. I'll tell you more when we meet. He offers £2,200 for the 8 or 10 concerts & *all expenses* for myself wife and servant!

I was afraid poor old Jaeger might feel left out so I invited him to Worcester for a day or two: he of course refused saying he could not ask the firm to let him off as he's been away so long, on his dreary errand. If it is not a busy time & *if you think well of it*—there may be many reasons for refusing— do tell him he may come to Worcester Festival if he likes. I shall not say a

---

[23] Elgar Birthplace parcel 398.

word more but leave it to you & shall perfectly understand: I could manage that the expense wd. be nothing. It wd give us the greatest pleasure to see him. We wd. do anything to have Jaeger with us!

I wrote a partsong & sent it up the other day—it is quite a short thing & will do for artistic singers but I fear it's not a gold mine & it certainly isn't a pot boiler—I think it's the best I've done & I put it to the memory of Mr Howson of Morecambe: one of the best men I ever met.

I have heard of no cottage yet.

Kindest rgrds
Yours ever
Edward Elgar

I have not been able to go to see Hatteral [but[24]] my wife has been: did you see 'The Quarry House'? I have some idea that it was too small.
Alice was delighted with the garden & grounds

The proofs of *Evensong Scene* reached Elgar, and he returned them with a note:

Plas Gwyn, Hereford.
Sep 3 1905
Dear Sirs:

I see on the enclosed proofs an enquiry as to more exp: marks in the accpt.
My views were written on the M.S.—but, if there is room, more marks can go in if desired—following the voc.parts.

Yrs v siy
Ed.Elgar

The music editor West noted: 'I have added one or two more. These will probably be enough.'

It was arranged for Jaeger to come to Worcester for the Festival, and Alice Elgar wrote to welcome him to their house party:

Plas Gwyn, Hereford.
Thursday [7 Sept. 1905]
Dear Mr. Jaeger

A hasty line to tell you we are so glad you are coming & shall expect you on Monday with much pleasure. Castle House[,] *College Green*[.] I do hope we shall have nice weather.

I wanted to ask you to send to Worcester or bring me a copy of the *German* Edn. of the 'Apostles'[.] I lost mine, alas! at Köln. May it be roan or somethg. like it. Of course I will purchase it.

[24] Elgar wrote 'by'.

I do hope you are keeping well & Mrs.Jaeger—my love to her, Excuse haste,

Vy siny
C.A.Elgar

I shd. like to be at the Rehearsal today.[25]

That was a London orchestral rehearsal for Worcester, where Jaeger saw Elgar, as he reported in his acknowledgement to Alice Elgar. She responded:

Plas Gwyn
8 Sept. 1905.
Dear Mr.Jaeger

So many thanks for your sweet letter, I *am* so glad you can come, it is good of Mrs.Jaeger to spare you—If you must go to the A[tkins']s you must absolutely only go for 1 night, as you come for a real holiday & are NOT to be worried, So wd. you fix Wednesday if quite the same as that wd. be rather the best for us, but you must dine with us on Wednesday & come back on Thursday—If you wd. rather go there another day, of course do, & all shall be arranged—

Love to Mrs.Jaeger & all being well, it *will* be nice—So glad my dear Knight looked well—

Ys. very sicy &
very welcoming
C.A.E.

I am [*illegible*] E.'s sketch book with *such* a lovely tune.[26]

Jaeger arrived, and took as energetic a part in the festivities as he could in his precarious state of health. At the end of the week Elgar accepted an invitation from Lord and Lady Charles Beresford to cruise with the Mediterranean Fleet. He quickly packed, and sent a note to Alfred Littleton about permission to use the words of *Evening Scene*.

Plas Gwyn, Hereford   *In train*
Friday [15 Sept. 1905]
My dear Littleton:

I am sorry I had to depart without seeing you & Mrs Littleton.

Enclosed I send the revise & Mrs.Patmore's two letters which cover the ground: as we were not able to consult perhaps the title will do: I am on my way to Greece! Crossing the channel tonight & go straight through to

Brindisi: get an Austrian boat there & join the fleet somewhere in the Greek Archipeligo!

> Kindest regards
> Yours ever
> Edward Elgar

A few days later Alice Elgar reported on her husband's Mediterranean progress:

Plas Gwyn, Hereford.
19 Sept. 1905.

My dear Mr.Jaeger

I hope you & Mrs.Jaeger returned none the worse for the fatigues—*What* a delightful & wonderful week it was—the appreciation of the works, & the personal affection shown to E. touched us both most deeply.

Now I trust he is nearly at Athens, does it not seem wonderful even to write the name? Our Dr. who was over on Thursday so *strongly* urged his going & he had not been as vigorous for some time as we cd. have wished, so I trust this will do him so much good, & it sounds entrancingly delightful. Of course I miss him most *dreadfully*.

I wish we cd. have seen more of Mrs.Jaeger & were *so* glad to have you, it was a delightful party.

Now could you, without trouble, help me in this. I am anxious to Collect all Edward's sketches, rough Copies &c, together, as I know they are of great interest. I can only think of a sort of portfolio Cases (preferably to *stand up* on shelves) Some of the music paper wd. require 16 in. in height. Do you think you cd. very soon send me ½ doz? (a purchase of course) I shd. think nice *lineny* wd. be best. I do want to collect & arrange them.

> Love to you both
> Yr. siny
> C.A.Elgar   PTO

P.S.

I so much want to know what has become of the full Score of the 'Apostles', it was over in the Cathedral & I inquired about it & Mr.Atkins promised he wd. see &c but I have heard nothing, & it is our only copy—& there is a blank in the house without it. I fancy it has E.'s name in blue pencil.

Just had a telegram from E. from Patras [—] all well—D.G.[27]

1, Berners Street, London, W.
Sept 20th 1905

Dear Lady Elgar,

Many thanks for your Kind letter. You have forestalled me, for I was on the point of writing to you last night, and only domestic incidents prevented me. Yes! it was a remarkable & wholly enjoyable Festival experience, & I thank you once more with all my heart for so kindly letting me enjoy the

---

[27] HWRO 705:445:8834–5.

prized privilege of joining your House party. I am convinced your other friends could not have appreciated the Honour more than, if as much as the ever devoted old mosshead, Japot, Jaggs, Nimrod! I fancy even you, dear Lady Elgar, could scarcely feel deeper joy & gratification than I do at the wonderful rise of our dear E.E & the phenomenal growth in the appreciation of his great works. It warms my heart, & makes me happy (& also *proud*) to have been one of those, who, like yourself, have believed in his genius for so long, & fought the good fight for his recognition staunchly & fruitfully through good & evil hours. The triumph is *yours* no less than his!

That Edward has safely arrived in Greece delights me. What impressions will crowd upon his wonderful Brain as he nears Athens & beholds from afar the Acropolis which stands—even in ruins—for all that is greatest & noblest in art & History. The journey will stimulate him & his creative faculty tremendously, I have no doubt & he will return strong in health & brimful of ideas. Only!—What about 'Apostles Part III' for B'ham next year!? I begin to fear me that we shall hope in vain to see our soaring expectations fulfilled.

Now Business: I send you by Parcel Post a case with *flaps*. Kindly tell me whether it is *something like* what you require? Of course your cases would be stouter & larger, with broader backs & larger flaps, to allow of the insertion (comfortably) of say $\frac{1}{2}$ inch or 1 inch (*kindly say which*) of thickness. I can think of nothing better, nor can our Binders, who lent me this case.

Do you want all cases bound in the same colour cloth, say brown 'Holland', or shall I select some (varied) nice colours? Or if you like, I can send you a batch of Specimen colours (cloth) to choose from. Kindly tell me. The cases could be made in 2 or three days & you may rely on getting something good & serviceable.

I sent you a Bill for specially binding that 'Apostel' Vocal Score. The price represents *net wages cost* of the Binders. The *copy* is not charged for, of course, except, in the usual business way, against Edward's *Royalty* account.

Hoping you are quite well & with my Kindest regards & devotion

Yours sincerely
AJJaeger

P.S. My Kindest regards to dear Carice & Ditto Miss Grafton[.]
My wife enjoyed the Worcester days hugely in spite of our temporary separation[28]

Plas Gwyn, Hereford.
12 Oct. 1905.

My dear Mr. Jaeger

First I must tell you I hope to see E. safely back on Saturday, having just heard he is safe in London. It is too trying for him to have to go to Norwich [for a Festival rehearsal on 13 Oct.] before seeing him!

---

[28] HWRO 705:445:8792.

I am so glad yr. cold did not get very bad & trust you are all well again.

Thanks for telling me about the lunch & the words about E. &c. Also about Lessmann's paper. I have not seen it & much wish to. A friend & I took the Allgemeine but it has ceased to come, I know not why. Is the 'Neue Zeitschrift' really 'Neu' & does it take its place. If you wd. send me word where to get it & the No. or date of the one with notice of the Intron. & Allegro, I shd. be grateful.

Now you *are* good & kind, the cases came yesterday, & are really beautiful[.] We had a great work last evening & already filled all but 4—They are lovely, & it is so deeply interesting to have the sketches & M.S. &c, where they can be seen, it was so interesting sorting them out. Now the want is, shelves deep enough to put them on! May [Grafton] will label them beautifully[.] You will be interested some day to come & look them through[.] *Very very* many thanks.

Best of greetings to you both

Yrs. very Scy
C.A.E

Many thanks about 'In the South' for Vienna.[29]

Then came a warm-hearted letter from the younger Boosey brother, George, whose health was beginning to be as precarious as Jaeger's:

295 Regent Street, London, W.
Oct 17 1905

My dear Edward

I was so sorry I was away when you looked in the other day as it was ages since I saw you. I have been away seedy & have only just got back to business.

I read all the accounts in the papers when your works are being given & am always *delighted* when you come out on top & you always seem to attract the largest house, it gives me great delight & I wish I could hear more of your works & enjoy them myself but they do not give us many chances in London. Are you at home now? if you are will you drop me a card to Sparsholt, Winchester & I will send you some game from my little place.

With kind regards to you both

Yours sincerely
George C Boosey[30]

Elgar went back to London for a Norwich Festival orchestral rehearsal on 20 October. There a last-minute suggestion for the *Caractacus* full score (now being engraved by Novello) reached him.

[29] HWRO 705:445:8833.   [30] HWRO 705:445:8171.

Langham Hotel, London.
Friday 10 a.m. [20 Oct. 1905]

My dear Jaeger:

I send this as I fear I cannot come across—I leave for home at 1.30., or rather, the train does.

By all means fire away at the final chorus of Caract:

It's a good idea & a pity the genius—whoever he is—that now thought of it did not think of it six months ago.

Yrs ever
Ed E.[31]

After the Norwich Festival, Elgar gave the first in a new series of professorial lectures at the University of Birmingham on 1 November. Then he wrote a final letter about the title of the Coventry Patmore part-song:

Plas Gwyn, Hereford.
Nov 3.1905

My dear Jaeger:

Just home.

Now Evening Scene seems best after all. I *did* like 'Curfew time'—but the curfew in the poem is ideal not real—& the title wd. be real & not ideal. If you stick to the printed title 'Evening Scene' it will save corresponding with Mrs.Coventry Patmore.

I think 'Evening scene' a little prosaic, but there you are.

The first line is too long for a title & will be shortened ridiculously in programmes.

I should like

Vesper   or better

Vesperal—a beautiful word which means everything & wd. make people think. I know I proposed it once before for some other thing [*Chanson de nuit*] but you thought it churchy which of course it is *not* really.

Yours ever
Edwd. Elgar

P.S. You will receive your modest desire for warmth in a day or two   Bless you.[32]

Jaeger had to leave for another winter in Switzerland, and his doctor had said he must have a fur coat. This the Elgars saw to for him. Elgar himself was away from home through mid-November conducting the London Symphony Orchestra in the Harrison tour of northern cities. From Hereford Alice Elgar wrote:

[31] HWRO 705:445:8293.   [32] MS in possession of Felix Aprahamian.

Plas Gwyn, Hereford
17 Nov. 1905.

Dear Mr. Jaeger

I want to send a few lines as I do not know when you have to start & I want to say how it is my *heartfelt* hope & wish that you will return home completely restored & that yr. dear wife will be able to bear yr. absence with something approaching to cheerfulness [—] with that, I trust, happy prospect to look forward to. I know it is very dismal for you both but trust it will be better this year & perhaps you will be able to find some little recreation—

I am thankful to say I have good accounts of E. so far. I was at Birmingham the 1st night of the Tour, it was simply *magnificent*, I wish you cd. have heard the Brahms Symphony [No.3], it recd. the *most* beautiful & poetic reading & as for in 'The South' it was like *magic* web of lovely sound— I never heard it as it really was intended to sound, like that before—even at very good performances.

I trust to see E. home next week & trust he will not be the worse for his fatigues—

With love to Mrs. Jaeger & every best wish & please let me hear when you have to go

yrs. sicy
C.A.Elgar[33]

A suggestion arrived from Alfred Littleton that Elgar should prepare his Birmingham University lecture notes for publication.

Plas Gwyn, Hereford.
Thursday [23 Nov. 1905]

My dear Littleton:

I could not possibly reply to your kind letter on the tour & could not prepare any of my lecture notes for the press. Some other time.

One thing: I have heard nothing from Baring or Sharpe as to the fee for the Concert in Cheltenham last Saturday week. I think it should be paid at once [—] isn't that usual?

I am tired out & have a bad cold.

Kindest regards
Yrs. ever
Edward Elgar

[33] HWRO 705:445:8832.

Plas Gwyn, Hereford.
Nov 26 1905
My dear Littleton:

I know you will forgive me for troubling you: but, I have received nothing from Harrison yet[.] I don't know if he is sending to you or *via* Sharpe[:] anyhow I want some money!

I daresay I shall hear from you in a post or two but it is very odd that neither of the concert givers should have sent the fees.

It is very wet & stormy & I am tied in with a bad cold

> Kindest regards
> Yours ever
> Edwd.Elgar

I am delighted to receive the Goetz Catalogue—thanks a thousand for getting it for me: it will go to Birmingham University

One of the professorial duties which interested Elgar most keenly was building up the University's music library.

Plas Gwyn, Hereford.
Nov 28 05
My dear Littleton:

Many thanks: I have recd. a full cheque from Sharpe.

My cold is better but not well & I am a poor thing.

I got frightfully sick of the tour although I found Mr Harrison a pleasant & amusing companion—but it was *cold*

> Kindest regards
> Yours ever
> Edward Elgar

I have recd. a p c. signed by all sorts of unreadable people including Max Hehemann from *Crefeld* glorifying Gerontius which they had just performed. I hope you saw the Vienna news of Gerontius

Plas Gwyn, Hereford.
Dec 10 1905
My dear Littleton:

I was glad to hear from you & sorry you are not down here in these lovely days.

It was very good of you to offer to help me about the library—long ago—I have been unable to avail myself of your help because for the present we are buying only *necessaries* & the orders go to the 'purveyor' via the librarian & give me little trouble. I think you can help me about Purcell: can we have the big complete Society's edition? If you can tell me about [this] I shall be grateful.

The enclosed letter may amuse you as it has us: I have not replied to it and I dont know if it would be worth while for a letter to be sent from Berners-st—Chanson de Matin might do for him. Please do what you think best BUT do let me have the priceless letter again. I am going to keep it

Kindest regards
Yrs sncrly
Edward Elgar

Unfortunately the correspondent's letter was separated and most probably returned. It has not been traced, but may have been a candidate for what Elgar later called his 'freak box'.

Life was not yielding much joy in larger matters then. His continuing lectures at Birmingham were being savagely criticized in the press as he spoke home truths about one group after another of the denizens of English musical life—composers, executants, critics. And he was struggling with the new oratorio for Birmingham—looking at the 1902 sketches for the unfinished section about Peter and wondering whether he could now add significantly to them. Alice Elgar reported as best she could to Jaeger, who was back in Switzerland in bad condition.

Plas Gwyn, Hereford.
14 Dec. 1905.
Dear Mr.Jaeger

We were very sad to find you were still kept at Lausanne & distressed to hear you had again been suffering. It must indeed have been a most wretched time & made yr. separation from yr. dear ones much worse to bear. I do hope by now you are at Davôs & will soon feel better & then if you can have some of the recreations that wd. help to pass the time, we trust by the Spring you will have made splendid progress—

This has been a very busy time as E. has had the Lectures crowded into such a short space of time. I wish you cd. have heard them, you wd. have enjoyed them.

They have been so dreadfully misquoted in such a misleading way, what he says is far over the reporters' heads, they cannot follow him in the least, & all the *beautiful* parts are left out. Yesterday was perfectly delightful, the audience did thoroughly enjoy it & were in a suppressed state of clapping all the time. The reports give *no idea* of what his Lectures are.

Now he is turning to Music again which is a great joy—

We are longing to be in the South, no doubt that is very ungrateful as we have had quite a spell of lovely weather & brilliant sunshine. Carice is looking very well & is busy with Studies & hockey & gymnasium & her pets &c.&c—I do not know if you know she has a lovely white Angora bunny—he is a very dear person & has a hot bottle every night for fear he shd. be cold!

May is doing some very good photography. I have some new German Literature[:] I cannot say I find it edifying so far! I do hope Mrs.Jaeger & the babies are well, I do feel so much for her having to be separated but hope all will be well & no more exile necessary another Winter.

Edward sends his best love & every good wish [—] he is sorry for all your weary trial you have been through—

Mr. Kalisch sent us a Card from Dresden where he had just heard 'Salome' & evidently was much excited by it.

Now it is past time we will hope to write again very soon.

> & with best greetings
> & best of wishes
> Yours Sincerely
> C.Alice Elgar[34]

Carice's white 'Peter Rabbit' became Italianized to 'Pietro d'Alba'—a name which was to serve Elgar for various pseudonymous purposes in the years to come.

Plas Gwyn, Hereford.
Dec 16 1905
My dear Littleton:

(*New oratorio*)

Do you think West could make the enclosed passage look better for piano. I can't *arrange* it well myself & spend hours trying to make 'bits' look like my scoring. Tell him the first two lines are very *smooth, full & rich* but quite soft in my orchestral idea. He can knock it about as much as he likes. I think the movement of the parts can be followed fairly from this.

I hope to begin sending some fair copy now soon

> In haste
> Yours ever
> Edward Elgar.

N.B. the enclosed is one of my favourite bits & I want it to go as well as it can on the PF.

Novello's files contain two revisions in John E. West's hand of passages in the piano reduction of what was to become *The Kingdom*. Both are in the central scene of Pentecost and Baptism, one around cue 73, the other at 109. On the other hand, the passage might have come from the first few pages of vocal score or the Lord's Prayer setting, both of which Elgar was preparing to send in.

---

[34] HWRO 705:445:8831.

Plas Gwyn, Hereford.
Dec 30 1905
My dear West:

Many thanks for your letter & kind revision of my pianistic effort—oh! this arranging for piano! Your suggestions are all adopted with thanks—those stems make all the difference to the look.

I am getting on & shall hope to send you some more soon.

All good wishes to you & yours for the New Year

Yours ever
Edward Elgar[35]

Meanwhile Elgar asked for libretti of sacred choral works by other composers. One was Julius Benedict's oratorio *St Peter*, produced at the Birmingham Festival of 1870 and published by Novello.[36] Elgar was to make some use of its suggestions.

Plas Gwyn, Hereford.
Dec 19.1905
My dear Littleton:

I am very much red-hot in my work. Will you cause copies of the *libretti* of the things named on the enclosed sheet to be sent to me. If the libretti are not separate the 8vo. words might come. I *should* like them before Christmas. I want to see what others have done

Yrs ever
Ed.Elgar.

1906

With the opening of the new year Elgar sent in the first few pages of vocal music for the oratorio:

Plas Gwyn, Hereford.
Jan 4 1906
My dear Littleton:

By this post I send the first scrap of the new work—title to be considered: it should be

'*The Kingdom of God*'

This portion is only the introduction but the rest shd follow soon: this portion must of course end a page.

Yrs ever
Ed:Elgar

[35] MS in possession of Stanley West.
[36] Elgar's marked copy of the *St Peter* libretto (by Joseph Bennett) is in BL Add MS 47906 fos. 107–112.

Plas Gwyn, Hereford.
Jan 15.06

My dear Littleton:

I send to Berners-st today—to p.52 of the new thing with the accompanying libretto—I can't send the whole libretto yet as I keep altering it as I go on
but I hope to get a rough copy soon for you.

I fear you are spoiling the children [—] they seem to be having a great time!
so many thanks to Mrs.Littleton & to you.

Yours ever
Edward Elgar

Polling day here!

Carice and May Grafton had gone to stay for some days with the Littletons at their
London home.

On 18 January he sent the vocal score of the Lord's Prayer setting, destined for a
place late in the oratorio. Some days afterwards he wrote to Jaeger in Switzerland:

Hereford
Jan 26 1906

Heart friend:

I have been very evil in not writing to you but I had not the heart to do so.
To-day we hear from Mrs Jaeger that you are seeing the proofs of my new
thing: I did not dare to suggest that you *should* see them & I dare not send my
own sheets, so—I could not write. I am so delighted to know that the firm
send the stuff on to you. So far it is the best thing I've done *I know*: remember
it's not piano music & won't sound well on a tin kettle.

We are so really glad about your skating & know it must be a pleasure & a
great help in many ways for health as well as recreation.

I was delighted to see [William Henry] Bell's works which he kindly sent to
me: & I have done what I can in the way of recommendation but people *are*
so *difficile*.

I must now go on with my work—but I have been *bursting* to write to you
for a long time.

A dove is born (hatched I mean) here to-day,—any omen think you?
Much love in which all join

Ever your
Edward[1]

A dovecot had been added to the growing menagerie at Plas Gwyn—begun ostensibly
for the amusement of Carice but also touching her father's quick sympathy with the
life of nature around them. The new arrival was named 'Bellerophon'.

Yet none of these distractions, nor his own assurances that the new oratorio
contained his best music, could conceal the fact that the composition was not
progressing smoothly. Its best ideas were almost entirely from the three-year-old

---

[1] HWRO 705:445:8758.

sketches originally planned for the 'Peter' section of *The Apostles*. Elgar's impulse toward oratorio writing was running low.

While the publishers engraved vocal score proofs of sections he had sent in, with Julius Buths poised to translate the libretto into German for a separate edition of the vocal score, and the Birmingham Festival authorities attempting to engage the very soloists Elgar wanted for the première, the composer himself faltered. By the end of January 1906 he had finished only the Prelude and the first scene in short score. He had detailed sketches for some further portions over the first half of the new work. Of its second half there was little beyond some notes toward a libretto. And the trip to conduct at the Cincinnati Festival in America was to occupy the whole of April and May. Elgar showed signs of nervous breakdown. Rumours began to appear in the press.

Once again his wife went to the publishers and to the Festival authorities. An entire oratorio on the scale of what had been completed for *The Apostles* in 1903 was impossible. Consultation with Elgar's doctor suggested that the most which could be hoped for the 1906 Festival was half a work. The fact was to be a secret—so well kept that it did not emerge for three-quarters of a century.

As Elgar sat down to write to Alfred Littleton in late February, he received the remainder of Novello's second £500 as a sign that the 10,000th copy of *The Apostles* vocal score had now been sold.

Plas Gwyn, Hereford.
Feb 21:1906

My dear Littleton:

Very many thanks for the cheque, I enclose the form receipted: I am so very glad the limit has been reached for the sake of the firm as well as for myself.

I have been waiting until things have definitely settled: I felt too much 'overdone' to think of completing the whole of this work: I have offered the first *half* and yesterday heard from Mr.Beal[e]—who has been away—that they are glad to do that much.

Now will that still suit you? I wd. prefer *not* to do it but it seems the only way to make things pleasant for everybody & so I suppose it must be done.

I have heard from Cincinnati & it is all settled aright: they ask me if I 'carry' scores & parts but I said *nay* & referred them to your firm.

With again thanks for the cheque & for so kindly looking after my interests now & always

Yours v sicy
Edward Elgar

P.S. I have today heard from Buths about the translation so I can send any information on doubtful points directly to him.

Meanwhile Elgar had completed the vocal score of the small Scene II, and had gone on to what was to be the central episode (Scene III) in the shortened plan, the depiction of Pentecost. By mid-March he could report progress.

Plas Gwyn, Hereford.
March 15 [*possibly* 10]. 1906
My dear Littleton:

I was very glad to receive your letter; I explained, or rather Alice explained for me, to the Birmingham people & they are willing to do the ½ of the new work: they will announce it when they think fit, but Beal[e] said they wd not refer to the length of the work &c. at present: but that is their affair.

I propose to send you a large batch next (or even this week) & they might *begin* with the chorus or as much as is ready if necessary—they will find enough to do.

We must now really decide upon the name. Has 'The Kingdom' become more reconciled to you or the reverse; tell me if you have thought of anything else: I don't feel satisfied about it but it is a name that can be bandied about in Shops &c without jarring on one's feelings.

I, or rather, we sail on Ap.6 Celtic.

I think & hope you will like the scene III—the waiting for the Holy Spirit—it looks odd on paper & may sound *frightful* on the piano (alas!) but it is about the best so far for colour &c. & will sound gorgeous with the orch.

Kindest regards
Yours ever
Edward Elgar

Thanks for your news of Cincinnati[.] I will see to the Chorus &c. It is very hard that we cant have Muriel Foster *or* Kirkby Lunn.

Then Elgar made a request which showed again the composer's care to anticipate the needs of performance. Early in Scene III came a soft passage with the female choral voices elaborately subdivided. If the choir were small, the 3rd contraltos would need assistance from the tenors (who were otherwise silent in the passage).

Plas Gwyn, Hereford.
March 15. 1906
Dear Sirs:

If the *voice parts* are being copied for printing will you kindly call attention to the note on the other side which I forgot to put on the corrected proof

Yours sincerely
Edward Elgar

See slip

N.B. p.70. bar after ⊡73 to (about) ⊡74.

Please engrave in full (small) the *3rd* Contralto part in the *1st Tenor* chorus part: to be useful for smaller choirs

p.71. 2nd score bar 2, please *alter*-Contralto 2 & 3 thus

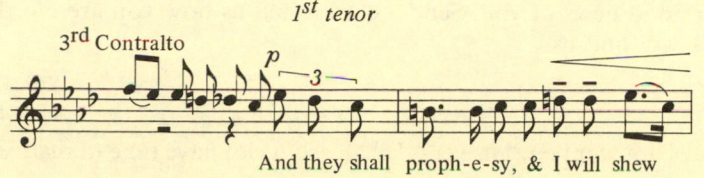

This is the passage actually needed.

EE

Jaeger, very unwell in Switzerland, had begun to receive vocal score proofs of the new work. He expressed some disappointment over the concluding chorus of Scene I, 'O ye priests'. This reaction worried Alice Elgar, who was doing everything in her power to raise her husband's flagging spirits.

Plas Gwyn[,] Hereford
17 March 1906.

Dear Mr. Jaeger

A few lines to tell you I am so glad the [*sic*] Davos has really done you good, am much concerned that you think you must suffer more treatment at Lausanne but trust that it will be completely successful—I trust you will be well & able to enjoy Summer in England & the dreary separation over—

I think yr. surroundings &c must have depressed you when you wrote—

It is curious that that Chorus did not fire you, it works up all who have heard it to a great pitch of excitement—& I think you might have given E. some credit for his really fine literary taste & poetic feeling in his selection of words—If you cannot feel the Sacerdotalism of any *Church*, there is the eternal priestdom of Elect Souls in all ages, who have stood above the lower minds & dragged them up; to those who believe by religion, & to others by art, literature & pure & noble character & aspirations; so instead of 'Matthias' meaning nothing to us, it is the type of Everything wh. can still infuse heroism, self sacrifice & great thoughts into all who are not dead to such things—

Wait to judge of the new work, & especially to *remark* to anyone on it, till you have heard E. play it—all those who have, & all those have been real musicians[,] think it the most original & greatest thing he has done. He is very very busy & has much to think of, & so soon to start for America so *please* not remark on anything I have said—He is better I am thankful to say but the strain of the work is very great for him & makes him very easily worried—He wd. send his especial love I know, did he know I was writing. We shall hope to hear good news of you, Send a card & tell us how you are c/o the Prof. N.York wd. find us.

> yrs. siny
> C.A.Elgar

This does not want *any* answer—I shall *really* not have time to read letters till we start—Please rest & not write.[2]

But Jaeger did write again, with enthusiasm over the opening pages of Scene III. Alice Elgar, in the thick of preparations for their American journey, responded in an undated note.

[n.p. *c.*25 Mar. 1906]

Dear Mr.Jaeger

One line today[.] I do hope we shall find you home all well with yr. dear ones.

I *am* so glad you think the Pentecost so beautiful, What follows is really astonishing.

> Best greetings
> C.A.E.

I am thankful to say E. is *so* much better & less worried over his work—[3]

To Elgar Jaeger had sent a postcard questioning a melodic resolution in the Prelude to the new work. Elgar replied:

---

[2] HWRO 705:445:8851.   [3] HWRO 705:445:8853.

[n.p.]
March 26 1906
Dearie Moss:

Many thanks for your p.c.

Your remarks about those *two* bars in the *intro* were quite right & they were *never intended* to go in—they are altered now. It is easy(!) enough to write a melody—except the last two bars: I am sure it is the difficulty of avoiding a 'barn-door' ending that has kept the modern school from symmetrical melody.

Meyerbeer is of course notorious for bad endings & Mendelssohn is almost as bad—or quite as bad in another way.

'Happy & blest' & [*sic*] fine opening ends

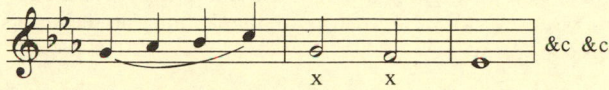

Wagner (Lohengrin) comes perilously near a bad end I think

lovely – but how about this?

Well: this is not to excuse my own infantile attempts & ineptitude but to shew you what I feel about 'tunes' & you with unerring instinct put your finger on two bars which I put in my sketch to remind me of my design—length &c. The bars are better now but I have taken 'jolly good' care not to make 'em more interesting than the real tune

We start on Ap 6. & I need not say, dear old man, how I hope to find you fit & well when we return: all good wishes are yours you know

Yours ever
Edward[4]

Jaeger's health, despite his second winter in Switzerland, was worse. Practically on the eve of his own departure for the United States, Elgar wrote on a postcard to his friend:

[4] HWRO 705:445:8757.

Plas Gwyn, Hereford
Ap 2 06

I cannot tell you how sad your news has made us: I hope & pray all may soon
be brighter. In the hurry of departure I can say no more. C.H.H.P[arry] is an
angel as ever. God bless him! If you *do* want anything you know all that's
mine is yours so go ahead.

    Love to you

Yours ever
Edwd. E.[5]

Next day the Birmingham Festival chorus master R. H. Wilson visited Elgar to go
through Scenes I to III of the new oratorio—all that was finished—so that much
could be rehearsed from proof copies during Elgar's absence. The balance of the
composition had to wait for Elgar's return at the end of May. On the day before his
departure Elgar wrote to Alfred Littleton to thank him for the firm's efforts to
promote his music in Germany.

Plas Gwyn, Hereford.
Ap 5. 1906

My dear Littleton:

    So much is rushed into these last few minutes that I fear this letter, which I
hoped might have been adequate, will be very short to catch the post.

    All thanks for what you have done about Berlin: I only fear that you are
taking *too* much trouble for what after all must be a very unremunerative
thing: I wish I were ambitious! I should probably feel more alive[:] however it
is pleasant to know that some appreciate what I have done & that you &
yours do so pleases me more than all.

    I have no more M.S. ready to send & I think there will be plenty of time
when I return.

    I think it would be well to let the Birmingham people have (as soon as
possible) all that you have: it's really a good solid slice & will give them
something to do

    Mr. Wilson the Chorusmaster has been here & we went thro' it & I told him
he could probably have it soon.

    I will be very careful about the proofs in America but I am taking them as I
hope to work hard at them.

    Now with again all thanks & kindest regards to you all

Yours ever
Edward Elgar

They arrived in New York in a heat wave, and spent one evening with Novello's
American agent H. W. Gray and the Damrosch brothers—Walter, who conducted
the New York Symphony Orchestra, and Frank, who conducted the Oratorio
Society. Then they went to Cincinnati, where they stayed at the Country Club for the
duration of the Festival. There Elgar began to score the finished portion of his new
oratorio. He reported to Alfred Littleton:

[5] HWRO 705:445:8756.

Cincinnati Country Club[,] Grandin Road
Ap 18. 1906

My dear Littleton:

One line to say that we are here safely & most comfortable: this is a clean, new, bright Club House up on the hills & we have, for the present, the whole place to ourselves.

We remained only one night in New York.

Sanford had a few people to dine. among them the two Damrosches: it is, quite privately, talked of having a three day festival in New York next winter & they want the first [American] performance of the new work: so if any enquiries should be made from elsewhere on this side, please do not give the first performance to others without much consideration. I saw Mr.Gray who was, as usual, faultless in manner[,] dress & everything!! He is coming on here soon.

I should like to have the remainder of the proofs here or in New York. I wish you were here [—] it is so very pleasant: the snapshotters & interviewers are soon disposed of & the rest is sunshine—at present.

I feel inclined to take a bath every few minutes as I have *four*—all varieties—at my disposal. Kindest regards to you all

Yours ever
Edward Elgar

Elgar's presence added greatly to the success of the Cincinnati May Festival. Back in New York with their American friend Mrs Worthington, Alice Elgar sent a postcard to Jaeger (who had now returned to his home in Muswell Hill for the summer).

50 West 52nd. St. N. York.
11 May. 1906.

Excuse card but must send a line to say how we *hope* & *trust* you are much better & think you may be home & trust Mrs.J is well & the babies.

You will like to hear the Festival was a *most* satisfying success & E.'s works made the most *profound* impression. People were so nice & most welcoming & hospitable. We hope to sail on 18th. & soon to hear good news of you. The Prof is to sail very soon too. Do you know *1200* people stood on the Gerontius night in the Hall—It was a wonderful sight[.] Best of greetings, E. is out or wd. send love

Yrs. siny
C.A.E.[6]

But the interruption of the American trip proved a serious distraction when Elgar returned home and tried to resume composition of his new oratorio. Alice Elgar wrote to Jaeger to warn him off too close enquiry:

[6] HWRO 705:445:8850.

Plas Gwyn
6 June [1906]

Dear Mr. Jaeger

E. has been so wretchedly unwell that he has not been able to write so I send a hasty line to say we are so glad you are safe home & hope & trust you are keeping well & are *really* better—

Do not trouble to write but rest *all* you can. I trust E. will be well again in a day or two but it is so hindering for him & he gets *so worried*. So that we must not hurry him or any thing—I do trust all the work will be finished before long & then he can recuperate[.] Meanwhile I prevent anythg. possible from worrying him.

With his love & best greetings to you & Mrs.Jaeger

Yrs. sicy
C.A.E.[7]

Even now, not four months from the date for the first performance, the title of the oratorio was still in question. Elgar wrote:

Plas Gwyn, Hereford.
June 6.1906

My dear Littleton:

Beale writes that they want to announce the *name* of the work at their meeting on Monday next: I told him it was not yet fixed (this was a week ago) but that it *could* be fixed at anytime; I was too ill to think of anything last week & so forgot to speak to you about it on Monday when you were here.

I still hanker after 'The Kingdom': why not 'The Kingdom of God' & leave people to drop the last two words in course of time. But you may have talked & thought it over since our last conversation on the point, so let me hear what you now think please.

Beale asks if they are to announce it as 'The Apostles Pt III' & I said no: but as I can only give them a one-part, that is a half-programme work, you might think that best to do.

In haste
Yours ever
Edward Elgar.

Littleton responded by return, agreeing to the shorter title, but demurring from the idea that Elgar's friend Canon C. V. Gorton should write an 'Interpretation' of Elgar's libretto for the new work as he had done for *The Apostles*. The soloists for Birmingham had now been chosen, and they included the young bass William Higley, whose career Elgar was eager to help.

[7] HWRO 705:445:8849.

Plas Gwyn, Hereford.
June 7: 1906

My dear Littleton:

Many thanks: well 'The Kingdom' be it.

I am glad Jaeger will do the analysis but I can never understand your objection to Gorton: his book has done more real good—if you know the people it has reached—than anything else: I shall of course say nothing to him about it.

I understand that Agnes Nicholls
                         Muriel Foster
                         John Coates &
                         Higley

are to be the singers. I have written to Higley telling him to take all the engagements he can: he has evidently misunderstood—I only suggested I *might* want him for U.S.A. in March [1907] but he had better remain here this next season: so will you write to him again[.] I need not say I did not mention the A.Hall to him

                         In great haste
                         Yrs v. sincy
                         Edward Elgar   PTO

P.S. My wife reminds me that there was some conversation—I had quite forgotten this—with Canon Gorton as to the old 'Interpretation' & a possible new one: however I'll leave it as it is, but I cannot for the life of me see what objection there [is] to its' being done.

Next day he sent a portion of the full score of Scenes I—III which he had begun in America. But the final scenes of *The Kingdom* were not yet written. Anxiety and depression fostered a heavy cold, and in response to the doctor's prescription of rest and change of scene the Elgars went for a fortnight to the mountains of the Welsh border. There they received an anxious enquiry from Jaeger. Alice Elgar's reply showed their troubles very clearly.

[*mourning stationery, as Elgar's father had died a few weeks earlier*]
Arden Bank[,] New Radnor[,] Wales

15 June   *Thursday*
Dear Mr.Jaeger

A few lines to answer yr. note to E. The Birm. announcement is right, he will explain when you meet.

You will be surprised to see above address, but E. has been so *wretchedly* unwell the Dr. sent him up here on Tuesday for bracing air, it has been so wretched to see him & he is of course dreadfully worried about his work being late; he is certainly better since he came but unfortunately there is a cold East Wind & grey mist wh. as he has a bad cold are *not* helpful. The air is splendid here & fine mountains & moors are all around—You shall hear as soon as ever he can let you have more M.S.

He sends love & we *hope* you are keeping well & all yours

Yrs. sicy
C.A.Elgar

We take this house by the week, so expect to be here till next Tuesday & longer if it suits E.[8]

A week later the news was better, and Alice Elgar sent Jaeger a picture postcard view of New Radnor with this message:

22 June 1906.

I know you will like to have a line to say E. is much better today & has been working hard & I hear a *lovely* tune—I do trust he will keep well now, it has been a dreadfully worrying time & he has worried so much over it so it is better not to write about it to him[.] You will see him I hope next week—This place is *beautiful*[.] Such wonderful mountain Solitudes, the best place for Composing I think. I do hope you are fairly well & Mrs.J. & babies

Yrs sicy
C.A.E.[9]

By now Alfred Littleton was becoming concerned about the lateness in finishing even the abridged scheme which had been agreed for Birmingham. Elgar wrote to reassure him:

New Radnor
Monday [25 June 1906]
My dear Littleton:

Very many thanks for your telegram about the rehearsal.

We arrive on Wednesday at 4.10 & go to the Langham: I am better but am not well.

This illness had quite upset my plans for everything. I now see my way D.V. to let you have the final M.S. of this portion in July[.] You can print in August & the Chorus can quite well learn the remainder in September: so all will be well. I very much regret causing any inconvenience but I find I cannot 'work up' my sketches when I'm ill

I have eliminated the 2nd bass part so the cast will be

Miss Nicholls
    ” Foster
Coates
Higley

In great haste
Yours ever
Ed:Elgar

[8] HWRO 705:445:8847.   [9] HWRO 705:445:8848.

Minutes after posting the letter, Elgar slipped on some wet stones and fell on a shoulder and knee. The shock put an end to their holiday. Later in the day they left for home, where several days elapsed before further work could be done. The first sign was a brief note to the firm from Alice Elgar on 29 June requesting further proofs of the last two pages of *The Kingdom* Prelude in piano score, as the same music was to provide a basis for the work's conclusion. But when Jaeger asked for the Lord's Prayer setting in the final scene, he was met with an agitated response.

[*mourning stationery*]
Plas Gwyn
1 July 1906.

Dear Mr.Jaeger

Edward asks me to write for him & tell you he cannot send you the 'Lord's Prayer' yet.

He hopes to send some new M.S. tomorrow. He is better I am thankful to say & at work again after the most painful interruption—

He is sorry for the delay, but please have a little more patience & all being well, the new work will be about his best, and in time convincing even to pagans, but you must PLEASE not worry or hurry him in any way—

Best remembrances

Yrs.sicy
C.A.E.[10]

As composition of the final scenes began to go forward more smoothly, Elgar was able to reply to Jaeger's suggestions for amending Scene III.

Plas Gwyn, Hereford.
July 3. 1906

My dear Nim:

I am better but cannot bend my knee yet!

Thanks for the copy stitched up: your suggestion on p.97 will *not* do as the syllable 'Je' is so unimportant, but my brave boy, on pp.99 & 100 I gladly accept your emendation & we will have B♭ for 'these' p.99 & C♮ for '—so' on p.100.

p.110 the cue shd be marked Celli

In haste
Yours ever
Edward
(the lame & blind)

I have 4 prs of spectacles now![11]

Then the composer's own emendations for Scene III brought a longer letter.

[10] HWRO 705:445:8846.   [11] HWRO 705:445:8759.

Plas Gwyn, Hereford.
July 7 06

My dear Jaggs:

I shall soon finish with you: look here: I want the *two* Soloists T. & B. [—] or rather under their names John & Peter [—] to sing *with* the chorus from 79 to 82 incl.:—see how you can do it without messing the plate—it's simply to add the names somewhere—see p.130 *Apostles* for example. [There the direction was 'John & Tenors' etc, and the same formula was now adopted.]

In the new Baptism (*refreshing*) theme [beginning a bar after cue 111] I endeavoured to shew the *movement in* the orchestra but I shall have to alter it as the rocking in the R[ight] H[and piano score] suggests Humperdinck—there's nothing in the Harmony or outline so its soon done. It's curious because there's *nothing* in my *orchestra* arrangement which is like H. only I tried to make it *feel* like the s[emi]quavers.

E.E.'s feeble attempt at arrgt.

shd be   Orch.   &c   This is

impossible—but I'll carve it all right. I expect it's engraved now so send it along.

That *surprise* or rather quiet astonishment theme is all right, eh?

I can bend my knee etwas but cannot do this yet.

Yours ever
Edward[12]

[*postmark*] Hereford
[9 July 1906]

My dearest Nim.

Only one line to say how very sorry we are to hear of the boy's illness and its attendant worries for Mrs Jäger & you[.] We can only hope that it will be the usual infantile trouble & be soon over

Love
E.[13]

In the midst of composing the final scene, orchestrating earlier portions, and correcting instalments of proofs for *The Kingdom*, Elgar had to consult with Alfred Littleton about the latest form of a much-renewed proposal that he should write a work for the Leeds Festival. His correspondence with the Festival secretary Frederick Spark (1831–1919) showed all too clearly the composer's hesitation and confusion.[14] The personality of Spark was antipathetic to him, and the Leeds Festival conductor was Stanford. Even so, Elgar had promised or half-promised and then withdrawn works from Leeds, and then produced similar works in Birmingham and London. Now Spark was trying to extract a promise for the 1907 Leeds Festival. Elgar wrote:

[12] Elgar Birthplace parcel 343.   [13] HWRO 705:445:8760.   [14] HWRO 705:445:5979–86.

Plas Gwyn, Hereford.
July 14: 1906

Private

My dear Littleton:

This is the third letter I have received during the last six months or so. I wish you wd. advise me what to do[.] You see 'they' will not do anything straight out: S[park] wrote asking me if I had a Mass &c.&c.

I know that 'they' (generally) do not want me, but they want to be able to say I have been asked. I am not conceited about it but I do strongly object to my being treated a third time in the way 'they' have done twice before. You see much as the Conductor wishes to leave me out they 'save their face' by putting in an orchl. work—or by asking an *impossible* thing very late.

S. wants to get all information he can *before* any meeting of the executive: anything to save the Committee offering me an invitation which I *might* refuse: they are so extremely touchy over it.

I have not made the position quite clear I fear but I will talk it over with you when we meet: *don't* trouble to write because there's nothing urgent.

I shall be in town on *Monday* for an hour or two &, if the dentist lets me off early enough I wd call at Berners-st about 3 oc'

Yours ever
Ed:Elgar

In London on 16 July he did consult with Littleton, but once again no new work for Leeds was forthcoming.

At last it was confirmed that Jaeger was to write an Analysis of *The Kingdom* for the Birmingham première.

Plas Gwyn, Hereford.
Saturday [21 July 1906]

My dear Nim:

I hope the boy, bless him! is going on all well: we are so very sorry for your trouble—it is really desperately annoying & we can only hope it will pass very soon.

Well: I played thro' Variatn N⁰ 9 ['Nimrod']—written by one Ass to the glorification of another old duck: you will never be more *dearly* idealised than that—better perhaps but not so sincere. I have been reading your analysis of the Apostles & very wonderful it is: I am amazed.

Now I hear with great joy that you are doing a like office for the Kingdom: I am sending you [—] or rather I will send if you wish [—] some commentaries on the Acts [of the Apostles, on which the libretto was based]—they are not long; that is, the portions necy to the work are not long. There are sundry points I want mentioned in the analysis. viz—*glossalalia*.

I am just completing the final revision of my notes [—] sketches: the whole thing is intentionally less mystic than the A[postles]:—the *men* are alive & working & the atmosphere is meant to be more direct & simple (mixed sentence but you will gather what I mean). But we will have a talk one day—I hope to be in town at the end of this week—possibly—& will try to arrange to see you if it be possible for you.

Send a p.c. saying if you will have the books.

> Love to you all
> Yours ever
> Edward Elgar[15]

Jaeger asked for the Biblical commentaries, sent some observations about tempo near the end of Scene III, and gave news of his little son's illness.

[n.p.]
July 23. 06

My dear Moss: We *are* so glad to hear you are about again & that Hans is going on all right.

I'll be sure to see you when I come—on Thursday belike.

I will not go into the points you name now—only one thing strikes me as being *plain* & you want it plainer—look at [111] bar after we start $\downarrow$ = 58. between [114] & [118] there is a *stringendo* which brings us, at [118] [,] to 'double as quick' as we started [,] viz— $\downarrow$ = 58—at [120] $\downarrow$ = 58 again so there's *no* change of time really. I will add, at [120], $\downarrow$ = $\downarrow$ of the preceding.

It was really the only way to write it

> Ever yours
> Ed:

I am sending you a book.[16]

Jaeger asked about the naming of musical motives in *The Kingdom*.

[*University of Birmingham stationery*]
July 24 06

My dear Nim:

Here's a book. You will find some useful things in it. You need not worry your Pagan head with more than the first four chapters—& some of the final Notes.

As to naming the themes we'll see to it. You will see there is no theme for *The Kingdom*—the Kingdom includes everything.

The work deals only with the Church in Jerusalem—You might hint that perhaps a further section is contemplated (it's partly written!) dealing with the church of the Gentiles. All else when we meet.

Glad the boy is better

> Yours ever & one day
> Edward:[17]

[15] HWRO 705:445:8762.   [16] HWRO 705:445:8763.   [17] HWRO 705:445:8764.

That day Elgar revised the final work on *The Kingdom* vocal score. On 26 July he saw Jaeger in London, and they discussed the Analysis. He went on to Dover for a little holiday, but was back in London after one day.

Langham Hotel, London.
Saturday [28 July 1906] a.m.

Authentic Moss:

The weather was so uncertain that I came back & am on my way home, so please send any proofs &c. (today & onwards) to Plâs Gwyn. Will you ask Mr.Pointer to see that the myrmidons of the Woolly Lamb [*Jaeger notes*: Oppenheimer, Printer [Geidel]'s agent] (on whom blessings!) do not muddle the turns in the orch. parts: as thus:–

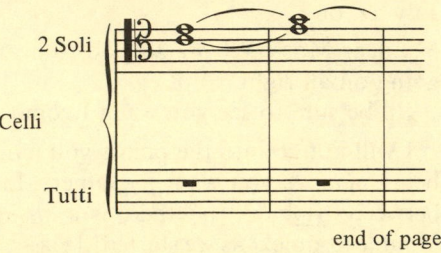

end of page

This is a 'nonsense' passage but it shews what I mean: the two soli will be at the same desk so that the turn is impossible.

Something, (I think pubd. *not* by you), had to be engraved over again from a similar cause.

Verb:sap.

It *was* good to see you again & your dear, old, *earnest* face. bless you!

But you cannot persuade me that it's worth while to write music

Oh! Send me today without fail (A[rtemus] Ward says 'there aint no such word as *fale*') a copy of the Lord's Prayer section as supplied to Birmingham, to Authentic Mossheads &, apparently[,] to everyone except

Your sorrowing
Edward.

My love to all at home[18]

37 Curzon Road[,] Muswell Hill
Sunday 29/7/6

My dear Elgar,

Many thanks for your dear letter, & *Bless you*!

Yes, send me anything that will help me to understand 'The Kingdom'. I should have the original shape of that 'Sacrum Convivium' theme, shouldn't I? When you come to London I must ask you a few questions, because I find it very difficult to *name* some of the *motifs*. I'm not generally slow at this sort

---

[18] HWRO 705:445:8765.

of thing, & I know the work *well*, as far as I have seen it (up to page 138) [just before 'The Arrest'.] I must also speak of Buths' translation which *I* won't have, whatever *you* may say! He takes such licenses with your music that I don't recognize the stuff. I have sent some pp back to him *twice* for correcting & I have virtually re-translated the 'What meaneth this' chorus, which he simply ruined. I can't understand him at all.

I am now back at 'No 1' [Berners Street] (my boy doing very well), so I shall see you, I hope. Till then Farewell.

I have worked all day at the Analysis, & am tired. So excuse a short scribble.

Ever yours
A.J.Jaeger

I say, I wish I'd written pp.105–8, 112–114 & *a few others*! I'm surprized you havent given that magic low G in the orchestral Bass, 2 Bars before 122 (p 122) to the *voices* (Bass) also. I hope you have put some weight into it in the *orchestra* to *fetch it out*. I should mark last bar p 118 *ritard al Andante* 120 [:] a *sudden* change at 120 both in time & tempo will endanger the *Andante* commencement (at 120) it will *wobble* for a few bars[.] *Prepare* the *tempo*. I should mark against the D flat Tune at 6 (page 4) *The Triplets always broadly*. They may be *hurried* & the *tune ruined*—and put over the Commencement (Gospel theme) *Con Dignita*, or something[.] The last scene pp 124 &c is *lovely*![19]

The 'last scene' referred to is not the last in the work, but the last which Jaeger had seen in proof, Scene IV (beginning on p. 124 of the vocal score). Later the same day Jaeger went over proofs of the last section of Scene IV, 'The Arrest'. This includes the soprano solo 'The sun goeth down', to be sung at Birmingham by Agnes Nicholls (1877–1959).

Later the same day Jaeger sent a well-filled postcard.

37 Curzon Road.
Sunday 29/ 7

My dear Elgar,

I have just spent an hour over the Scene 'The Arrest' which is *perfectly beautiful & wonderful*. Look here: ask Agnes Nicholls whether she couldnt make *three times* the (*emotional*) *effect* if you wrote [at cue 162]

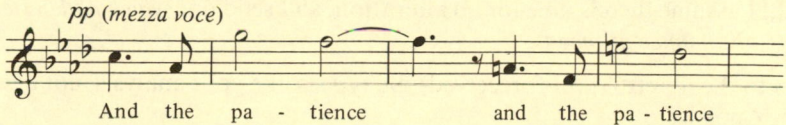

That makes ME *choke*; Agnes would set the floodgates of the whole Room open. The rise of sevenths & then the drop of one tone is as (emotionally)

[19] HWRO 705:445:8775.

beautiful a thing as I know. There will be *no* strain for the Voice, and *no* 'cheap', and [*illegible*] effect. Agnes will *cry* over that if she has a Heart

Try it with a singer, or ask A.Nicholls

You will get a proof to-morrow or Tuesday. I say, *what* SHALL I do about all the motifs from 'The Apostles'? I *can't* quote them all. The Analysis would become an Encycl. Britannica Vol!

> Much love!
> AJJgr

Oh! the latter part of 'The Kingdom' is marvellous![20]

Plas Gwyn, Hereford.
July 30. 1906
My dear Jaggs:

Here are some *few* pages which end a page [of the printed score] so I send 'em.

I am delighted to get your cheery card saying that the Soliloquy ['The sun goeth down'] is good. I will look to your good suggestions when I receive the proof.

Hope all is well at home now.
So hot here!

> Yours ever
> Edward

Please send a wire acknowledging the arrival of the Score—*if you get it*!!
*It's rather a 'tall' bit**
            Perpend
*bit of scoring I mean[21]

That day Jaeger, back at his office, wrote to Elgar again. He enclosed a letter from elsewhere, and discussed typography for *The Kingdom* libretto. This letter is not now to be found, and its absence makes some points in Elgar's reply obscure.

Plas Gwyn, Hereford.
Augt 1: 1906.
My dear Nim:

Only time for a hurried line: as to the omission I *intended* it [—] but, as you ask[,] I assume there's time for an alteration, so I send one *which had better go in by all manner of means.*

as to the libretto (proofs received) the type is like your analysis, not like the 8vo. Apostles.
There are several alterations in the headings necy.

You will see how the difficulty about *Italics* was overcome if you look at *Apostles* libretto: all the *ital.* words are a size larger than the corresponding

---

[20] HWRO 705:445:8776.   [21] HWRO 705:445:8761.

roman—or the *Ital* names are smaller—I can't, with my worn out old eyes, see which it is.

I have received [']The Arrest' & its not bad apparently.

Glad you like it: I adopt, dear godfather, your suggestions.

Thankfully
Yours ever
Edward   P.T.O.

P.S. I return Mr Maclean's letter: *I have nothing to do with it*! Many people have written to me (including Zavertal) about it but I know nothing.

I will of course do as you wish if I get the chance[22]

Ladislas Zavertal (1849–1942) had conducted the Royal Artillery Band in an early performance of the *Imperial March* before Queen Victoria in 1897.

The progress of *The Kingdom* scoring was documented in letters to Jaeger and to the firm.

[*mourning stationery*]
[n.p.]
Augt 1:1906

Dear Sirs:

By this post registered I return
   proofs corrected with corresponding M.S.
   2 pages amended V[ocal] sc. MS.
I take the opportunity to send also pp 97–116. full sc.
Kindly send a telegram on the arrival of the parcel

Yrs ffy
Edwd. Elgar

The next six days produced no fewer than fifty new pages of score:

Plas Gwyn, Hereford.
Augt 7: 1906

My dear Moss:

This is a music pen

Herewith pp 117–168 full score [—] *please send a wire*!

Also a few pages of proof, V[ocal] sc.

also libretto.   the caps. (in place of Italic) will *not* do.—try the *larger* size italic for the text. I shewed it to Mr Alfred [Littleton at his house in Hereford] yesterday & he said you might try it that way, as in the Apostles:

I forgot to say that

A)   Bars 1,2, line 1 page 141 V.sc.
B)   ,,   1,2, line 2 ,,   ,,   are from old Hebrew tunes.

22 HWRO 705:445:8766.

A) 'Al Elleh' [—] Hymn of Weeping
B) 'Hamabdil' [—] Hymn of Parting

You see PARTING & WEEPING are in the scene [of 'The Arrest'].

   see pp 8. 29. of the Augener book which I used for the Morning Psalm in the Apostles

In haste
Yours ever
Edward

(I scored 70 pages in the week)[23]

His progress was so rapid that Alice Elgar, who set out the 'frame' for her husband's orchestral scoring from the octavo vocal score bar-lines, ran out of vocal score proof from which to work.

Plas Gwyn
Thursday [9 Aug. 1906]
Dear Mr.Jaeger

Do you think you could be very kind & send me some proofs[?] I have ruled &c out for E. to page (oct[avo vocal score]) 155, the last that came, & now am at a standstill as E. proceeds at a [*sic*] such a prodigious pace that I shall not have it ready for him. If I could have some quite uncorrected ones it wd. do, as I cd. rule it & fill in vocal parts afterwards.

I do hope yr. little son is nearly all well again—Best remembrances

Yrs sincy
C.A.Elgar

And Elgar himself wanted full score proofs.

Plas Gwyn, Hereford.
Augt 9: 1906
My dear Moss:

Can I have a copy of the cleanest proof of the full score as it 'comes along'?

I have some orchl parts but nothing to correct by really & I cannot try to remember all that I wrote in Cincinnati in April—though I might do so with an effort.

I want to get the orchl. parts played thro as usual so if there's any desperate hurry you must let me know.

In haste yours ever
Edward Elgar

Jaeger, whose health was more and more fragile, felt he could not finish *The Kingdom* Analysis. All were very concerned, and Alfred Littleton relieved him of some of his office duties so that he could complete the work. Elgar wrote:

23 HWRO 705:445:8768.

Plas Gwyn, Hereford.
Augt 19 1906

My dearie Moss:

I have been unable to steal a minute to write.

I *am so glad* you are going on with the Analysis & hope you have an easier
time with it; when can you come down?

I am getting on all right with the score.

Much love from us all to you all

Yours ever
Edward[24]

It was arranged for Jaeger to come to Hereford for a few days beginning 25 August to
consult over the Analysis.

Plas Gwyn, Hereford.
Tuesday [?21 Aug. 1906]

My dear authentic Moss.

By this post some score on the receipt of which I crave a telegram.

Don't worry.

there's only *one* 'stop' in the whole work—top line page 6. This may be
better marked thus // & knock out the comma.

on pp 30 & 53 [of the vocal score] the commas only shew a sort of breath
mark making the word following a little pointed: the commas shd. *not* be in
the PF. part which is continuously slurred on.

I added more of these commas at [Frank] Damrosch's request & I think
[the Birmingham Festival chorus master R. H.] Wilson—I forget about W.
though. Frank D. said it made the chorus *understand* so much better.

There is no *hush* wh. you are afraid of

Am I a fool?

   No. (I'm not at all sure)

Now: how long can I keep the proof of Prelude full score: when shall I
receive the wind? I want to play, or rather, get it all played through by
Mr.Austin & I haven't enough to make it worth while.

If the parts will not be coming yet I can return the sc: pro tem.

Much love
Yrs ever
Edward.[25]

[24] HWRO 705:445:8769.
[25] HWRO 705:445:8767. This letter was written when *The Kingdom* full score had begun to
appear in proof, together with some orchestral parts. Dr Young (*Letters to Nimrod*, p. 264)
suggests 31 July 1906. This is a possibility: Frank Damrosch's proposals would have been made
during Elgar's time in New York in the spring of 1906; and by early July the Novello copyist
Dodd had begun to produce parts. On the other hand there is no sign of any full score in printed
proof so early, and Alice Elgar's diary records no visit by John Austin until 16 September. *The
Kingdom* score was finished on 31 August.

On 24 August Elgar sent in pages 261–300 of the full score. The next evening Jaeger arrived for consultation about the Analysis. Alice Elgar, who met him, described him in her diary as 'far from well'. He stayed, at the Elgars' insistence, for three days. Then, on the last day of August, Elgar finished the full score of *The Kingdom*.

That day he received a handsome present from Alfred Littleton and Dr Charles Harriss (1862–1929). Harriss was an Englishman resident in Canada, the promoter of Empire concerts in various parts of the world, and keen to get Elgar to conduct in Canada. He wrote from Littleton's Hereford house, to present a large brass doorstop in the shape of a griffin holding a shield.

Hatteral, Hereford.
August 31st 1906.

Dear Sir Edward.

The undersigned hope you will accept with their compliments the 'Door Porter' sent herewith. May you 'find' help to keep open the door of friendship to

> Yours ever sincerely
> Charles A.E.Harriss
> Alfred H Littleton[26]

Plas Gwyn, Hereford.
Sep.2.1906

My dear Littleton:

This one line of thanks for the Griffin supplements my telephonic joy of yesterday. It was most kind of you & Dr.Harriss to think of me & give me this beautiful brass. Come & see it soon.

> Yours ever
> Edward Elgar

And the griffin figured in the Elgar household ever afterward.

Back in London, Jaeger wrote about the grand new headquarters for the firm in a handsome building designed especially for them at 160, Wardour Street. But *The Kingdom* score and parts were not going smoothly.

1, Berners Street, W.
Sept. 3 1906

My dear Edward,

Dodd confesses himself beaten by 'The Kingdom'. He cannot possibly do the Wind parts of the whole work & we must therefore employ another man on the portions from 123 ('The Sign of Healing') to End. I am very sorry, but a man can but do his best, & that Dodd is doing.

Are you likely to call in [?]

You might arrange with Rivers when he can send you Wind parts of a big

[26] HWRO 705:445:6780.

[*illegible*]. (He is doing the Duplicates.) *We* (the office) are now at 160 Wardour Street attached to our *works* in Hollen Street which you know. I *may not* be here to morrow or Wednesday because I *must* finish that Analysis which worries me. I have only about 40 more to do,—the most impressive, *Holiest purest* portion of the work. Those last 30 or 40 pages are marvellous[,] dear man, & as uplifting as anything I know.

Ever thine, with much love
AJJgr

The enclosed is [Havergal] Brian's Partsong which I'm told is so *awful*. What say you?
By the way, *Rivers* & the *Shop* are still at *No. 1* [Berners Street][27]

As for Jaeger himself, his health was worse than ever, and there was talk of his retiring permanently, though he was only forty-six. When his letter came, Elgar was in London attending rehearsals for the Hereford Festival.

Langham Hotel, London.
Wedy a m [5 Sept. 1906]

My very dear Moss:

Thanks for your letter & p[ost] c[ard]. I have been so busy or I shd. have come up [to Muswell Hill] to see you & now I can't as I leave tomorrow

I have decided to adhere to the new version & have sent the amended score to Berners st.

Alice tells me you write sadly of yourself to her—well I can only say how sorry I am that you are depressed & wish with all my soul I could cheer you. She does not tell me *what* you say but I shall learn that tomorrow, Only for the moment be assured that anything we can do shall be done to our last coin

Bless you
Yrs ever
Edward[28]

Poor Jaeger could not attend the Hereford Festival, for he had been ordered by his doctor to the seaside to try to recruit his failing strength for another journey to Switzerland. That would take him away from England during the week of the Birmingham Festival, so he would miss *The Kingdom* première as well.

Plas Gwyn, Hereford.
Wedy [12 Sept. 1906]

My dearie Jaggs:

Thanks for your letter to which I can only send a hurried line: $\frac{1}{2}$ of the Analysis has come & you shall not be bothered with it.

I am glad you are 'placed' amongst *nice* English sea & shore. Blessings on you.

[27] HWRO 705:445:8774.   [28] HWRO 705:445:8296.

I am torn in pieces this week by people.

I will not tell you of the [Hereford] festival: the old effect of the building is grand as ever.

I will not go into your private affairs now: I only say do not worry yourself but do all you can to get better & don't tell us we can't understand or sympathise because, of course, we know that already: you old Moss.

> Love from all
> Yours ever
> Edward.[29]

Amid proof corrections for *The Kingdom* score and parts, Elgar read through Jaeger's Analysis and made considerable alterations. On 25 September he conducted the first orchestral rehearsal of the new work in Manchester (since many of the Birmingham Festival orchestra were Hallé players). Alice Elgar sent a card to Jaeger:

Plas Gwyn
Thursday [27 Sept. 1906]

You will be glad to hear the Rehearsal at Manchester was *splendid—* Gorgeous Seas of Sounds. The band broke now & again into irresistible applause. E. is at Aberdeen & I hope having this lovely weather. Trust you all better[.] Gt. haste

> Yrs Siny
> C.A.E.[30]

Elgar had gone to Aberdeen to receive an honorary degree. On his way home he sent Jaeger a postcard.

[*postmark*] Birmingham
[29 Sept. 1906]
on train

Hope you are allright have been unable to write

> Love
> EE.
> LL.D. Aberdeen

Jaeger had written of his impending departure for Switzerland, and Elgar took the first moment to reply:

Plas Gwyn, Hereford
Sep: 30: 1906.

My dear Jaeger:

I only recd. your letter this a.m.—we came from Birmingham on Saturday for a quiet rest.

I do hope you will have a comfortable journey & that all will go well. I

[29] HWRO 705:445:8770.   [30] HWRO 705:445:8844.

need not say how sorry we all are that you have to go away again. As to the Music—never mind. I am quite tired of the musical world & want room for energy—the musical world is too small for me.

I forget all about the rehearsals already!

Send us a p.c. & let us hear all about you.

> Much love
> In awful haste
> Yrs ever
> Edwd.[31]

On the eve of *The Kingdom* première in Birmingham, Jaeger wrote to Dora Penny ('Dorabella' of the *'Enigma' Variations*) about the preparation of his Analysis.

37 Curzon Road, Muswell Hill N/
2/x/6

My dear Miss Dora,

Here is my wretched analysis, written under great difficulties (of ill health). I hope you may find *some*thing in it to interest you. Of course you can't—in fact nobody can [—] guage [*sic*] the qualities of work by Elgar from the few quotations in an analysis written by a Duffer like me. My stuff was knocked about by Elgar & my 'governor' after I had passed the proofs for the press— to take out some of my 'appreciatory' remarks, and in this process of bowdlerizing two words have dropped out & other bad things have happened for which I'm *not* responsible. So forgive *me* these 'faults', anyhow. The thing was *much longer* originally.

I'm off tomorrow or Thursday for another 6 months stay abroad trying to 'get better'.

I have been *very* bad, but am picking up again. I fear I shall not have time to say Goodbye to you & your dear Mother & sister; I'm very busy 'getting ready'—writing innumerable letters, amongst other things.

But I remembered my promise to send you my analysis, and here is the little thing.

Goodbye now, and *keep well, you* & Your dear ones,—That's the main thing; nothing else seems to matter!

With my kindest regards to your dear mother[,] Your sister & your kind, good self

> Very Sincerely yours
> A.J.Jaeger.[32]

The première of *The Kingdom* on 3 October was the central event in the 1906 Birmingham Festival. Directly it was over, score and parts corrections were urgent, because of an imminent performance in London under Allen Gill. Elgar wrote from Wychnor Park, where he was staying after the Festival with Maud Warrender's sister Lady Margaret Levett.

[31] HWRO 705:445:8772.   [32] MS in possession of Mrs Mary Fraser.

Wychnor Park, Burton-on-Trent.
Sunday [7 Oct. 1906]

My dear Littleton:

I seize really the first moment to write a line.

The Kingdom went very well—not superlatively as the Chorus was rather 'inelastic' in those portions where they are implicated with the Soloists.

I wish you had been there.

I am hoping to come to town on Wednesday to correct the Score & parts: they sent off the whole orchl. material at once to the firm as Mr.Gill had a rehearsal on Saty.

Would you let me know if it will be possible to have the whole thing (score & parts) at Wardour st on Thursday morng? I wd. then arrange to come up— but the parts &c. may be engaged.

We return home tomorrow.

> Kindest rgrds
> Yours v.sinly
> Edward Elgar

Amid the rejoicing over this newest Novello publication, the best that Boosey could offer was a miniature score series of the *Pomp and Circumstance* Marches.

295, Regent Street, London, W.
Oct 9:1906

Dear Sir Edward

By this post I have sent you some proofs that I have received from Geidel.

The print is very small, but it is clear & bright. The size of the book would leave room for a little enlargement up & down, but the side margins cannot be reduced. Unfortunately photography does not enable us to enlarge in *one* direction only!!

Of course these little books are not for a conductor's use, but merely as an aid to the eye to keep company with the ear as the procession goes along,— *so*—we must not expect too much from them.

I hope that you keep strong,—equal to all the demands made (& accepted) on mind & body, and able to bear the plaudits of the public with calmness & philosophy.

> With many longings,
> I am Yours very sncy
> Jas.Leighton

A dweller in a 'Land of Hope'[33]

Elgar went to Novello's offices on 11 and 12 October to correct orchestral parts of *The Kingdom*. While there he looked at Julius Buths's German translation of the libretto as *Das Reich*. This Elgar discussed with a younger member of the firm, Harold Brooke (1880–1956), a nephew of Alfred and Augustus Littleton who had

---

[33] HWRO 705:445:8168.

recently transferred from the editorial department to the publishing office to begin to replace as far as possible the irreplaceable Jaeger. Brooke was an excellent linguist (as well as a skilled and experienced pianist). Back at home Elgar wrote to the firm.

Hereford
Oct 13 1906
Dear Sirs:

'The Kingdom'
Referring to my conversation with Mr.Harold Brooke concerning the German translation—I find Luther has Geduld = patience
Bauleuten = builders
Prof.Buths may have taken his version from Ps.22 for the last passage: I have not the O.T. in German: but wd. you ask him to see Acts 4,11 where the Ps: is quoted?
Will you please *insist* that *Patience must* be in even if we alter the phrasing of the music completely.
Builders also should certainly go in or the 'idea' fails.*

Yrs V trly
Edward Elgar

*'The stone. . . . has become the chief corner stone.'

Plas Gwyn, Hereford.
Oct 22.1906
Dear Sirs:

I sent a telegram this morning concerning the German title: as the word 'Gottes' will appear, will it be now necessary to consider Prof.Buths' suggestion as to stating that the work is a continuation of 'The Apostles'? I see no objection to such a statement but I think he may have wished it, as 'Das Reich' (without Gottes) wd. have a very different feeling in Germany from that called up by 'The Kingdom' in England. Please settle it as you like best.
I return the proofs of the three pages v.s. & Prof.Buths' letter

Yrs v try
Edward Elgar

Das Reich it remained in translation, despite the political implications.
There were further cards and letters to Jaeger in Switzerland:

Plas Gwyn, Hereford
Oct 18 06
My dear J.

How & where are you? We have been very quiet since Birmingham: you never send a word as to yourself. The weather is now dull & gloomy, & we are preparing for winter[.] Good luck to you [—] we all send love

Yrs ever
Ed E.[34]

[34] HWRO 705:445:8773.

[n.p.]
30 Oct. 1906
Dear Mr.Jaeger

We were very glad to hear of you & hope the treatment is helping you on fast—We are so glad to hear your cough was better. It certainly sounds very hard work, & must require immense courage to plunge into the cold as you describe but I trust you feel better & then all labour will seem light. I am afraid there cannot be much variety in the days so perhaps a letter may amuse you. I daresay you have heard long ago about the Birm. Fest. It really was a very good first performance of 'The Kingdom' & was most thrilling to hear & the vast audience were most profoundly impressed—It is most *wonderful* to hear, the female voice choruses, 'Come from the four Winds' different from anything else—It is impossible to imagine anything more beautiful that[*sic*] A.Nic[h]olls' singing of the 'Eventide'. Of course in a Cathedral the effect of the whole wd. be still more overpowering. Last week the performance of Gerontius at Southport was very fine. The Chorus was simply marvellous, such delicacy, such expression, it has to be heard to be imagined—The audience seemed spell bound, all through.

It has been such wet weather, Instead of being able to be out & have some sort of holiday after such a pressure of work, Edward has hardly had any at all—& now the Lectures have to be got through—

Hanley Choirs are singing a lovely programme of Brahms, Elgar, Jensen, Möllendorf &c, partsongs at the Malvern Concert Club Concert on Saturday, I am so looking forward to it, especially to hearing the 'Evening Scene'.

Carice is very hard at work & enjoys her studies so much. May is busy but has had no weather for photography.

Now we do hope you are getting on well, & have a good account from home—With best remembrances,

Yrs. sicy
C.A.Elgar[35]

[*n.p., n.d., probably included with the preceding: the folds match*]
My dear Jaggs:

What a drastic cure! *How* I should like to join in it: we would skip together in fine form.—dear old boy, I hope you are getting on well: it seems very lonely with you away and all the good Americans gone home. I have not heard from Sanford since his party left here after the Hereford Festival

Love to you now & always

Yrs ever
Edward[36]

[35] HWRO 705:445:8842.   [36] HWRO 705:445:8771.

In fact Elgar was thoroughly depressed, and it told on his health. He was suffering from eye trouble when he lunched with Alfred Littleton in London on 26 November. On the doctor's recommendation he tried another cure in December.

Gwalia Hotel, Ltd., Llandrindod Wells.
Dec 14 1906
My dear Littleton:

One line to say that drinking these peculiar waters has done me good: my eyes have been worse since I saw you but now the inflammation has departed into my *hands*—not much but gout is indicated
Love to you all
I go home tomorrow

Yrs ever
Edwd.Elgar

A request from the choral conductor Nicholas Kilburn for a separate edition of *The Apostles* Prologue brought an offer from the firm to print the Prologue and pay an extra five guineas. This Elgar ultimately accepted. Then Alice Elgar wrote to say that they were forced to give up a planned trip to Italy for the winter. The real reason was that Elgar felt too depressed.

Plas Gwyn, Hereford.
18 Dec.1906.
Dear Mr.Littleton

Edward asks me to send you a few lines, as after much thought, we feel we must give up our Italian journey. It is of course a very great disappointment & I hoped such great things from the change for Edward—We feel convinced however that we could not undertake it without financial anxiety & the only course is to abandon it—

We thought we wd. rather tell you of this change of plan ourselves, & I know you will be sorry, with all your kind thoughts for E. about it—He was much better for N.Wales, & his eyes, but is not quite so well now & his eyes resent any work. We must try & go down to Devon & Cornwall where he can be out of doors more than here—

With united best remembrances to you & Mrs.Littleton

Yrs.siny
C.A.Elgar

But after Christmas other counsels prevailed:

Plas Gwyn, Hereford.
Dec 26 1906
My dear Littleton:

All good wishes for the New Year.

After much deliberation my wife & myself start to Naples on Friday—I pass thro' town & shall call if I can squeeze out a minute; but in case I cannot do so will you be so good as to send some money! I don't in the least know if I deserve any but if possible I shd like a fifty-pound cheque sent to my niece (May Grafton) here crossed Lloyds Hereford and wd. you pay into *my* acct at Glyn's Mills Currie & Co[,] 67 Lombard St[,] E.C. one hundred: I am awfully sorry to trouble you but the doctor insists on rest & we have hurriedly decided to go.

A line to Poste Restante, *Capri* will find us: we sail on Friday calling at Genoa &, of course, Naples.

Love to you all at home

Yours ever
Edward Elgar

1. Elgar in the study at Plas Gwyn, 1906, with the sketches of *The Kingdom*

2. Novello's offices at 160 Wardour Street

3. Novello's shop at 160 Wardour Street

4. Elgar in the music room, Severn House, Hampstead, 1912

From Naples Elgar wrote about the projected American trip in the spring, to include the New York Oratorio Society performances of both *The Apostles* and *The Kingdom* conducted by their composer, and an honorary degree at the new Carnegie Institute in Pittsburgh.

Parker's Hotel, Naples.
Jan 11:1907.
My dear Littleton:

I recd. a letter from the Oratorio people in New York, I refused to accept: they offered 1500 dollars: but the difficulties were these: if the Pittsburgh people [*i.e.*, Andrew Carnegie] had objected to pay my expenses (and I could not in the time ask them)—the amount wd. be ridiculous. Then I do not know anything of the soloists: again they only give the same number of rehearsals for *both* works that they give to *one* by Pierne (I think *Pierne* but am not sure) So I could not very well go & be worried to death by bad singers and curtailed rehearsals with a fair prospect of getting nothing

It is bright here but cold & I do not improve, one thing, I don't want to; & that may be a reason.

Thanks for sending to May [Grafton] &c.

We leave here for Capri tomorrow and then Rome: but I am bored to death.

> Our love to you all
> Yrs sinly
> Ed:Elgar

Grand Hotel Quisisana, Capri
Feb 5.1907
My dear Littleton:

I have decided to go to U.S. after all. Gray cabled about Chicago also & said *do come*: so I relented.

I shall probably go straight from Naples.

We have been having most dreadful weather: raining for days & gales. We have had nothing like the severe weather we have heard of on the mainland: we can see miles of snow but there is none here.

We may go to Rome for a day or two but at present the weather is too uncertain.

Between times we get walks on this lovely island & the air, when breathable at all, is *most* delightful

> Our love to you all
> Yours v sincly
> Edward Elgar

Rome
Feb 21 07

My dear Littleton:

Many thanks for your letter: I am glad to hear you are better & *may* see you in a day or two.

We leave this on Saturday for Paris & home: I must take my wife to Hereford and I sail by the Carmania March 2 (Cunard) I shall be at home (D.V.) on Tuesday or Wednesday till I sail. *If* trains fit I shall 'hop' out in London.

We heard of you being at Hereford from the children who were radiant at having you & Mrs Littleton in Hereford again

If Pointer wants me he had better write home: if a stitched up score of the Kingdom will be ready it might go to the ship. I am 'seeing' better but my eyes are not right.

At Chicago I do some orchestral things. I forget the date but Gray has arranged it all.

> Kindest rgrds
> Yrs ever
> Edward Elgar

A letter from H. W. Gray in New York confirmed Elgar's arrangements for New York, Chicago (where he was to conduct the Theodore Thomas Orchestra), and Pittsburgh.

21 East 17th Street, New York
Feb 19.07

Dear Sir Edward

Your two letters safely received & everyone is delighted. This arrangement is quite independent of the Pittsburgh show so you will have no trouble on that score. I have written to Chicago & sent your list, but think you will get a letter from [Frederick] Stock, the Conductor, before this. We will give you the best time possible & you will like the Oratorio [Society] crowd. I am sure you will approve or would not have urged your acceptance. There is quite a general feeling that both works need you as a finishing touch. Dr. Damrosch will have things in good order for you & you will only need to 'touch the button'.

Your trip to Capri ought to, & I hope will, put you in good condition for our strenuous life also for the trip over, may it be a pleasant one. Don't forget the 'Weepers Ivy' whatever you do; we might have a Potato Dance or something.

I trust Lady Elgar is well & won't mind the extra travelling.

Yours truly
H W Gray

P.S. Don't forget to let me know the ship you sail on.[1]

On 1 March, the day before Elgar sailed, Harold Brooke went to Plas Gwyn to go through proof sheets of *The Kingdom* full score. The following day Elgar sailed from Liverpool, and his next letter was written from the home of his friend Mrs Worthington in New York.

The Wyoming[,] 55th Street & Seventh Avenue
March 30.1907

My dear Littleton:

I hope you are all well & finding spring weather: here, after snow &c, we have some really lovely days, quite warm & brilliant.

The two things [*The Apostles* and the American première of *The Kingdom*] went fairly well: some points good but usually too 'assertive' for me. All are amiable & mean well. I have read nothing & don't believe what my friends say! so I am not in a position to say much about my work.

I am anxious to get home & have a quiet summer, it is scarcely restful here but amusing up to a certain point.

Gray has been most kind & of the greatest assistance, I leave here on Tuesday next for Chicago, I hope under his personal guidance but he is not yet sure of his plans. We return on the Campania Ap 20 & I shall hope to see you at Hereford soon after.

My love to you all.

Yours ever
Edward Elgar

I went to Parsifal yesterday—it is an outrage!

Initially *Parsifal* had been given staged performances only in Bayreuth. The Americans had begun to produce it in 1903, but it was not seen complete in London until 1914.

After Chicago, Elgar went to Pittsburgh for his Carnegie Institute honorary degree. Its millionaire founder, Andrew Carnegie, had seemed to promise heavy expense fees for the visit; in view of this, Elgar had accepted the low figure for his engagements with the Oratorio Society in New York—only to find Carnegie's promises in Pittsburgh unrealized. On the return voyage he wrote:

[1] HWRO 705:445:5455. Another letter from Gray, dated 8 January 1907, begins 'Dear Mr President' (HWRO 705:445:5614). This was perhaps addressed to Elgar, but it is almost entirely taken up with private jokes now unintelligible.

R.M.S. 'Campania'.

Ap 25 1907   At sea & rolling very much

My dear Littleton:

I am nearing home & am right glad to feel I shall (D.V.) soon be there. I have not much to say & will reserve 'talk' until we meet; I trust this may be soon.

I have much to say about the disgraceful way old Carnegie has treated his 'guests'—& the old *fibber* put me in quite a false position with Damrosch & the secretary of the Oratorio[.] He told them he was paying me <u>600£</u> ($3,000) to come. *Now* he refuses to pay any of his 'guests' more than 16£ (lowest possible fare!) each way & they are all at much expense!

Do come down to Hereford soon.

Much love to you all

Yours ever
Ed: Elgar

On his return there was another proposal from the secretary of the Leeds Festival, Frederick Spark: would Elgar conduct *The Kingdom* at Leeds in the autumn? This was arranged through Novello, and Elgar wrote during a visit to London:

Langham Hotel, London.

Wednesday [15 May 1907] p m

My dear Littleton:

I was too much rushed this morning to come round & I hope to go out to suburban friends this p.m.

I shall be back anyhow tomorrow and will call at Wardour st about 12: if you should be away or invisible let me hear if you can.

Mr Spark was here to-day & I saw him and agreed to that floating early choral rehearsal

So all is well.

Would it be possible—without any trouble to anyone—for you to give me a *sort of* idea as to how my royalty account is going on? It will depend upon that—now old Carnegie seems hopeless—how we proceed about our Italian winter arrangements. But you must not trouble yourself.

Volbach (Mainz) writes that they are giving the Kingdom next season and I am thinking of conducting the work in Heidelberg.

Yours ever
Ed Elgar

I should have called to-day to see Mrs.Littleton [at their London residence in Lancaster Gate] but I understood the family is in a festive mood: so I'll pay my respects tomorrow

Mrs Littleton was in failing health, and every attention was welcomed.

Elgar had done no noticeable creative work since *The Kingdom*. As his fiftieth birthday approached in June 1907, he found himself in reminiscent mood. Looking through old sketches of anthems for St George's Catholic Church in Worcester written during his organist days there twenty years and more ago, he rounded and polished two of them as an *Ave Maria* and *Ave Maris Stella* for the publisher. They could join the *Ave Verum*, already published under similar circumstances in Novello's 'Cantiones Sacrae' series.

Plas Gwyn, Hereford.
May 24:1907

My dear Littleton:

By this post I am sending to Wardour st two little things from the old sketches & Church things: they *may* do to go with the tiny 'Ave verum' but the editor must decide: the 'Cantiones Sacrae' is what I mean. They are tender little plants so treat them kindly whatever is their fate.

We miss you very much but the weather has not been good.

Your daughter, whom the household dares to call Rose, (which familiarity I cannot attain to), has just left looking very well

Yours ever
Edward Elgar

It was the beginning of a close friendship between the Elgars—especially Alice and Carice—and Rose Littleton.

Alfred Littleton wrote to ask whether the new anthems should go under the 25 per cent royalty agreement, or be treated as *The Apostles* Prologue, for which the firm had just paid 5 guineas to publish separately.

Plas Gwyn, Hereford.
May 28:1907

My dear Littleton:

I should prefer that all things published now shd. go in under the present agreement: except of course 'extracts' from things pubd. before the agreement; e.g. the Prologue to 'Apostles' which the firm wrote [about] the other day.

'Rosie' is coming to dine tonight so I shall have a chance to shew my acquired knowledge.

I have been mowing the edges of the back lane with a scythe; hence the extreme jerkiness of the writing

Ever yrs
Edward Elgar

After another winter in Switzerland, Jaeger had been sent to Germany in his search for ever more elusive health.

Plas Gwyn[,] Hereford
May 28. 1907.

My dear Moss:

I have been wofully busy & have scarcely been 'at home' yet. I do hope you are feeling satisfied—as satisfied as may be possible under the circumstances—with your new surroundings. I forget where *Westfalen* is but I am going to look at the map presently: curiously there was long ago an old family here, of German extraction I think[,] named *Westfaling*, so spelt & there is a Westfaling street in this city.

S.S.S[anford] is in Paris safely bless him & I hope he may have a peaceful & restful time: he has been really ill during last winter & an angel to many as usual.

I had a mixed time in America—mostly very pleasant but the unpleasant times were jokable, so all passed well.

We are altogether enjoying the summer when the weather will let us: some days hot & then very cold as is today. There is really no news: all goes steadily on: I shall be fifty next week they tell me, but I don't know it: I have my pipe & the bicycle & a heavenly country to ride in—so an end. I take no interest whatever in music now & just 'edit' a few old boyish M.S.S.—music is off.

We all send love & best of wishes to you, let us hear soon how you are taking to the new spot.

> Yours ever
> Edward.[2]

On the day of his fiftieth birthday, 2 June 1907, Elgar wrote a little part-song to a poem by Arthur Maquarie entitled *Love*: he dedicated it to his wife, in tribute to their years together. Alice Elgar wrote:

Plas Gwyn, Hereford.
7 June 1907.

My dear Mr. Jaeger

Edward is writing hard, so I am going to send a few lines & thank you for him (& myself) for yr. cards & all yr. good wishes for him on his birthday. You have written him such *beautiful* wishes in such beautiful words, it touches us very deeply.

Your cards make our hearts ache to think you are still so unwell, & still having to stay in exile. We do trust & pray you are recovering from this attack which must have been so dreadfully anxious & trying for you & that the new Dr. & treatment will soon have some good effect. *How* glad we should be for better accounts, I cannot tell you & I am sure you know—

Edward's head has been *full* of music ever since his return & he has been continually sketching & playing. He has sent Messrs.N[ovello] 2 lovely Motetts & the other evening wrote a lovely pt.Song, & is just waiting for permission for the words wh. I trust he may soon receive. & now he is orchestrating another Pomp & Circumstance March [No. 4] a *splendid* one— one to rouse every spark of martial fire. The occulist [*sic*] still orders him to rest his eyes. The weather has been, & is *most* trying [—] So chilly & gales of wind & torrents of rain, & the country all the time trying to look so lovely. For a birthday treat we took a motor & had a drive on Monday [3 June] all round by Birchwood, it was very touching to see it all again & the views were most lovely. Carice has just learnt to ride a bicycle & enjoys it so much but of course has not very much time as she is very busy with studies. Edward's love & every wish that our hearts can send you for improvement

V.siny
C.A.Elgar

[*on reverse*]

My dearest Nimrod: how I did make 'you' sound in Chicago! A fine orchestra (100) & they knew (via dear old Theodore Thomas) *everything* of mine backwards: I shed a tear over it. Now I'm busy & must not use my eyes much so I am doing trifles: poor things but mine own boyish thoughts. I wax old but not infirm. I wish you would send better news of yourself but we hope for that next time.

All love to you
Yours ever
Edward

The first pt of the 4th march is good: the middle *rot* but pleasing to march to.[3]

Pomp and Circumstance March No. 4 took its place in the series published by Boosey, outside the Novello agreement. Boosey's terms were the same as for *Pomp and Circumstance* No. 3, £50 down—but with an increased royalty of 4d. on all arrangements published. The new 'trifles' Elgar worked at were the *Wand of Youth* pieces.

In response to a query from the *Musical Times* editor Edwards about the origin of *Dream Children*, which had appeared in 1902, Elgar wrote:

The University, Birmingham.
June 6. 1907.

My dear Edwards:

I am sorry I could not let you have a reply as early as you suggested: I was away at the University all day yesterday.

Now as to Dream Children; I really can tell you *nothing*! They (or it) were (or was) written for small orch: as published; the pianoforte solo is an arrangement. They were (or it was) written long ago, or rather sketched long

[3] HWRO 705:445:8855 and 8779.

ago & completed a few years back. I really know nothing of the first performance & I have never heard them (or it).

I am sorry my answers will not deserve marks.

What weather:

> Kindest rgrds
> Yours v sincerely
> Edward Elgar.[4]

The correspondence with Alfred Littleton resumed after the Elgars returned to Hereford on 14 June. Elgar apologized for not seeing Littleton in London: he had been sitting to the Italian sculptor Cercigliari-Melilli for a statuette.

Plas Gwyn, Hereford.
June 16 1907

My dear Littleton:

I was so sorry I cd. not see you, principally owing to that sculptor business; what a ghastly nuisance it is!

Alice convoyed a little part song [*Love*] to Wardour st—unimportant but perhaps worth printing.

The score of the Kingdom arrived yesterday & I send very many thanks & admiration for it: it is really a splendid 'book' [—] the printing could not be better & is worthy of the glorious Hall in Wardour Street from which it comes

> Yours ever
> Ed:Elgar

On 22 June Mr and Mrs Littleton attended a function at Windsor. Elgar had considered going, but decided against it.

Plas Gwyn, Hereford.
June 30. 1907

My dear Littleton:

I hope you & Mrs.Littleton are all well after the exertions of the week & that the ceremony went off well amidst pleasant surroundings *and* weather?

I have returned revises of the two little Latin things & with them two adaptations (*in anthem-wise*) with English words. I hope you will approve.

I wrote to the firm about the one set of words & am pursuing enquiries: the other set ['Jesu meek and lowly'] are in the Anthem book No.664 so I suppose they are usable [*sic*]: please cast a fatherly eye over these two things.

> Kindest regards
> Yrs ever
> Ed.Elgar

---

[4] BL Egerton MS 3090 fos. 85–86.

Side by side with the revision of early anthems, Elgar was revising his earliest music of all, written for the children's family play in Worcester forty years earlier. Through the summer of 1907 he shaped much of it into an orchestral suite which he called *The Wand of Youth*. On 7 August Alfred Littleton came over to Plas Gwyn with his granddaughter: Elgar played through the *Wand of Youth* music on the piano, and Alice Elgar's diary records that Littleton was 'absolutely *delighted*'. Four days later the orchestration was finished. Alfred Littleton collected the manuscript from Plas Gwyn and posted it from Hereford to Wardour Street:

Hatteral Hereford.

Aug 12. 1907

Dear May

With this I send M.S. Score of a new orchestral Suite by Elgar—(in 2 envelopes) He would like the score engraved as *quickly* as *possible*. Can Brause do it. He ought not to undertake it unless he can promise proofs of the whole in about a month. If he can't do this it must go to Germany and they must be told to do the whole thing in 3 or 4 weeks.

With regard to size I think it should be royal 4to—but Elgar rather favours large 8vo. Please let me know what you & Brause think about this.

You will notice memorandum about ruling bars in sections [of the orchestra: each bar-line running down through woodwind, broken and commencing again at brass, broken again before timpani, and so on.] I think this is a good idea & I am inclined to think we ought to do it with all Scores.

I should like to see a specimen page before the work goes right on: but this need not cause any delay.

Please acknowledge receipt of the M.S. to Elgar—but do not write to him more than this—please write all you have to say about it to me.

When you write please let me know how Brause is getting on with [Dvořák's] 'Spectre's Bride' German edition—vocal score & vocal parts— Rosencrantz knows when these have to be ready for a performance in Vienna. I should also like to know how he is getting on with vocal parts of Bach's B minor Mass.

I hope this is all clear & that the M.S. will reach you safely.

Yours sincerely
Alfred H Littleton

C. J. May telegraphed news of the score's arrival, together with his opinion favouring the larger format—which was used.

The Elgars meanwhile had gone for a holiday to the Welsh coast. On return they found a letter from Jaeger: he had returned for the remainder of the summer, but the journey itself had made him ill.

Plas Gwyn, Hereford.
Augt 24: 1907
My dear Moss:

I was delighted to see the postmark on your letter & overjoyed to hear that you had arrived. I hope the temporary ailment resultant from the journey & this awful climate is passing rapidly away. I am not writing at length now because I am just back from the sea & had on Friday to rush to town: back yesterday. I fear I have no musical news for you: my eyes are not really workable & I have done only some ancient trifles this summer & I seem to have forgotten all about music: you know I have no ambition & so there's an end.

Now, dear Moss, this is only to bring you our love & best wishes: I shall hope to *see* you soon.

Best regards from us all to Mrs. Jaeger

Yours ever
Edward[5]

Elgar spent some days at Frank Schuster's country home, The Hut, where on 1 September he played *The Wand of Youth* Suite to Henry Wood. Wood then wrote to Alfred Littleton:

4, Elsworthy Road, London, N.W.
September 13th 1907.

Dear Mr.Littleton,

A couple of weeks ago I spent a Sunday with Sir Edward Elgar, and he played me a new Suite, which you are publishing. Would you care to reserve the first performance if I could put the work into my first Symphony Concert at Queens Hall, November 2nd. It is such a very delightful little work, and Sir Edward is quite agreeable to its being produced at one of my concerts, so perhaps you will let me have a few particulars as to when the parts will be ready, etc., as I should not like to announce it and then have to postpone it, while on the other hand I naturally want it to be a novelty. With best wishes,

Faithfully yours,
Henry J. Wood

(In the event, Wood conducted the première with the Queen's Hall Orchestra on 14 December 1907.)

Elgar completed his orchestration, and on 29 September sent instructions to Novello for their copyist to give extra cues, for performances with reduced instrumentation. Then he went to the Cardiff Festival, where he heard Parry's *A Vision of Life* (set to a text by the composer himself and published by Novello). Then Elgar went on to the Leeds Festival. From there he wrote to Jaeger.

[5] HWRO 705:445:8778.

Queen's Hotel, Leeds.
Tuesday [8 Oct. 1907]

My dear Nim:

I have thought about you so very much during these festival times.

I say! that 'Vision' of Parry's is *fine stuff* & the poem is literature: you *must* hear it some day.

I hope you are better: I heard of you via that dear good woman Mrs. Worthington & wanted to climb up to you [at Muswell Hill] but could not.

This is only to bring my love—I've really nothing to say

> Yrs ever
> Edward[6]

Jaeger had been forced to retire from Novello, and the firm were seeking ways to help him financially. The company secretary Clayton sent him a cheque for 20 guineas to buy the copyright of Jaeger's Analysis of *The Kingdom*. Jaeger responded:

37 Curzon Road, Muswell Hill[,] N.
Oct. 16/ 07

Dear Mr Clayton,

I enclose Copyright-assignment & receipt for Cheque (£21) for the 'Kingdom' Analysis, and need hardly say, how greatly obliged I am once more for the Firm's largess [*sic*]. At the same time I do wish you would have allowed me to *prove* in the 'practical' way I proposed, *how* deeply grateful I am for all the firm have done for me. It would have filled me with a sense of satisfaction & a certain 'pride'. But I suppose I must not indulge in such dreams; and when I make up my Bank Book (I have just finished doing so!) I have to come to the sad conclusion that perhaps such 'satisfaction' & 'pride' would be misplaced in a poor fellow like unto myself. So I will once more thank your Firm most sincerely for their Kindness. Candidly, I don't think the 'Kingdom' Analysis worth £21, especially after Elgar knocking it about in the way he did. But—comme vous voulez!

I certainly feel somewhat stronger [—] can take longer walks, eat heartier (vegetarian) meals, and enjoy my cold bath & subsequent air-bath (windows & door wide open) & exercise (wet & naked) more. But I still cough a good deal. But then my new doctor told me I should have to do that for some months yet—a cryptic utterance, which may mean anything! Well, I cough away & hope that's the right thing. I have no fever, sleep pretty well, on the whole, &—hope on. Dum spiro spero.

---

[6] HWRO 705:445:8780.

I mean to call at No 160 [Wardour Street] one day soon & then I may perhaps have the pleasure of seeing you. And I hope I may find you in good Health.

Yours, very faithfully & gratefully
A.J.Jaeger

My Dr wants me to do some light work at Home. Cant I do some reviewing for the M.T.?

Plas Gwyn, Hereford.
Oct. 25. 1907

Dear Sirs:

I shall be much obliged if you will transfer to Mr A.J.Jaeger any rights I may have as to copyright, fees and royalties in the following three analyses written by him, viz:
    The Dream of Gerontius
    The Apostles
    The kingdom.
The transfer to take effect from the date on which the last royalty account on these works was made up & all profits due to me since that date & in future to be paid to Mr Jaeger

Yours faithfully
Edward Wm.Elgar

Plas Gwyn, Hereford.
Oct 25. 1907

My dear Littleton:

Enclosed I send a formal letter to the firm; is it sufficient? Do not trouble to answer as I shall see you so soon but perhaps you will get matters *en train* in case I have to sign formal papers

Yrs ever
Ed:Elgar

It is the least I can do for Jaeger & I have sent him a note saying I have done it

Plas Gwyn, Hereford.
Oct 25. 1907

My very dear Nim:

I have today asked Messrs.Novello to transfer all rights & royalties I may have in the Analyses of Gerontius, Kingdom & Apostles to you from the last making up of the accounts. I am very much 'wanted' by my poor relations, just now more than ever, so I apologise to you for not making the transaction retrospective: this I wished to do but I *cannot*. So forgive your friend & please accept the little I can do.

I hope you are going on well & when I pass through London on my way to economize 'in the South' [*i.e.*, spending the winter in Italy] I hope I may see you

> Love
> Yours ever
> Edward Elgar[7]

Jaeger wrote to Novello:

37 Curzon Road, Muswell Hill.
27/x/7
Gentlemen,

Please pay no attention to Sir E Elgar's letter re transferring his rights & Royalties in the Analysis of Gerontius, Apostles & Kingdom to *me*. I have written to him that I cannot & will not accept his generous offer.

> Yours sincerely
> A.J.Jaeger

But Elgar would have none of it. From Alfred Littleton's London home he wrote:

50 Lancaster Gate, W.
Wedy [30 Oct. 1907]
My dearest Jag:

All right! many thanks for your letter about those analyses—but you are a dear good chap—BUT E.E. is going to have his own little way for the first time in his life

> Love
> Edward[8]

In the year since *The Kingdom*, Elgar had produced little beyond the *Wand of Youth* Suite and *Pomp and Circumstance* March No. 4. Littleton was anxious to get other things from him. In particular he wanted to commission a Marching Song on behalf of the Worshipful Company of Musicians. He sent Elgar a book of verses with several especially marked. Between the Cardiff and Leeds Festivals Elgar responded:

Plas Gwyn, Hereford.
Oct 1:1907
My dear Littleton:

I have been through the songs for Marching again & again & I fear the result remains disappointing.
88; will not do—the men do not like to be reminded of their dialect
17; I. impossible

---

[7] HWRO 705:445:8781.   [8] HWRO 705:445:8782.

II. Do

III. Better, but *I* cannot use it

IV. The Best of the set. but not the right 'stimmung'

94; No good

34; do.

9; Good but too '*fighting*'

69: Dialect—will not do.

You see I cannot do anything with them: I am sorry but it is so. Now you had better see if the words will inspire some other minstrel.

I am rather seedy after scrambled meals & no meals at Cardiff &c &c.

> Kindest regards
> Yours ever
> Ed:Elgar

He was trying to get permission to use the words of Arthur O'Shaughnessy's Ode *The Music Makers*, but had so far not found the late author's representative. Some proofs had reached him of *The Wand of Youth* in John E. West's piano solo version, based directly on Elgar's own short score. The weekend between the Leeds Festival and the North Staffordshire Festival at Hanley found the Elgars staying again at Wychnor, from where Elgar wrote to Littleton.

Wychnor Park, Burton-on-Trent.

Oct 13 1907

My dear Littleton:

I am so glad that you are better: we are resting here after Leeds on our way to Hanley.

I am glad you think the title will do.

West has sent on the proofs of the PF. arrangement of some of the nos. & asks about the 'other numbers'. I conclude I am right in saying *he* is to arrange these. Those sent are (I think) those of which I made *sketch* arrangements. The things look very nice & *eatable*

As to the Ode it is called simply Ode—but I will give exact title of the volume when I reach home.

I am truly grieved about those marching verses but I really cannot *feel* any of them.

We reach home soon & I will write again

> Yours ever
> Edwd.Elgar

Home at last after all the Festivals, Elgar acknowledged the payment (through Novello) of his fee for conducting *The Kingdom* at the Leeds Festival.

Hereford
Thursday [17 Oct. 1907] a.m.

My dear Littleton:

Very many thanks for sending the Leeds cheque & for arranging that it should come.

Just this moment home & find heaps to do.

By the way I've not yet seen the 2nd. proof of the Score of the Suite.

Yrs ever
Ed:Elgar

Littleton suggested making *The Wand of Youth* available to Henry Wood for his première rehearsals in proofs pulled directly from the engraved plates to save time. He asked Elgar to confirm that the O'Shaughnessy Ode began with the words 'We are the music makers . . .'. But he returned to the question of a Marching Song; and he also wondered whether they should at long last bring out the big piano *Allegro* which Elgar had written for Fanny Davies in 1901, and which she had performed again recently in public. Finally Littleton invited Elgar to join him at a Musicians' Company Dinner in London on the following Monday.

Plas Gwyn, Hereford.
Oct 23 1907

My dear Littleton:

First many thanks for your kind invitation which I gladly accept for Monday night. I arrive (solus) at Paddington at 4.15 & will come straight to you.

Now as to many other things:
I do not think the P.F piece in its present form entirely satisfactory—I have the M.S. now & may re-cast it. Its *too* long!

I have written to Wood about the kind proposal you make to have the score & 'pulled' parts ready for rehearsal.

The first line of O'Shaughnessy's Ode *is* 'We are the music makers'.

Now the marching song. I fear the consequences, I do not think it would be used for the purpose intended. Booseys, who are in touch with Military Band life, have a book of songs &c for soldiers with the band arrangements, but it has never been used. I wish you wd. get a copy & look at it—as far as I remember it is good selection, but I saw it since I saw you so could not speak of it before. What I fear is this: there isn't going to be any singing by the soldiers. Now I am keeping those songs you sent until Monday & will bring them with me & my final reply also.

In my paragraph about the P.F. piece (reference to which arose out of the Riga lady's letter) I forgot to thank you for seeing to the answering of that long epistle

Yours ever
Edward Elgar

So many thanks for extending the invitation to Alice—she does not come to town until the end of the week.

When Alice Elgar arrived, they would be *en route* for their winter in Italy.

In London at the beginning of November, Elgar went through *The Wand of Youth* Suite No. 1 with Henry Wood, to prepare for the première in six weeks' time. On 5 November Alfred Littleton saw the Elgars (with May Grafton) off at Victoria Station. Four days later they were settling into the flat they had taken in Rome.

Via Gregoriana 38/III Roma
Nov 9:1907

My dear Littleton:

We are here all safely & find our flat very simple but comfortable & a glorious view: it is really one of the best situations in Rome & the walks on the Pincian are at our door almost which is most convenient for Alice.

Please let Wood have all the material for his performance as soon as you can as there may be errors in the parts & he may have an early opportunity to rehearse—I do not think you had better print for sale until his performance is over, in case of mistakes &, for the first time for years, the parts go to the first performance without my playing them thro' with Austin.

I can't tell how much I shall be able to work here: there are 'voices most vociferous' & pianos most pianiferous in the street which is otherwise quiet. But I'll report later

Kindest rgds
Yrs sincy
Ed Elgar

P.S. Our journey was most successful: May & I were not very good travellers but I think your coming to see us off (which was most kind) gave us good luck.

Amongst the post reaching him in Rome was the newly printed vocal score of *The Kingdom* in German, and a request from the tenor Paul Reimers (1878–195?) for the composer to give his sanction to altering a passage in it.

38 Via Gregoriana P.3[,] Roma
Nov 23.1907

My dear Littleton:

I recd. the enclosed a few days ago & *today* have received the copy of 'Das Reich' referred to.

Will one of your people write to Herr Reimers & tell him I cannot possibly alter the passage. I remember his artistic singing with pleasure in Rotterdam. You will see that his letter requests an alteration of the only real *tenor* bit in the work & his pencilled propositions alter the melody into nothing[.] A tenor who has not an 'A' at the low pitch must be a curiosity.

In great haste
Yours ever
Edward Elgar

All well here & settling down. Cold with a good deal of sun

There was also a card from Jaeger, who was now too ill to go to Switzerland for another winter. Elgar was beginning at last to work on his Symphony, and his wife undertook to answer.

38 Via Gregoriana P.3[,] Roma
9 Dec. 1907

Dear Mr.Jaeger

So many thanks for your card, we were so glad to have it but grieve that you could not send a better report of yrself & trust you are better again. I fear you have had some bad weather & bad fogs wh. must be dreadfully trying for you. I know you will like to hear something about our surroundings & about E. especially. He loves his Rome very much & loves going for long exploring walks, one day impressed by the Palatine, going back to the wonderful days of the Caesars, another day to the wonderful Churches & *their* associations, & to gaze again & again at the wonderful Juno. The beautiful Villa in wh. the marvellous bust used to be more worthily housed has now, with its beautiful gardens, all disappeared. The ground on which it stood is the new quarter, a mass of huge, modern Hotels—& now Juno stands in a hideous little room in a Museum, but nothing can diminish her greatness.

No concerts have begun yet, music, except horrible piano-organs & pianos[,] *seems* necessary to modern Romans, & the Church Music we have heard so far, is DREADFUL, the very tone of the organs makes you *fly*, if you can—

I am longing to be at Queen's Hall on the 14th. I do love those tunes so much. I hope you will be able to be at a Rehearsal?

When Pianos &c allow of any quiet, E. has been writing, & I TRUST you will hear the Symphony, yet, & many times. Carice & May so enjoy being here—& are keenly interested in all they see.

Prof.Volbach sent us a telegram & papers about the great success of 'The Kingdom' at Mainz, which is very nice to hear of. The Abbé Perosi was here the other day & played his new Composition to E. the Pater Noster from Dante's Paradiso—it sounded very sweet & beautiful.

E. was rather laid up with a cold but is now out again I am glad to say. Please give my love to Mrs.Jaeger. I do trust her Gloucester journies are a great success & not too tiring for her—

Best of remembrances & best of wishes

Yrs. sicy
C.A.Elgar

[*note added by Elgar:*]
Much love, dear Nim, glad to hear you were at rehearsal: the weather here is *possible* but too hot sometimes; wish you were here

Yours ever
E[9]

Mrs Jaeger was going to Gloucester and Stroud to give lessons two days a week in the effort to support her children and ailing husband. The connection had been secured for her by Herbert Brewer, the organist of Gloucester Cathedral.[10] Lorenzo Perosi (1872–1956) was director of music at the Vatican, and eager to have Elgar's approval for his compositions.

The *Musical Times* editor F. G. Edwards had sent a set of hymn-like verses by T. T. Lynch, beginning 'How calmly the evening once more is descending', with the request that Elgar set them for publication in his journal. This Elgar did, sending a covering letter.

38 Via Gregoriana P.3[,] Roma
Dec 2: 1907

My dear Edwards:

Good luck to you!

Here's the little setting of those simple words—homely but '*felt*'. If it is printed for January you may *try* & send me a proof but there is scarcely time for that—posts here are vague.

However the thing is *so* simple that a proof is scarcely necy
—In greatest haste

Yours ever
Edward Elgar[11]

Elgar also informed Alfred Littleton, who had meanwhile sent a new version of marching-song words:

---

[9] HWRO 705:445:8854.
[10] Information from the Jaeger's daughter, Mrs Mary Fraser, 1983.
[11] BL Egerton MS 3090 fo. 88. A proof was sent, and Elgar returned a few corrections on 17 December.

38 Via Gregoriana P.3[,] Roma
Dec 2 1907

My dear Littleton:

I have had a slight chill & have been laying low.

Edwards sent me some simple words for the M.T.—I am sending him a setting *direct*—but he will of course consult you about it. The setting is very simple—the words wd. not stand elaboration—but it may be *too* simple for your requirements

I have recd an amended version of the Marching song & will report progress shortly

Carice has had a swelled face & is very sorry for it—but we are bearing up

Love to all
Yours ever
Edward Elgar
P.T.O.

P.S. I have received a long letter from Mr. Vogt (Toronto) about a possible visit for me to Canada. I have asked him to write to *Gray* who knows what is going on & if it could be managed in conjunction with other things: this refers to Spring 1909 (not 8)

Augustus Stephen Vogt (1861–1926) was conductor of the Mendelssohn Choir in Toronto, Canada. His plan resulted in an initial visit to Canada by Henry Coward and members of his Yorkshire choirs, and in 1911 a world tour by the Sheffield Choir with Elgar as guest conductor through the eastern United States and Canada. Nothing came of the negotiations with Novello's New York agent H. W. Gray for Elgar's presence in 1909.

Next day Elgar began a big sketch for the opening of his long-awaited Symphony. This beginning seemed finally to eliminate any interest in completing the *Apostles* trilogy. He wrote immediately to Charles Beale of the Birmingham Festival, and to Alfred Littleton.

38 Via Gregoriana P.3[,] Roma
Dec 3 1907

Private

My dear Littleton:

I promised Beale I would let him know as to an oratorio—the final one of the series—for the next Birmingham festival. I have to-day written definitely & finally to give up the idea.

The surroundings here are noisy (pianos, &c.&c.) & I think I shall not write anything at all under the circumstances. In any case I am sadly disappointed with the commercial results of the last oratorios & for the sake of my people must not waste more time in attempting to write high 'felt' music: I fear you will be sorry but I have thought it seriously over & have decided

Yours always
Edward Elgar

But not a word about the Symphony beginning.

Meanwhile he had been busy with other part-songs. On 5 December Alice Elgar had written verses entitled 'A Christmas Greeting', for him to set to music as a present for Sinclair's choristers at Hereford Cathedral. He finished the setting on 8 December, and the following morning Alice posted it to Novello.

A week later he was ready to say something about the Symphony.

Rome
Sunday Dec.15.07
My dear Littleton:

Thanks for your letter and for all the news. We have complained of the piano *practising* & have some mitigation—I have bought some *heavenly* M.S. paper & have scored some of the symphony! But I see little signs of its being finished

Do get out a duet arrgt of the two [*Wand of Youth*] Suites soon. I was glad to write the little tune at Edwards' suggestion & had no thought of the price! never mind that.

Please take care of the enclosed letters: I send them in case anything shd. be made public &c. & you might think it worth while to say something on my behalf: so far as I am concerned the matter goes no farther—but I fear the poor fellow is crazy! I have not been to Bournemouth for ten years & certainly (as I told Mr.Godfrey) have never criticised the orchestra.

We are all '*bearing up*'[:] love to you

Yrs ever
Ed Elgar

In the wake of the correspondence about a Marching Song, McNaught sent out to him 'Reveille' by the American poet Bret Harte.

160, Wardour Street, London, W.
16 Dec 1907
My dear Elgar,

You will remember that I pressed you to compose a biggish male voice chorus (unacc) and you said find me the words. I have sought in many places in vain and at last I came on to the enclosed. I do hope you will like the poem for the purpose. Mr.Littleton agrees with me as to its suitability.

We have had an enquiry from Morecambe as to your coming 'Marching Song'. If it could be in the Morecambe programme it would be a capital start.

I hope you and Lady Elgar are flourishing. With best seasonable good wishes and kind regards to you and her

Believe me,
Yours sincerely,
W.G.McNaught[12]

12 HWRO 705:445:8250.

The dark ambiguities of Harte's poem suited Elgar far better than any conventional Marching Song. 20 December found him hard at work on the setting, and a week later it was sent to Novello with these letters.

38 Via Gregoriana P.3[,] Roma
Dec 27 07

My dear McNaught.

Your august demands have been obeyed & I am sending a Manuscritto Racommandato to the firm. (It's not bad!) Cast your docto-fatherly eye—or both eyes [—] over the proof—I think I have hit the difficulty—the grade of difficulty I mean—there's enough to do but not too much

All good wishes for 1908.

Yours ever
Edward Elgar.[13]

38 Via Gregoriana P.3[,] Roma
Dec 27:1907

My dear Littleton:

Many thanks for your letter: I will reply to some of it soon: this is only to say that I have *perpretated* [sic] a setting of the words McNaught sent & have sent it to Wardour st. Let me have proofs soon as it takes so long to correct them & get them backward & forward[.] The setting is of *medium* difficulty—fit for the big competitions & not too (I hope[)] disastrously complicated & harsh.

We are having some rain but are all well & send love to you all

Yrs ever
Edd. Elgar

I bought a TAYPOT at a sale. Please break this news to your daughter Rose.

1908

McNaught was delighted that his suggestion had borne fruit.

160 Wardour Street, London, W.
1 Jany 1908

My dear Elgar,

I am so glad you have taken to the 'Reveille' so kindly.

The setting is splendid—the high B at the end will be a roof raiser up in the North and I hope in Wales.

Mr Clayton is seeing to the words—as to permission—and when that is settled the world will soon come into its inheritance.

[13] MS in possession of Diana McVeagh.

I must look out half a dozen of so more sets of words as I have been so lucky. So be prepared!

With most sincere good wishes for the New Year and kindest regards to you and Lady Elgar

Believe me
Yours sincerely
W.G.McNaught[1]

38 Via Gregoriana P.3[,] Roma
Jan 4 1908

My dear McNaught:

I was glad to hear that you are not disappointed with my effort. I think it should make a bonnie noise. Would you give yourself the trouble to look over a proof, *before I see it*, with an eye—two eyes—to expression marks & stage directions—I overdo this sort of thing (—necessary in orchestral stuff—) as I put down all my feelings as I write & then haven't the heart to take 'em out. So take a lancet—pen I should say [—] & with Doctorial solemnity relieve the spasms—if any abound.

I am inscribing a part song to you! If you'll let me

All good wishes
Yours ever
Edward Elgar[2]

160 Wardour Street, London, W.
Jany.8 1908

My dear Elgar

I will with great pleasure [—] in fact I may say with fiendish joy [—] go over your expression marks.

I thank you very much for your kind intention to dedicate a Part Song to me.

It is a great honour

Yours sincerely
W.G.McNaught[3]

The part-song to be dedicated to McNaught was a setting of part of Shelley's 'Ode to the West Wind'. It was one of a set of four. The others were from Tennyson, Byron, and 'Pietro d'Alba'—his own *nom de plume* drawn from Carice's pet Peter Rabbit. The last, entitled *Owls*, was finished on the final day of 1907.

Early in January 1908 came the news that May Grafton's father Will (the husband of Elgar's sister Pollie, with whom he had lodged in his bachelor days beginning at the time of the Graftons' marriage in 1879) was dangerously ill.

[1] HWRO 705:445:8251.
[2] MS in possession of Diana McVeagh.
[3] HWRO 705:445:8252.

38 Via Gregoriana P.3[,] Roma
Jan 12 1908

My dear Littleton:

We have been in great distress of mind over May's father's illness: the poor child had to fly off at a moment's notice—we hear she has arrived at Worcester but know nothing further: we hope for better news.

This is only to say that I am despatching 3 partsongs somewhat *advanced*: please have them printed in type (not engraved) in the ordinary way & *do* let me have proofs soon, I want to *see* something to excite me further. There should be four in the Op. but I send *now* only Nos. 2, 3 & 4. The last is a 'clinker' & the best I have done.

Rather cold here but gorgeous sun & blue sky

Love to all
Yrs ever
Ed.Elgar

Next day came the news that Will Grafton was dead. He had always been a favourite of Elgar's, and the shock was great. He managed to send the outstanding part-song to make up the four of Op. 53. But the progress of the Symphony was badly affected, especially when he came down with influenza.

38 Via Gregoriana P.3[,] Roma
Jany 30 1908

My dear Littleton:

The enclosed came the other day

I have been ill with influenza in bed 10 days—I think this has settled any idea of music which has waned frightfully during the last month.

I hope you & Mrs.Littleton enjoyed Brighton: it has been very cold here & bright: now warm, tremendous storms of rain & thunder &c &c

The *noises* of this place are beyond belief. New York is quiet in comparison

Ever yrs
Edward Elgar

A picture of their life in Rome was sent by Lady Elgar to Jaeger back in England.

38 Via Gregoriana P.3[,] Roma
3. Feb. 1908.

Dear Mr. Jaeger

It seems a long time since we had your card & we are thinking of you & so much wishing to hear better accounts than when you wrote. I fear the weather has been most horrible & fear you must have felt it. I only hope Mrs. Jaeger & the children have not suffered any ill effects from it.

Here we had about a fortnight of the most beautiful weather, such bright, light air & gorgeous sunshine, sharp frost at night & cold in the mornings &

in the shade. I am sorry to say E. cd. not enjoy it as he has been laid up for just a fortnight with severe cold & a strong touch of influenza, you know how wretched & depressing that is. He is better I am thankful to say & allowed out again but still has a cough & now the weather has changed & it is raining in torrents. It *can* rain here. Of course since E. has been laid up we have not been able to see much of interest—but I hope as soon as it clears again we may have some excursions. I *long* to see the Hills they look so lovely & opalesque in the distance—& there are so many interesting places to see.

Before he was ill E. had his head full of *lovely* new tunes[.] I hope he will soon be set up again & busy again.

There have been no Concerts here yet. Strauss is to conduct one here soon, & E. has been invited to conduct one. The New Hall does not seem to be ready yet. It is impossible to describe the 'how not to do anything' of the people here, one wonders how Italy can have been *steeped* in art for so many centuries & can care so little about it, seemingly, in *this*.

We had a sad time before E. was laid up as 'May' was summoned home, her father being very ill. Soon after her return he passed away—from heart. It is so sad for them & E. has been much distressed, being much attached to this brother-in-law. It was so sad to send off poor May on such a long journey with her anxious heart, & such a break up to our little party here.

I *did* wish myself at Q's Hall to hear the 'Wand of Youth', & the Bavarians on Sunday & many things.

We suffer from many pianos here—one too near was playing a piece the 1st. evening we arrived & we hear it almost daily with no improvement!

Carice is looking so well I am thankful to say & has enjoyed the wonders of Rome immensely. She is having Italian lessons too—

The flags all round are flying at half mast in memory of this horrible Lisbon tragedy, which is truly dreadful.

Now goodbye for today & we shall much hope for a p.card soon. Edward sends his love & every affectionate wish,

Love to Mrs. Jaeger

Yours Sincerely
C.A.Elgar[4]

The Lisbon tragedy was the assassination of King Carlos of Portugal and the Crown Prince on 1 February.

Work on the Symphony was not easily resumed. Elgar referred to his lack of progress again, when later in the month he answered a letter from Henry Clayton about a proposal to fit the Elgar arrangement of the National Anthem to words beginning 'My country, 'tis of thee' for use in the United States.

[4] HWRO 705:445:8858.

38 Via Gregoriana P.3[,] Roma
Feb 20 1908

Dear Mr.Clayton:

Many thanks for your letter about the national anthem of the U.S.A. [*sic*]

I see no objection to the publication of my version of 'God save the King' with the American words provided the title page can be so worded as to acquit me of any connection with the enterprise. I should not think this would be difficult: you might let my name appear only in a foot-note—'The choral & orchestral arrangement is that of the British(?) National Anthem by EE.' or something of that sort.

Many thanks for your enquiries: I have had influenza & as far as rest & quiet go our visit is quite hopeless & I can write nothing here except short trifles

Yours sincerely
Edward Elgar

Meanwhile Alice Elgar had written to Alfred Littleton, enclosing an enthusiastic letter about Elgar's part-songs from Mrs Peterson, who conducted a women's choir in Melbourne.

38 Via Gregoriana P.3[,] Roma
15 Feb. 1908—

Dear Mr.Littleton

I am glad to be able to tell you that Edward is fairly well again, he was, as I daresay you know, laid up for about 3 weeks with severe cold & influenza. Now he is out again & making the most of this lovely Spring day, & asks me to write to you for him.

First I enclose this very nice & interesting letter. I am sure you will be interested to read of the immense enthusiasm for the Pt.Songs. Edward will acknowledge the letter, but would you be so kind as to have any sent to her that you can, & the new ones as soon as ready? Edward is so glad to have the proofs of the Pt.Songs, he has been looking for them, he has them now all except 'The Réveillée' [*sic*], but I am to ask if you would very kindly have some duplicate copies of proofs sent him, as when he returns the proofs, he has not a line of them by him—

Now, this is a plea of my own, which is, may we *please*, have his M.S.[S.] back again, not here but when we return, or if it wd. save trouble, they will be quite safe if sent to Plas Gwyn, 'not to be forwarded'.

I was sorry to hear Mrs.Littleton had been so unwell, & hope she is now much better.

I am just allowed in the drawing room again after 10 days of influenza, so you may think this whole last month has been somewhat dreary. I am thankful to say we are both better now & Carice has been extremely well. We have had very bright days with hot sun but hard frosts & very cold in the shade. I hope now it will be milder & more equable & that we shall be able to have a few excursions & escape the *noise* of Rome for a few hours—

With best of remembrances from Edward & me, & my love to Mrs. Littleton

> Yrs sincy
> C.A.Elgar

160, Wardour Street, W.
Feb 21.1908

Dear Lady Elgar

I am delighted to hear that Sir Edward is better again and able to go out. It is too bad that your Italian visit should be interfered with by influenza—we can stay at home and have that. I hope by this time that you are also quite well again and that you are all looking forward to an enjoyable time.

Mrs. Peterson's letter is splendid—I did not know that the Australians could be so enthusiastic—We are sending Mrs. Peterson a number of things—and will send Sir Edward's new partsongs as soon as they are ready.

The rest of the proofs shall be sent in duplicate and we will send Sir Edward more copies as soon as they are properly printed. We will take care of the M.S.S. for you—they have not been used for printing from and so are quite clean.

I am glad to say my wife is better for her stay at Brighton—although she is still not very strong.

I am very glad we were able to obtain permission for the use of the words 'We are the makers of music' and I hope Sir Edward will be able to complete the music. I am looking forward to this as one of his most important and successful works.

Everybody is delighted with the new partsongs and we are hoping soon to be able to hear them sung.

> With kindest regards
> I am
> Yours very sincerely
> Alfred Littleton[5]

The executor for the author of the Ode, Arthur O'Shaughnessy, had been found to be Canon A. W. Newport Deacon. He readily gave permission, and looked forward to the result of Elgar's setting: he was to wait several years.

The recently completed part-songs continued to occupy the attention of McNaught, immersed in adjudicating duties.

5 HWRO 705:445:8253.

160 Wardour Street, London, W.
Mch 9. 1908

My dear Elgar,

Your card and the proofs of Reveille are to hand. As I promised the work shall be revised in sight of an authorised edition of the poem.

There is considerable anxiety as to the Marching Song. That and the Emperor's letter are the two great topics at present

The ff > sf *must* do the March *Merke*.

I have been gazing at 'There is sweet music' and am longing to hear it done by a real live choir. It will give some conductors a bad quarter of an hour

I have decided not to use it on a sight test at Morecambe.

Yours ever sincerely
W.G.McNaught

♩ = M.44 for Sweet music seems slow for some parts.

But I can see that anything like a jaunty rhythm will upset the idea

WMc[6]

There is Sweet Music was written in two keys simultaneously and for eight parts.

Elgar heard again from Jaeger, both directly and indirectly. Jaeger, trying to fill his listless hours with some useful work, had resolved to write an analysis of Elgar's latest part-songs. Worried by Elgar's continuing inability to complete his big projects, he had confided in their American friend Mrs Worthington—who had telegraphed Jaeger's worry back to Elgar himself.

Rome
Ap 26 190[8; '1905' *written in error*]

My dearest Nimrod: Your very welcome p.c. has just arrived & I hasten to send the reply you ask for. I was delighted to receive your last jolly long letter & should have written in answer to that but—my hand *jumps* when I write as you will see from this letter & I avoid writing as much as I can—sort of cramp & rheumatism mixed. I am *so* glad you are writing some notes & reviews & that you take pleasure in it.

It seems odd to think of anything of mine being worth writing about—I mean I remember my *first ptsong* in 1890 or thereabouts 'My Love dwelt in a Northern Land' [—] Now a stock piece for superior *poetic* choirs: *then* it was said to be crude, ill-written for the voices, laid out without knowledge of the capabilities of the human voice &c&c!! How funny it all is! Now I have made a sort of name by writing some big things & can only get *commissions* to write rot—ah! & a! I must *talk* to you some day about my avoiding work on great things—I have too many people *now* alas! (& the clog gets heavier every day) to allow me to think of anything I would wish to do: it is painful but it is the only reward I get: I say this because I saw a portion of the letter you sent to Mrs.W.—More of this when we meet.

Now: All you said more or less represents what I meant. I do not think I

[6] HWRO 705:445:8228.

have overdone the [expression] marks[:] you see nothing emotional is ever performed in strict time & it takes conductors *years* (literally) to find out a reading: you have only to think of the way people play Brahms (Symphonies or anything) now & compare it with the want of 'reading' they obtained even ten years ago. I have only put sort of *emotional* marks for the conductor to do the best he can with. I wish you could have heard the *Morecambe choir under Howson* sing four or five years ago: you wd then fully appreciate what I have tried to do.

Now as to the stuff. No.1 [*There is Sweet Music*] is of course written as it is for *convenience*—As to 'Owls'—it is only a fantasy & means nothing. It is in wood [*sic*] at night evidently & the recurring '*Nothing*' is only an *owlish* sound.

One word as to my treatment of the words, not only in this op. but always. I hold that *short* syllables may be sustained occasionally for the sake of effect: just as an actor does. There is one dear good man against whom I wd. not *think anything* but the greatest admiration & that is Parry. But he almost if not quite annoys me in the way he sets the words which swarm in our English—two syllables, both short, the first accented e.g. *petal.* Set in an ordinary way a poem sounds like reading a newspaper paragraph. I remember insisting on doing a poem of Tennyson [*The Lotos Eaters*, set now by Elgar in *There is sweet music*] by P.—I liked it & studied it with the chorus for months & had great difficulty in getting them to *take* to it: they did it very well—I preached & preached Parry. After the concert a very well educated lady—musically & artistically, in fact cultured in every way, said to me 'We have done our best to please you & I am sorry you insisted: I shall never read the poem again with any enjoyment'. This of *course* simply on account of the *driven* accents. Occasionally an Actor says '*Murrr*-der!' instead of 'Murdèr' & why should not we? You will note that I threw over from the first the convention of commonplace part-music—You know the sort I mean—where every idea requiring *force* is put to a high, intolerably high note for every voice: I often mark a *low* note to be sung loudly: naturally I *know* what the effect will be & that the poor dears cannot force it out beyond the other, maybe *well-lying* parts: yet only the other day one of your best chorus-masters said *I* know nothing of writing for the voice *or* choral effect—asked why[,] he pointed to a ff on a C for Sopranos: this sort of thing is annoying as it shews what sort of idiots we write for. If the clown had an ounce of artistic sense he wd. have seen that the note was to help the contraltos & lead into a *diminuendo* impossible to obtain in any other way.

As to the words: you will find they read all right. I omitted '*Be*' in Alto, No.3. p 9. on purpose:—it gives force to the E♭ *Through.* You must remember that a modern partsong is to be listened to & not read. If you *hear* any one of these, the words flow right on correctly. I added '*Can*' on the last p. to oblige McN[aught]'s idea of a better ff—which was a good thought.

All else you have seen. I cannot find your letter & must rush out now.

You are an old goooose to think (Mrs W's letter) that I was annoyed: I am only somewhat heartbroken; I cannot afford to get a *quiet* studio where I might have worked & my whole winter has been wasted for the want of a few more pounds: it seems odd that any rapscallion of a painter can find a place for his 'genius' to work in when a poor devil like me who after all *has* done something shd. find himself in a hell of noise & no possible escape! I resent it bitterly but can do nothing. It is just the same now at Hereford, noise has developed in the neighbourhood—I dodged it doing the Kingdom at great expense by going to Wales but I can't do it again: my lovely works do not pay the rent of a studio!

Much love to you & great rejoicing that you are having a change

Yours ever
E.E.

P.S. Sgambati (dear man) has some wonderful things—given him by Liszt [—] the first copy of the score Siegfried Idyll sent by Wagner to Liszt in Rome with a little writing on the title. Also the *first* exemplum of *Faust* Berlioz sent by B to Liszt! & above all (1868) the full score Meistersinger sent by W. to L. with words on the title 'De profundis clamavi!' at the top[,] a date &c. below & *Richard*. How wonderful to see & touch.[7]

Giovanni Sgambati (1841–1914) had been one of the Elgars' most welcome companions in Rome. He spoke English, as his mother had been an Englishwoman. He had been a pupil of Liszt, had befriended Wagner, was himself a distinguished composer and altogether one of the leading figures in Italian music.

Elgar had at last set the *Marching Song*, with words by Capt William de Courcy Stretton. The work became the property of the Musicians Company, of which Alfred Littleton was a member. After returning from Italy in early May, Elgar was invited by the Company Master, Charles T. D. Crews, to dine on 3 June so that he 'might formally present you with a cheque for the Marching Song in the presence of the Officers . . .'.[8] There was also a suggestion of Elgar writing a full Communion Service.

Hereford
June 1:1908

My dear Littleton:

Many thanks for yours of the 28th May: I am *awfully* rushed with accumulated rubbish which must be seen to. I fear I shall not be in town in June—I must work & things which might enforce my attendance in London are too uncertain to build other engagements on.

I shall be delighted to meet Mr.Crews some day: in the meantime I don't quite know what a *full* Communion Service includes. I shall be very pleased to try my hand: will you send me two complete services containing the whole of the things necessary to be set—very simple things will do[,] preferably by authors I hold in awe & reverence, Wesley to wit.

I have been turning over some M.S.S. & find the score of accompaniment I wrote for Worcester to one of the old Carols [*The Holly and the Ivy*]. it was used with Novello's edition: I think you had it once to look at. I have a sketch

---

[7] HWRO 705:445:8784. Paragraphing at the present paragraphs four and five is editorial.
[8] 21 May 1908 (HWRO 705:445:6715).

of other ACCPTS to carols. Would they be of any use—they are *only* for orch—no use in any possible arrangement I think. The one we did was very effective & (about Christmas) the possibility of having an orchl. accpt might lead Societies to revive a carol or two.

I'll send you the one rough score if you like.

> In haste
> Yours ever
> Edward Elgar.

P.S. I know it's not *necessary* to tell you that a song which Boosey proposes to publish shortly has been in his hands since 1899 or 1900—so it has to remain with him—under the old agreement relating to it. I had forgotten the song's existence!!

Elgar's 1898 arrangement of *The Holly and the Ivy* for the Worcestershire Philharmonic Society Chorus and Orchestra was never published.

The song of 1886, *Is She Not Passing Fair?*, however, occasioned one of Elgar's few surviving letters to Arthur Boosey written at this period. After all these years, Elgar had yielded to Boosey's persuasions for another song by finishing off this old effort and sending it in. Boosey wondered whether it should appear, as past songs had appeared, with the name of a favoured singer on the title page, with the superscription 'As sung by . . .'.

Plas Gwyn, Hereford.
June 30 1908

My dear Boosey:

All right about the song: I think we have no singer worth (from a *commercial* point of view) paying a royalty to in perpetuo—the old days of Lloyd are gone for ever: so do not *tie* yourself to anyone if you can help it.

> In haste
> Yours ever
> Ed:Elgar

Please give me *four*pence on this song.

The higher royalty was agreed on 7 July.

Meanwhile the correspondence with the ill Jaeger went on. Jaeger had learned that his article on Elgar's recent part-songs was not to be published immediately. Elgar, on the day after his own fifty-first birthday, wrote with all the depression that birthdays and other anniversaries of time passing usually brought him.

Plas Gwyn, Hereford.
June 3 1908

My dear Moss:

I was glad to receive yours of May 26th. & to know that you had been west & had some fresh air: here it is very lovely but too suffocatingly *stuffy*: I can't write—there are too many other composers singing their own or traditional compositions loudly on every bush. I am sorry your article is put off. I wish the M[usical] T[imes] could *lead* instead of follow. I am glad you are able to write & feel 'good' about it: I look forward with interest to your 'stuff'.

I can only write sadly about myself—I have done some good work in my life & now I can only get orders (which will keep my people in necessaries) for rot of kinds & I *must* do it. I have no intention of completing my oratorio cycle or whatever it is—I am not allowed to beg a dispensation of a benevolent providence who objects to the world being saved or purified or improved by a mere musician. Of course I have the thing—the biggest of all sketched—but I cannot afford for the sake of others to waste any time on it. Alas!

Well: I am well & strong except my eyes & must be thankful to be allowed to breathe somebody else's air I suppose & walk on somebody else's roads—but I am not thankful at all.

What an object lesson is poor dear Madam Albani: one of the best of women: she has sung to these delightful English their own *oratorios* & sacred things for years.—her husband loses all their money—she has to advertise for pupils! Now look at a battered old w—e like Melba & Co:—!!! My beloved countrymen and women wd. & will subscribe anything to keep her if necessary—it makes ones blood boil—where is providence? NOTHING

> Goodbye
> Yours ever
> Ed Elgar

Nikisch's Variations were odd. but they never muddle you & you sound well. Bless you![9]

The Elgars had heard Arthur Nikisch's performance of the *'Enigma' Variations* at a London concert on 20 May.

Jaeger sent his manuscript article on the part-songs. Lady Elgar responded, giving the first hints that Elgar was back working at the Symphony:

Plas Gwyn[,] Hereford.
12 June 1908.

Dear Mr.Jaeger

I must be allowed to send you a few lines to tell you how immensely I appreciate your beautiful & valuable article on Edward's pt.Songs.

You have shown such true insight into their depth of meaning & so truly recognise all their wonderful, poetic atmosphere like a *true* interpreter. Such an interpreter is a necessity between the genius & the outer world; the thoughts of a genius are always in advance of the ordinary world's understanding, & intense gratitude is due to the one who can see the new & beautiful thing offered to the people & reveal it to their more slowly perceiving eyes.

Everything that you have said is so absolutely true & it is a record of the capability & mind of the Composer—Any curtailing would be a very great disappointment

Edward is so absorbed in some work (I trust you will hear some day) that I know you will understand the delay in his reply to your letter.

I do hope you are feeling better these milder days & that Mrs.Jaeger & the Children are well. I have had such a busy time since our return re-settling the house &c.

With best remembrances

Yrs. sincy
C.A.Elgar[10]

But the *Musical Times* editor, F. G. Edwards, insisted that Jaeger's article be curtailed.

37 Curzon Road, Muswell Hill[,] N
13/6/8

Dear Lady Elgar,

I am greatly obliged for your kind words respecting my article & very glad that you like it. You are of course quite right in saying that an 'interpreter' is generally needed between genius & the public, & it is because I feel the truth of this so much, & fear that there will be comparatively few conductors or singers who will appreciate those partsongs at their *real* worth, that I wrote what you have read. For I fancy I *can* get right at the heart of E's works & realize from the printed note what the effect of a PERFECT performance (none other must be taken into account) must be. These pieces are so much more than stereotyped partsongs. They are wonders, pieces of E's very being, of his heart & soul.

I thought my 'interpretations' would be welcomed by amateurs & conductors, & especially by the *M.T.* But I'm told I 'must not give a chance to scoffers'! Did 'scoffers' undo me (or E. for that matter) over my 'Gerontius' analysis in 1900? If there were scoffers, they must feel supremely silly now, because they failed to appreciate E's wonderful work & tried to make me look a fool. I didn't mind & I laugh at them now.

What annoys me is this,: that after being a writer for the M.T. for some 16 years & having done some of the best critical & analytical work for the paper; after all my successes in hailing new composers, conductors, &c with Enthusiasm, I am still treated like a novice who wants careful Editing. And I'm truly surprised that dear, kind Mr A.H.L lets that old fogey of an Editor persuade him into agreeing with him. I feel more & more that it's futile offering now good work to the M.T.

However, the 'stuff' must be boiled down, as I have marked it, and you see from enclosed (which please destroy) that Mr E[dwards] wants my 'copy' at once!

I hope E. is not cross with me—I wrote my letter in quite a fever & you

[10] HWRO 705:445:8857.

know I would not 'explode' as I did if I were not such a 'ridiculous' admirer of & believer in E's gifts, & wanted not to see him *the* composer of the day, *the* deliverer of messages such as no other composer has the genius (& the *heart & soul*) to conceive. E. MUST be great in his works, & great in his contempt of the world which may not repay him as is his due.

I went to a Philharmonic (Beecham) concert this afternoon—the first concert I have been to for years. I heard Delius's 'Appalachia' a typical example, I take it, of the crazy 'colour' school. Well, D. is a genius in a way, & I heard sounds from the orchestra such [as] I have never heard before. Some of the Scoring is perfectly marvellous, I fancy; but—apart from the length of the thing (70 minutes) which is impressive, or oppressive, there is nothing to remember, nothing to dwell over, nothing to take to your heart & hug. Colour, Colour, colour, awful Harmonies, a vulgar nigger tune varied in a number of impertinently long sections. no melodic ideas. only colour & Harmony. And 70 minutes of it! I met some friends afterwards & ventured the opinion that the first great *melodist* coming along will sweep the Whole colour-school into the Sea of forgotten failures. The Human race wont alter its hearing apparatus within a few years, nor its primitive love of *rhythmical tune*. That the great melodist must be a colourist also seems true, for the charm of colour such as E & Delius have on their palettes is great & undeniable.

I fancy E will develop more & more as a strong, original melodist, & see his special mission in that direction. Colour & Harmony can never move us & lift us out of ourselves (Delius would have done that with his stuff this afternoon if it were possible). But finely presented noble tune will go to the Hearts of all, now & always.

To me E. has only begun his career as a *great* man, as a genius. Excepting, say, the prologue to 'King Olaf' (one of the finest things I know), his early works (before Gerontius) do not sound the note of *Genius*. Gerontius & the 2 oratorios are full of it. So I look forward to E's future with high hopes. He will grow stronger & stronger, more original & beautiful, more melodious, & more inventive in Colour, Harmony & Form with every passing year. He will be *the* great melodist, & hence *the* great composer for the world's *need* of *Heart*-music. I have heard Delius; I am more than ever an upholder of the Banner of Edward Elgar as *the man of the times*.

Sincerely yours
A.J.J.[11]

Plas Gwyn, Hereford
15 June 1908

Dear Mr.Jaeger

Thank you *much* for yr. beautiful letter, you know how I appreciate all you say.

I enclose yr. beautiful article & I must tell you that for our joy & its great value, May has copied it all out, for our private selves—so it is not lost—

[11] HWRO 705:445:8791.

Now can you not arrange that the whole article can be published in something else, do try that. Why not in Mr. [H. W.] Gray's Musical Review?

Mrs.Worthington is here for a night & sends her love & says she is coming to see you. *She* will have it put in the N.Y. Review so do arrange that.

E. sends his love, you have heard from him by now, & he wants to say to you 'the Sym. is A I'[:] it is *gorgeous*, steeped in beauty. he is quite absorbed in it.

Best greetings

C.A.E. in such haste.[12]

Elgar had already made arrangements for Jaeger to receive the composer's part of the royalties resulting from the oratorio Analyses, and this he confirmed to the company secretary.

Plas Gwyn, Hereford.
June 13 1908

Dear Mr.Clayton:

Many thanks for the two cheques: I am sending on the one resulting from sales of the Analyses to Jaeger[.] I have, however, signed two receipts which I think will be correct whatever happens to the amount—I sincerely hope Jaeger will submit to receive it.

Kind regards
Yours sincerely
Edward Elgar

Plas Gwyn, Hereford.
June 13 1908

My dearest Moss:

Here is your royalty on the 'analytical notes['] of 'The Apostles' & 'The Kingdom': Mr.Clayton sends me a *separate* cheque to keep it *separate &— you must* have it. So shut up & swallow it.

I can't answer your letter at this moment. I can't say I have anything more *important* to do, but it must be done & done now. Oh! such a tune

Yours ever
Edward.[13]

It was the 'motto' theme of the Symphony, and he was beginning to see his way to the big work.

Yet the publication of smaller pieces needed his attention. He wrote to Alfred Littleton about the *Christmas Greeting* composed for Sinclair's choristers with optional men's chorus parts.

[12] HWRO 705:445:8856. Gray's American periodical was later called *The New Music Review*.
[13] HWRO 705:445:8786.

Hereford

June 15.1908

My dear Littleton:

I sent to Wardour St the copy Sinclair had made of the Xmas piece: it is not well written & does not contain the T.&B. Chorus. I pointed this out in my note to the firm which accompanies it: but it may do to print from & save copying—I do not think you need mind using the original M.S. for the printer. Sinclair will not mind the *laying out* marks[.] Anyhow I hope you need not go to the trouble of making a new copy on his (or my) account. It was a very great pleasure to see Mrs.Littleton & you again: we trust she stood the journey well & is better

Kindest regards
Yrs ever
Ed Elgar

The Wand of Youth Suite No. 2 was now being readied for publication. The piano solo arrangement had been made by John E. West.

Hereford

July 12 1908

My dear West:

I find the arrangement excellent & thank you for the trouble you have taken.

One or two suggestions are on the proof but don't adopt them unless you think fit.

Yours ever
Ed:Elgar

That day it was decided to make minor alterations in the words of *A Christmas Greeting* to broaden its appeal. Lady Elgar did this, and next day took it to Alfred Littleton's house in Hereford.

All this time Elgar's mind was elsewhere—'immersed' (as Lady Elgar noted) in the Symphony. Some evidence of this state of mind emerged in his response to F. G. Edwards's request for some notes about *The Wand of Youth* Suite No. 2 for *The Musical Times*. First, on the morning of 17 July, Elgar telegraphed: 'So sorry cannot say anything more re suite except list of movements'.[14] Then, later in the day, he did send some rough notes to the editor at his home in Potter's Bar, Middlesex.

---

[14] BL Egerton MS 3090 fo. 90.

Hereford
July 17: 1908

My dear Edwards:

Who was Potter & why did he possess a Bar?

What sort of a Bar?

Wand of Youth

Here is a little line—I *cannot* do this sort of thing but from these rough notes you may jape up something to suit you or on reading it again it might go as it stands almost

I *did* write you a lovely article—condemned by the family as too intimate & *touching*—can it be??[15]

The Symphony must wait

———————

But, Oh. Edwards! perpend:

Potter, <u>his Bar.</u>

This is my theme: I cannot conceive that Potter kept a tavern; the occupation is too common to be identified in this *public* way.

Potter surely did not levy toll at a private 'pike': a sort of sedentary highwayman? the thing is not possible

I conceive Potter as a philosopher: high & serene musing on & clarifying problems far beyond usual human knowledge; I see him brought face to face with some impenetrable riddle before which the mighty intellect—even that of Potter—quailed, paled & failed.

Surely this was Potter's Bar. It being granted that the Bar of Potter *was* something of this kind we propose, in our next, to clear up the mystery of this 'Stond or impediment' (Bacon) which apparently prevented Potter from taking his place among the other acknowledged philosophers of all time.

Yours obediently*
Edward Elgar

*Obediently?—not at all!!!

Kindest regards[16]

Elgar was famous among his friends for his 'japes' and foolery. This letter affords a rare glimpse of such a thing developing under his pen—his brain sharply stimulated by the creative effort of the Symphony, whose first movement was by now practically within sight. The letter was followed up two days later by another continuing the foolery.

[15] A sheaf of notes, partly handwritten by Elgar with corrections, partly typed by his niece May Grafton and with further manuscript corrections, is in possession of the writer.
[16] BL Egerton MS 3090 fos. 91–93.

Hereford
July 19: 1908

My dear Edwards:

In answer to your long letter concerning Potter's Bar, which I have not received, I can only say that the points you raise are too trivial.

I *am* aware that soap & music are given to the world in bars; surely you will not contend that Potter was a musical composer because he has left one bar? In our young days we spoke of Purcell's Ground & thought it covered the whole ground; we say Bach's Mass, or Beethoven's Violin Concerto; those great men having left behind them one only of the compositions named— always in the possessive case. But Potters *Bar*! produce the bar & we can judge its musical value.

I hold it were trifling on your part to suggest that Potter, whom I assume to have been a man of intellect, made soap: even if he did condescend to soap he must necessarily have made more than one bar. I wish you would treat Potter seriously; if you really believe that there were many Potters in the district, artists in china, first prove to me that the parish affords a clay proper to the uses of potters.

You are not sincere in this I fear or it may be you are merely torn in doubt; I gather this from the fact that you omit an apostrophe: this is of course a palpable subterfuge; I call upon you to be manly enough to declare your convictions as to the plurality or singularity of Potter by this simple means.

I reserve the remainder of your letter concerning Potter till a more convenient time.

Yours always
Edward Elgar

P.S. Potters Bar can have no heraldic significance: ignorant novelists speak of a bar sinister, a thing which cannot exist, & the simple bar is to[o] 'obvious' an[d] ordinary to be associated solely with Potter. The same objection wd. hold in the case of two Potters or a thousand Potters. Potter was acutely English; this I am prepared to swear; the equivalent of barre in French is *bend* in English: we should then have Potter's Bend—barre being impossible in our tongue & Potter was not of any race but our own. We have a proper pride in Potter & I refuse to give him up or multiply him.[17]

Elgar's friend W. H. Reed wrote of his musical thinking:

Like Beethoven, he allowed an idea, which may have occurred to him as a short phrase, to germinate and transform and throw out branches... He liked to see how it shaped—how it presented itself to the eye as well as the ear. Fugitive phrases he would redraft and play with by inversion, augmentation, and other devices as if they haunted him.[18]

[17] BL Egerton MS 3090 fos. 94–95.
[18] *Elgar as I Knew Him* (Victor Gollancz Ltd, 1936) pp. 129, 131.

The 'Potters Bar' letters show the same process translated to verbal and intellectual foolery, but they show it very clearly.

Alfred Littleton sent the new Novello full score of Dvořák's G major Symphony as a sample of the firm's score printing. With it came a proposed arrangement for piano solo. These were intended as guides for the printing of Elgar's Symphony.

Plas Gwyn, Hereford.
July 23.1908

My dear Littleton:

Many thanks for sending the score of Dvoraks 4th Symphony: it is *beautifully* engraved but, from a practical point of view, *much* too much spread out I think, the frequent turning of the pages is particularly trying to a conductor.

As to the M.S. piano arrangement I don't know what to say: it is excellently done & seems very playable—perhaps a little difficult for the ordinary person in places: anyhow it *looks* like real piano music & is effective. I am not sure as to the value of the suggestion to call the arrangement a 'Sonata' after the Symphony, I think you might well try the experiment & see how the world receives it. I am in favour of the idea but can form no opinion as to whether the name wd. attract or repel piano players: If ever my Symphony is finished (it is going on) I should like Herr Sigfrid Karg-Elert to arrange it.

Have you the full score or parts, or both of Pierson's *Jerusalem*. I have your copy & wd. like you to issue the *Sanctus* 8vo.—but only if the orch is available. Tell me this first & I would *edit* it if necy

We hope Mrs Littleton is better.

> Ever yours
> Edward Elgar

The oratorio *Jerusalem* by Henry Hugo Pierson (1815–73) was published by Novello, but nothing further emerged from this suggestion. Littleton's wife was now very ill; and most of Elgar's energies were taken up with the Symphony.

None the less Elgar was to conduct the première of *The Wand of Youth* Suite No. 2 at the Worcester Festival in September. And before that he was booked to conduct a concert at Ostende. On his way through London on 10 August, Elgar left the first two movements of the Symphony at Novello's offices. Using the example of the Dvořák score, he wrote a card to Alfred Littleton at Hove, where Littleton had taken his wife. Elgar's card seems not to have survived, but its contents were reflected in Littleton's note to his printing manager C. J. May.

2 Palmeira Court[,] Hove[,] Brighton
Aug.10.1908

Dear May

I have a post-card from Sir E.Elgar saying that he left today at Wardour Street two movements of the Symphony. Please get Mr.Pointer to look over the M.S. and then send it *at once* to Germany to be engraved[.] Pointer ought to do his part in one day but in any case he must not have more than two days & the M-S. must go off to Germany as early as possible this week.

You will remember that Elgar wants the score to be got into as small a number of pages as can reasonably be done to avoid continual turning over

Please let me have a line to say that this is all being done.

> Yours truly
> Alfred H Littleton

Elgar sent a postcard from Ostende, and a full report on his return.

Langham Hotel, London
Sunday [16 Aug. 1908]

My dear Littleton:

We are safely back so far but the steamer was so late yesterday that we could not get through to Hereford as we had intended.

Everything was a great success at Ostend & most pleasantly arranged & carried out. A splendid orchestra & a joy to conduct.

Poor Rosenkranz [Novello's representative] suffered from his tooth & I fear had a bad time. He returned on the same boat but it was so crowded (nearly 700) I could not get to him.

A fine gathering* of Belgian musicians

	Vincent d'Indy
*they met to adjudicate on	Edgar Tinel
an opera competition	Paul Gilson
	Matthieu [Emil Mathieu]
	Jan Blockx.

& the director & the conductor of the Monnaie, Bruxelles[.] Ruiskopff gave a lunch & we were all photographed[.] I wish the picture cd. go in the M.T; I spoke to Rosenkranz about it but I do not know what he was able to do.

I wish you had been present—it was all so inspiriting & gay. The good lady did not know her songs & we had to omit the Gerontius selection as it wd. have made the programme too long. All thanks to you for doing all you did.

We trust Mrs.Littleton is better & that you are well

> Yours ever
> Edwd E.

The contralto who did not know her music was Tilly Koenen (1873–1941).

Returning home to Hereford next day, Elgar quickly settled to scoring the Symphony's third movement Adagio. On 23 August he sent it to Novello.

Everywhere people were asking about performing his music. When an enquiry came from the United States about an American première for the Symphony, Elgar made up his mind to demand a lot of money. He was still feeling sore about the financial disappointments of his trip there in 1907. Now the position was complicated

by the interest of Elgar's friend, Professor Sanford, who sponsored Walter Damrosch's New York Symphony Orchestra. But Elgar was determined, and resolved to
use Novello as his negotiator—despite a warning from Henry Clayton that there was
such a thing as asking too much. Clayton, constrained to write to New York on
Elgar's behalf, made it clear to Novello's New York agent H. W. Gray where the
demand came from, and when a copy of this letter arrived at Plas Gwyn, Elgar was
not at all pleased with its tone.

Plas Gwyn, Hereford.
Augt 28 1908

My dear Littleton:

Many thanks for your letter & enclosures, which I return.

I wish Mr.Clayton had written more on behalf of the firm & not so much
on my own account. Do not misunderstand me: I am not at all ashamed of
wanting fees &c. but the whole letter throws the onus on *me*: this gives a
different feeling, and a wrong one I think, to the whole affair: Gray
immediately refers to me as the prime mover & it makes negociation
impossible.

Of course W.Damrosch has a good position but not the highest, neither
has his orch. the best; it was thought 'they' wanted to get the Symphony to
get a little possible credit—not to give me a lift. If the N.Y.Symphony people
will only pay an ordinary performing fee it wd. be better to let other
orchestras have the work if they wish it. I cannot see what bad effect asking
for a high fee will have—which Gray seems to think possible: if nothing is
shaping regarding the tour no harm can come of anything I do. I am not
disposed to let America have anything cheap. I went there with high artistic
ideas & except at Cincinatti [*sic*] & Chicago they shewed me the worst side of
the U.S.A. character & failed to appreciate my unselfish conduct, &, as might
have been expected, treated me badly.

Please do not let Gray think that Damrosch or anyone in America had the
slightest influence on me in writing the Symphony as you know I have been
'symphony-writing' for years! The idea is too absurd!

I think the whole thing must wait. Do not let any copies go to *U.S.A.* at all.

I understand the Sym: is announced by the [London] Symphy orch in
London on Dec 7th.— I know nothing of this. do you?

In great haste. Hoping Mrs.Littleton is better.

Yours ever
Ed Elgar

P.S. I must be in town next week & might see you between [Worcester
Festival London] rehearsals. I go to *the Hut*[,] Bray[,] Berks tomorrow

It was there, at Frank Schuster's country house, that Elgar was to begin to score the
Symphony Finale from his sketches.

Alfred Littleton, the consummate diplomat, suggested allowing New York to make an offer for the Symphony première in America. In that way both Walter Damrosch and his brother Frank could be involved directly. New York on the whole offered the best site for this première. Elgar replied just before leaving for The Hut:

Plas Gwyn, Hereford.
Augt 30 1908
My dear Littleton:

I am so very sorry to have been or rather for *being* such a trouble to you.

Your letter is just the thing: only I would omit the lines I have taken the liberty to cross out: but if you think best please reinstate them. As to ① —I would not mention the sum again for this reason; the 'sort-of-talked-over' offer was probably in conversation with Sanford, who is *their* president &, I believe, backer. I *remember* it all but, as I told Clayton & you, the whole thing was controversial & 'in the air'.

Let them make an offer as you say that will be best.

2) For the same reason as above I suggest *N. York* in place of W.D.

3) I fear the effect of this par:—Gray will probably talk over things with *both D's*. & Frank D. thinks he has done a great deal—& I believe he has done. Chicago has not done *much* since Theodore Thomas died; Cincinatti of course had the festival only. You see they are all friends & will treat things differently from the *agents'* way. I hope you do not think all these quibbles too worrying: the *nuance* in dealing with or amongst friends is what I meant when I said in my former letter that negociation becomes impossible

> Again many thanks
> Yours ever
> Ed: Elgar

Shall you be coming to Worcester or Hereford at all? & how is Mrs. Littleton?

Mrs Littleton's illness prevented any Festival excursion for her husband. His next letter to Elgar enclosed several proposals. One was from the conductor at Brighton, Joseph Sainton (1878–19??), asking Elgar to conduct *Gerontius* there in December. The other was to conduct two concerts at Eastbourne: this Elgar feared might tread on the toes of the conductor of the Municipal Orchestra at Bournemouth, Dan Godfrey (1868–1939), a doughty protagonist of British music on the south coast.

In his reply, Elgar gave Littleton the news that he had just resigned from the Professorship of Music at Birmingham.

The Hut, Bray, Berks.
Sep 1:1908
My dear Littleton:

Many thanks for your letter—yes I suppose the Brighton affair must go on. Your idea of fees will do.

One thing important about *Eastbourne*: I have been asked for so many *years* by Godfrey to go to Bournemouth & he has asked me again now

(I think you may have his letter) & I think I ought to go there if possible. Godfrey has done so much English music &c.

Private I have resigned my Birmingham post— this will not be known until announced from B.—I give up on the grounds that I cannot remain in England during the winter: so the Brighton date must not be fixed too late— as my acceptance of the Brighton offer must depend on the date entirely.

The weather here is truly awful.

> In haste
> Ever yours
> Ed:Elgar

Later that day he went to London for Worcester Festival orchestral rehearsals. These included the new *Wand of Youth* Suite No. 2. Henry Wood asked Elgar to conduct its London première with his Orchestra at Queen's Hall. Elgar asked him to work through Novello.

Langham Hotel
Sep 5 08

My dear Littleton:

Your wire reached me—or I reached it—late last night.

Wood called on me & asked the questions regarding the Suite & Symphony—he wants *me* to conduct both (52/10/-) for two concerts. I demurred—saying the Suite is not important enough for a serious symphy. Concert—he said they might include something with the Suite say, 'In the South'[.] I told him I did not know what arrgts. the pubrs. had made about performances & that he had better write to Novellos: he wants the first performance of the Sym *under my conductorship* at Qn's Hall: I forget how far the Philharmonic negociations went. I send this on now as I am on my way to Worcester & will hope to write further tomorrow.

I really am in great trouble lest all these accumulations of proposed engagements shd. be a bother: I had no idea the things wd. be so numerous: naturally I am delighted for you & the firm to do these things but they have grown to such an extent that I feel I ought to ask you again if you would not prefer to give it up & I wd. employ an agent. Please say frankly what you think of this—I fear my business must begin to be a nuisance

I saw some proofs of the Sym. it looks *fine* in print!

> Yours ever
> Edward Elgar

P.S. If you have not settled any performances which wd. not fit in with Wood's proposal you might send a line to Worcester [where the Elgars were to stay for the Three Choirs Festival] & I would settle this with Wood myself.

These letters indicate the growing complexity in the concert-managing side of Novello's relations with Elgar—especially with performances of the new Symphony in prospect. Elgar concluded a letter to Littleton on 18 September, devoted otherwise entirely to dates and schedules, with a P.S.: 'I forgot to say anything about the little [*Wand of Youth*] Suite [première] at Worcester: it was an immense *pleasant* success. I wish you had been there.'

Jaeger had managed to hear *The Wand of Youth* Suite No. 2 by attending the London rehearsals for the Worcester Festival. (There also Tilly Koenen, despite her derelictions at Ostende, rehearsed badly for Worcester—only to be replaced at the last moment.) That night Jaeger wrote:

37 Curzon Road, Muswell Hill
3/9/8
My dear Edward,

I had a happy day to-day, for I heard once more, after many many months' starving, some *music*. Your works struck me with *all the force* I felt years ago, when I studied them & I was as deeply moved (Tilly K. notwithstanding) as ever. I shed a few happy, silent tears over so much beauty & my whole being was thrilled, elevated & purified & braced up. I feel morally & physically better for having heard your music, & I thank you. It was a wonderful experience, after many months in the Desert, to drink those refreshing, strengthening draughts of divine water of Healing.

Do let us have that third oratorio directly you have completed your Symphony. You owe it to us who *do* appreciate your genius fully & to whom your music *is* an inspiration and a moving power & the 'most beautiful of God's revelations' (Goethe). If we are only a few hundred or thousand to-day, be sure that we shall number *all* genuine music lovers in days to come.

Your works are too new, too original, too great to be appreciated by the average amateur or musician straightaway. Be happy that you made so many converts in so few years. And fear no rival! Your music has a greatness of conception & ideality & an *ethical value* possessed by the work of *no* living composer I know of. You are unique, a single & perhaps sometimes rather lonely wanderer in Elysian fields & on Olympian heights, yet surrounded by the love & admiration of many, many genuine 'disciples'. Go on, & give us more. Never cease. Be sure that the Best that is in you is just good enough for us greedy, starving enthusiasts. Make *no pause* when the Symphony is finished. By that time you should just be in the *right mood & trim to go on* with Part III of your sacred Trilogy.

Glück auf!! and may you be helped in your work by the love of your friends, including

Your old Nimrod.[19]

Elgar responded after the Festival, in the midst of work on the Symphony Finale.

[19] HWRO 705:445:8789.

Plas Gwyn, Hereford.
Sep 19:1908

My dear Jaggs:

We *did* want you at Worcester & were a learned party.

I loved having your letter & all you said about rehearsal was cheering.

As to the symphony—the general key is A♭—the signature of one flat means nothing—it is convenient for the players. The first movement is in 'form' 1st & 2nd. principal themes with much episodical matter but I have—(without [definite *deleted*] intention to be peculiar but as a natural feeling)—thrown over all key relationship as formerly practised*: the movement has its 2nd. theme on its 2nd presentation in A♭ & as I said, the movement ends in that key.

You will find many subtle *enharmonic* relationships I think & the widest *looking* divergencies are often closest relationships

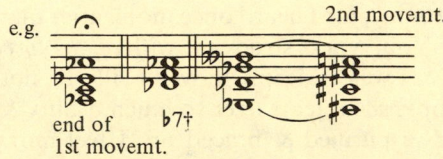

or (if you *play* it)

[† Elgar's writing here is not quite clear, but the figured bass notes are the likely explanation.]

This is a sort of *plagal*(?)[*sic*] relationship of which I appear to be fond (although I didn't know it)—most folks run through *dominant* modulations—if that expression is allowable [—] & I think some of my twists are defensible on *sub*-dominant grounds. All this is beside the point because I *feel* & don't invent—I can't even invent an explanation—*no excuse is offered*—Although when a dear old Mosshead asks I try to be good: after all I am only an amateur composer—if that means I compose for the love of it—I certainly *am* an amateur letter-writer for I only write for the love of Nimrod

Whose I am ever.
E.E.

*I am not silly enough to think (or wish) that I have *invented* anything: see Beethoven's late Quartetts passim.[20]

[20] Elgar Birthplace parcel 343.

Against the first sentence of this letter Jaeger noted 'this is no doubt wrote sarcastic as I know they were a very *jolly* party'.

Dan Godfrey had written to Novello to suggest 14 November for Elgar's appearance in Bournemouth, and Littleton conveyed that proposal to Elgar. The reply came from Lady Elgar, who also enquired about progress over printing *A Christmas Greeting*:

Plas Gwyn, Hereford.
25 Sept.1908.

Dear Mr.Littleton

Edward is so absorbed in the Finale of the Symphony that he finds it almost impossible to write anything else—so he feels sure you will not mind my writing for him—

First about Bournemouth, he wishes me to say he cannot go on the 14th November & will be so much obliged if you would kindly let Mr.Godfrey hear this.

Edward *hopes* to finish the Symphony this week & probably will take it up on Monday or very early next week.

He asks me to write also with some urgency about the Christmas Music, he has heard nothing of it, & has had no proofs at all. He knows that people, especially Girls' Schools, will be arranging their music & thinks no time should be lost in announcing & advertising the work, & that it should most necessarily be announced in the Oct 'Musical Times'[.] I think this is all I have to report for him.

We much hope Mrs.Littleton is getting on well, & is stronger. We miss Rose very much & it is very sad to think Hatteral [*i.e.*, the Littletons' house in Hereford] is bereft of you all.

All best greetings from us all

> Yours very Sincerely
> C.Alice Elgar

P.S!
My dear Littleton:

I have been kept back a little & am now going to 'deliver the goods' next Monday.

I know you will not mind my wife writing for me.

We *must* go abroad in January so the Phil is impossible

> Yours ever
> EE

The Philharmonic Society representative, Alberto Randegger had asked whether Elgar could conduct for them on 2 February 1909.

The Symphony was finished on 25 September. Immediately Elgar had one of his typical nervous reactions, and instead of going to London repaired to his bed. Three days elapsed before he felt able to make the journey with the Finale score.

After finishing the Symphony Elgar wrote a song, *Pleading*. The words were by

Arthur Salmon, who had sent a book of his verses in the hope that Elgar might find something to tempt him. Besides 'Pleading' there was another poem, 'The Haven of Desire', and on 3 October Salmon sent his enthusiastic permission to use both. This letter Elgar included when sending *Pleading* to Novello. (He sent direct to the firm as he did not wish to disturb Alfred Littleton, whose wife had died on 1 October after a long illness.)

Plas Gwyn, Hereford.
Oct 8 1908
Dear Sirs:

Enclosed I send M.S.S. of a little simple song (in 3 keys)—kindly have it engraved as early as possible as I want it out very soon.

I enclose Mr Salmon's letter regarding the words (he refers to *two* sets—I have only set one as yet) Will you kindly arrange with him in the usual way

Yrs v try
Edward Elgar

P.S. I hope to set the other poem soon. but you need only refer to 'Pleading' at present[.]
I shall be glad if there can be no delay in this matter

'The Haven of Desire' was never set by Elgar.

On 12 October Elgar went to London for a week, during which he conducted the London première of *The Wand of Youth* Suite No. 2 and orchestral rehearsals for the Norwich Festival. Back at Plas Gwyn, he engaged John Austin to go through Symphony parts in proof on 24 October. The parts were late, with the result that Elgar and Austin had to work hurriedly over the 25th and 26th, before Elgar left for the Norwich Festival.

During that Festival (which included a performance of *King Olaf*), he corrected further Symphony proofs. These he left with the publisher on the return journey through London on 2 November. Back at home, he telegraphed next day:

Doctor Richter coming here Thursday [5 Nov.] please let me have remainder of full score third & fourth movements at once

Edward Elgar

He and John Austin were busy with these almost until the moment of Richter's visit, which in fact took place on Friday 6 November. Together they went through the Symphony in preparation for its first performance, and fixed dates for rehearsal.

Two days later Elgar wrote to Alfred Littleton:

Plas Gwyn, Hereford.
Nov 8 1908
My dear Littleton:

I hope you are well & like this cold weather. I have not troubled you about my small matters lately as everything goes on all right.

I *do* hope the little song may be successful—I have sent a note to

Mr.Clayton about it and also about another South Coast (St Leonard's[)] Concert as he has very kindly arranged the other 'events'.

The performances at Norwich were excellent & old 'Olaf' was very exhilarating.

Richter has been here and I have played him the Symphony & he is delighted. There will be a preliminary *run through* at Queen's Hall on the 23rd at eleven o'clock—*I* conduct. Would you care to come? It wd. give me very great pleasure if you would

I am busy with the proofs. I have sent (to save time) a note to Mr.May about the scores & he will probably talk to you about it: as the miniature score is only for the public to follow I do not think we need put in the 'conductors'' page of directions: what do you think?

[Ernest] Newman writes enthusiastically about the Symphony.

> Kindest rgrds from us all
> Yours ever
> Edward Elgar

Please let me have the priceless enclosure back some time: shew it Edwards!

Unfortunately there is now no trace of the enclosure. But the anticipated success of the Symphony was such that it had been arranged to print 500 copies of a miniature score for immediate sale.

From his sickbed on 3 November, A.J. Jaeger wrote to his old firm about publishing Elgar's simple setting of verses beginning 'Lo! Christ the Lord is born!' by Shapcott Wensley (librettist of *The Banner of St George*). At the publishers' request, Wensley revised the words, and this 'old carol' was discussed in Elgar's next letter, together with the newer *Christmas Greeting* and the Symphony:

Plas Gwyn, Hereford.
Nov. 10 1908

Dear Sirs:

I have returned the last movement. (full score) of the Symphy. by an early post

I am sorry the new 'Christmas Greeting' has been delayed so long: I fear it is too late now for the Schools', (etc.) Xmas Concerts: if a circular cd. be sent this week to the mistresses & perhaps, music masters of the chief & possibly other schools this week [*sic*], possibly it wd. be brought under their notice in time for breaking up concerts &c.—otherwise we cannot expect any sale at all until next year—that is twelve months hence.

As to the Old Carol: I shall be very pleased for you to issue it: it has not been issued in any other form to my knowledge. Would you ask Mr.S.Wensley to consider the fourth line in each Stanza? in the traditional words there is throughout a strong accent on the *first* syllable (see the Music) & this must please be retained. I have, with much diffidence, pencilled in the sort of thing that wd fit the music except in the last stanza. Kindly let me see it before printing. If printed in v.s. the last two F Fs in the vocal bass must be on the fourth line* & not as in the short score[.] All else seems correct.

I return Mr.Jaeger's copy of the poem.

Yours faithfy
Edward Elgar

* If printed in short score the upper Fs had better go in the present 8ves small for PF.

Amid further Symphony proofs, he found a moment to write to Jaeger of an invention from 'The Ark'—the former dovecote, now an amateur laboratory.

Plas Gwyn, Hereford.
Nov 11:1908

My dear Jaggs:

I am truly grieved you shd. be so worried & can only hope you are better now: I am sorry also that my work is to miss your ever helpful introduction. but I cannot think of my loss when you are ill, bless you!

You will perhaps be amused—I hear that the 'new Sulphuretted Hydrogen Machine designed by Sir Edward Elgar' is to be manufactured & called the 'Elgar S.H. Apparatus'!! I will not offer to send you my invention—you would soon tire of it—although a nice toy.

I have many proofs of the Sym to finish & some diagrams of the machine to *draw* & send to the makers by this post so goodbye

Love
Yours ever
Edward[21]

On 23 November Elgar conducted a first rehearsal of the Symphony with the London Symphony Orchestra in London. Richter was present, and took away the manuscript (at present the only copy of the full score), as he wrote to Novello, 'to be able to enter into the Spirit of this great masterpiece'. Also in the audience for Elgar's rehearsal had been Alfred Littleton and his son—now a Novello director.

2 Palmeira Court, Hove, Brighton.
Nov 29.1908

My dear Elgar

No amateur & few if any professional musicians have the right to give any opinion on so important a work as your Symphony after one or even several hearings. But I was so much struck with my son Jack's remark that I cannot help sending it on to you. His words express the greater part of my own feeling and I should think the feeling of most of those who were fortunate enough to be present. He said it was the noblest music he had ever heard—I hope to hear the Symphony many times but doubt if I shall ever be able to add anything to this.

[21] HWRO 705:445:8788.

I hope you are now enjoying the quiet of home after the excitement and anxiety (if you had any) of the first hearing of your work—

With kindest regards to you all

> I am
> Yours very sincerely
> Alfred H.Littleton[22]

Once again the ultimate enthusiasm came from Jaeger, making out the music as best he could at home from proofs of Karg-Elert's piano transcription.

37 Curzon Road, Muswell Hill
26/xi/8

My dear, great Edward,

I was allowed to come down today for the first time for a month, and I spent some happy quarter Hours over your Adagio in the Symphony (P.F. arrangement.)

My dear friend that is not only one of the very greatest slow movements since Beethoven, but I consider it *worthy of that master*. How original!, how PURE, noble, elevating, soothing. &c &c. I can't find the words. How exquisitely beautiful in every detail. I cried happy tears of 'Wonne' over so much beauty. It's the greatest thing You have done. I almost admire most of all the PURITY of Sentiment & the absence of all sensationalism. The movement was written by a good pure man, & only such a character can feel & invent such music. I detected one or two places, where the great adagio of the Choral Symphony was recalled to my memory. Nothing in the way of a reminiscence (the Satz is *quite* your own), but just the feeling of nobility of sentiment. At 104 we are brought near Heaven. That is a lofty & inspired thought.

Until today I had only *looked* at the printed pages, & though I thought the music very fine, I was not prepared for this revelation of Beauty. You see, poor old mosshead *must* have his old Broadwood to help him. He is such a rank amateur. Yet he's not a bad Critic when he can HEAR sounds.

I must go to bed, though I Know that haunting Adagio won't let me sleep soon.

I wish I were near you that I might press & kiss your hand & say: thank you, my friend, for this great piece of music.

> My love to you
> Always yours
> A.J.J.[23]

Elgar's reply is missing. It was, as it almost had to be, self-deprecating. But Jaeger would have none of it.

[22] HWRO 705:445:3798.   [23] Elgar Birthplace parcel 398.

37 Curzon Road[,] Muswell Hill[,] N.
4/xii/8

My dear 'poor conventional chemist'.

I like that! 'poor conventional chemist' is good. I protest against your suggestion that I 'romances' regarding the personality of the composer of that wonderful Adagio in the Symphony. I fancy I know your character as well as most of your friends, & better than many, & I meant what I said, and I feel sure your wife, who should Know you by this time, will agree with me. As regards the [*one line removed*] only innocent chaff & harmless.

Now I want to say that I do not 'see' only the Adagio, but since I have been able to spend many happy hours over your Sym. at the P.F. I see it *all* & feel most intensely all it implies & expresses,: The tremendous strife, alternated with delicious moments of hope & faith, imploring, sighing, smiles & happiness. I love it all, but of course the dramatic fights against the unsympathetic world, the proud assertion of your manly self & your belief in yourself & in your powers thrill me most. There is one passage over a Pedal F# where the Fiddles sweep upwards with

(I quote from memory, having lent my proofs to Miss Wright; so excuse any misquotation!) where the discords on the Pedal F# bite like acid into my musical feelin. But 'I likes it'. And there are as many passages that affect me as powerfully as anything you have ever done, or as anything in modern music as far as I know it.

The Scherzo is a real joy & one of the biggest things of the Kind in all Symphonic literature. And then that mysterious Lento with its abysmal depths of tone colour & the astounding Finale, an overpowering outburst of optimism & joie de vivre that carries one away in spite of oneself until the superb peroration crowns the whole splendid structure. [*illegible*] It's a great & masterly work & will place you higher amongst the world's masters than anything you have done. Ill as I am (& I feel so ill to-night that I want to go to the nearest Ry Station & throw myself under a train to end my misery) I hope to go next Monday [7 December, the London première]. I have bought a ticket & am looking forward to what I fear will be the last great [*last line or two removed*][24]

The Symphony had met with such success at its première in Manchester on 3 December that the London première four days later was more than sold out, and was the scene of an extraordinary reception. Jaeger was there, and he wrote a famous account of it to Dora Penny:

I never in all my experience saw the like. The Hall was *packed*... After the

[24] HWRO 705:445:8790.

first movement E.E. was called out; again, several times, after the third, and then came the great moment. After that superb Coda (Finale) the audience seemed to rise at E. when he appeared. I *never* heard such frantic applause after any novelty nor such shouting. Five times he had to appear before they were pacified. People stood up and even *on* their seats to get a view.

1909

After this, everyone wanted to hear the Elgar Symphony. London orchestral programmes for weeks ahead were quickly rearranged to include it. The authorities at Brighton, where Elgar was shortly to make a conducting visit, wanted it too. Walter Damrosch wrote of several performances in America. Even small concert societies with inadequate resources asked for it. For those who could not play or hear the original, there was a proposal for an organ arrangement of suitable passages.

Elgar himself was in another phase of post-creative depression. His health suffered, and thoughts of going south for a holiday inevitably brought up the question of money, as he suggested to Alfred Littleton on 24 January. A reply was undertaken by Clayton.

[160, Wardour Street]
January 26th [190]9

Dear Elgar

Littleton, who is attending a Court of The Musicians Company today, has asked me to write to you.

First I send you the Brighton cheque for £36.5.0. I have sent a receipt on your behalf; so, as the transaction will not pass through our Books, a mere acknowledgement from you will be all that I want.

As regards performing fees for performances of the Symphony *already taken place*, which amount to 7 all told in England, you have been paid for the three you conducted yourself. We owe you Thirty-five Guineas for the other four—Thus:—

Manchester.	Richter	£10.10.0
London	,,	10.10.0
do	,,	10.10.0
Brighton	Sainton	5. 5.0

Then Siloti has already paid us for *one* performance—and there will be at least £50 already due from Damrosch—but we have not received anything yet.

The £100 I sent to your Bank a few weeks ago was debited to your account generally, & it makes no difference whether it is charged to Symphony Performing fees, or to Royalties on the Sale of Publications. A lot of performances are coming on (see list) & in a few weeks' time we shall have several more sums credited to your account. So if you want more money don't hesitate to drop me a line.

The enclosed letter came for you today.

I am very sorry to hear you are queer—you had better accept Littleton's offer & go to Brighton. It is a wonderful place to pick one up. It saved my life once after Scarlet Fever.

I ought to have added that we credit you with £5.0.0 for Siloti's first performance & £5.5.0 (when we get it!) for Loewe's Vienna performance.

Yours sincerely
Henry R.Clayton[1]

Alexander Siloti was conducting the Symphony in St Petersburg, and Ferdinand Löwe (1865–1925) in Vienna.

But amid all this good news, Elgar noticed that no performing fee had been added to the hire charges for score and parts in respect of his own performance with the Queen's Hall Orchestra (under Robert Newman's management) on 16 January.

Plas Gwyn, Hereford
Jan 28. 1909
Dear Clayton—

Your letters recd. for which thanks (one at least has been sent to Her*t*ford) & delayed.

I cannot go to Bournemouth—if I get better I shall be away: at present I have a coldy cough.

Thanks for the Brighton Festival cheque.

I cannot understand about the performing fee for the Symphony: surely Queen's Hall (Newman) pays the same as the London Symphony orchestra. The fact that I conducted has nothing whatever to do with it—they pay me always 25 guis: whatever is done & they shd. pay a full performing fee for each time the symphy was done. I cannot *think* how it came about.

I hear the Sym has been done in Chicago & Cincinnati by Damrosch

In haste
Yrs sincerely
Edward Elgar

[160, Wardour Street]
February 1st [190]9.
Dear Elgar

Many thanks for your letter of the 28th.

I am awfully sorry that you are not satisfied with the arrangements which we made with Mr.Newman for the production of your Symphony at Queen's Hall under your direction. I can assure you that both Littleton and I have a good deal of anxiety about performances of this work. Our object has been to

[1] Clayton's letters survive as office copies on thin paper.

get as much as possible in the shape of performing fees for your benefit, and at the same time, as I put it to Littleton, not to kill the goose for the sake of the eggs of gold. And I can assure you it needs very delicate handling. For we know of several cases where the idea of performing the work has been abandoned, where we quoted £15.15.0 or £10.10.0—*fees which included our charge for the loan of the music*. Even in America, where big fees are the order of the day, we have quite a struggle to get £3.3.0, for ourselves, per performance for the loan of the music, in addition to the fees that Damrosch is to pay you. Therefore when we knew that Newman was going to pay you Twenty-five Guineas for conducting, & us Five Guineas for the loan of the music, we felt that the Total Thirty Guineas was about as far as we could ask them to go.

Of course I see your point that your personal services in conducting have nothing really to do with the right to perform, & that, if you had not conducted, someone else would have been paid to take your place. But I think Newman & Co. would reply to that argument that when they ask a composer to conduct his own work for an agreed fee it is understood that he will grant them the right to perform the work he is going to conduct, & that if not he would state so at the time. The first arrangement made for you to conduct the Symphony was, we understood, made between you & Henry Wood, & the only note of it that I have is that you were to be paid 50 Guineas for conducting 'The Wand of Youth' (No.2) on October 17th and The Symphony on Jan 16th.

I certainly think Newman would have demurred to any further claim on our part for a performing fee unless it had been mentioned at the outset.

Knowing of this arrangement made by yourself, & assuming as we did that it covered the right to perform, we adopted it as a basis of subsequent negotiations when Newman discussed with us direct your terms for the 2nd and 3rd performances. So if a mistake has been made it is due to the fact that we never quite understood what you meant when you agreed to the 50 guineas fee with Henry Wood. At the same time had you consulted us in the matter I am quite sure both Littleton and I would have advised you not to demand a performing fee in addition to your own conducting fee. It is better to ask too little than to frighten people by asking too much—& although we are not likely to undervalue your services as conductor we are anxious not to make your work too dear. You must also remember that although you conducted your own work at the three Concerts in question, Wood also was engaged on each occasion; so that the argument that, if you had not conducted the work someone else would have been paid to do so, loses some of its force: for if you had not been there Wood would no doubt have conducted the entire concert, and on that account Newman would no doubt look upon your fee as an extra outlay on account of the inclusion of your work in the programme.

We are doing all we can to keep up the performing fee tariff & for this reason have refused 3 applications for permission to perform it at *Symphony Concerts* in London. viz. Albert Hall, St.James's Hall. & now The Coliseum where Sainton wants to perform it on Sunday March 7th. We have said 'No' to all these, because directly people get to know that they can hear the work on Sunday by paying 6d. or 1/- for a seat the market for good prices at good concerts, & good performing fees will quickly begin to fall, & your interests will suffer. But Sainton is pressing us to give way as a favour to him. I don't see how we can, do you? Littleton will be here tomorrow & I think he will agree with me. If you have any views about this, please wire them in the morning.

In any case I hope you will rest assured that, whatever we do about the Symphony, will be done for the best, according to our views, & that your interests will not be overlooked.

Yours sincerely
Henry R.Clayton.

Plas Gwyn, Hereford.
Feb 2.1909
Dear Clayton:

All right & thanks for your letter: I am sure you do your best for me but the incredible meanness of Queen's Hall annoys me, more than I should reasonably let it do so, after the exuberant protestations of Edgar Speyer & the rest. Wood is paid an annual salary so that point is not quite as you assumed. They pay *any* foreigner 4, 5, 6, 7 or even 8 times the amount given to me & lose largely over the visitor because they say its good for art. It annoys me that the money they really make out of me is spent on other people.

This is all by the way but it relieves my feelings

Kind rgrds
Yours sincerely
Edward Elgar

He went for a few days to Llandrindod Wells in search of health, but returned little improved. The question of an organ arrangement from the Symphony had by now become a confusion of many opinions—not least that of Novello's music editor John E. West. Elgar was tired of it all, even when Karg-Elert's piano arrangement of the entire work arrived at Hereford in a finished copy.

Plas Gwyn, Hereford
Feb 15 1909
My dear Littleton:

I arrived home on Saturday & am not at all well—cold affecting liver of course: it stops *all* work & I must be contented to be idle musically the rest of my life I suppose, as going away is not possible. Alas!

However I have been quite disillusioned as to the musical world for some years & have no ambition so I say farewell to it without the slightest regret. As to the organ arrgt.—please arrange with Atkins if you think well & let him

know West's ideas but do not send anything to me: they can quite well settle
it between them.

The piano arrgt. looks fine [—] I shd. like ½ doz *here* if possible.

I *may* come up to dine at Marlborough House on Wednesday if I am well
enough & might see you but it's quite uncertain

I return West's notes & enclose an extract from a private letter from
N.York—what does it mean? Has Gray only enough parts for *one* orchestra
or is it only an excuse: if Gray is keeping the thing in Damrosch's hands he
should be receiving special fees?

Kindest rgrds
Yours sny
Edward Elgar

P.S. The Daily Mail telegraphed on Friday asking me to set a new poem by
the Poet Laureate; a *Marching Song* for these new territorials—I refused—
but can't these men be brought to know there *is* a marching song already.

Elgar did go up to dine with the King on 18 February, and was in the royal party
attending a concert at Queen's Hall that evening. While in London, he was told by
Alfred Littleton of the old man's plan to marry his cook—a woman who was to look
after him faithfully through the remaining few years of his life. The reaction of
Littleton's daughter Rose was still unknown. Back at home, Elgar wrote a short
note—during the hours of a concert at Hereford which included part of *The Wand of
Youth*.

Plas Gwyn, Hereford.
Feb 19 1909

My dear Littleton:

I have just arrived & find your letter which is a more cheering greeting than
I expected—before you told me.

They (May & Carice) are away at the Concert so I shall hear of Rose on
their return: my wife is better but not out of doors yet

Yrs ever
EE

The following months saw little creative work and less correspondence with
publishers. On 23 February Elgar tried his hand at verse-making for one of his own
march-tunes. But when he consulted Arthur Boosey in London next day, Boosey
advised against publishing it. At Novello, E. J. Pointer submitted mixed-voice
arrangements of *The Snow* and *Fly, Singing Bird*, which he had shown to Elgar and
secured the composer's approval. And the question of arranging the Symphony for
organ was sorted out. Atkins was to arrange the Adagio as an entire movement, West
was to put together a selection of themes from all the movements. His sketch for this
reached Elgar in Italy, where he had gone with Lady Elgar in April to stay with their
friend Mrs Worthington.

Careggi
May 16 1909
My dear West:

Many thanks for sending the organ arrgt sketch. I suggest sundry things which wd. be perhaps useful in making the piece longer—as I at first suggested your arrangmt is admirable.

At the end of p.2 please take in the repetition f as you have it on p 4—to *two* bars from end of p 5—(these pp. refer to your M.S. Then for the 2nd theme your *simpler* arrgt. is best for the purpose only please keep in 4/4 as suggested in my writing. Continue this theme (your own arrgt of course) to p.25 of PF arrgt. then *link* as suggested to fullest possible repetition of the big theme as suggested: the chords on the oblong sheet are from the *finale*—I leave you to fill them in, or out, in keeping with the rest of your arrgt.

I hope you are well & am sorry to trouble you so much.

Kind rgds
Yrs sincy
Edwd. Elgar

I enclose some proofs, please pass on[2]

In Italy Elgar returned to composition. The first result was a part-song, *The Angelus*, to a translation of traditional Tuscan words.

Villa Silli[,] Careggi
May 13.1909
Dear Clayton:

I enclose a short pt song—one, I hope of a Series—will you have it set up in 8vo. the usual way for me to see a proof as soon as possible

I heard yesterday that Mr Alfred Littleton is on the way here & we are looking forward very much to seeing him.

Yrs snly
Ed:Elgar

When Littleton arrived they all enjoyed wonderful spring weather. But the visit was cast in shadow by the news that the long illness of Jaeger had reached its close on 18 May.

Careggi
May 21: 1909
Dear Mrs.Jaeger:

Thank you most sincerely for your great kindness in writing: you know our deepest sympathies & prayers are with you & yours. The news came as a

² MS in possession of Stanley West.

great shock & I cannot realise that the end is come & I am overwhelmed with sorrow for the loss of my dearest & truest friend.

May God bless you

Yrs ever sncly
Edward Elgar[3]

It was inevitably with Jaeger in mind that Elgar wrote his next work, an *Elegy* for strings commissioned by The Worshipful Company of Musicians. Its origin, however, had been the death of the Musicians' Company Warden early in June 1909. Alfred Littleton persuaded Elgar to write it, but the origin of his request was described several years later in a letter from another member of the Musicians' Company.

140, New Bond Street, W.
Jan.20th.1916.
Dear Sir Edward Elgar.

I cannot tell you with what pleasure I received your letter and the, to me, so precious manuscript accompanying it! Still more, however, do I appreciate your kind thought in thus remembering my interests!

It was on the 11th. of June, 1909, when leaving the grave-side of the Rev.Robert Hadden, whose death took place under such tragic circumstances, that I happened to express to Alfred Littleton who accompanied me, my regret that we had no Dirge of our own which could be performed at the service just held, and attended by Liverymen of our ancient City Guild, the Musicians Company, the oldest existing Body connected with music. Alfred Littleton who was in sympathy with my idea, kindly spoke to you on the subject; with the result that what to me has always seemed a most inspired piece of music was composed!

When any member of our Guild, who has won the regard of his fellow-liverymen, passes away, we now have this Dirge performed, and each time I hear it, it grows in impressiveness and tends to raise one's thoughts to a better world above!

With renewed thanks for your kind thought, and deed, and with kind regards to Lady Elgar and yourself.

I am,
yours sincerely
Arthur F.Piel[4]

The *Elegy* was finished and posted to Littleton after Elgar's return to Hereford:

[3] MS in possession of Richard Brookes.
[4] HWRO 705:445:6787.

Plas Gwyn, Hereford.
Jun 24 1909

My dear Littleton—

Here is the little Elegy you asked for—if it will not do, never mind—tear it up.

It is not very original I fear but it is well meant

Ever yours
Ed.Elgar

Hereford
June 25 09

My dear Littleton:

Many thanks: I am much interested in reading of Mr.Hadden & keep the cutting for the present—or probably altogether as I am sending it to Mrs. Worthington who was a Hadden of New York.

The little piece I sent yesterday makes no pretension to be anything but quiet, somewhat sad & soothing. I forgot to say it is meant for *all* your strings & there is a Double Bass part—one of course will do: if you think it worth while to play the piece. I see you refer to it as a *Dirge*—I have put Elegy on the copy but please alter it—I think I like Dirge best—but the little piece is such a trifle that it is scarcely worth while to dignify it by a title at all. So please do exactly as you think best

In haste
Yours ever
Edward Elgar

So *many thanks* for your great kindness to May & Carice

The girls had been staying with Littleton's daughter in Lancaster Gate.

Besides the *Elegy*, Elgar had recently completed a big part-song to words by the early Italian poet Cavalcanti, translated by Dante Gabriel Rossetti. This he proposed to dedicate to Alfred Littleton.

Plas Gwyn, Hereford.
June 27:1909

My dear Littleton:

About your chorus. I am returning final proofs of the music & have asked the printers to await your instruction regarding the title *page*.

As the thing is to be produced at the festival would it not be best & more important-looking to issue it separately—that is to say in the usual yellow cover & *not* in the part-song book: I should propose to put
'Go, song of mine'
Chorus (unaccompanied) in six parts &c &c
& drop the part-song altogether. It would, I feel sure, be better for the future

of the work—will you think of it & settle it very soon as they will be wanting copies for practice & the title, at present is on the first page of the music.

In greatest haste
Yrs sincy
Ed:Elgar

Littleton agreed that *Go, Song of Mine* should be issued separately in the standard Novello format for paper-bound oratorios.

Plas Gwyn, Hereford.
Wednesday [14 July 1909]
My dear Littleton:

Thanks for yours—I am so sorry I could not come again but I came straight on from Bray.

I saw Sinclair & had a talk with him & he puts in the pt.song [for the Hereford Festival] all right: it will be done in the original form i.e. without accompaniment and under its proper title & 'entered' as Chorus (in 6 parts)—as was the case with the Cornelius pt songs.

I am so glad Nikisch has spoken—Failing to get him to lunch or any other meal at Mr.Schuster's I called on him & had a long & interesting talk—but I think I told you this before

Yours ever
Ed:Elgar

The great Hungarian conductor Arthur Nikisch (1855–1922) had said publicly that as Brahms's First Symphony had once been hailed as 'Beethoven's Tenth', so Elgar's Symphony could well be called 'Brahms's Fifth'. Nikisch was planning numerous performances in England and on the continent.

From this point onward, Elgar's correspondence with Novello was less and less with Alfred Littleton, whose age was telling heavily against his health since the death of his wife. In any case, the agreement covering fees and royalties for all Elgar's works made the arrangements more automatic, and there was less reason to communicate about creative progress and problems, as had been done so fully in the past in the letters to Jaeger and more recently in those to Alfred Littleton.

The bulk of the Novello correspondence now was with the company secretary Henry Clayton, who acted as Elgar's unofficial concert agent. It was a difficult role, and Clayton filled it with resolution and tact for many years. These are in no sense publishing letters, and there is little of permanent interest in the very lengthy procession of provincial concert forces, fees, and dates to which almost all of these letters are exclusively devoted. They tell next to nothing about Elgar the man and composer which the reader of the present correspondence does not already know well.

1910

For a Memorial Concert to benefit Jaeger's widow and children, Elgar had agreed to bring forward for first performance three songs with orchestral accompaniment to words by Sir Gilbert Parker. They were from a projected cycle of six. The poet had addressed Elgar a month earlier:

20 Carlton House Terrace[,] S.W.
Dec. 2/ 09
Dear Sir Edward Elgar/

I am delighted. Do as you will. It is enough for me to have the Master of English Music enshrine my words and give them a chance of life beyond their own moment. &c&c.[1]

Elgar sent this permission to Novello together with two of the full score manuscripts—little more than a fortnight before the concert date of 24 January.

Plas Gwyn, Hereford.
Jan 7:1910
Dear Sirs:

I have a general permission from Sir Gilbert Parker to use his poems which are privately printed. I have written to him asking him about printing the three songs for the Jaeger Concert & shall hear shortly.

I send the full scores of two songs: the *letters* for rehearsal will do for the complete work: you will be careful to notice that these three songs do not (in the complete work) follow each other. Perhaps the orch. parts had better not be printed, although if *each string part of each song* makes a page it would be safe to do so.

If the parts are to be M.S. for this Concert I must pay for them—the Concert fund must not suffer. 5 Vio I. 5 Vio II. 4 Viole. 4 ea Celli & Bassi wd. do for these accpts.

I enclose Sir G.Parker's letter which please take care of & return to me.

Yrs sincly
Edward Elgar

Please send Sir G.P. a few prospectuses of the Jaeger Concert.

He wrote to Novello's publishing manager Harold Brooke over the *'Enigma' Variations* programme note for the Jaeger Memorial Concert, with special reference to Jaeger himself. This letter survives in a copy made for Novello's archives.

[1] Copy fragment in Novello archives.

160 Wardour Street
Thursday [13 Jan. 1910] a.m.

Dear Mr. Brooke,

I do not like this note—please alter it as marked.

'Something ardent & mercurial, in addition to the slow movement (No. [*i.e.*, Variation] 9)[,] would have been needful to portray the character & temperament of A.J.Jaeger (Nimrod)[.']

I think the proof correction is clear but I have copied out the altered portion.

Yours sincerely
Ed. Elgar

P.S. The *words* (songs) are all right [*i.e.*, are used with Sir Gilbert Parker's permission].

A letter surviving from the publishers of the *Bavarian Highlands* songs shows how difficult it was for any smaller publisher to give the kind of service Elgar and his music now required:

32, Great Portland Street.
Feb 2nd., 1910

Dear Sir Edward Elgar,

In view of the fact that you require a Royalty on the full Score of your Choral Suite 'FROM THE BAVARIAN HIGHLANDS', we have decided to dispense with its issue for the present. The cost of production would involve an outlay of between £60 & £70, and there is little or no profit on the actual sale of this style of publication.

With Compliments.

Yours very truly,
pro JOSEPH WILLIAMS, Limited.
Florian Williams, Secretary.[2]

One exchange of letters with Clayton at Novello shows the extra dimension of the publisher's work in collecting the performing fees demanded for Elgar's Symphony— over and above the royalty agreement on sale of scores and Elgar's own fees when he conducted:

[160, Wardour Street, W.]
February 8th: [19]10.

Dear Elgar

I enclose account of all the British performances, & some of the Foreign, of your Symphony, with cheque for £208-19-0 in settlement. As regards the performances at *Hull, Middlesboro, Doncaster, Nottingham,* & *Leeds* (Choral Union) I assume that the fees arranged to be paid, were paid to you direct,

[2] HWRO 705:445:8208.

but as I was ill at the time I have never definitely ascertained. But I fully anticipate that everything was done in the usual course.

As regards Great Britain we have now paid everything, so as to clear it up, altho' in 8 cases *we* have not yet been paid.

As regards foreign performances we still owe you for:

			Elgar's share
June 1909.	Sydney Philharmonic	£15.15.0	£10.10.0
Sep 2. 1909	Eastbourne—(P.Tas)	10.10.0 (not paid)	7. 7.0
Sep 9 1909	Hereford Festival	15.15.0	10.10.0
Oct 5 1909	Birmingham Festival	21. 0.0	16.16.0
Oct 21. 1909	Newcastle Festival	15.15.0	10.10.0
Oct 26 1909	Hull	5. 5.0	Nil
Oct 27th 1909	Middlesboro	5. 5.0	Nil
Oct 28th 1909	Doncaster	5. 5.0	Nil
Oct 29th 1909	Nottingham	5. 5.0	Nil
Nov 2. 1909	Leeds Philharmonic	15.15.0 Not paid	10.10.0
Nov 3 1909	Leeds Choral Union	5. 5.0	Nil
Nov 7 1909	R.A.H. (Sunday Concert)	15.15.0	10.10.0
Nov 11 1909	Queen's Hall Orchestra at Exeter	12.12.0	9. 9.0
Nov 24 1909	Glasgow Choral (*Dundee*)	15.15.0 not paid	10.10.0
Nov 29 1909	Edinburgh	15.15.0 not paid	10.10.0
Nov 30 1909	Glasgow Choral	15.15.0 not paid	10.10.0
Dec 4 1909	Glasgow Choral	15.15.0 not paid	10.10.0
Dec 7 1909	Liverpool Philharmonic	15.15.0 not paid	10.10.0
Jan 31st 1910	London Symphony O.	15.15.0	10.10.0
Feb 3rd 1910	Norwich (Bates)	15.15.0 not paid	10.10.0

Foreign

Feb 26 1909	Boston	10.10.0	7. 7.0
” 27 1909	Boston	10.10.0	7. 7.0
Mar 5 1909	Pittsburg	10.10.0	7. 7.0
” 6 1909	Pittsburg	10.10.0	7. 7.0
May 4 1909	Louisville	13.13.0	10.10.0
Octr.25 1909	Budapesth	12.12.0	9. 9.0

Foreign performances not paid

Bonn—Nov.25.	7.10.0
Munich Dec.20.	10. 0.0
Frankfurt ?	15.15.0
Rome Jan 6.	15.15.0

£208.19.0

and 5 *American* performances (Boston Symphony Orchestra) which have only just taken place. I have postponed accounting to you for these, as it appears likely that we shall have to wait some considerable time before we are paid ourselves. As a fact we are experiencing some difficulty with Bonn & Munich in obtaining payment. Rome neither answers letters nor returns the music, & Frankfurt completely ignores our repeated requests that they will *fix the date* of their performance. They have already had the music over 4 months.

We always have a lot of trouble with these foreigners. The worst of it is they will not return the music after the performances, so we do not know what they are up to, & lose control accordingly.

Mr.Alfred Littleton has asked me to deal with your letter addressed to him, so I add a line to let you know that I have to day sent to Landon Ronald a Folio Copy of the Symphony Full Score, & am now having a proof copy of 'The Torch' pulled for Miss [Viola] Tree [both requests from Elgar].

> With kind regards
> Yours sincerely
> Henry R.Clayton

There are no performances of the Symphony now booked for any place in Great Britain, & we have no enquiries about possible performances!

Elgar had been staying by himself at Queen Anne's Mansions, London, to work on the slow movement of the Violin Concerto. He returned to his home in Hereford on 9 February, as his wife noted, 'keen over his new musics'. But when he opened Clayton's letter next day, she noted: 'Tiresome publishers' letters, no cheering news. E. much depressed & beautiful music driven away.'

Plas Gwyn, Hereford.
Feb 10 1910
Dear Clayton:

Many thanks for the cheque—formal receipt for which is enclosed: I am sadly disappointed about Hull, Middlesboro, Doncaster[,] Nottingham & Leeds—I appear to have been thrown into the bargain, or the Symphony was—this is exactly what I so strongly objected to in the case of Queen's Hall a year ago & it was not to happen again. It is of course too late to do anything about the L.Symphy Orchestra 4 northern concerts (as above) but did Mr.Embleton expect *not* to pay the performing fee? or has it been simply let go by?

I hope you will look sharply after the American performances. I have a programme of Chicago October 22 & 23 (*Stock* conducting) last year (two performances) which I do not see in your list: have you had notice of these?

Thanks for sending the score to Mr Ronald & the proof of Song to Miss Viola Tree.

As to the future of the Symphy—we cannot expect it to go on but it is not worth while to consider any reduction at present I think. Ronald is doing it on the 24th inst. & there must be a few performances next autumn: by that time we may have some new work & could consider the position. I hear that Nikisch is taking the *Variations* on tour with the [London] Sym.Orch: & these cost nothing. Why should we give away the Symphony—I wd. prefer it was never done again.

Kind rgds
Yours sncly
Edward Elgar

[160, Wardour Street, W.]
February 11th. [19]10.

Dear Elgar

Thanks for your letter of yesterday's date. It has made me rather uncomfortable, for if anyone is to blame for letting off the Hull, Middlesboro', Doncaster[,] Nottingham & Leeds people too cheaply, I fear I must bear it. I would gladly bear the blame, even if censure accompanied it, but the thought that your pocket may have suffered as a consequence of my action, makes me, as I have said, uncomfortable.

I have used the expression 'may have suffered' because in my own mind I am convinced that your pocket has not suffered, but has really derived a benefit from the arrangements made in each case. As regards the four Towns controlled by Sharpe I am morally certain that if I had claimed the usual £10.10.0 performing fee, beyond what Sharpe agreed to pay, he would not have performed the Symphony at any of the Towns—& his action after the performances justifies my belief, for having agreed to pay you 35 Guineas for the first Town & 25 Guineas for the other three, he afterwards withheld the extra £10.10.0 for the first Town on the ground that having agreed to 25 guineas for the other 3, the first would obviously be at the same rate.

We resisted this on the ground that he made a separate Contract for each place quite irrespectively of the others, & that he was bound by his Contracts. He still demurred & we ultimately referred the matter to you, & you gave way.

It is not likely that a man who struggled so hardly for that Ten Guineas would have paid Forty Guineas more. Embleton also would I believe have cried off if we had added a performing fee to your fee for conducting; for of recent years Embleton has become ever so much more inclined to save than was the case a few years ago. In each case we asked as much as we thought *the performance could stand*, & we have always been most anxious not to ruin your chance of securing a Conducting fee by piling on other expenses.

This is a sound policy to follow, but I can imagine your replying that we had no business to follow any policy that you had objected to; for your letter this morning contains the expression 'this is exactly what I so strongly objected to in the case of Queen's Hall a year ago, and it was not to happen again.'

As that is your view of what happened at that time I think I had better enclose the correspondence which conveyed quite a different impression to my mind. I read your letter of Feb 2nd 1909 as being in a sense your acceptance of an argument which I had put forward although you did not altogether endorse it. It certainly never occurred to me that you intended by it to take away our freedom of action, or to warn me that the Queen's Hall case 'must not happen again'. So if there is a blunder I am responsible for it, for I have entirely misunderstood your letter of Feb.2nd [1909].

For the future however I shall know how to act & I will ask for a performing fee whether you conduct or not. But I honestly believe you will lose money by it.

As regards American performances I am writing to Gray today for a complete statement of all performances of the Symphony in America & Canada.

I find that when I was away ill (viz at the end of November) he wrote mentioning performances at Chicago on Octr. *28th* & *29th*—New York Nov.7. & Philadelphia (no date) but he gave us no particulars of any performance & he has since ignored the whole of them. I will at once take up the matter & follow it out. It was your letter of this morning which put me on the enquiry.

I cannot find any record of any arrangement made with Landon Ronald for his performance on the 24th instt. but no difficulty is likely to arise with him.

With kind regards
Yours sincerely
Henry R:Clayton

Mr.C.J.Longman of Longmans Green & Co. has sent us a Folio edition of 'The Dream of Gerontius' [Newman's poem in manuscript facsimile] to be sent to you—I have ordered it to be posted to you tonight. His address is 39 Paternoster Row, E.C.

Plas Gwyn, Hereford.
Feb 12 1910

Dear Clayton:

Many thanks: 1st for Longman's parcel containing the costly Gerontius;—of which another copy has already been sent me!

Also for the Irish letter—I really do not want to go—the date will be a tie & I cannot see any way to promise this so far ahead: the matter had better drop so far as I am concerned:

As to the symphony performances: I quite agree that the probability is, or was, that if you had stipulated for the performing fee the five concerts wd. not have taken place—but then I wd. much prefer that they had *not* done so.

To go over old ground—these people pay, say Richter, £50 & do not get a fuller room than when I go there—they lose gladly;—they get me *and* the symphy for ½ that amount & complain—that's the matter in a nutshell & I will not do it again. At Queen's Hall they had an absolutely full house—the next Concert they engaged Clara Butt 105£ shewing they must have made this profit—at least one must infer that they did—the third concert was a *full* house—but not crammed[.] They had these three really *trying* concerts from me for 75£—then paid Debussy about 200£ for a concert which only ¾ filled the house—I am not *complaining*. I only state what happens & I do not see why I should earn money for people to spend on others.—& that is really what it has come to. Do not think anything more of these past matters but we will have no more in the future.

Kind rgrds
Yrs snc'y
Edward Elgar

P.S. I really cannot stand the advt. which you send of Gerontius—about the enormous expense &c.—It quite puts me 'off'
Thanks for the old letters—returned herewith

During much of the spring of 1910, Elgar was at work on the Violin Concerto. Moreover he had promised the Second Symphony for the London Musical Festival at Queen's Hall in May 1911. Beyond that was the long-considered prospect of setting *The Music Makers*, and even a revived dream of the final oratorio for the trilogy. But privately Elgar was restless. Dissatisfied with Hereford, he had rented a flat in London; and his stays there were fragmented by conducting engagements. Throughout all this he had none the less managed to deliver the first two movements of the Concerto to the publishers, and was hard at work on the Finale. He was aided in the work by W. H. Reed, who now became one of his most intimate friends. Elgar wrote from his London flat:

58, New Cavendish Street, W. Just leaving for Lincoln
Thursday [2 June 1910] a m

My dear Littleton

I was sorry to miss you yesterday & am glad you like the look of the Concerto[.] I wish you could have heard Mr. Reed play some of it—I wanted to arrange it here but it was too difficult—(the problem of meeting I mean not the Concerto).

I have kept your Albert Hall proposition before me & have the poem but I am waiting until I get home on Saturday—everything depends upon my finding a quiet & possible place to work in—not in the immediate future but in a few months: if that can be arranged I do not see why you should not have the choral work, the Symphony ready[,] the Violin Concerto *and* the IIIrd Oratorio—But I cannot work now under disagreeable conditions. We shall see more in a month or two.

Kindest rgrds
Yrs v sy
Edward Elgar

By the time Elgar sent in the Concerto Finale in piano score a month later, all the leading concert societies were contending for the first performance, offering high fees, combinations of several performances, and (where they could) Fritz Kreisler as soloist, for the Concerto was dedicated to him. Elgar had half promised the Concerto première to the Philharmonic Society.

Then Robert Newman came into Novello's offices. He represented the Queen's Hall Syndicate, and said that the Syndicate were securing the services of Kreisler for the first performance. On that basis, Clayton allowed Newman to take away piano score proofs of the first two movements to show to Kreisler. Elgar was furious, and telegraphed on 29 June:

Do not give Newman or anyone else proofs on any account. I am much upset at the idea. Please recover proof if possible. Edward Elgar

Plas Gwyn, Hereford.
June 29:1910

My dear Littleton

I am sorry you cannot be with us this week & hear the Concerto: we are to be away next week.

I am very much annoyed that Mr Newman should have had copies of the concerto—*I* should have seen Kreisler first: it is inconceivable that my music should be shewn to K. by Newman and it is treating N. different from the other societies &, to my mind, is quite a mistake.

I have given no promise to the Philharmonic: they have asked for a new work & I have said it would be a great pleasure &c. to me to produce something: the concerto was mentioned but no question of performing fee which must now be adjusted in the usual way & if the Phil. cannot pay a performing fee as high as the (say) L.Sym orch they *cannot* have the first performance.

As to the Piano Concerto I meant that the programm for Nov. contains a concerto (Caesar Franck) to be played by Pugno—not one of mine. I hope to send the last movement of the Violin Concerto in a few days now.

Please send me Kreisler's address in case I have to communicate with him

Yrs v sncly
Edward Elgar

This elicited a letter of apology from Clayton:

160 Wardour Street W.
June 29th. 1910.

Dear Elgar,

Your telegram reached me this morning. I am very sorry that I blundered in sending Newman a set of proofs of the first two parts of your Violin Concerto.

He telephoned to me on Monday & asked whether he could have a rough set of proofs at his Office on Tuesday Morning. I enquired why he wanted them & he replied that they were hoping to make a Contract with Kreisler to play the work, that Kreisler would be at his office yesterday, & that they could not very well make a Contract with Kreisler to play the work until Kreisler had had an opportunity of looking at the work. As Kreisler's name has already been very much coupled with your work, I saw no harm in letting Newman have the proofs for that purpose, so I sent the proofs to Newman yesterday morning (i.e. clean proofs).

On receipt of your telegram I sent round to Newman's Office & tried to recover the proofs, but Kreisler, who has gone to Paris & returns tomorrow has them with him—I will try and recover them on Friday.

We are so in the habit of supplying proof copies of unpublished Choral works to the artists who are to take part in their production that it never occurred to me that there could be any objection to a set being sent for the purpose for which Newman required them—In fact I thought I was helping in some small degree to clinch matters with Kreisler, whose name has been so much to the fore in connection with the first performance of your work. I even thought that Kreisler might be annoyed and prejudiced against the work if we declined to supply the proofs.

However I hope no great harm has been done—& I shall of course take care that no one else is allowed to see the proofs until the matter has been referred to you.

With many regrets that what I have done has vexed you.

Yours sincerely
Henry R.Clayton

The Philharmonic Society, Queen's Hall, the London Symphony Orchestra, and Landon Ronald's New Symphony Orchestra were 'all *fighting* hard' (according to Lady Elgar's diary) for the première when Elgar went to London on 1 July to meet Kreisler at Novello's offices. The great violinist was 'much impressed. He said at one passage "I will shake Queen's Hall!"'

The Philharmonic Society's offer of two performances of the Concerto with Kreisler, each carrying a performing fee of £100 in addition to Elgar's regular conducting fees, won the day. All these negotiations were carried out through Novello.

Time to prepare the score and parts for the première, scheduled for 10 November, was short enough. Elgar's preference was to have the full score engraved and corrected first: this would allow time for the production of a miniature score in time for the première (as was done with the Symphony), as well as an authorized version against which to correct orchestral parts. But this method was not followed, either in the engraving at Geidel's firm in Leipzig or by the now anonymous denizen of Novello entrusted with the preparation of the Concerto.

Plas Gwyn, Hereford.
Oct 4 1910

private

My dear Littleton:

I have written a strong letter to the firm about the printing (reading) of the Concerto. I wrote (with the m.s. score I think) that *as usual* we should correct the score first—the score was never hurried, [(]as it should have been) through the German office. Now we have to hurry to allow of the small score being done in time. Also West has been reading *some* of the string parts with his portion of the score! It is really too absurdly vexing as apparently all the real correction of the parts will now come in my busy time when I can get no assistance.

I know it is now too late to do anything different. I only tell you the reason of my writing. Harold Brooke has done *nobly*! but you promised me once that I should never be troubled again with ——!!

Yours ever
Ed.Elgar

Several private trials of the music with Kreisler and a semi-private performance with piano at the Gloucester Festival in September, brought Kreisler more and more closely into final revisions to the solo part. Elgar wrote to Harold Brooke:

Plas Gwyn, Hereford.
Oct 7 1910

Dear Mr.Brooke:

Many thanks for your note. I return everything to-day (looked over)

I note that I may expect some parts at the end of next week—by that time it will of course be impossible to rectify any errors (that may be discovered in playing through the parts) in the full score!! Why, oh! why, was not the full score done first, a month ago, as I said? It is too foolish.

Yours sincly
Edward Elgar.

When you send the parts I must have a (latest) Score with them.

N.B. One or two passages in the Violin *Solo* I have marked Ⓚ —they are Mr.Kreisler's bowings—if he is in London you might *shew* him & [*sic*] final proof & ask him *what* he wants on these doubtful points. If you *cannot* see him print the passages as they stand—there is nothing in them of any *real* importance.   EE

Some of Kreisler's suggestions resulted in the recomposing of solo passages in printed proofs.[3] All this was done against a background of Elgar's conducting engagements and restlessness at home in Hereford. While Lady Elgar looked at new houses, he spent more time in London.

---

[3] Later given to Charles Sanford Terry, and now in the British Library.

Queen Anne's [Mansions, London, S.W.]
Wedy [12 Oct. 1910]

Dear Mr Brooke.

Many thanks: I do not know if you were able to catch Mr Kreisler but I think the points are fairly clear—that is[:] it doesn't matter much either way.

Please see p 20 Vn.Solo (two bars before 91 [)] & decide about engraving the notes in their proper place—(also two bars before 77 [)]. *Here* add an E to the first C[:] see slip—(this is one of the Kreisler queries—but failing him I settle it as on the slip)

I want the bar lines in the *Solo* pt Cadenza taken out where marked—it looks *free* & better.

I remain here for some days & am anxious to correct all I can. I fear I cannot come out as I have had a bad sting on my ancle & cannot use my foot much.

> Kind rgrds
> Yours sincy
> Edward Elgar

Q Anne's
Oct 14 1910

Dear Mr Brooke:

Here are the final proofs (of P.F. and Solo) of II & III.—Now—when do you want to print? Mr.Kreisler will be here on the 15th & we are to play together between that date (probably on Sunday the 16th) & I could then ask him about one or two minor points such as the harmonics on *p.11.Solo*. These few things are however not very important and need not affect the printing if you want to commence at once

As to p.11—IF the passage is marked do not put oooo but *armonici* (italic) where *placed* in the Solo pt will do—being a *tone* direction only it is not wanted in Score or P.F.

> Yours sincerely
> Edward Elgar

I want to know, as soon as possible, the 'course of events' regarding the orchl. parts. Can I have them *all* (at Hereford) on Saturday *next week*[?] I could then return by Monday evening!

Sessions with Kreisler on 15 and 17 October brought a few more emendations. Back at Hereford on 23 and 24 October, John Austin helped with final checking of orchestral parts against the score. A triumphant première on 10 November was followed by many performances, a number of which Elgar conducted. He was meanwhile attempting to bring together his disparate sketches for the Second Symphony (promised to the Queen's Hall Syndicate in May 1911) into a final pattern.

During the autumn of 1910, Elgar had been persuaded by Ivor Atkins, the organist of Worcester Cathedral, to collaborate in preparing a new edition of Bach's *St Matthew Passion* for performance at the Worcester Festival in September 1911. Elgar was to deal with musical matters, and Atkins with the words. Novello would publish the result. Although Atkins went to Hereford frequently to consult about the edition, it came in Elgar's busiest time of preparing the Violin Concerto for its première and composing the Second Symphony. In the event, Atkins appears to have done most of the work. None the less Elgar's name was so valuable that each of the collaborators was paid a hundred guineas. As often happened, however, major creative worry told on Elgar's health.

1911

The new year opened with an invitation from Alfred Littleton, now Master of the Musicians Company, to accept Honorary Freedom of the Company.

Plas Gwyn, Hereford.
January 10. 1911
My dear Littleton:

I have been laid up with chill—as usual in the Winter [—] & regret I have been unable to write for some days. All thanks for your kind invitation to the Musicians' Company's dinner—I fear it is quite impossible as I must return here immediately after the Concert next Monday (or Tuesday)

It is most kind of you to think of the Hon. Freedom of the Company for me & some time I will accept the honour with very great pleasure but we must talk of dates when we meet.

I am all behind with my work & I have grave fears for the 2nd Symphony, but I must decide its fate next week—I have been too cold to do anything

We all send best wishes to you all.

Yours v sincerely
Edward Elgar

The official letter offering Elgar Honorary Freedom of the Musicians' Company[1] arrived just as he was finishing the first movement of the new Symphony.

Plas Gwyn, Hereford.
Jany 29:1911
My dear Littleton:

I have received a very flattering letter from the Clerk of the Musicians' Company & I have accepted the honorary Freedom—but I shall be in *US.A* in April & cannot possibly be present on the date proposed—perhaps some other time, if it is necessary for me to be present: thank you for proposing me for the Honorary Freedom.

[1] Dated 25 Jan. 1911 (HWRO 705:445:5014).

The first movement of the symphy is ready for the printer & I am sending it to *you*. I got *Pointer* (a private arrgt of my own) to look over the first 28 pages & the thing so far is in *clean* form—after that your readers must follow the usual 'style'. But the troublesome time over the Concerto *must on no account* be repeated & you must please be very firm & keep the entire correction away from ——. I cannot face it again.

Please get the score engraved first and at once: if you insist Geidel could let you have it in[,] practically, a *few days*—they did for Boosey the Coronation Ode in a very short time[.] So please hurry matters post haste as I *must* correct the score before I go to America: there is time if the score is put in hand at once & the engravers quickest possible despatch insisted upon.

Kindest regards—I look to you to see to all this & let Mr Brooke (for choice failing Pointer) take charge of it

Yrs v.sny
Edward Elgar

Elgar had accepted a proposal from Dr Charles Harriss to conduct his works in America as part of a Coronation-year world tour by the Sheffield Choir. He was to be away from late March until May. Another proposal had come from the patron of the Leeds Choral Union, Henry Embleton. Elgar wrote:

Hereford
2 FEB 1911

My dear Littleton

I was delighted to receive your letter about the Symphony (II) & am glad you heard a note or two—it *is* decidedly joyous [—] 'Spirit of Delight' sort of thing—but ends sedately

I have sent a p.c. acknowledging the receipt of the enclosed letter—I don't remember the writer: you see it opens the whole question of 'Gerontius' in Italy: I think it might be worth while for you to see Mr.Bonifacio & hear what he has to say. Embleton was very keen about taking his choir & San Martino was in favour: I cannot say if it's any good but you might enquire &c &c. If you don't think it worth pursuing never mind

Kindest rgds
Yrs sny
Ed Elgar

The 'Spirit of Delight' was a reference to Shelley's poem beginning 'Rarely, rarely comest thou, Spirit of Delight!', which Elgar wished to use as an epigraph to the Second Symphony. Alfred Littleton suggested printing the entire poem above the music.

Plas Gwyn, Hereford.
Feb 20 1911

My dear Littleton

Many thanks for your letter. I will think over your idea about the Stanzas. I proposed to put only the first two *lines*—in the score—which suggest all the rest—& let the programme makers put the whole poem.

I return Dr.Harriss' letter & have made a note of the dates.

In greatest haste
Yrs v sincy
Edward Elgar

By this time Elgar was well into the final construction of the Symphony Finale. It was finished on the last day of February, and on 3 March Elgar delivered the movement to Novello's offices in London.

A trip to Brussels to conduct the First Symphony with Eugène Ysaÿe's orchestra resulted in a bad cold just as Elgar was preparing to sail with the Sheffield Choir to Canada. His daughter Carice was also down with tonsillitis. He managed to complete a setting of words from Psalm 5, beginning 'O hearken Thou unto the voice of my calling', requested by Sir Frederick Bridge for the Coronation of King George V and Queen Mary in June.

Hereford
March 16 1911

My dear Littleton:

Excuse scrap. I have an *awful* cold & chill—I may be able to go to Canada as the horrid thing is at present only in my head—there's plenty of room there you'll say! I am not allowed out.

—This is only to say I have finished the Offertory for Sir F.Bridge & have sent the voc.sc arrgt & full score to him by to-night's post.

Pointer is coming tonight so all goes well. but I'm afraid I am rather a trouble to you

Kindest regards
Yrs ever
Ed.Elgar

Carice goes on steadily better but slowly

When E. J. Pointer arrived next day to go over Symphony proofs, Lady Elgar noted: 'He sat up by E.'s bed & they worked thro' the proofs of the 4th Movement.' The departure for Canada was put off.

During the next days there were long letters from Clayton about conducting engagements for the remainder of 1911 and beyond. Elgar was taking over chief conductorship of the London Symphony Orchestra from the retiring Hans Richter. There had also been the proposal that Eugène Ysaÿe should play the Violin Concerto at a Philharmonic Society concert. This Ysaÿe had cancelled, for reasons which were still obscure.

22 MAR 1911

My dear Littleton—

Many thanks. I am better & have had the shortest possible walk & have booked my passage for Saturday next.

I leave you to settle the fee question: I dictated a full reply to Clayton's letter which I hope covers the ground: I am awfully sorry to be so troublesome.

As to the Daily Mail: I fear that's my misfortune though not exactly my fault. A man came down here to see me about the (now-happily-abandoned) Children's Song at the C.Palace[.] I was *interviewed* on the subject for publication (the thing never came to anything) but the few words I said on the [new] symphony were not so intended. I have seen nothing of it[.] I will be more guarded another time.

As to Richter—the announcemt. that he will continue to conduct Opera rather knocks the retirement idea & consequent presentation into the background don't you think? I don't see how it can be proceded [*sic*] with at present.

I sent the letter to you, H.J.Wood and, I think, *L.Ronald*, Legge, S.Loeb[,] Kalisch[,] Pitt, Percy [—] there were several 'floaters' who had temporising cards &c. & who do not count.

Regarding Ysaÿe & the abandoned Philharmonic performance of the Concerto—We have had friendly letters from the Ysaÿes, saying that Eugene is going to play the Concerto at Brussels next winter—Could *you* suggest to *Ronald* (The L.S.O. have Kreisler in October [—] 23rd I think) to capture Ysaÿe: say in November—it wd. be a great draw & a feather in Ronald's crown? I don't understand the Phil's attitude at all.

I have had a letter from Sir A. Bigge (the matter was brought before the King) & H.M. is very pleased that I should dedicate the Symphony to the memory of his father, King Edward—I am submitting a dedicatory sentence & you shall have it as soon as possible. I hope you will be pleased at this.

I always intended the work for King Edward but of course cd. not use his name without permission.

> Forgive scrawl
> Yours ever sincly
> Ed.^d Elgar

Carice has been allowed down for a few hours to-day—but has to be *carried* upstairs: but she is really better[2]

Programme notes for Queen's Hall concerts were now written by Mrs Rosa Newmarch, and she had applied for details of the Second Symphony for the première programme note. The request reached Elgar during his American tour with the Sheffield Choir.

---

[2] MS in possession of H. S. P. Brooke.

New York
April 13

My dear Littleton

I hope you are well & all flourishes with you & yours.

I am all right & wearing through—but bored to death with noise & irritation—the tour goes on well & all pleasantly with that, but I mean interviewing & general vulgarity &c.

With this I send a few very rough notes which I hope will be in time for the programme book (Mrs Newmarch) Please use them as you think best—I fear they are very late & were intended for you a fortnight ago but on my return to N.Y. (between Buffalo & Cincinnati concerts) I find them still here! so I do the best I can.

I have really no news: the concerts seem to be a great success & the audiences are really enthusiastic: I had a talk with Dr.Harriss at Buffalo & all seems satisfactory.

I seem miles away—I mean worlds away & get very little news.

> My kindest regards
> Always sincerely yrs
> Edward Elgar

Gray has been most kind & helpful & is just the same as ever: I hope he's prospering but I do not know. He has given two dinners!

N.B. This is not to be printed *literally in extenso*: it is only a *guide* Phrases may be used if suitable   EE

Symphony No.2
(Motto) 'Rarely, rarely comest thou,
Spirit of Delight'

Shelley

To get near the mood of the Symphony the whole of Shelley's poem may be read, but the music does not illustrate the whole of the poem, neither does the poem entirely elucidate the music.

The germ of the work is in the opening bars—these in a modified form are heard for the last time in the closing bars of the last movement. The early part of the 1st. movemt consists of an assemblage of themes. I wish the theme at 11 to be considered (& labelled) as the second principal theme

—The spirit of the whole work is intended to be high & pure joy: there are retrospective passages of sadness but the whole of the sorrow is smoothed out & ennobled in the last movement, which ends in a calm &, *I hope & intend*, elevated mood.

(N.B. *private*

The second movement formed part of the original scheme—before the death of King Edward;—it is elegiac but has nothing to do with any funeral march & is a 'reflection' suggested by the poem.)

The Rondo was sketched on the Piazza of S.Mark.Venice: I took down the rhythm of the opening bars from some itinerant musicians who seemed to take a grave satisfaction in the broken accent of the first four bars.

The last movement speaks for itself I think: a broad sonorous, rolling movement throughout—in an elevated mood.

The reappearances of the first theme are obvious & I need not point them out.

Please note the new 'atmosphere' at 27 (suggested at 24) with the added Cello solo at 28 —remote & drawing some one else out of the everyday world: note the *feminine* voice of the oboe, answering or joining in, two bars before 30 [;] note the happiness at 30 —real (remote) peace: note at 33 the atmosphere broken in upon & the dream 'shattered' by the inevitable march of the Trombones & Tuba pp.

In the 2nd movement at 79 the feminine voice *laments* over the broad manly 1st theme [—] and may not 87 be like a woman dropping a flower on the man's grave?

Fine

E.E.

The Coronation service in June was to be enriched not only with the anthem *O Hearken Thou* but also with a recessional *Coronation March* from Elgar. This was the subject of his next letter to Alfred Littleton, written on board the ship bringing him back to England after the Sheffield Choir tour (where he had missed his first engagement through delayed sailing because of illness).

On Board the Cunard R.M.S. 'Mauretania'.
May 4

My dear Littleton

I am sending this directly I land to say that so far so good—I am safe on the ship & have done all the work—save & except Montreal. I am hoping to get to Hereford for a few days before the strenuous London times—& will let you have the score of the March at once.

The tour has been an enormous success I think & should do a lot of good—but I will tell you of it as there is too much to write & some of the experiences were weird

Gray was most kind & helpful & did *everything* possible in N.Y.

I shall probably find some news from you & others when I arrive at home but at this moment my mind is a perfect blank regarding England.

Kind regards
Yours sny
Edward Elgar

Elgar arrived home on 9 May, and the next days were filled with scoring the *Coronation March*, correspondence with Clayton over engagements, and preparation of the Second Symphony parts. He wrote from the London house he had taken on a short lease.

75, Gloucester Place, Portman Square, W.
May 17:1911

My dear Littleton

I am tired out (6 hours) but I must send one word of praise & congratulation to you on the splendid way the score & parts have been produced—there were several absolutely trifling errors (such as *arco* omitted) but not one serious mistake—in fact the only *error* was the 1st Horn had E♭ instead of ♮—This is really wonderful—I do not take any credit to myself(!) for my awful M.S. Score but Pointer & Harold Brooke deserve a real word of glory.

Ever yours
Edward Elgar

The first performance of the new Symphony, conducted by Elgar at Queen's Hall on 24 May, came nowhere near the success of the First Symphony two and a half years earlier. A second performance a week later attracted a thin house. Two other performances had been booked in June with the aim of introducing Elgar as principal conductor of the London Symphony Orchestra. On the day after the first of these, and on his way to a Royal Levée, Elgar wrote to Alfred Littleton:

75, Gloucester Place, Portman Square, W.
June 9 1911

My dear Littleton:

In great haste as I have to be at the Palace & am going out of town for Sunday

No one came to the concert last night so I have told the *L.S.O.* that I receive no fee of any kind (performing or otherwise) for this concert (8th) or for the concert next week (15th)—most depressing!

I hope to call in on Monday & look thro' the orchl parts of the March.

I hope you have stood your great amount of work well

Ever yours
Edward Elgar

Ten days later it was announced that Elgar was to receive the Order of Merit—his country's highest mark of artistic distinction—in the Coronation Honours. Among the flood of congratulations from old friends and new, one must stand for all. Charles Volkert of Schott, from whom Elgar had purchased violin pieces for his lessons with Pollitzer in 1877, sent a postcard of Wendelsteingipfel in Bavaria, where he was on holiday, with this message:

St John's Day 1911 [*postmarked* 24 JU 11]

My dear Sir Edward

Please accept my hearty good wishes to this well merited and great distinction, and say something nice to Lady Elgar.

My 2nd daughter & I walked up to the highest mountain & sang 'God save the King' near the Cross on Coronation Day.

Your old admirer and sincere friend

Chas.Volkert[3]

But Coronation Day, 22 June 1911, found Elgar so depressed that he refused to attend the Coronation or to allow his wife to do so. (Carice went with Alfred Littleton and his family.) The deepest causes of Elgar's depression remain matters for speculation, but there can be no doubt that the relative failure of the Second Symphony to please its audiences, contrasting unhappily with the success of the First Symphony, led him to conclude that his creative day was drawing in. It was not the first time he thought this; but the Coronation atmosphere spread abroad a sense of casting out the old along with bringing in the new.

On 27 June Elgar went to Novello's offices, to find few performances of either Symphony booked for the future. He returned to his rented house and wrote two letters to terminate the agreement by which, since 1904, Novello had paid him a 25 per cent royalty in exchange for the near-exclusive contract to publish his works.

75, Gloucester Place, Portman Square, W.
June 27.1911

Dear Sirs:

Enclosed I send formal receipt for the annual royalty acct. & some performing fees. The account is very disappointing & I must as soon as possible make some other plans: with very much regret I must ask you to accept this as notice to terminate the agreement existing between us as to publishing;—I believe twelve months' notice is required but I have not Mr.Littleton's letter here which forms the agreement.

I need not say that I send this notice with very great regret but I see no other course open to me.

With many thanks for the care that has been taken of my interests,

Believe me
Yours v.try
Edward Wm. Elgar

75, Gloucester Place, Portman Square, W.
June 27:1911

My dear Littleton:

I am very sorry that I feel compelled to send a formal letter to the firm giving notice that our agreement—or whatever it was—must end—I believe twelve months' notice is required.

[3] HWRO 705:445:4950.

I do this with very great regret as the personal friendship to you has grown so strong—but I feel that the time has come when it is necessary to make—or rather to prepare to make [—] other plans.

The present account is very disappointing—I must try & subsist on 'sums down' on publication which other publishers give me—however it is not necessary to go into details

I thank you sincerely for all your care of my interests & regret that the publication—i.e. the sale of my works shd not have been more successful.

Kindest rgrds
Yrs v sincerely
Edward Elgar

160 Wardour Street W.
June 29.1911

My dear Elgar

I need hardly say that your letter received yesterday caused me some surprise and regret—but I quite agree that you have nothing to do but to consider your own interests and make any arrangements which you think will prove advantageous—

I shall always be proud of the connection of our house with the production of your works—particularly of your earlier works when publishers were not so accessible to you as they naturally would be at the present time—and I am also proud to think that we may have been of some little use in helping the rapid progress which has culminated in the high position you have reached—

Trusting that whatever new arrangements you may make, may prove satisfactory to you in every way

I am
Yours very sincerely
Alfred H Littleton[4]

The reply on behalf of the firm was drafted by Henry Clayton and signed by him with the firm's signature.

160, Wardour Street, London, W.
June 29th.1911

Dear Sir

We are favoured with your letter of the 27th.inst. signifying your desire to terminate the publishing agreement which you made with us in 1904. We need not say with what regret we have received this intimation of your decision in the matter.

We have consulted the letters which constitute the agreement between us, & find that Mr.Littleton's letter of April 14th.1904. suggested a notice of 12 months on either side. Your letter of June 7th 1904 however, in repeating the

---

4 HWRO 705:445:8255.

terms, mentions Six months' notice on either side. The point however is immaterial; as to restrict your freedom of action in any way is the last thing we should wish. Please therefore entirely disregard the question of notice

Yours very truly
Novello & Co.Ltd.[5]

75, Gloucester Place, Portman Square, W.
June 30.1911

Dear Sirs:

Many thanks for your letter of yesterday's date referring to the termination of our publishing agreement.

I am writing more fully on the matter to Mr.Alfred Littleton as we have generally discussed matters together & I will explain my position to him.

Believe me
Yours v try
Edward Elgar

75, Gloucester Place, Portman Square, W.
June 30 1911

My dear Littleton:

I am very grateful to you for your kind letter about the termination of our agreement. I want to tell you at once that I have made no other arrangements and have not contemplated making any. I am not dissatisfied with the firm, although there are some minor points we might have adjusted—not worth considering really apart from the big question, which is as follows.

I have never deceived myself as to my true commercial value & see that everything of mine, as I have often said, dies a natural death;—if you look at the accounts you will see that a new thing of mine 'lasts' about a year & then dies & is buried in the mass of English music: under these inevitable circumstances it seems to me that the royalty system we adopted in 1904 cannot really be satisfactory to either of us. I am now well on in years & have to consider a 'move' & make a new home—under the depressing state of my music I have to reconsider this entirely & shall probably go abroad or to a cottage in the country & leave the musical world entirely.

My reference to a 'sum down' refers to the fact that other publishers have offered me in the past, a substantial sum for a new work: under the present strain this wd. suit me better & there is no reason, that I see, that your firm shd. not do this: only I have *no* work on hand & contemplate no large work in the future—I may *think* of large works but I shall not write them; to write them is labour lost. I hope I may see you. I write thus hastily to assure you that nothing was farther from my mind than any 'break' with the firm except that the royalty system does not seem to suit my needs: I thought that a

---

[5] HWRO 705:445:8256. The draft in Clayton's hand is preserved in the Novello archives.

formal notice was absolutely necessary for the firm as a Ltd. Company:—
Also the notice (12 months) which the firm waives if I like, had better be
adhered to

> Kindest rgds
> Yrs sincy
> Ed:Elgar

It did not mean that Elgar would never write another work to be published by
Novello. It did mean that, after the expiration of the year, they would bid—or not—
against other publishers for whatever he might produce.

The end of the summer in 1911 brought more unhappiness. The violinist Eugène
Ysaÿe, having given Elgar a great reception in Brussels and promised to play the
Violin Concerto, had not in fact given his scheduled performance with the Philharmonic Society. This may have had something to do with the performing fee which was
charged (by Elgar's desire) whenever the work was played. Now, as Ysaÿe prepared
to play the Concerto at the Norwich Festival, he sent the publishers his request for the
orchestral material, so as to try over the work with his own orchestra in Brussels.

Godinne
5 Sept.1911.

Messieurs.

Sur le point de terminer les études du Concerto de Elgar dont vous êtes les
éditeurs, et désireux de le voir avec Orchestre à Bruxelles avant de le faire
connaître à l'étranger, je viens vous prier de me dire si vous voulez mettre
gracieusement à ma disposition le partition et le materiel complet d'orchestre; Mon ami, Monsieur Elgar, m'ayant dit qu'entre lui et moi il ne
saurait être question *d'aucune droit à payer* pour l'execution de l'oeuvre. Je
suppose que vous serez du même avis et que je pourrai faire connaitre le
Concerto partout où les moyens artistiques m'en serant fournis sans les
conditions spéciales que vous avez assignées a l'exécution.

J'attends votre rèponse dont les plus courts délais et vous prie d'agréer
l'assurance de ma haute considération.

> E.Ysaÿe

The following draft reply is preserved in Novello's archives:

London
12/9.11.

Mr.Ysaye

Surely Mr.Ysaye will recognise that the composer of a great work like the
Elgar Concerto should have some financial return for all his time & labour he
bestowed upon it.

This return can only come from performances of the work when a large
audience is attracted by the work itself and by the distinguished performer
who plays the principal part in it.

Surely some fractional part of the receipts of such performances should fall
to the share of the composer. Sir Edward is not a member of the 'Genossen-
schaft' and will therefore receive nothing from that Society. When the work
is performed by Mr.Ysaye, he can certainly arrange that the giver of the
concert shall pay a small fee to the composer who provides one of most
important items of that concert.

In order to make this quite easy we would propose to reduce the fee to
fs.125. pr. performance or fs2000 for 20 performances in one season.

The whole of this amount less a small percentage for use of the material
would be paid to the composer.

Notwithstanding all we have said we will not charge any fee for your
concert on 30 Sept.

On the same day the firm received this telgram from Ysaÿe:

Sans confirmation notre accord ni materiel devrai renoncer Elgar 30
septembre   Ysaye

It was followed by a letter.

Godinne
13 Sept.1911
Monsieur.

Après l'entretien que j'avais eu avec Monsieur Rosenkranz, au cours
duquel j'ai expliqué clairement les raisons qui me forçaient à ne pouvoir
souscrire au nouveau rêglement affecté a l'exécution du Concerto d'Elgar,
j'avais cru et espéré non seulement recevoir *de suite* le matériel dont j'avais
besoin pour étudier l'oeuvre avec les moyens dont je dispose ici-même, mais
aussi qu'il ne serait plus un moment question d'un droit a payer ni pour moi
ni pour les Sociétés philharmoniques auxquelles je proposerais l'oeuvre. Je
vois par la lettre que vous m'ecrivez que je me suis trompé, qu'il y a
Marchandage, que vous me tenez un langage qui s'éloigne singulièrement de
l'idée artistique qui est la seule qui m'ait guidé, moi, pendant le long travail
de Concerto. Je ne discute pas les raisons d'interêt qui vous font agir; je me
refuse d'entrer dans une discussion pénible à ce sujet, je crois seulement qu'il
est peu possible que le Compositeur vous ait invité à m'écrire les misérables
considérations dont la lecture fait mal au coeur. Je regrette de devoir vous
apprendre que je renonce à exécuter le Concerto d'Elgar; cette résolution
m'est dictée par une raison de dignité où les transactions commerciales n'ont
rien à voir.

Recevez,Mr, mes Salutations.   E.Ysaÿe

Two notes in Novello archives show the next moves.

Telegram sent in answer to this to say our representative would come &
see him

Concerto material sent to Ysaye on 13th Sept: Score, 8-8-6-6/5 [strings], 20 Wind. No Charge

This was because Elgar himself was so keen that Ysaÿe should play the Concerto. The files contain this undated pencil notation:

Mr.May saw Elgar with reference to this matter & he reports that Elgar seemed very anxious that Ysaye should play the work, but stated that the question of fee was a matter for the firm to decide & he suggested that a nominal fee should be quoted for say 10 performances.

At the same time Mr.May thinks from Elgar's remarks that he would be very pleased if we would allow Ysaye to play the work even if he was *not* disposed to pay any fee.

The firm then confirmed the position by letter, a draft of which is preserved.

Londres
14/9.11
Monsieur Eugene Ysaye,
Illustre Maitre,

Vous confirmant notre lettre d'hier nous vous informons que le matériel d'orchestre (partition, parties & doublures) vous a été éxpedié hier par la poste. Ce matériel n'etant pas publié, nous ne pouvons le vendre. Ne pourriez-vous arranger à Bruxelles etc (Concert anglais)

Alfred Littleton noted with this draft:

It is curious to think that while Mr.Isaye is in receipt of a larger fee per performance than any other violinist he should consider it just that the composer—who provides the music which he plays—should be content with nothing & presumably live on air.

At this point Littleton explained the matter to Elgar.

2 Palmeira Court[,] Hove, Brighton.
Sep 17.1911
My dear Elgar

I think you know that we have been in correspondence with Isaye about performances of the Concerto on the Continent. My brother thinking the matter important and wishing to please Isaye sent Rosenkranz to Belgium to see him but of course he could not settle anything definitely at a first or introductory meeting. A day or two after this Isaye wrote and his letter was brought down here to me by Rosenkrantz [*sic*].

I drafted what I thought to be a very careful & diplomatic reply. I did not insist on payment of a performing fee but I endeavoured to explain the justice of the point that some fee should be paid by somebody. But justice is something that Mr. Isaye does not appear to care about or understand—and in reply we receive the enclosed rude letter.

In writing as I did I thought I was carrying out your idea—with which I entirely agree—that if a work of yours is the attraction of a concert or even only a portion of it you ought to be paid something whether small or large & this fee I proposed to Isaye was ridiculously small. If by any chance you should think it advisable to try and bring Isaye round again—you can of course write & say that we exceeded our instructions & propose any terms you might think proper. I mention this now to save time and because I know it will be a disappointment to you if Isaye does not play the concerto. He has evidently devoted a great deal of time to the study of the work & will not want to give it up lightly.

He has telegraphed to [Robert] Newman to say that he will not play the Concerto in England. This is most unreasonable as the question of performing fee does not concern him in any way. It is agreed to in each case and will be paid by the concert givers as it has been paid many times before—

The *great artist*! thinks of nothing but collecting his own exorbitant fees and it seems to me that the words 'transactions commerciales' and 'Marchandage' apply much more to him than to anyone else. I should like to show the whole thing up in the public press—

> With kindest regards
> Yours very sincerely
> Alfred H Littleton

I have told them at Wardour Street to send you the previous correspondence including copy of my letter.

Robert Newman was concert manager for Henry Wood, who conducted the Norwich Festival.

On the same day he wrote to Elgar, Littleton wrote to his own publishing manager, C. J. May.

2 Palmeira Court[,] Hove, Brighton.
Sep 17.1911

Dear May

I have written to Elgar and sent him Isaye's letter. Will you please send him at once all the other correspondence including my draft & Rosenkrantz's last letter. Will you please write to Newman & say that we wrote to Isaye merely pointing out that it was only just that the composer should receive some small fee from the *concert givers* when the Concerto was played on the continent. We did not insist in any way as we thought the matter was under discussion—

It is most unreasonable that he should decline to play the work in England as there is no dispute about the performing fee and in any case it does not affect him *in any way*—

I hear he has spent a very large amount of time in studying the work—&
will not like losing this—and Mr.Newman who knows him so well might very
likely bring him round at least as far as England is concerned.

Yours sincerely
Alfred H Littleton

We must not write direct to Isaye any more—

A series of telegrams followed. On 20 September Elgar telegraphed to the firm:

Still unwell. Professor Terry will call this afternoon about 4.30 to consult you
for me regarding Violin Concerto Ysaye performances.   Edward Elgar.

Two days later Elgar received a 'Reply Paid' telegram from Henry Wood:

Very many thanks for wire[.] Monday will be too late for Saturdays
conference[.] If you could wire Novello instructing them to agree Ysaye
conditions all will be well not only in England but on the continent as I am
sure Ysaye will play your concerto everywhere and give a superb performance   Wood

This caused Elgar to send another wire to Novello:

Received telegram Henry Wood begging me accede to Ysayes terms[.]
Understand final conference tomorrow presumably for Norwich[.] Have
begged Wood consult you[.] Letter follows   Edward Elgar.

Plas Gwyn, Hereford.
Sep 22 1911 4.pm
Dear Sirs:

I have just recd. the encld. telegram from Sir Henry Wood—in reply, & in
a letter sent by this post, I have said I cannot understand Ysayes attitude at
all & have asked him to take you into his confidence—if this has not already
happened—& see if anything can be done

When I was conducting one of Ysaye's concerts in Bruxelles last March we
were talking of the possibil[it]y of his playing the Concerto & I promised I
wd. conduct the first performance which he proposed to give in Bruxelles for
nothing. I have heard nothing since & am quite at a loss to understand what
he means.

I suppose I must give up everything for the sake of art & must leave you to
decide

Yrs try
Edward Elgar

That day Lady Elgar had gone to London to see her solicitor. She wanted to break
a trust fund established long ago, so as to have funds to buy a large house in

Hampstead which Elgar liked, and where he thought he could continue composing. The next morning she received this telegram from Elgar (who had remained in Hereford), beginning with their private code-word of greeting:

Anemone[.] No interesting letters and no news[.] Say to Novello hope Ysaye performances can be arranged at almost any sacrifice[.] Love

Alice went to Queen's Hall, where she met with Henry Wood, Robert Newman, and Alfred Littleton's son. Alfred Littleton himself remained in semi-retirement in Brighton, from where he telegraphed to Elgar:

You will of course do as you think best[.] I cannot take part in giving way to such a person[.] Littleton Brighton.

Next day he wrote to his son:

2 Palmeira Court[,] Hove, Brighton.
Sep 24.1911
My dear Jack

The Isaye affair is as you say most extraordinary. The colossal impertin-ence of saying he will not play the concerto in *England* if any fee is paid—goes beyond anything—I am very much afraid Elgar is inclined to give way to Isaye even on the England point. I have written to him pointing out how wrong this would be—and saying that we will not give way under any circumstances[.] Please tell Uncle Gussie this and see that nobody does anything contrary to this position. If the parts are asked for they must be sent with a bill for £2.12.6 charged for the particular performance on the particular date whatever it may be—

With regard to the performing fee we must of course wait for Elgar—but if he gives way I don't see how we can ever make a charge to anybody else.

Love to you all

Your affectionate Father
Alfred H Littleton

Littleton was right. Elgar gave way, telegraphing to Ysaÿe:

Pour vous aucunes conditions.

He wrote to Alfred Littleton:

Plas Gwyn, Hereford.
Sep 25 1911
My dear Littleton

I am so much obliged to you for your letter: I quite feel with you but I felt I *had* to give way to Ysaye: so I wired this morning saying he must have his way: Wood & Newman seemed disgusted I think at Y. but laid great stress on their having *three* performances arranged—besides Norwich & I could not well stand in the way of this & I dreaded the sort of 'Scandale' & the quite misunderstanding way the press wd. treat the matter. Since I telegraphed to Ysaye—Newman has just wired that the concerts are *off*—he says 'Sorry for troubling you but have recd. letter from Ysaye this morning which prevents his Concerts taking place Newman'—so the very reason I gave in to—is now vanished.

I am sick of it all. I am better & hope to be in town soon & shall see you

> Kindest rgds
> Yrs sncly
> Ed:Elgar

When he arrived at Norwich, Ysaÿe would hear nothing of the Elgar Concerto but had signified he would play the Beethoven instead. Henry Wood recalled:

... His performance ... was easily the worst I ever directed. In the slow movement his memory went to pieces—indeed, I do not know what he would have done had not Maurice Sons [the leader] prompted him as he went along, playing the solo part on his own violin. Ysaÿe managed to get through but, fond as I was of him, I did think he walked away with two hundred and fifty guineas that night at the expense of much anxiety on my part.[6]

1912

Ysaÿe was determined not to be dictated to over the Elgar Concerto, as he showed again when Arthur Nikisch wanted to arrange a first performance in Berlin with him. The concert agent Wolff advised engaging Emil Telmanyi, as Ysaÿe was 'impossible'. But Ysaÿe never returned the orchestral material sent him in September, and by the beginning of the new year 1912 there were rumours of Ysaÿe performances of the Concerto in eastern Europe, where he must have imagined that the arm of Novello would not reach. Russia remained outside European copyright conventions. Clayton wrote:

[160, Wardour Street, W.]
January 9th. [191]2

Dear Elgar

Your Violin Concerto was performed at Bremen on the 3rd instt. and at Berlin yesterday. In both cases we were made aware of the fact by the music dealers, who wrote to us for miniature scores & V. & P. arrangements for sale.

We at once wrote for particulars & found that Ysaye was to play the Solo part on each occasion & that at Berlin the Orchestra was to be the Berlin

[6] *My Life of Music* (Gollancz, 1946), p. 252.

Philharmonic under Nikisch. On hearing these details we wrote & said that there would be a performing fee of £7.17.6 to include the loan of the music.

We have written several times to Bremen, but can get no reply. But from Berlin we heard yesterday (from Wolff the Concert agent) that Ysaye has told them that you have given him permission to perform the work anywhere (on the Continent I presume) without any fee! We have replied that we do not know of any such arrangement, but that we will communicate with you on the subject: & we warned them that in any event we should expect to be paid a fee for the loan of the music. I may add that in neither case have we been applied to for the loan of the music, & that Ysaye has obviously lent the music which we sent to him in September *for a special occasion*

It seems to us that we are likely to lose not only the performing fees but also the entire control over the work on the Continent, if Ysaye is to be at liberty to retain the Score & parts, and play the work wherever he pleases.

In the two cases mentioned neither Ysaye nor the Concert givers intimated to us their intention to perform the work. We discovered the fact solely as a result of orders reaching us for the miniature scores etc . . . . from the Bremen & Berlin music sellers.

The situation is an awkward one & needs careful handling. But before taking any step we ought to know whether it is correct that you have made an arragement with Ysaye, &, if so, what that arrangement is.

Will you enlighten us on that point.

Hoping you are better & that you are pleased with your new home

Yours sincerely
Henry R:Clayton.

Elgar replied from the house in Hampstead which he and his wife had at last purchased. The telegraphic address was a typical Elgarian play on words—a mirror-arrangement of his distinctions 'Sir' and 'OM'.

Severn House, 42, Netherhall Gardens, Hampstead, N.W.

Telegraphic address

Jan 10th 1912   *Siromoris, London*

Dear Clayton:

I fear the Concerto-Ysaye business will prove to be a nuisance: what occurred was this: Y. was down to play it at Norwich & also at three concerts at Q's Hall: I heard—I forget how (I think I heard from *Novellos* in the first instance) that he refused to pay a fee &, subsequently, refused to play if anyone else paid a fee,—I mean the concert givers. Wood & Newman pressed me to give way to Ysaye on the point of fees saying *they would pay* the performing fees. I wrote to Alfred & he could not advise one way or the other, in fact left it to me; so I wired to Ysaye asking him what the matter was as I did not understand the position—he replied that the matter was contained in his correspondence with Novello: Queen's Hall pressed me further (very urgently as the concerts had to be announced—or rather fully advertised, they had been announced,—or withdrawn.) & I telegraphed to Ysaye as near as I can remember '*pour vous aucunes conditions*'. Of course I had in my mind Norwich & Q's Hall. I did not gather the fact that you had supplied him with the orchestral material—this fact makes the real difficulty.

Y. is evidently interpreting my telegram in a very wide sense & I don't see what can be done as long as he HOLDS *the orchl. parts*

I am better but have not been out of the house (which is a delightful home & I hope you will see it soon—we are not 'in' yet)—we cannot get the telephone (applied for months ago) put in so I send my regd. telegraphic address.

I wrote to Alfred about the Coliseum work & the manager will put the publishing possibilities before you

> Kind rgds
> Yours siny
> Edward Elgar

The final reference in Elgar's letter is to the 'Imperial Masque', *The Crown of India*, which Oswald Stoll had persuaded him to write. Its story will be taken up on page 760.

Next day Novello wrote again to Ysaÿe. The lengthy draft in the firm's archives, written in Clayton's hand, went over all the old ground and added:

We have now laid the matter before Sir Edward Elgar and we have his reply. He assures us that he did not give you the permission which you claim. No doubt you have misunderstood the meaning of the concession which Sir Edward made to you.

No answer was received, and early in the next month Clayton wrote to Elgar again.

[160, Wardour Street, W.]
February 5th. [191]2
Dear Elgar

The Ysaye trouble is becoming acute and serious. We learned on Friday that he gave a third performance of the Violin Concerto on Jan 13th, this time at Konigsberg on the Russian Frontier. Again he has not consulted us either as regards the performing right, or the use of the music . . .

We wrote to him on Jan.11th. asking him to return the music, & explaining to him that his performance of the work without our sanction in Germany or elsewhere was irregular, & that you had not authorized any such performance. He has ignored our letter. So we have determined to take action against him in the Belgian Courts to establish the performing right in the work, unless in the meantime he agrees to hand over the music.

Before we do this we shall make one more attempt to persuade Ysaye to return the music, & I think we must ask for your co operation. I send you a copy of what we wrote to him on Jan.11th. Could you not write & tell him that you have read that letter, that it agrees with your view of the case, & that you would be personally obliged to him if he would end this unpleasant controversy by returning the music to us. . . .

We have every reason to believe that Ysaye is now on his way to Russia, or in Russia, & that he will play your work there without any licence from us or from you. We have of course no rights in Russia, but as he can only perform the work there, by unlawfully detaining our music, which was sent to him for another purpose, I should think the Belgian Courts would take that fact into account in awarding damages against Ysaye.

The fact that Ysaye is playing your work without fee is known all over Germany, & it is supposed that he has your authority, even though we warned the Bremen & Berlin people, *before their performances took place*, that he has no such right. Last Saturday week Kreisler rang me up & asked me to send the music to Vienna for him to play the work there tonight. Having arranged all about the music with me, Kreisler mentioned what Ysaye is doing, & *objected on that account to pay any performing fee himself*. I asked him whether he considered it fair to you that while he is being paid to play your music you should go unrewarded. He replied that it was his own Concert, & that he was not being paid. I retorted that the combination of Elgar & [Kreisler] was a guarantee of substantial profits, which would be his, but which you would not share. He still demurred, so I had to tell him pretty plainly that unless he agreed to pay the fee I could not without your authority send the music to Vienna. He did not like the idea of the matter being referred to you, & promptly agreed to pay the fee. But I should not be at all surprised if we have some difficulty in getting that music back from Vienna.

I have told you all this so that you may realize the situation. Directly I heard of Ysaye's agitation to be allowed to play the work without fee, I protested to everyone here that if we gave way to him it would be almost impossible to justify our charges to Kreisler and Zacharewitsch, & to lesser lights like Margaret Holloway. Things have turned out exactly as I have anticipated—Kreisler has made his protest, & the rest will follow suit. In my opinion the bottom will be knocked out of the work unless we bring Ysaye to book.

By the bye, can you send me any letters or telegrams which you received from Ysaye about the middle of September about the Concerts. I think it must have been about Septr.25th. that you wired him 'pour vous aucunes conditions', for you wired us on that day telling us that you had had to agree to Ysaye's terms. I want particularly to see Ysaye's letter or telegram to you, which caused you to wire that message to him.

Yours sincerely
Henry R:Clayton.

Severn House, 42,Netherhall Gardens, Hampstead, N.W.
Feb 6 1912

Dear Clayton

I am just off to [conduct at] Leeds & have only time for a hurried word[.] I
am writing direct to Godfrey about his programme [of Elgar's works at
Bournemouth] which will save you time & trouble

Yes—the Oxford people paid me on the spot Decr. 6 [25 guineas for
conducting *The Kingdom*]

As to the two Agreements I enclose *one* signed but the other says seven
copies as six [allowed the publishers for sending to reviewers etc]—isn't this
unusual[?] it shd. I believe be 13/12—the Vn. & PF. arrgt. scarcely comes into
the ordinary Sheet music [,] Piano piece, or Song category?

As to the performances of the Concerto (Ysaye &c) I fear I cannot turn up
the correspondence as things have been so much disarrayed in moving but I
will cause a search to be made. I gave way *entirely* to oblige Queen's Hall &
with them (same orchestra & conductor) Norwich Festival & only to save the
awful trouble in rearranging the programmes & QUITE PRIVATELY the Queen's
Hall people said they wd. see the fee was paid in each case irrespective of any
views Ysaye might hold—then I wired to Ysaye—as I said before I had no
knowledge or perhaps recollection (I *may* have been told) that Y. had the
orchl. material

Kind rgds
Yrs sincerely
Edward Elgar

If a letter is necessary how wd the *enclosed sketch* do? Perhaps the end
paragraph is too *angular*?

[160, Wardour Street, W.]
February 7th. [191]2.

Dear Elgar

Many thanks for your letter.

Thanks also for the return of the Assignments of the Violin Concerto. I
stamped the one you signed this morning at Somerset House, and tomorrow
morning the Copyright and the Performing-right will be duly registered at
Stationers' Hall, & the Official Certificates, which is what we are playing for,
will be in my hands about Monday next.

The other assignment of the V. & P. arrangement is quite correct. We allow
7 copies as Six on *all Folio music except* Orchestral Scores and Band parts. I
have never heard of any exception either at home or abroad. It is moreover a
valuable concession to the Trade, & by means of it our Travellers frequently
induce Country dealers to order half a dozen copies when they would

otherwise order only two or three. It is an absurd custom, but it is too well established to be interfered with, I am afraid.

Your letter to Ysaye exactly meets the case, but A.H.L has suggested two trifling alterations which perhaps you may care to adopt. I agree with him that 'evading' is some-what point blank as compared with 'not conforming to'.

If you will write the letter & will send it to me I will have it registered, *unless you think that that would be an unnecessary precaution as between you & Ysaye*. His Brussels address is:—

> Profr. E.Ysaye
> 48,Avenue Brugmann
> Bruxelles.

Can you let me know *who played the Solo part* at the recent Cambridge performance of the Violin Concerto (Feb 1st.)

Also let me know whether the Leeds people are paying you your fee for tonight's performance *direct*.

I want to see you at the first convenient opportunity about *an apparent desire* to play *both* your symphonies in Buenos Aires!!

> Yours sincerely
> Henry R:Clayton.

Severn House, 42, Netherhall Gardens, Hampstead, N.W.
Feb 13 1912
Dear Clayton:

I have been without one single moment. I now send the letter for Ysaye [—] please see that it is quite correct.

I also send the agreemt signed.

Mr.Louis Pecksai played the concerto at Cambridge (and very well indeed).

The Leeds people paid me [£]52/10/- the other evening.

I am interested in B.Ayres—is it on a ship? I met the conductor last summer (name forgotten) of the scheme of the Hamburg Amerika Line—to take a large ship with an orchestra of 100 & visit S.America &c &c—I will come down as soon as possible.

> Yrs sny
> Ed Elgar

He enclosed the original and a copy of the following letter. The original was posted to Ysaÿe by registered mail on 13 February; the copy was retained in Novello's archives.

Severn House, 42,Netherhall Gardens[,] Hampstead, N.W.
9th Feby 1912   *copy*

Dear Mr Ysaye

Messrs Novello inform me that you still have the Orchestral Material of my Violin Concerto.

I sent you a telegram only referring to the three proposed Concerts in London in September and October last and Norwich Festival as Messrs Novello gave me permission to deal with those performances.

I have no power to give you full use of the Concerto and if you cannot agree to Messrs Novello's terms, which of course concern me very materially, I shall be obliged if you will return the Orchestral Material.

I am deeply sensible of the honour you do me by performing the Concerto and I am sure you do not wish to do very considerable harm to me by not conforming to the ordinary course of business.

> Kindest regards
> Yours faithfully
> Edward Elgar.

Again there was no answer, but Novello received a programme showing that Ysaÿe played the Concerto in Vienna, with the Wiener Tonkünstler-Orchester under Oskar Nedbal, on 23 February. In mid-March Clayton wrote his final letter to Ysaÿe.

[160, Wardour Street, W.]
March 14th [19]12

Dear Sir

On January 11th we addressed to you, at your house in Brussels, a letter in which we called your attention to the fact that the performing rights in Sir Edward Elgar's 'Violin Concerto' are reserved, that Sir Edward Elgar had not authorized any of the performances which about that time you were giving on the continent; and that the score and band parts which you made use of on those occasions are our property; and that they were lent to you *only* with a view to your rehearsing the work in anticipation of certain English performances, which had been arranged when we sent you the Orchestral Material.

You have not favoured us with a reply to that letter; which we much regret, because, if you do not answer our letters, we can see no prospect of terminating the unfortunate misunderstanding between yourself and us, without invoking the assistance of our lawyers, and that is a step which we are anxious to avoid, or to postpone until the last possible moment.

May we now respectfully ask you to be good enough to return to us the music which we sent to you on Sept.13th 1911; and may we also inform you that Sir Edward Elgar has recently assigned to us all his rights in his 'Violin

Concerto' viz:—his publishing rights, and his rights of public performance.

We therefore are the only people who are in a position to authorize performances of the work referred to.

Yours faithfully
Novello & Co.Ltd.

This appears to have brought the Ysaÿe performances to an end. He never played the Elgar Concerto in England.

We must now return to take up the main thread of Elgar's relations with his publishers. Just as he was preparing to move into the large and expensively refurbished Severn House (as he himself named it) in Hampstead, there came an unprecedented offer. Oswald Stoll, principal of the Coliseum Theatre, wanted Elgar to write music to an 'Imperial Masque' by Henry Hamilton to celebrate the Indian Coronation of King George V and Queen Mary, to take place later that year. *The Crown of India* would then be played as part of the Coliseum's daily programme of music-hall turns. If the composer could conduct the run of his work, his profits would be greater still. Having moved into Severn House barely a week earlier, Elgar wrote to Alfred Littleton:

Severn House, 42,Netherhall Gardens, Hampstead, N.W.
Jany 8.1912

My dear Littleton:

I have not been very well & had to give up going to Cologne for the 2nd Symphony: I am better now & have been eating something occasionally.

I have agreed with the Coliseum to write the Music to a Masque—this for a Sum down & half profits, subject to a 1^d a copy to the author of the words; I have asked the Manager to communicate with the firm as to publication but of course the Coliseum holds the half share. I write in haste to catch post as the matter is only just concluded

Best rgrds
Yours v sincy
Edward Elgar

The Masque is going to be very gorgeous & patriotic—Indian Durbar—& will last only 30 mins: I shall write the music at once & it will not interfere with other things—I think you will like the idea.

Littleton came up to Severn House on 12 January, and made a note for his files 'that the Firm was prepared to deal with the matter on the basis of a sum down on account of Royalties'. For the Elgar-Novello agreement had still some months to run.

Severn House, 42,Netherhall Gardens, Hampstead, N.W.
Jan 17: 1912

My dear Littleton:

I have written to Mr.Stoll's manager, Mr.B.Shelton, suggesting that he should call upon you in reference to the publication of the Masque.

We are nearly blown away here to-day

Kindest regards
Yours v sincy
Edward Elgar

When Shelton arrived at Novello's offices, however, there was no discussion as to Novello publishing *The Crown of India*—and the cause appeared to arise from Elgar's own actions. Henry Clayton sent to Elgar a summary of events.

160, Wardour Street, W.
January 25th.1912.

Dear Elgar

You will, I think, be expecting to hear the outcome of a visit which we have had to day from Mr.Shelton, who called upon us. I imagine, in consequence of the letter which, you told our Chairman in yours of the 17th.instt., you had sent to him. I see your letter of the 17th. says that you had suggested to Mr.Shelton that he should call upon us in reference to the publication of your Masque; and we were consequently expecting that he would be prepared to discuss the matter more or less on the lines of the verbal proposal made to you by our Chairman when he was with you, I think, on the 12th.instt., that would be, roughly, on the basis of a Sum down and a Royalty. Mr.Shelton, however, has evidently put an entirely different construction upon your wishes in the matter. He absolutely declined to discuss the business on the basis of publication by Novellos. He said that his Principal had already made other arrangements, that the particular kind of music in question was not in our line at all, that our Contract with you had come to an end, and that we had no locus standi!!

When we demurred to his last two pronouncements he informed us that at all events we were out of Court on the question of the existence of the Contract on which we were presuming to rely, and that he had seen our letter to you waiving our right to the 12 months notice for which our Contract provides.

As he had informed us that he had seen our letter to you waiving the right to notice, we thought it was time that we showed him that we are not the unprincipled people which he must have thought us to be after our Chairman's emphatic statement to him a few weeks ago that that Contract was still in force. So we showed him your letter to our Chairman of June 30th.ult, which concludes with the following remark:—

'Also the notice (12 months), which the Firm waives if I like, had better be adhered to.'

No doubt you had forgotten the fact that you had written that letter; for Mr.Shelton was evidently much surprised, and having read your remarks, & having taken a note of the date of the letter, he admitted that that letter put a very different complexion on the case as it affects us.

We told Mr.Shelton that, although our rights were still regulated by the Contract made in 1904, we were nevertheless willing to discuss the business on the lines suggested to you by our Chairman on Jany.12th.

He however declined to discuss matters with us at all, and he left saying he would report to his Principal, and would leave us to settle matters with you.

To that we replied that that would be entirely in accordance with our views, & would be only what was customary in our transactions with you.

For my own part I felt convinced that that would be the easiest, & quite a simple, solution of the difficulties which have arisen.

Yours sincerely
Henry R:Clayton

Since moving into Severn House, Elgar had been affected with giddiness, which it was feared was related to a disturbance of the middle ear. A rest cure was prescribed, and Elgar referred to it in his reply to Clayton.

Severn House, 42,Netherhall Gardens, Hampstead, N.W.
Jan:25.1912

Dear Clayton:

I am sorry about the Masque: I quite thought our agreement was at an end and more than sorry if you have not met with all the courtesy & consideration which shd have been given you.

I hope to be able to see you on Monday—but you will have understood about my enforced semi-idleness—that is to say I am only allowed to do what is absolutely necessary.

Leaving the question of publishing on one side for the moment I will only say that I do not think the Masque is in your line at all & I do not see how your firm could make it a commercial success as others, who exploit this sort of thing, might do. However I want you to understand that I asked the Coliseum to interview you about possible publication before I knew of any offers from other Publishers.

I am glad to hear the Concerto &c are going on. I had a rapturous acct of Leipzig—via Harold Brooke I think

Yours sincerely
Edward Elgar

P.S. I know of *no* arrangements having been made with other publishers—

Within a few days, however, everyone knew of an offer from the firm of Enoch & Sons. The English branch of this firm had been founded in 1869 by Emile Sigismond

Enoch (1844–1924). Enoch's dapper charm and linguistic accomplishments (he spoke English as a native) had built the English firm into a notable competitor with Boosey in the field of ballads. Enoch had secured the publication of Humperdinck's music for *The Miracle*, a pageant-play which Max Reinhardt had produced with supreme success under Charles Cochran's management at the London Olympia in 1911.[1] Enoch's offer for *The Crown of India* promised continental performances in addition to those at the Coliseum: '& it would be a great commercial loss to me' (Elgar wrote to Alfred Littleton) 'if these were not arranged'.[2]

So Novello released Elgar from the arrangement which he himself had asked to carry on for the final year. The firm's letter survives in a draft in Clayton's hand preserved in Novello archives.

Jan.31.1912.

Dear Sir

Having now carefully considered the question of the publication of the music which you have written for the Indian Masque, about to be produced at the Coliseum, we have decided, if in your opinion it is to your interest that the work should be published elsewhere, not to interfere with any other scheme of publication, which you have in view, by asserting our right to the work under the terms of the existing Contract.

We cannot help expressing our great regret that you should have formed that opinion, but, having done so, will you please consider that as far as we are concerned you have a free hand in the matter.

With compliments
             We are dear Sir

Severn House, 42,Netherhall Gardens, Hampstead, N.W.
Feb 1:1912

Dear Sirs:

I am just leaving for Cambridge [to conduct a concert] but hasten to send you a word of thanks, necessarily very hurried, for your generous letter (about which I will write or see you on my return) concerning the publication of the Masque

             Yours very truly
             Edward Elgar

The files contain no further letters from Elgar to Novello about *The Crown of India*. But he sent a personal letter (now missing) to Clayton offering him a gift and expressing such gratitude that it prompted this reply:

[1] Information from Enoch's granddaughter Yvonne Enoch, 1981.
[2] In a brief letter of 31 Jan. 1912, concerned otherwise with concert arrangements.

42, Regent's Park Road, N.W.
March 18th.1912.

Dear Elgar

Many thanks for your exceedingly kind letter. I feel completely over-whelmed, and I am at a loss to find a way of expressing my own feelings without running a risk of hurting yours. Your letter itself is a reward more than ample for any small services which I have been able, by the accident of my position at Novellos, to perform in your interests; and I value that letter more than any gift with which you could possibly supplement it. I hope I am not proud, or ungracious: I know I am not ungrateful. But I must urge two reasons why I must beg you to allow me to decline any further acknowledg-ment of anything that I may have done that meets with your approval.

First I would plead that I take a pleasure in all the voluntary work that I undertake. If it is successful, its success is my reward. If I am rewarded in any other way my efforts lose their charm to me personally, because they thereby become less spontaneous, & I am put under obligations. In my private life, as well as in my business life, I hold many honorary appointments, but if I were to gain anything but good will through holding them I should be anxious to resign them all.

Secondly—Whatever work I undertake at Novellos is performed by me as an Official of that Firm, and I feel very strongly that to the Firm, and not to me, belongs the credit of anything that has through my agency been creditably done.

Therefore please let me record my very grateful appreciation of your kind letter, which I shall treasure all the more because, I find that, arising out of business relationships such letters are rare. But please don't seek to put me under any further obligations, but let me go on making myself as useful as circumstances may permit.

With my very grateful thanks

Yours sincerely
Henry R:Clayton[3]

On 8 February 1912 Enoch & Sons entered into a contract with Elgar, the librettist Hamilton, and Oswald Stoll to publish *The Crown of India*: the terms were £600 advance against royalties.[4] Yet Enoch was in no position to produce orchestral material. He therefore subcontracted this work to the firm of Hawkes & Son (in later years to be amalgamated with Boosey). This led to a curious arrangement: while Enoch produced a complete piano-vocal score of the Masque and controlled the orchestral parts and abbreviated score produced by Hawkes for use in the theatre, Hawkes & Son were allowed to print and publish on their own account a five-movement Suite in full score. Elgar himself was keen for the publication to take place, and he sent on to Enoch a letter from Oliver Hawkes (d. 1919) with his recommenda-tion to Enoch.

[3] HWRO 705:445:8257.
[4] Contract later in the archives of Messrs Edwin Ashdown, who purchased the Enoch firm.

Severn House, 42, Netherhall Gardens, Hampstead, N.W.
March 21:1912

Dear Sirs:

I have received the enclosed from Messrs. Hawkes: they should have permission to issue the original full score of the movements constituting the Suite and the March & any separate numbers: it will be of no use for first class concerts without the *full score*. I recommended your firm, I think via Mr. Broadhurst [Enoch's assistant], to hold the right of publishing the full score of the *complete masque*. I am sorry if there has been any misunderstanding—but it will be useless to issue the orchl. parts without the full score (except in the popular edn. which will go only in theatres & restaurants &c)

> Believe me
> Yrs v tr[ul]y
> Edward Elgar[5]

Alas for Elgar's hopes of better treatment by smaller publishing houses: neither Enoch nor Hawkes was in a position to make use of Elgar's fame as Novello would have done, and the music itself was of a different character. No full orchestral score of the entire Masque ever appeared, and the whereabouts of Elgar's manuscript is now unknown. Hawkes's printed score of the Suite was issued in a small number of copies, of which only a few examples are now in existence. And Enoch's well produced piano-vocal score sold so much below expectation that when I visited their successors, Messrs Edwin Ashdown, in 1982, some copies of the seventy-year-old first edition were still in stock.

Elgar conducted the first fortnight of *The Crown of India*, which opened at the Coliseum on 11 March 1912. Perhaps as a consolation to Novello, he finished and sent off a big setting of Psalm 48, *Great is the Lord*, which he had sketched in the summer of 1910 in the wake of the Violin Concerto: the psalm-setting contained strong echoes of the Concerto's themes. But Elgar's health was worse than ever. One eminent consultant diagnosed 'gout in the head', and a new rest-cure was prescribed to keep Elgar confined to the house for much of April. His last engagement before beginning this was to conduct the Second Symphony at a concert promoted by Henry Balfour Gardiner (1877–1950) on 27 March. Two days later he wrote to Clayton, for Novello were still managing his concert affairs, and continued to do so for many years.

Severn House, 42,Netherhall Gardens, Hampstead,N.W.
March 29 1912

Dear Clayton:

Many thanks for Mr.B.Gardiner's cheque: I return his letter to you.

I have to undergo (if that's the word) this gout cure commencing next Monday—I think after all I shall remain *here* in seclusion—so if there is anything floating that you want me to see to let me hear before Monday if possible.

I have nothing really to say. I am sending a gigantic Anthem to the firm

---

[5] Ashdown archives.

which I fear will be commercially not much to you—the organ part is important & must be on three staves: it is very big stuff of Wesley length but alas! not of Wesley grandeur.

> Yours sincerely
> Edward Elgar

Elgar spent most of April 'in cold storage', as he said. On 3 May Alfred Littleton came to lunch at Severn House to report on the negotiations which he had taken over at Elgar's request with the Leeds Festival. Now that Sir Charles Stanford had departed as chief conductor, it was arranged that Elgar should share the conducting at the 1913 Festival with Arthur Nikisch and Hugh Allen. Also it was mooted that Elgar should write a new orchestral work for the Leeds Festival: in the event he fulfilled an old scheme to write a symphonic 'study' of Shakespeare's Falstaff.

Before that, Elgar was to complete another long-contemplated project for the Birmingham Festival in October 1912. This was his setting of Arthur O'Shaughnessy's Ode, 'We are the music makers', and it was understood from the beginning that Novello were to publish it. But this would be a major work, and barely five months remained before the scheduled première. Late in May he was still struggling with his sketches. On the 23rd, Lady Elgar noted in her diary: 'E. not very happy over his work—not "lit up" yet'.

At Novello, Clayton had undertaken negotiations for Elgar to conduct at a Brighton Festival in November. They wanted a new work, but were unable to meet Elgar's fee, so Clayton suggested they should give the second performance of *The Music Makers*.

Severn House, 42, Netherhall Gardens, Hampstead, N.W.
May 23 1912

Dear Clayton: Brighton.

Many thanks for your letter which, I fear, has given you trouble regarding the lengthy negociations: I quite agree that your suggestions are for the best & I should have agreed to them at once but I waited to be able to tell you about the new Ode—it [is] for *chorus* & *Contralto solo*—orchestra & organ of course: it should last 25–30 minutes. I am hoping to send some M.S. to you soon. I send the exact title

> In greatest haste
> Yours sincly
> Edwd. Elgar

Ode—*'The Music Makers'*. for Contralto solo & Chorus [—] words by Arthur O'Shaughnessy.

Throughout much of June he worked at the short score, sending it in to Novello portion by portion for printing and sending to the Birmingham Festival Chorus to rehearse. Proofs of earlier sections (such as the reference to Babel in stanza 3) were arriving for correction side by side with new composition, as Elgar prepared the penultimate part of the work for his wife to take down to Harold Brooke with this note:

Severn House, 42,Netherhall Gardens, Hampstead, N.W.
July 12 1912

Dear Mr.Brooke:

Here is some more & the rest is short & will be with you very soon.
I also send the words. I have made a sad mess of
'Babel itself IN (not with) [our mirth;']
I suppose it was unconscious cerebration—working to the Babel idea. I note
that more proofs are coming & rejoice thereat—therefor & therefrom

Yours (as you demean yourself[)]
Edwd.Elgar

Six days later he sent the final portion of vocal score. Through the summer he
corrected proofs, completed the orchestration, and rehearsed Muriel Foster in the
contralto solos of the work. One letter written later to Harold Brooke shows the same
difficulty with tempo markings that McNaught had experienced in *The Banner of St
George* at the beginning of the century. A similar notation in *The Apostles* had caused
trouble since 1903. At cue 32 in *The Music Makers* Elgar marked '♪ = 112 (♩ of
preceding bar)'. As soon as other conductors saw it, they wondered what it meant.
Elgar wrote:

Severn House[,] Hampstead, N.W.
Nov 28 1912

Dear Mr Brooke:

Please leave IN the superfluous time direction—I took it out of the full
score because it came on a page by itself.
It is EXTRAORDINARY how the simplest change puzzles people—as in the
final Chorus of the Apostles—♩ = ♩—now here we say ♪ = ♩. of the preceding—giving the metronome marks. Sir F.Bridge on going thro' the work with
me said 'these directions are by no means clear'—so I give up.
Neither Richter or Steinbach ever understood the change in the Apostles!

Yours sincly
Edward Elgar

The first performance, conducted by Elgar himself, had taken place on 1 October
1912, and it seemed to make a considerable impression. This was summarized in a
letter written by Clayton in response to an expression of interest from William
Hannam on behalf of the Leeds Festival in 1913 (for which *Falstaff* was commissioned). Hannam was now exploring the possibility of including *The Music Makers*
as well.

[160, Wardour Street, W.]
November 8th. [191]2.

Dear Mr.Hannam.

Many thanks for your letter which I will keep quite private until I see Elgar, & afterwards as far as I am concerned. I will also ask Elgar to keep your secret until you announce your programme.

As regards 'The Music Makers' we honestly believe that we have got a really good Elgar work. We have heard a good many opinions expressed about it by well known musicians, & people who frequent musical circles, & there can be no doubt that the work has made a great impression. The Chairman of our Company heard the work produced at Birmingham, and he had a talk with R.H.Wilson—the Birmingham Choir-trainer—about it. Wilson told Littleton that both he & the Chorus were enchanted with the work, & that during rehearsals the Choir seemed to be quite excited about it. Dr.Vogt, the conductor of the famous Mendelssohn Choir, of Toronto, heard it at Birmingham, & he told me he considered it a very fine thing. (He mentioned, incidentally, that it was a pity that Elgar conducted it! So I assume from that that he meant that the work itself was worthy of a better presentation than it got at Birmingham.) I believe that the Mendelssohn Choir are going to do the work.

Already we have booked Fifteen performances. The second performance takes place at the Brighton Festival on the 13th instt.—Elgar conducting. and the third at the Albert Hall (Royal Choral Society's Concert) on Novr.28th. Bridge conducting.

Elgar wrote to me on October 29th. to tell me that Steinbach, who conducts the Lower Rhine Festival next year in May or June, has expressed his intention of performing the work at that Festival; and that we would probably have to get out a German Edition. I need hardly say that I wrote & told Elgar that we are quite prepared to do all that is required of us in that way.

I think the work is now well launched, & that a successful career is assured for it. I don't think it can possibly fail to pass the severe test of a Leeds Festival programme, & I hope for everyone's sake that it will find a place there.

Perhaps you may like to know of other performances in the near future: they are:—

    4th Performance—Sunderland Philharmonic   N.Kilburn—Novr.20th.
    5th Performance—Worcester Festival Choral Socy. I.Atkins—Nov 26th.
    6th Performance—Liverpool Philharmonic   Sir F.Cowen—Feb.18th.
Thanking you for your letter

Yours very sincerely
Henry R:Clayton.

Yet the excitement which had been generated by the appearance of Elgar choral works in the past was largely missing now. Elgar's letter of 29th October contained more than a hint of weariness:

Severn House, 42,Netherhall Gardens, Hampstead, N.W.
Oct 29 1912

Dear Clayton: . . .

Ode

Steinbach *says* this is just the thing for the Lower Rhine Festival (*he* conducts) this [next] year in May or June. I have given him a copy & he will return in a fortnight or so &, of course, may quite have changed his mind. If it comes off (the Ode not his mind) there will be a German translation to be thought of. Please understand that I do not press this—my ambition has been dead for years & it seems that all the honour & glory is only an infernal expense!

> Kind rgrds
> Yrs sincerely
> Edward Elgar

Clayton wrote back the same day assuring Elgar of the firm's desire to have a German translation made in case Steinbach did take up *The Music Makers*. Elgar replied:

Hampstead
Oct 30.1912

Dear Clayton

Thanks for yours: if the translation *is* done why not *Buths*—he does not I think pretend to be a poet but in this case we want a musician first & we know he did the other things well. I shall be glad if you will send a copy to him anyway—I am writing to him but of course shall not say or suggest anything about translation

> Yrs sny
> Ed:Elgar

Nothing definite had been heard from Steinbach by the beginning of December, when Clayton met Elgar to discuss Hannam's proposal to do *The Music Makers* at the 1913 Leeds Festival. But the idea was ill-fated, and Elgar's conducting for that Festival was arranged without including *The Music Makers*.

Still he had hopes of the Steinbach performance.

Severn House, 42, Netherhall Gardens, Hampstead, N.W.
Dec 27 1912

Dear Clayton:

Please send Professor J Buths[,] Ehrenstrasse 17[,] Düsseldorf a.R. a copy of the Music Makers

I asked for this long ago I believe & he's just written to say he has never received it.

When *Steinbach* was last here he said he is going to do the Ode at the Fest & verbally engaged Mrs.Goetz to sing it—he also said he should write to you at once (a month or more ago) about a translation &c.&c. Has he done so? If not had we better not send him a reminder?

> Yrs sincy
> Edward Elgar

Yet without any definite commitment from Steinbach (or anyone else) to perform *The Music Makers* in Germany, Novello were reluctant to go to the expense of a translation.

1913

The beginning of 1913 was a bad time for Elgar. A trip to Italy in January and a cure at Llandrindod Wells in February were ineffectual in raising his spirits, dogged by illness and giddiness. A visit to his sister Pollie and her family in Worcestershire left him no better. On 23 April he conducted *Gerontius* in Wales at Mountain Ash, where the Elgars stayed with Major and Mrs Gray. He wrote afterwards:

Severn House, 42,Netherhall Gardens, Hampstead, N.W.
Ap 29.1913
Dear Clayton:

Many thanks for yours of the 26th.—I am not very well but got through the Welsh business: I will of course send a letter to the choir which did very well—their only faults arose from inexperience of orchestras: I return the letter—the writer must have an odd opinion of composers & conductors and soloists! There was no applause when the work ended—in the enormous room half the people knew nothing about it—*each person brought a baby*! (which cried—*all* of which cried continuously)—why we shd. be expected to go back when nobody apparently ever knew we had been 'on' I cannot see. The room was too large—the executive means too small (the orchestra was ridiculously small)—the audience ignorant & unwieldy. But the chorus was good & enthusiastic.

All this is of course *private*.

Our host & hostess were charming & *most kind*

> Yrs sincy
> Edwd Elgar

It was late May before he settled to the composition of *Falstaff* from his sketches. The work was in theory to be thrown onto the open market, but he kept in touch with Novello about it. In June Clayton sent on a letter of enquiry about *Falstaff* from Ferdinand Löwe, who had conducted several of Elgar's works in Vienna. Elgar replied:

Severn House[,] Hampstead, N.W.
June 22.1913

Dear Clayton—

'*Falstaff*'

Thanks for your letter about Vienna: the thing is getting on & the score will be ready shortly—some is of course done now

It should last about 20 minutes.

If you wd. kindly tell Dr.Lowe this & incidentally say I wd. go to Vienna.

Nikisch is anxious for the German translation of the Ode for Berlin. Steinbach sd. he was expecting it for this Autumn—is anything being done?

Schillings wants me to go to Stuttgart & Nikisch proposes I should conduct also—but directly anything (hitherto) has been sd. about terms——vanish! I am coming down to see you

> Yrs sny
> Edwd.Elgar

[160, Wardour Street, W.]
June 24th [191]3.

Dear Elgar

Many thanks for your letter of the 22nd instt. We have written to Dr.Lowe at Vienna as suggested.

I think it would be well if you could come at your leisure & have a talk with A.H.L about a German translation of the Ode. If Steinbach means business we are quite ready to go ahead, but after mentioning the matter to you last October, he appears to have let the matter drop. For he has not written to us, & we have heard nothing since the enclosed correspondence passed between you & me.

You will see from mine of October 29th. that we must obtain permission from Canon Deacon [the poet's executor] to make a translation.

> Yours sincerely
> Henry R:Clayton.

Elgar had promised to score his setting of Psalm 48, and already Clayton was relaying enquiries.

Severn House[,] Hampstead, N.W.
July 7:1913

Dear Clayton—

I think there wd be no difficulty in letting you have the score of the Anthem by the second week of Sept or even a week earlier so that ought to satisfy Mr.Crowe.

As to the Ode in German: Steinbach (in *the Spring*) said he wd do it at an early concert (presumably Gürnzenich) next autumn—will you write to him?—you can say I told you this. Nikisch is (or rather said he was) going to speak & desire [Siegfried] Ochs to do the Ode in Berlin[.] Of course nothing can be done until they *see* a translation I suppose—& it seems all talk

Yours sncy
Edwd.Elgar

None of these hopes came to anything. The Lower Rhine Festival had passed, and at the end of July Fritz Steinbach had his secretary write to say that he would not be able to find room in the next season's programmes for 'das Chorwerk von Elgar'. Clayton sent this on to Severn House with what comfort he could muster.

By this time *Falstaff* was well advanced, and Novello had accepted it. The decision had come a month earlier, recorded in Alice Elgar's diary:

July 10 1913. A. to Novello for E. to see Mr.Littleton about Falstaff— Were they going to have it? A.Littleton wanted it. So it was arranged.

Next day she took the first portion of *Falstaff* full score to Novello.

It was virtually the last appearance in Elgar's affairs of Alfred Littleton, who died in the following year at the age of sixty-nine. From now on Elgar's dealings at Novello were mainly with Henry Clayton and Harold Brooke (for music editing).

Elgar finished the *Falstaff* score early on the morning of 5 August, the day he and his family left for North Wales, where they had taken a holiday house for four weeks. There he wrote his own analysis of *Falstaff* and corrected proofs.

Tan yr allt.   Penmaenmawr
Aug 12 1913

Dear Mr Harold Brooke

I was so glad to see yr initials on the proofs: I was afraid you were away from home so I sent the corrections the other day to 'the reader'; however you will forgive this I hope.

Many thanks for yr. valuable suggestions [missing from the archives], most of which I have adopted

Kindest rgrds
Yrs sny
Edward Elgar

Now that he was no longer in Worcestershire or Hereford, Elgar no longer had the services of John Austin in correcting orchestral parts. Austin's place was taken for that function by W. H. Reed, now leader of the London Symphony Orchestra. Reed and Elgar met at Frank Schuster's country house near Maidenhead on 21 September to go through the wind parts.

As with the Symphonies and the Violin Concerto, a miniature score of *Falstaff* was made available in time for the first performance, at Leeds on 2 October. It seemed to show again how certain Elgar was of his orchestration even before hearing it. The young Adrian Boult was enormously impressed to see Elgar hand a copy of the printed miniature score to Nikisch at the final rehearsal in Leeds on 30 September.

But for once there were corrections to be made afterwards. On the morning after the première, Elgar wrote:

Hotel Metropole, Leeds.
[n.d., *envelope postmarked* OC 3 13]
Dear Mr Brooke.

I think on p 71 f.score (in the parts & large score) the pause had better be placed over the last crotchet in the second bar

—This is easier for the band to understand—we had one very small slip there last night.

Seven bars after 146 put *con sord.* for Trpts & Trombones—*senza* at pause on next p.

I think that is all—I don't know how to thank you for all your kind trouble.

Now all is at an end; farewell.

Yours v.sincerely
Edward Elgar

And again a fortnight later:

Severn House[,] Hampstead, N.W.
Oct 15.1913
Dear Mr.Brooke:

The only further correction I want to make in Falstaff (I forgot it this morning) is in the *Side drum* PART—never mind the score if it is inconvenient to alter it: fifth bar after 118 should be ⟨music⟩ *not* as printed in the

miniature score

Kind rgrds
Yours ever
Edward Elgar

When Brooke queried the notation for trombones, however, Elgar was on firm ground.

Severn House
Nov 7
Dear Mr.Brooke:

I am sorry I left the B.Trombone vague. I wrote the 3 Trb pts for the new seven valved insts.—they have these low notes (Bless them!) The B.Trb. can

manage the low D so only the first C must appear small in the upper octave—
but you know the compass of Trombones better than

Edward Elgar
(Bless him also)

Falstaff seemed to be a success, and before the end of the year W. G. McNaught
(who now edited *The Musical Times*) could send this list of performances:

'Falstaff'

1st	Performance	October 2	Leeds
2nd	,,	November 3	Queen's Hall
3rd	,,	November 24	Helsingfors
4th	,,	November 27	Manchester
5th	,,	November 28	Queen's Hall
6th	,,	December 6	Moscow
7th	,,	December 10	Vienna
8th	,,	December 14	Royal Albert Hall
9th	,,	December 14	New York

2nd Symphony

So far there have been 27 performances here and abroad. The 28th will take
place at Rome on January 25. I cannot find that any other modern symphony
except your first has had anything like this success.

W.G.McN

Something like the above will go in the January M.T. It would go well with
an article on orchestration don't you think?

W.G.McN[1]

    Yet it was not like the First Symphony atmosphere at all. People everywhere were
curious to hear Elgar's latest work, but one hearing seemed to satisfy them. Landon
Ronald, to whom the work was dedicated, felt a proprietary interest (though he
confessed privately he could not 'make head or tail of it'[2]). He conducted the first
London performance on 3 November to 'an array of empty benches', according to
C. W. Orr, who was present. Ronald's second London performance three weeks later
fared hardly better. On 3 December Henry Clayton concluded a letter to Elgar: 'I
have arranged with Ronald to p[l]ay "Falstaff" at the Albert Hall on Sunday week
Free of all charges—yours & ours.'[3]
    Ronald was none the less a loyal friend to Elgar and his music. Seeing Elgar's
depression after the *Falstaff* première and for weeks afterwards, Ronald invented a
considerable distraction. He had been for many years musical adviser to The
Gramophone Company ('His Master's Voice'). He suggested to Jeffrey Stephens,
another Gramophone Company retainer, and the brother-in-law of Muriel Foster, to
interest Elgar in conducting records.

¹ HWRO 705:445:2838. Undated.
² Recalled by Sir Adrian Boult, 1975.
³ HWRO 705:445:3760.

Recording an orchestra was a difficult business in 1913: recorded sound could only be captured through a horn which transmitted the sounds into acoustical impulses to guide the recording needle. Everything which was to be heard must be close to that horn. Even rearranging the orchestra so that all the least powerful instruments were to the front, no more than forty players could be crowded into the tiny wood-lined recording rooms of the time. Many instrumental parts had to be reassigned to more powerful instruments: violoncello and double bass parts, for instance, were given to trombones and tubas. The result sounded less than lifelike, especially when played on machines of the period. This limited the sales of orchestral records, and the resulting dictates of commerce meant that orchestral selections had for the most part to be confined to a single four-minute side each. There was then no prospect of recording Elgar's major works.

Yet Stephens invited Elgar to lunch on 3 December, and to that luncheon he also brought W. W. Elkin, the publisher of light music who had applied to Elgar without success in earlier years. The result was an Elkin contract for two light orchestral pieces (which Elgar proposed to add to his Op. 12, containing at present only *Salut d'amour* of 1888). One was *Carissima*. The other was to be called *Soupir d'amour*: but its ache of longing made it inappropriate for what Elkin and the Gramophone men had in mind. In the end Elgar sent *Soupir d'amour* to Breitkopf & Härtel, who published it as *Sospiri*, finely orchestrated for strings with harp and organ. The other number for the Elkin contract he supplied many months later, in 1915, with an orchestration of one of his earliest characteristic melodies, *Douce pensée* of 1882. The new orchestration was appropriately entitled *Rosemary ('That's for remembrance')*.

For these two little works Elkin contracted on 23 December 1913 to pay no less than a hundred guineas for the copyrights. Of this sum, only one quarter was advance against royalties of 3d. per copy on home and empire sales, 2d. elsewhere. The little pieces were to appear in arrangements of all sorts. In addition, 'two-thirds of net royalties received in respect of mechanical instrument reproduction to be paid to the composer'.[4] If Severn House was proving expensive to maintain, here was clearly the sort of music which would help Elgar most.

1914

On 21 January Elgar conducted a recording orchestra of about thirty players in two 'takes' of *Carissima*, the second of which was chosen for publication in April. (It was in fact a première, for the first public performance did not take place until February.) From 'His Master's Voice' Elgar received £50 on account of royalties of 5 per cent.

By the end of January Elgar had completed five new part-songs—two with words by the seventeenth-century poet Henry Vaughan, and three from Russian poems in versions by Mrs Rosa Newmarch. On 1 February W. G. McNaught came to lunch at Severn House, and heard Elgar play through the new part-songs. He strongly urged Elgar to send them to Novello. Elgar wrote to Clayton:

[4] Elkin contracts and letters, unless otherwise noted, are now in Novello archives.

Severn House, 42,Netherhall Gardens, Hampstead,N.W.
Feb 3 1914

Dear Clayton:

I have completed five songs for chorus; Dr.McNaught, who has seen them, suggests the description 'Choral Songs'.

Would the firm be disposed to give me a sum down, say one hundred & twenty five Guineas free of restriction & an immediate royalty of 25% on the marked price for these pieces?

I received only last night permission to use three of the poems (£1/1/- each) the other two are non copyright (17th century)

Yours sincerely
Edward Elgar

Clayton consulted Alfred Littleton, still Chairman though living in retirement near Brighton, and his brother Augustus, who was now taking more of the firm's affairs into his own hands. Alfred Littleton telegraphed 'Chairman concurs'. Augustus telegraphed from Cannes, where he was staying: 'Must agree Elgars terms'. And he followed this up with a letter to Clayton which showed how differently he was to look upon Elgar's affairs.

Le Grand Hotel, Cannes.
Feb 6.14

My dear Henry

I sent you a wire this morning saying must agree Elgars terms. I don't think we ought to hesitate a moment. The price is high amounting to extortion, but the point is that plenty of other houses would jump at the stuff at the price[.] We must fight these people until the position becomes absolutely absurd, then we can retire. This is a very different matter to the Indian ballet. Here we are on our own ground and if the Part songs catch on we shall make money, anyway we cannot afford to throw up the sponge just yet. The future must take care of itself, and if Elgar repeats himself, which he won't in his own interest just yet, we must consider each case on its merits. But you must on no account do the Part songs at Fourpence. They should be at least sixpence, and the Tonic [Sol-fa] the same. Our system of publishing the Tonic versions at a much lower rate than the O.N. is absurd. Both versions serve the same purpose and should be the same price at any rate when the work is purely Choral. The higher price won't stop the Partsongs going if they catch on, if people grumble we must quietly let them know that the higher rate is owing to the composers greed. Competition gets keener every day, and composers getting scarce and some of those slipping through our fingers. I don't want any more Elgar symphonies or concertos, but am ready to take as many partsongs as he can produce even at extortionate rates.

If they don't show an immediate return of the money they ought to prove good capital investment. But each case wants individual consideration

Yrs sincerely
Augustus Littleton

Clayton translated this into a gracious acceptance:

160, Wardour Street, W.
February 7th.1914.

Dear Elgar

Excuse my delay in replying to your letter about the Part-Songs. All my senior Co-directors are away & it was accordingly necessary for me to communicate with them. This I have now done, & I am glad to be able to write, which I now do, and accept your terms, i.e That we pay you One hundred & Twenty-five Guineas, & a Royalty equal to Twenty-five per cent of the price of each partsong, to commence at once & to be paid on all copies sold subject of course to the usual exceptions.

In your letter there is a passage which I do not quite understand, perhaps you will tell me what you mean. I am quoting from memory. I think you say 'One hundred and Twenty-five guineas free of restriction'. I have no doubt we shall agree to it, but I am not at all clear what it means.

When can we have the M.S.S.?

I have found out all about the complaint from Wilhelmj of Riga about the 150 marks Fee, for a performance of your Violin Concerto. It seems that it was not our quotation at all. The quotation was given to Wilhelmj by Jost of Leipzig—

Jost got a quotation from us first for £6.6.0 & later, *when he said the price was impossible*—£5.0.0.

Wilhelmj has now sent us Jost's quotation to him viz 150 Marks!!!!

We have now written to Wilhelmj, & have told him that there is no need to do the business through Jost, & that we will supply everything for £5.5.0—So I hope business may result.

Yours sincerely
Henry R:Clayton

This must have been Adolf Wilhelmj (1872–1915), son of the great August Wilhelmj, who died in 1908.

Severn House, 42,Netherhall Gardens, Hampstead,N.W.
Feb:8:1914

Dear Clayton:

Many thanks for your letter of the 7th. accepting the terms for the five Choral-songs. The phrase I used I think was 'one hundred and twenty five guineas free of restriction': I quoted it from an offer made (*not for these works*) by another firm & I was told it meant that sum 'down' clear—*not* an anticipation of royalty—& this I gather is what your letter agrees to. I am sending the M.S.S. by hand on Monday morning: the things are ready for the printers but I have asked Dr.McNaught to look at one passage with his practical eye—but that will not delay anything. I should like to say how glad I am that Novellos have these things.

With this I send the letters referring to Mrs.Newmarch's translations: she told me that Mr.Norman O'Neill had set some as *songs* some years ago but that no reservation was placed upon them: I wrote to Mr O'Neill practically offering to withdraw my pt songs if he felt they wd. clash with his songs, of course pointing out that they *would not* clash: I enclose his reply which is quite satisfactory & you might like to file it (His publishers might at some future time raise the question for instance) with the other letters. Will you send the 3 guis to Elkin Mathew[s] for Mrs. Newmarch or shall I? You can debit me with it.

You will see what Mrs.Newmarch says about 'The Modern Greek Song' in answer to my question as to *title*—she leaves me to do as I like,—I said there was nothing Greek about the words & the title was too cumbrous: neither of those titles she suggests will do & I am not much in favour of 'Love's tempest', although that is more *useful*. 'The Tempest' alone is not enough, as I hope, for all our sakes that this big thing may be a success amongst the larger competitions[.] I should like to find a good title—Here again Dr. McNaught would help invaluably.

I am glad to hear that you have communicated with Wilhelmi of Riga. [Georg] Schneevoigt is very keen for me to go there & to Helsingfors & perhaps further—but the matter is awkward to arrange owing to the time—the length of time the journeys take.

Thanks for your letter of the 3rd.—I hope Atkins may do the Psalm [48 at the 1914 Worcester Festival]. By the way was it ever done at Chichester (?)—I forget the place proposed but I scored it for you last year: were the parts used? I am writing to Atkins & will tell him it is scored.

The Canterbury affair [a performance of *The Apostles* with the Leeds Choral Union] promises to be a great event & I want to talk to you sometime about judicious 'advertising': the Dean expected some (the usual) opposition-al outcry about paying for music in church, so the paragraphs which have already appeared will not affect the main issue.

Kind rgrds
Yours sincerely
Edward Elgar

P.S. I have great hopes that the '*Serenade*' (choral-song) will make an effective little piece for small orch. &c. &c—the M.S. now sent is however the original form.

On the same day Elgar wrote to McNaught, as an experienced choral conductor, about the passage which concerned him in the 'Choral Song' he was ultimately to entitle *Love's Tempest*.

Severn House, 42, Netherhall Gardens, Hampstead, N.W.
Feb 8 1914

My dear McNaught.

I am delighted to tell you that the firm have taken the five partsongs (*Choral-songs*) you were so kind as to listen to last Sunday. I am sending the M.S. tomorrow Monday & have written to Mr.Clayton saying I was asking you to cast your godfatherly eye on 'The Modern Greek Song'—we cannot call it that & Mrs Newmarch gives me full permission to do as I like regarding a title—two which she tentatively suggested will not do—you may see what I have said to Mr.Clayton about it: it wants a good *solid* title.

Now: I am not sure if I have written the enharmonic passages p i in the easiest way for *voice reading*—please advise.

p.2. (& the corresponding passage later) B[ass] (& Alto): you will see what effect I want—[(]*tremendous* energy)—perhaps (*B*) the first three bars are all right; but, most wise, at the fourth bar shd. it be (B & A)

see slip*

roar - - ing, roar - - ing

That is to say will it give them more chance to breathe & roar more lustily if the words are repeated?

This affects A also. *But it* CHOPS *it up sadly & sounds barkingly* see* SLIP And would you advise—I think not—omitting the Alto in the first of these 'roaring' bars—here & later—so as to obtain, perhaps, a greater cumulative effect by adding them to the second bar of the roar?

All wise! chorally
        orally
        morally
I sit at your feet
      & have the honour to be

            Your obedient servant
              No. I'm not!
            Your affectionate friend
            Edward Elgar

P.S. If you *do* think the alterations worth making a stroke of the pen wd do it—you need not send the M.S. back.[1]

Enclosed with this letter was a sheet of music paper imprinted 'M.L.Perosi—Vaticano.' On it Elgar wrote:

NB. (This piece of paper is out of one of the notebooks given to me by Perosi in Rome. Bless him!)
This is what I want really & should write it so for *wind instruments*

---

[1] Novello archives.

p.2. M.S.

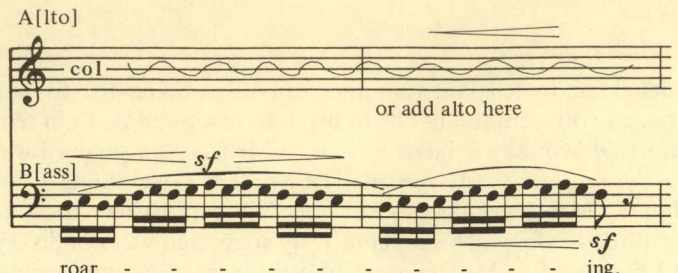

I should like this best if you think it would not stand in the way of the thing's triumphal(?) progress.

The same thing occurs on p4. M.S.

The piece is very quick so that it would not be *exhausting* I think to take the whole passage as marked here.[2]

   McNaught's reply is most unfortunately missing from the files. In the printed score, the alto part begins only in the second bar quoted. McNaught suggested some re-notation of an enharmonic passage (perhaps that leading up to the bars quoted in Elgar's note), even though this would produce a strange result in the tonic sol-fa version. And it seems that the title *Love's Tempest* was now fixed upon, for Elgar replied:

Severn House, 42,Netherhall Gardens, Hampstead, N.W.
Feb 13 1914

My dear McNaught

   Many thanks—I have pro formâ submitted the title to Mrs. Newmarch. I bow, respecting the enharmonic passage—but, perpend, a nice hash up of keys, tones & such like will you make, all conscienceless in the Solfa!—I can see you doing it!—all because I can't read

   The dedications are fixed & Blackpool may change colour before I write another pt song—oh! I have two or three T.T.B.B. in making but they must wait

                                                        Yours ever
                                                        E.E.

P.S. There is a flippancy in the capital N of your signature which augurs well: it looks like a bird of paradise[3]

    [2] Novello archives.   [3] Novello archives.

On 1 March McNaught came up to Severn House to go through the Choral Songs once again with Elgar. Three days later Elgar wrote about an offer from Robin Legge to write a piece about the new Songs in *The Daily Telegraph*.

Severn House, 42,Netherhall Gardens, Hampstead, N.W.
March 4:1914

My dear McNaught:

I have had a telephonic word with Legge & I shall see him over the ~~part~~ choral songs next Tuesday.

Will you ask the diabolus ex machina to let me have a set of proofs—final proofs as early as he can?

I will then send them to Legge.

'REGISTER' if you like

Yours ever
EE[4]

Legge's long and laudatory article appeared on 14 March under the title 'SOME NEW ELGAR. Five Choral Songs.' In addition to analysing the music, Legge made some more general points:

... When I heard them played through I seemed to like that one best which I heard last! But that was merely a momentary feeling. In the matter of sheer originality and individuality Elgar has never reached a higher mark; that itself is remarkable considering the smallness of the form, for none of the choral songs occupies more than a few pages. ...

He used to be accused of composing orchestral music to be sung by choirs. The accusation may now be allowed to die for ever, for certainly he has learnt his lesson, as so many of us have, from the amazing development of choral technique in recent years, and here he has given us the proof of his knowledge in his highest degree.

Meanwhile Clayton was dealing with the copyright of the Choral Songs. His next letter is interesting for its reference to the Copyright Act of 1911 (which came into force on 1 July 1912). Clayton himself was an authority on copyright, and he had in fact helped to draft this legislation. One of its enactments recognized the rise of the gramophone in providing for 'Mechanical Instrument Royalties'. This in turn brought into being a number of schemes for tabulating and collecting these royalties from records, player-piano rolls, and similar devices. Elgar had joined the scheme begun by W. W. Elkin, who published *Carissima* and had been closely involved with its gramophone recording. So the agreement Clayton presented for the Choral Songs now specifically excepted the mechanical rights from the copyright purchased by the firm for 125 guineas. (The exception was to carry an irony, for a quarter century would pass before a single one of the Choral Songs was recorded, and more than sixty years before they were all on disc.)

[4] Novello archives.

160, Wardour Street, W.
February 10th.1914.

Dear Elgar

Many thanks for your letter. I quite understand your meaning attached to your words 'Free of restriction'. I thought you meant what you tell me, but of course the words quoted might mean a very great deal more.

I have handed the M.S.S. to McNaught so that he may be able to consider any points about which you wish to consult him.

I have also sent a cheque to Elkin Mathews for Three Guineas as requested. I need not trouble you about that. It only remains for me to send you a cheque for the 125 Guineas—So I enclose it herewith, with receipt Form, & an assignment for your signature.

I hope the assignment carries out your views of the arrangement correctly. I know you have joined Elkin's Society for the Protection & administration of your Mechanical Instrument rights, so I suppose we cannot include them in the assignment—I have excepted them accordingly. The words last interlined are a consequence of the new Copyright Act which prevents an author from assigning his Copyright, otherwise than by Will, for a longer period than 25 years from his death

Yours sincerely
Henry R:Clayton.

Severn House, 42,Netherhall Gardens, Hampstead, N.W.
Feb 11::1914

Dear Clayton:

Many thanks for your letter of the 10th.—enclosed I send the formal receipt. Thanks also for seeing to Elkin Mathews for the words.

I have read the assignment which is all in order & I will return it signed as soon as I can get a witness.

You will not forget that I suggested that, someday, the Serenade might make an instrumental piece—I suppose any such arrangements, sanctioned by the firm & by me, are covered by the assignment.

Yours sincerely
Edward Elgar

Novello were not the only firm paying Elgar big fees then. During this same month Elgar wrote an imposing song for Clara Butt entitled *The Chariots of the Lord*, for which Boosey paid him a hundred guineas in addition to an immediate royalty of 3d. a copy—to increase to 4d. after the sale of 40,000 copies. Such was the optimism for ballads six months before the outbreak of the First World War. For a less sensational ballad, *An Arabian Serenade*, Boosey agreed in July to pay 4d. on each copy sold, but without a sum down.

A note to McNaught, written the same day as his last letter about the Choral Songs, seems to refer to the score of Psalm 29 ('Give unto the Lord'), long promised for St Paul's Cathedral. (The printed music was in the hands of the organist, Sir George Martin, by 24 March.)

Severn House, 42,Netherhall Gardens, Hampstead,N.W.
March 4 1914

My dear McNaught

Here is the thing now[.] I hope you can make it out
I like the sudden change to beginning of p 10

Yours ever
EE

The Anthem was orchestrated in April.

At the same time Elgar sent to Novello a short 'Harvest Anthem for Parish Choirs', *Fear Not, O Land*. The publishers gave him 50 guineas for the copyright, exclusive of mechanical instrument rights. The proofs were read by John E.West, to whom Elgar wrote.

Severn House, 42,Netherhall Gardens, Hampstead, N.W.
June 11:1914

My dear West:

I recognise your hand on the proofs of the little anthem & I have adopted all, I think, of your suggestions.

I am still vague about marking the organ part—two manuals scourge me a great deal. Is it necessary to put any indication at the opening—& please look at p.2. the query (last stave) and my answer—if 'la melodia marcato' is too Italian perhaps *marcato* wd. be enough—on p.3 I have put *Clar.* to shew the solo effect desired but perhaps this is unusual & if adopted should be followed by other indications such as Diap[ason]s. 3 bars after R[ight] H[and] E♭—& what about *Sw & Gt*?—is it usual in these small anthems to mention these. & 'coupled' &c. I am only anxious to make the thing Serviceable.

Kind regards
Yours sincy
Edward Elgar[5]

The correspondence with Clayton took up other matters. On 12 May Arthur Maquaire had written from Paris to ask for some Elgar music for a concert he was giving—'un choix de pièces pour piano (celles qui se prêtent le mieux à la grande virtuosité) et d'un choix de mélodies pour ténor et soprano, voire duos ou trios s'il en existe?' This request occasioned Elgar's next letter to Clayton, written on the day after a performance of the Violin Concerto by Kreisler at Queen's Hall.

Severn House, 42,Netherhall Gardens, Hampstead,N.W.
May 15 1914

Dear Clayton:

The Concerto was a huge success again yesterday & I am strongly advised to withdraw all performing fees! Lady Speyer told me she had seen Ysaye &c. &c. & said that the only thing that stood in the way of the worldwide

[5] MS in possession of Raymond Monk.

success(?) of the work was the terrible attitude of Novellos—I said all I could to combat the latter part: but, shall we let the work go free for the future? I am quite agreeable

I return the French things: I have really nothing of the kind they want & it seems a small tinkering affair & my work could not be represented adequately—will you break this fact as gently as you can to Mons.Maquaire

Yours sncly
Edward Elgar

Of course if you like to do it you could send the Songs of mine which you publish but cui bono? they are in English. The Sea Pictures (Boosey) are in French & obtainable in Paris but I will not send or name them to M.Maquaire as they require orchestra.

[160, Wardour Street, W.]
May 18th.1914

Dear Elgar

Thanks for your letter of May 15th.

I wrote to Mr.Arthur Maquaire of Paris, & pointed out that you had not given much attention to purely pianoforte music, à la grande virtuosité, & that the utility of your Songs for his Concerts would be handicapped by the fact that the words were English. I sent him a complete list of your works, & suggested that he should give his attention to some of your Orchestral works.

As regards the performing Fees on the Violin Concerto I certainly think it would be well to give them up, but I would not do so until after the Summer holidays when all our standing Contracts will have expired.

I will talk over the matter with Gussie Littleton & will write to you later about it. My idea would be to make an announcement in the September Number of 'The Musical Times' which we could send out as a Press Paragraph.

The Announcement must be very carefully worded, because if we cease to ask for performing fees we must on no account do or say anything which could be held to be an abandonment of the performing rights, which we might want to exercise at any moment for the prevention of the lending of Scores & parts by one Society to another. The performing right is the only weapon of defence which we can employ in such cases—so the right must not be abandoned, even though the fees are not demanded.

Yours sincerely
Henry R:Clayton.

Elgar's reply about the Violin Concerto was delayed for more than a month. He began his letter with reference to another matter—a proposal received from Holland to conduct his works there early in the following year.

Severn House, 42,Netherhall Gardens, Hampstead, N.W.
June 27 1914
Dear Clayton:

Very many thanks for yours of the 25th re Amsterdam &c. I prefer Feby 6 & 7: as to the programme wd. you, when settling the dates, ask 'them' (whoever 'they' may be) to consult me direct—I will feel my way as to the works: I might have a specimen programme or two to judge the usual length required &c. &c.

As to performing fees Concerto &c.—can't we make the announcement *now*: you see if we wait until September it will be too late for soloists &c. to include the work in the winter programmes: there may be still some reason for keeping back the announcement but wd. there be any objection to my informing Ysaye? Lady Speyer was very keen about his doing it when I talked to her at the last Kreisler performance & I would ask her to write to Ysaye & see if the thing could be reopened on friendly terms: but I will not move in the matter until you say yea.

Kind rgrds
Yrs sny
Edw.Elgar

They had a conference over the whole question of performing fees.

[160, Wardour Street, W.]
July 6th.1914.
Dear Elgar

By a curious coincidence since we had our talk with you about performing rights I have had two applications for the Violin Concerto.

Wood is going to perform it at the Promenade Concert on Tuesday Evening Septr.15th. with Louis Pécksai.

And Frank Bates of the Norwich Philharmonic Society wants to do it next Season on April 29th.1915, with either Szigeti, Anton Maaskoff, or Isolde Menges.

Of course at present neither of the applicants has any idea that we are giving up the performing fees, & so I could easily get Ten or Twelve Guineas for the two performances.

But we must *make a beginning* some where, & it would be hard lines on these two applicants to postpone the step merely to get their fees. Moreover Bates's performance will not take place till April 29th.1915, which would involve a long postponement of our announcement.

So I propose to tell these two Gentlemen that they can now purchase all the material, or they can hire it from us, but no performing fee will be payable.

I will prepare some such announcement for the August 'Musical Times', which I will submit to you. I wont write to them till tomorrow, so as to give you an opportunity of communicating with me if any further point occurs to you.

Yours sincerely
Henry R:Clayton

Severn House, 42,Netherhall Gardens, Hampstead, N.W.
Monday July 6 1914

Dear Clayton:

It is good news about the Concerto. To meet the case or cases now wd. it do to announce that the parts can be *bought*—& if people still wish to hire put on an extra guinea or so on the hire for me; would that be practicable? You might then perhaps 'inform' the two applicants what the (new) hiring fee is & take no further notice to them—

In haste
Yrs sincy
Ed.Elgar

160, Wardour Street, W.
July 7th.1914

Dear Elgar

Thanks for your letter. I think I understand your meaning—viz. that we are to advertize that the Score & parts of the Violin Concerto are now For Sale at prices to be announced, but that we are also to announce that the Score & parts can be still obtained on loan, & that whenever we *lend* we are to add One Guinea for you. I see no difficulty about that, & it is an arrangement which will work almost automatically, which makes it acceptable.

I enclose a draft of the proposed announcement for you to alter as you think suitable. We may as well settle it at once, & we shall then be able to make an announcement in the August 'Musical Times' without worrying you at the last moment.

Yours sincerely
Henry R:Clayton.

M.T. for August—?Set up as an advertisement for the Leader Page

ELGAR'S VIOLIN CONCERTO

The Publishers take this opportunity of announcing that, by arrangement with the Composer, they have decided to publish the band parts of Elgar's Violin Concerto forthwith. The Orchestral Score (Conductor's Copy & miniature edition) has already been published.

The Score and parts will still be obtainable on hire from the Publishers as heretofore.

Whenever the Score and parts are or have been obtained directly from the Publishers, either on purchase or hiring terms, no additional fee for the right to perform will be charged until otherwise announced.

Severn House[,] Hampstead, N.W.
July 8.1914
Dear Clayton:

I think the paragraph will do well: I do not know if it wd. travel outside the scope of the announcement to say after *Score* 'Folio and Miniature editions'—it feels to me it looks 'important' but you must judge.

I quite understand about the addl.guinea—I am glad you think that plan feasible

Yours v sincly
Edward Elgar

The outbreak of war on 4 August found the Elgars on holiday in the remote Scottish Highlands, cut off from up-to-date news reports. Elgar wired to Novello for news, and was answered by Alfred Littleton's second son A. J. B. Littleton.

The Gairloch Hotel, Ross-shire.
August 7:1914
My dear Jack Littleton

I do not know how to thank you for your telegrams. I owe you for one & must continue to owe you for change is short here & I have to consider every penny of *change*—money in bulk is to be had.

Mails here are vague & awfully late.

Best regards from Lady Elgar & Carice & myself

Yours sincly
Edward Elgar

Hampstead
Oct 6 1914
Dear Mr Harold Brooke:

So glad to hear all is well at home & that you are a soldier
I have looked thro the proof which is now I think all right.

Yours sncly
Edward Elgar

Elgar's next music was a recitation with orchestra of the Belgian poet Émile Cammaerts's *Carillon*, memorializing all the ruined churches of Flanders. Elgar had been persuaded to do this for a collection of works by Allied artists to be entitled *King Albert's Book*, to benefit Belgian war charities. The music was printed in piano score, and it was separately published by Elkin, whose contract Elgar signed on 30 November: it called for a royalty of 6d. on home and colonial sales, 3d. abroad. Once again the composer was to have two-thirds of mechanical royalties; and these were this time considerable. After a tumultuous première performance in early December, The Gramophone Company rushed ahead plans to record a slightly abridged version on two discs with the actor Henry Ainley reciting the poem in English and Elgar conducting. The records were made at the end of January 1915. They sold very well.

1915–1916

Early in 1915 Elgar was persuaded to undertake a more serious project. It embraced the setting of three poems, from Laurence Binyon's collection of war poems entitled *The Winnowing Fan*, for chorus and orchestra. Elgar took his title, *The Spirit of England*, from a line in the first poem of the three; but the climax was to be in the final setting, of 'For the Fallen'. After his music had progressed far enough to play sketches for friends, it was discovered that another setting of 'For the Fallen' had already been accepted by Novello from the Cambridge composer, Cyril Rootham. Elgar generously withdrew, as he wrote to the poet: 'There is only one publisher for choral music in England: Mr.Rootham was in touch with Novello first—my proposal made his M.S. wastepaper & I could not go on.'[1] This decision had been prompted by the firm itself, as a letter from Clayton makes clear.

160, Wardour Street, London, W.
March 26th 1915

Dear Elgar

Many thanks for your letter. It is very good of you to stand on one side for the benefit of Dr.Rootham, & I am very sorry indeed that our commercial views of the matter should be the cause of interfering with the plans of an artist like yourself.

We could not however get away from the conviction that if two settings of the verses in question were published about the same time, one of them would certainly prove a failure, & with you in the field we naturally feared that Dr.Rootham's work would be the one to suffer. In such cases the disappointed composer invariably blames the Publisher.

Moreover at the present time we do not regard lightly the prospect of publishing a work which, through being handicapped at its birth, is likely to prove a failure.

I repeat we are very sorry about it, & are much obliged to you for your kind action in the matter.

I have cut my right hand rather badly with that domestic weapon the razor, & have had to write this with my left hand—

Yours sincerely
Henry R.Clayton[2]

Yet the friends who had heard Elgar's sketches had recognized a masterpiece. Sidney Colvin, a colleague of Binyon's at the British Museum, had first made the suggestion: now he and his wife together protested to Elgar against the decision. They were joined by another Museum colleague, Richard Alexander Streatfeild, who went to Augustus Littleton and convinced him to publish both settings. Elgar was then persuaded to continue. He finished his 'For the Fallen', and almost on the eve of its première a year later Rootham vigorously protested. This elicited the following explanation by Streatfeild to Rootham.

---

[1] 31 March 1915; MS in possession of the Binyon family. The exchange of letters with Binyon is printed in Moore, *Edward Elgar: a Creative Life*, pp. 674 ff.
[2] HWRO 705:445:6349.

British Museum, London, W.C.
28 March 1916

Dear Sir,

I fully understand that I am taking what you may well consider an unwarrantable liberty in venturing to interfere in a private matter, but I cannot refrain from doing so in the hope of removing a misunderstanding which seems to have arisen between you and Sir Edward Elgar regarding your respective settings of Laurence Binyon's 'For the Fallen'. I should explain that I am a friend of both Elgar and Binyon, and was consulted by both of them on this matter, and that I also took a small share in the negotiations with Messrs.Novello that ended in the publication of both works. It is on this point that the whole misunderstanding seems to rest. Your setting of 'For the Fallen' was, I think, under Messrs.Novellos' consideration, when Elgar informed them that he was engaged upon three poems in the same book, & offered the work to them. Messrs.Novello, not unnaturally, wanted to secure Elgar's work, and thinking that it might not be profitable to publish the two works together, contemplated the possibility of rejecting yours. Elgar then, with what seems to be unexampled generosity, said that he would not permit this. You, he said, had been first in the field, and he would not stand in your way. He declared, therefore, that, rather than allow your work to be rejected, he would withdraw his own and lay it aside. This, as you can imagine, was a great blow to Elgar's friends. However I need not linger over our disappointment, except to say that we consulted in the hope of devising some means of rescuing Elgar's work from destruction—for the benefit of ourselves & of the whole English world. We decided that I should have an interview with Mr.Augustus Littleton & should endeavour to persuade him to publish both works. This I did with no very great difficulty, though I need no[t] trouble you with the arguments that I employed. He agreed to publish both works, & of course Elgar resumed work upon his setting of Binyon's poem. That was the main thing that we, his friends, were aiming at, and having secured the publication of your work, we felt that Elgar's hands were once more free.

Now, this is where we seem to differ, for, if I understand the position correctly, you maintain that Elgar's withdrawal in your favour was intended to be final, that he had no right to resume work upon his setting of the poem, and that he broke his word to you and, generally speaking, behaved in a dishonourable manner. I must say at once that no one who knows Elgar could possibly entertain such an idea for a moment. He is the soul of honour and is absolutely incapable of an unkind or ungenerous action. His offer to withdraw in your favour was, to my thinking, a piece of unexampled magnanimity, but you mistake his motive completely, if you suppose that he acted as he did, simply because he discovered that you and he had set the same words. *That* weighed nothing at all with him, nor was there any reason why it should. It is by no means an uncommon occurrence for two composers to set the same words and in this case, owing to the difference of scope and treatment, there could be no question of rivalry between you and Elgar, & it was the general impression of those who were consulted that neither work would interfere with the success of the other. Besides, Binyon tells me that he made it perfectly plain to you, that you were not to have the exclusive right of setting his poem, & you must have known perfectly well that there was a strong probability of the poem being subsequently set by some other composer.

What urged Elgar to his generous act of self-abnegation was the fear, that, if he allowed Messrs Novello to publish his work, yours would be rejected. When that fear was dispelled, by Messrs Novellos' acceptance of both works for publication, there was no possible reason why he should not finish his setting of Binyon's poems. It is painful to me to think that you seem not only to contemplate with serenity the thought of Elgar's destroying his work, in order to enhance the success of yours, but even to desire such a consummation. I can only hope that what I have written will have the effect of removing the misconception of Elgar's action which you at present entertain.

Yours faithfully,
R.A.Streatfeild[3]

Rootham was not mollified, and a shadow was thus cast for Elgar over his greatest piece of war music. Unfortunately the Novello archives contain no further correspondence about the matter. 'To Women' and 'For the Fallen' were published by them in the spring of 1916. The opening number, 'The Fourth of August', was delayed for a year because Elgar could not at first decide how to set lines referring to the enemy. The delay had nothing to do with the Rootham affair.

If Novello published Elgar's finest war music, Elkin took other works, no doubt hoping for a success to match *Carillon*. During the spring of 1915, Elgar was persuaded to write a commemorative work on the fall of Poland. This took the form of an orchestral piece, *Polonia*, interweaving his own themes with Polish folk tunes and melodies of Chopin and Paderewski. On 24 June Elgar signed Elkin's contract for its publication. The terms were for two-thirds of both performing and mechanical instrument rights. Although an abridged recording was made in 1919, it sold poorly, and performances were few. Even the first performance, on 6 July 1915, was not well attended, though it unquestionably touched the large element of Polish sympathy in the hall that night. Next day Elkin wrote:

8 & 10, Beak Street, Regent Street, W.
7 July 1915
Dear Sir Edward,

A line to congratulate you heartily on the success of Polonia last night. It was a pity the audience was so small, but they certainly amply made up for their lack of numbers. While it was very pleasant to hear the appreciation of the music, it was (as I think I mentioned to Lady Elgar) almost more so to notice the really warm & almost affectionate note one could distinguish in the reception given to you personally.

Yours very sincerely
W.W.A.Elkin[4]

[3] HWRO 705:445:3731 (copy in Streatfeild's hand, apparently sent to Elgar).
[4] HWRO 705:445:4737.

Polonia was suggested for inclusion in a provincial tour with the London Symphony Orchestra being planned for Elgar by the impresario Percy Harrison for early 1916. There was the question of producing sufficient copies and parts of the music (still in manuscript) for this purpose. Elkin, in a note dated 25 August 1915, 'suggested [to] make copy of score & pay for it out of fees'. The fees would come particularly from the Harrison tour concerts. One duplicating process was offered by the orchestral hire librarians Goodwin and Tabb. Elgar answered this suggestion from the house in Sussex he had taken for a short holiday between continuing performances of *Carillon* at the Coliseum. One run, with the Belgian actor Carlo Liten, had finished in early August. In October Elgar was scheduled to conduct it again with the daughter of his old friends Mr and Mrs Edward Speyer: she was Lalla Vandervelde, married to the Belgian minister-in-exile in charge of refugees in England. Elgar's reference to not finding a tune may refer to *Le drapeau belge*, another Cammaerts poem, which Liten was eager to recite with Elgar's music.

Hookland, Midhurst
Friday [27 Aug. 1915]
Dear Mr. Elkin:

Very many thanks—It is really lovely here & I wish you could see it—

I do not know Madam Vandervelde's ideas: I persuaded her to hear Liten as she wd. see his *stage effects*—which were violent but good in their way—I have heard nothing since—I like the words but I cannot find a tune for them—you must find a lyrical person

I have been thinking much about *Polonia*—in the present state of that country what shall we do? Goodwin & T. never sent me the specimen page of their process—have you seen the completed proof page they promised

> Kind rgrds
> Yrs sny
> Ed: Elgar[5]

An exchange of telegrams (missing from the files), and perhaps a little more correspondence intervened before Elkin's reply:

8 & 10, Beak Street, Regent Street, London, W.
9th Sept., 1915.
Dear Sir Edward,

> '*Polonia.*'

I duly received your wire in reply to mine, and have quoted the terms to Harrison. If he accepts them, it will simplify matters a little bit with regard to the production of the score and parts. On going into the matter, Goodwin & Tabb find that the score will make about 65 pages instead of 50, and of course the expense is increased proportionately. As far as I can see at present it is likely to amount to about £70. What I propose is that if Harrison agrees, we shall put that sum and anything else received in respect of performing fees

[5] MS in possession of Mrs Robert Elkin.

against the cost of production, and that if at the end of next year there is still a deficit, it shall be divided equally between us.

This is not exactly a business arrangement, but in the hope and belief that our association will prove mutually profitable I am quite ready to make it if it suits you. In the event of Harrison not agreeing we should have to find some other arrangement.

Since the above was typed, Harrison has offered 18 guineas, and I have replied regretting that we cannot reduce our terms.

I am sorry to have to trouble you with business matters while you are away, but with things as they are, it is unfortunately unavoidable.

I hope you are enjoying this glorious weather.

> With kind regards
> Yours sincerely,
> W.W.A.Elkin.[6]

So once again, as in the 1890s, Elgar was asked to subsidize the publication of his own work. It made an unhappy contrast to recent years of the Novello contract: but that was before the war, and in the wake of his biggest successes. Now he replied from Walls, near Ravenglass in Cumberland, where he and his wife were holiday-making with the Stuart-Wortleys: 'I agree to the proposition about "POLONIA."'[7] In the end, the score was printed (in an edition so small that copies today are almost unknown), and *Polonia* was included in provincial concerts Elgar conducted in February and March 1916.

Meanwhile Elgar's largest work for some years was taking shape. It began with a proposal from the *Daily Telegraph* critic Robin Legge that he should write music for a play by Algernon Blackwood and Violet Pearn, based on Blackwood's novel, *A Prisoner in Fairyland*. The play, to be called *The Starlight Express*, was to be produced by another acquaintance of the Elgars', the actress Lena Ashwell, at the Kingsway Theatre. The most appealing private aspect of it was the play's striking similarity to the childhood drama sketched by Elgar himself at the end of his own childhood nearly fifty years earlier.

He agreed to write the *Starlight Express* music, and arranged with Novello about borrowing tunes from *The Wand of Youth* Suites published by them. But when it came to the new music, publishers seemed reticent. Lady Elgar noted in her diary on 26 November: 'E. very hard at work—much telephoning: L.Ashwell, Elkin, Enoch, Novello, &c &c'. In the end the publishing negotiations were taken up as a favour by Landon Ronald. Before these were concluded the two vocal soloists, Clytie Hine and Charles Mott, arrived at Severn House to rehearse their parts.

December 6 [1915] . . . E. very rushed—Mr.Mott at 9.30. Very good & nice. Lunched with Landon [at the] Guildhall [School of Music] who explained the business he had, like an angel, settled for E.

This was a proposal that Blackwood's agents, Messrs Hughes Massie, should collect fees for Elgar also on all foreign productions of *The Starlight Express*: but these were in the event chimeras. Meanwhile there was still no contract for publication.

---

[6] Typewritten copy now in Novello archives.
[7] This sentence, copied on to the Elkin copy letter, is all that now survives of Elgar's letter of 18 Sept. 1915 to Elkin.

On 9 December Landon Ronald wrote that he was 'endeavouring to fix an appointment to see Mr.Clayton to-morrow morning'. The mission was unsuccessful. At last on 11 December:

'Mr.Elkin here later—to discuss publishing Starlight. Novello gave it all up—Kind Landon arranging things . . .'

Elkin's contract, which Elgar signed on 22 December 1915, provided a payment to the composer of 25 guineas only, plus royalties and large percentages for mechanical rights and concert performances. Elkin was hedging his bets, and he was quite right to do so. The production, though Elgar's music was universally praised, was taken off after a month. In the end, the only tangible result was a series of eight gramophone records which Elgar conducted in February 1916. In view of the fact that the production had been closed for more than two months when the records appeared in April, they did remarkably well.

As *The Starlight Express* closed, there commenced a stage production of Elgar's second piece of recitation with orchestra, *Une voix dans le désert*. This was far more elaborate than *Carillon*, for it involved a singer as well as reciter, and invited elaborate stage treatment. Elkin had been chary of it until the stage production was actually arranged at the Shaftesbury Theatre. He then brought out a piano score only, with a cover reproducing a charcoal drawing by Alfred Craven. Elkin wrote:

8 & 10, Beak Street, Regent Street, W.
3.2.15 [*sic*]
Dear Sir Edward,

I have a prejudice about giving away things that dont belong to me! Having only to-day acquired the drawing of 'Une Voix' I hope you will now accept it as a little souvenir of the piece—with a corner for its publisher!

Yours very sincerely
W.W.A.Elkin

PTO
It is in charcoal, & I think ought to be what is known as 'set'.[8]

But the Elkin contract for this and a third Cammaerts recitation, *Le drapeau belge* (which had still to be finished), was not generous: modest royalties on the sales of sheet music, three eighths of mechanical and performing rights, and sale of the copyrights for one shilling.

Elgar bore Elkin no resentment. Late in March, when Elgar was laid up with a cold, Lady Elgar noted: 'A[lice] to arrange about a typewriter for E. It came up & E. spent hours practising & writing wild flights.' One of these was to Elkin:

Severn House, 42,Netherhall Gardens, Hampstead, N.W.
29/III/1916.
Dear Elkin,——

The occasion(!) demands a decent sheet of paper;BEHOLD! I am shut up with a very bad cold and am sorry I even ventured out yesterday, although I

---

[8] HWRO 705:445:6754. The drawing is now at the Elgar Birthplace.

fully believe the germ must have been attracted to me some time before then: anyhow you are not held responsible

I have heard nothing from the Coliseum about rehearsal, perhaps there is not going to be one.

Please be lenient about mistakes to-day, the margin-spacer—*and* the warning-bell are both shaky am [*sic*] give the Operator fits.

I will not disturb you with further eloquent discourse but will only remind you that speed is what I go in for; accuracy is the virtue of Slaves.

> With very kind regards,
> Yours sincerely
> Edward Elgar.
> (TYPIST)[9]

In May 1916 came the premières of the last two numbers of *The Spirit of England*. The première performance with the Leeds Choral Union was followed by an entire week of performances in London (coupling the new works with *The Dream of Gerontius*) in a series of concerts organized by Clara Butt for the benefit of the Red Cross. Some weeks later the man who was now the Novello chairman, Alfred Littleton's younger brother, wrote:

160 Wardour Street W.
June 28.16

Dear Sir Edward Elgar

I was present yesterday at the Royal Choral Society committee meeting— when programmes for next season were discussed. It was proposed to include in the November concert your work For the Fallen. I suggested that considerable interest would be added to this concert if your work The Spirit of England, complete, was performed and my suggestion was favourably received by the committee. Will you very kindly let me know when you think you will be in a position to send us the music for the completion of the work. I think there is a strong probability that it would be given at the R[oyal] A[lbert] H[all] in November if it can be completed in time.

> With kind regards

> Yrs sincerely
> Augustus Littleton[10]

But the stanzas depicting the enemy in the first number still caused Elgar to hesitate. The first number did not appear until the middle of 1917.

There was a further loosening of ties with Novello. By mid-1916 they had ceased to act as his sole concert agent. From that time many of his affairs in this direction were in the hands of Ibbs & Tillett, the successors to N. Vert.

---

[9] TS in possession of Mrs Robert Elkin.
[10] HWRO 705:445:3734.

1917

Elgar's health grew worse and worse. He conducted when opportunity offered, but composed little. In February 1917, in response to a request from an old friend, he wrote a ballet after a fan drawn in sanguine by Charles Conder. *The Sanguine Fan* was performed twice as one number in a charity matinée, and Elkin agreed to act as its publisher. The documents are lacking, but he printed only 'Echo's Dance' in piano score, and kept Elgar's manuscript full score in case of requests for further performances. They were few.

In March 1917 Elgar went on with a project which had been requested fourteen months earlier by Lord Charles Beresford. This was to set to music a number of the verses in a little work by Rudyard Kipling called *The Fringes of the Fleet*, about the small peacetime coastal vessels now equipped with guns and war-gear for Channel patrol. The idea was for another series of music-hall performances at the Coliseum, and publication by Enoch.

Kipling and his agents had proven very difficult to deal with, and the poet was clearly less than enthusiastic. At last he agreed, stipulating a very high royalty (3d. of a total selling price of 1s.6d. per song) on sale of the music. But the income this time was to come from performances.

The production of the four songs at the Coliseum in June, with Charles Mott and three other baritones in costume and Elgar conducting, scored a big success, and a considerable run was in prospect. A fortnight into the run, Elgar added a fifth song, dedicated to the four singers. The words were not by Kipling, but by Sir Gilbert Parker. The new song, *Inside the Bar*, was offered to Novello. They rejected it in a letter sent over the initials of the publishing manager C. J. May. The beginning of May's letter mentioned Clayton (who had recently written to say that the firm still had the manuscript of *The Light of Life*, in case Elgar wished to reclaim it[1]). Altogether it could suggest that Clayton and May were taking direction from their new chief, Augustus Littleton, in disengaging from Elgar's affairs.

160, Wardour Street, W.
July 1917 [*Elgar date-stamped receipt* 1 AUG 1917]
Dear Sir,

Mr. Clayton handed to us last week the mss. of your setting of Sir Gilbert Parker's 'Sailor's Song'.

We have since heard the Song sung at the Coliseum under ideal conditions, but we think, that so much depends on the conditions that, when deprived of them, the Song is not likely to prove successful amongst those choirs who favour the more ordinary form of Glee or Partsong, & that its circulation is on that account likely to be restricted. Under these circumstances we are returning the mss. with many thanks to you for giving us the opportunity of considering them.

Yours faithfully,
Novello & Co. Ltd.
CJM[2]

[1] HWRO 705:445:6827.   [2] HWRO 705:445:3736.

Enoch was happy enough to purchase the copyright for ten guineas and a 25 per cent royalty after the first five hundred copies were sold.[3] The rarity of the publication today causes one to wonder whether even that sales figure was reached.

Another sign of the new order at Novello was a long contract, dated 15 September 1917, spelling out royalties (generally at 25 per cent) on a wide range of works and arrangements dating back almost to the beginning of the contract arranged by Alfred Littleton in 1904. No one could complain: it was sound business practice. But gone were the days of the gentlemen's agreement.

1918

Near the beginning of the new year came a letter from the man who had printed the most beautiful of all Elgar editions. It was W. H. Broome, who in 1901 had produced at the Old Bourne Press a folio of the *May Song*—printed on William Morris's press, with a special small edition on vellum. After all these years, many copies remained unsold.

Avalon, Grange Road, Bushey, Herts.
January 16th 1918

Dear Sir Edward,

Herewith please find a/c and cheque value £20.6.0 in settlement of sales of the May Song up to date. The sole reason of my not troubling you about the sales was that the result was so disappointing after all the trouble taken (putting expense on one side), that I had not the heart, so have left it until now that I am settling everything upon giving up my business. Since February 1916 I have sold only 2 Violin & Piano copies.

The May Song can still be procured from Miss N.Platt, 5 Albert Studios, Albert Bridge Road S.W.11, the trade having been notified and the collecting houses having it in stock. Miss Platt is my late manageress, and carries on the printing of the Old Bourne Press; the press upon which the work is done together with the furniture belonged to the late William Morris of Kelmscott fame.

I was most disappointed with the hand made paper and Vellum editions of the May Song. Five hundred were printed of the former and only 150 sold; the vellum was an edition of 10, out of which 2 only were sold. The paper was offered at 3/- and the vellum at 2 guineas piano, and $2\frac{1}{2}$ guineas violin & piano, just a little under half of the cost price and even then it was of no use.

[3] Contract dated 8 Aug. 1917 (later in Ashdown archives).

Have come to the conclusion that music is not like books in this respect, for hand made paper editions, and especially vellum copies, are much sought after. I advertised in several papers and sent band parts to all the princip[al] orchestras throughout the United Kingdom. However, I had the joy over the work, printing from wood blocks designed by Walter Crane etc. so must not feel it was all loss.

With good wishes for the New Year,

> I am,
> Yours very faithfully,
> W.H.Broome

JANUARY 15th 1918

MAY SONG
Account of Sales

Piano.

PRINTED				
1901		Free	500	
October	1,000	Review etc.	40	
1904		Sold	1,169	
January	1,290	In stock	581	
	2,290		2,290	

Violin & Piano

PRINTED				
1901		Free	500	
October	1,000	Review etc,	40	
		Sold	252	
		In stock	208	
	1,000		1,000	

Sold Piano solo . . .	1,169		
Sold Violin & Pf . .	252	Royalty 4d	
		7 copies as 6 . . .	
	1,421		£20.6.0[1]

Even years after this Broome was still in possession of many copies. In 1926 he sold them, together with the copyright, to Elkin. Elgar then made the suggestion that if he autographed all the remaining vellum copies they might finally sell. Broome responded:

---

[1] HWRO 705:445:3993.

Avalon, Grange Road, Bushey, Herts.
April 27 1926.

Dear Sir Edward.

First let me thank you for your suggestion re the May-Song; Mr Elkin purchased it from me last week after a very pleasant chat or two. I sincerely hope you are pleased. On Friday last I handed over to them the copies as per my last a/c to you ending March 30 1926.

Am sending the vellum copies per passenger train on Monday (key to trunk also labels for return herewith) and as I cannot pay for the return carriage (for all goods per passenger require prepayment) will you kindly arrange for this for me P O enclosed. I feel sorry to put you to this trouble.

Thanking you ever so much for your promise to autograph copies

> Yours very sincerely
> W H Broome

P.S. Envelope for return of key

> WHB.[2]

The autographs were added. Yet sales were few. As late as 14 June 1976, what may have been the final vellum copies were sold at Sotheby's, still in new condition.

In March 1918 Elgar's long bouts of illness culminated in an operation which removed his tonsils. It was a serious affair for a man of his age, but he returned home after a week, and three days later began to write a string quartet. The same day he wrote what may have been his last letter to W. G. McNaught at *The Musical Times*.

Severn House, 42,Netherhall Gardens, Hampstead, N.W.3.
March 25th 1918.

My dear McNaught,

Your welcome parcel of M.T. back numbers found me in an evil hour; I have had some trouble with my throat and did not dally with fate but went straight off to an operation and the resulting getting well,––which is worse than the disease!

I am at home again and creep about as becomes one who has lost much both in flesh and fine weather. I have read those sketches about S[terndale] Bennet[t] and am going to ask Sir A. Mackenzie to let me see the autographs at the R[oyal] A[cademy of] M[usic].

I wish somebody would write an account of people to whom music has been dedicated, (I could have written 'dedicatees', but I scorn to be

---

[2] HWRO 705:445:6809. Broome acknowledged receipt of the trunk with the autographed vellum copies on 29 May 1926 (HWRO 705:445:6810).

pedantic)—there are so many names which don't seem to exist apart from some quartet or other small composition; and then I should like to know all about the Grosshändler TOST to whom Haydn dedicated a whole string of IVtets [—] nearly a dozen! I expect it is all in Pohl but I haven't got P. Do ENCOURAGE, say, Selfridge, as a useful Grosshändler, to order some quartets from me. Best regards,

Yours ever
E.E.[3]

Less than seven months later McNaught was dead, and Elgar thus lost one of his last really close and old friends at Novello.

None the less, Harold Brooke, a generation younger, was endeavouring to play the role of a Jaeger as well as he could. In April 1918 he sent a suggestion for remaking *Caractacus* into an opera. It was a proposal often made, and always greeted by Elgar with interest, as now. He replied from Frank Schuster's country house:

The Hut[,] Bray on Thames
Tuesday [16 or 23 Apr. 1918]

Dear Mr.Brooke.

Many thanks for your letter. I am glad to hear you are recovering well—I have had a bad winter & am still 'down' after a throat operation.

I have often thought of 'Caractacus'—the first two scenes wd. knock into one act well—but there is no one to produce anything now & no one to sing!

Very kind regards
Yours sncy
Edward Elgar

As in the past, nothing came of the idea.

---

[3] TS in possession of Diana McVeagh. C. F. Pohl's standard biography of Haydn had appeared first in 1875 (Vol. 1) and 1882 (Vol. 2).

1919

Harold Brooke came closely into the picture a year later, when Elgar sent to Novello three pieces of chamber music (about which only a little correspondence survives). Brooke was a skilled and experienced pianist, and in revising the piano part of the Quintet especially he gave much welcome help. On 6 June 1919 Lady Elgar noted: 'Harold Brook[e] came up with questions re Quintet—much talk—he is devoted to E.'s works.' A vaguely dated note written from the Elgar's country retreat in Sussex suggests that the experience of several private performances, together with Brooke's suggestions, resulted in a complete revision of the Quintet first movement.

Brinkwells, Fittleworth, Sussex.
Monday [?19 May 1919]
My dear Brooke:

Quintet.

I am sending the new m.s. of the first movemt by letter post & you shd receive it on Tuesday morning. I have ans[were]d all the ?? I hope & have made some minor corrections in blue—I hope all is clear.

Yours sincerely
Edward Elgar

I think, NOW, it looks better than the 2/2 [—] especially pp 9–11

Elgar's figure is a model for the piano figuration first occurring shortly after cue 4 in the music as finally printed.

Another letter may refer to the same passage:

Brinkwells, Fittleworth, Sussex.
June 14 1919
My dear Brooke:

Quintet

So sorry to trouble you—the pencil arpeggio is all right: so go ahead.

I will give the proof of the first movement a good look over & post it back at once.

Do not send the M.S. of the 3rd movement yet.

Kind regards
Yours sny
Edward Elgar

Brooke asked whether he wanted back the second movement manuscript.

Brinkwells, Fittleworth, Sussex.
June 19: 1919

My dear Brooke:

Many thanks for yours of the 17th.—I do not think I need have the original M.S. until proofs come—*then* I had best have *everything*! There were a few very minor points—e.g. the high *G* in the slow movemt is after all ♩•— the D crochet vanishing[.] Don't worry over this [—] I will put it right.

So I await in fearful & feverish impatience   Proofs!

Yours ever
EE

By the time of writing his next letter two days later, Elgar had received a proof of the second movement Adagio, together with Brooke's suggestions for notating two piano figures in the third movement, Finale. The passage beginning four bars before cue 46 Elgar nicknamed 'straddlebug'. Over this he had also consulted William Murdoch (1888–1942), who had already played the piano part of the Quintet in two private performances. Elgar also suggested bringing the passages to the attention of H. Elliott Button, Novello's expert on musical notation and currently at work on a book about the subject. The other passage, beginning at cue 45, Elgar nicknamed 'tadpole'. Brooke wrote out the passages for inclusion with his queries. Elgar annotated Brooke's fragments, and sent them back with his letters of reply. Occasionally Brooke returned the fragments with further remarks. Elgar began this exchange with a reference to fishing at Brinkwells.

Brinkwells, Fittleworth, Sussex.
Longest day [21 June 1919]

My dear Brooke:

If I am not amiable this evening blame not me but a large trout which broke my line & got away!

I fear the pace is too quick for your L[eft] H[and] idea [in the third bar before cue 46]. I think the passages had better stand as I have green-inked them. Mr Murdoch said the dots were of no use (in the straddlebug passage—the small scrap) & suggested a slur over just to shew the 'cut off' from the last two bass notes > > .

This will not do —please leave all to R[ight] H[and] except the > > & put a *Slur* (not dots[)] right over each of these passages. [E.E.]

You will accept, as a peace sacrifice, my acceptance of your improved bars 4 & 8 [after cue 45]. I am not sure if the slurring of this tadpole passage (larger sheet) shd. be above [the notes] or below—as I have done it, or the reverse.

better *over*? slurs as written here [E.E.] I think this is not so good, as it doesn't show the hands so clearly. [H.L.B.].

adopt suggestion overleaf [E.E.]

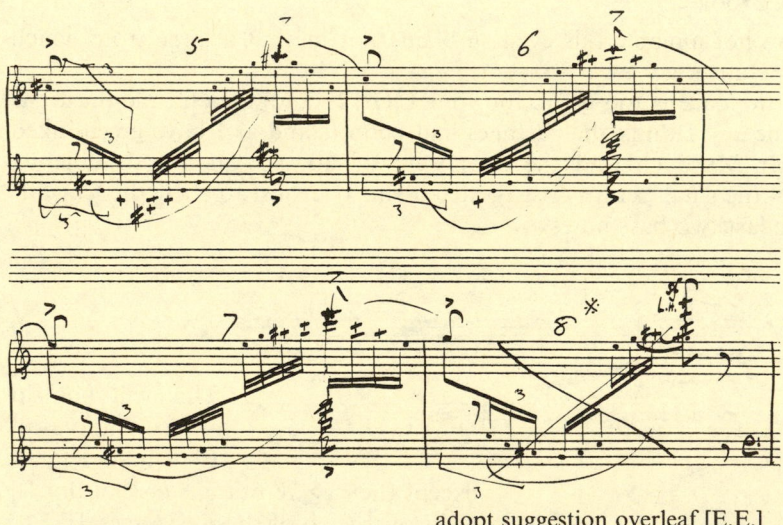

adopt suggestion overleaf [E.E.]

[*overleaf*] Alternative suggestions [H.L.B.]

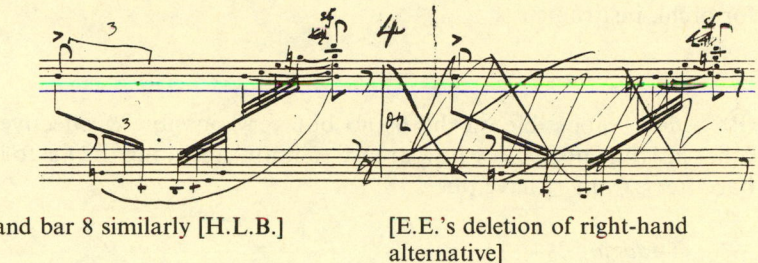

and bar 8 similarly [H.L.B.]   [E.E.'s deletion of right-hand
                                alternative]

> Yours sincerely
> Edward Elgar

Delighted to have two letters at once. The Adagio looks beautifully laid out.
You will have to wait for the metro[nome speeds]:—I have none here.

With this letter Elgar also enclosed another sheet discussing three passages:
A = twice before cue 54, once after cue 57, again after 58; B = ninth and tenth bars
after cue 32; C = after cue 59.

Quintet

Mem[oran]d[a]

Ⓐ In the last movement a Viola passage (4 times in as many keys)

please write thus

(this will save any time words[)]

Please shew this B & C to H.E. (His Eminence) Button for his book [on Musical Notation]. I meant to draw his attention to the difficulty in writing for orchl. inst[rument]s

Ⓑ —*fp* is impossible on the piano but very possible & effective on most other instruments[.] Now how are we to know how long the *f* is to last?—9th bar after 32 q.v. I have put

(*Adagio*)

I want the *f* short—a semiquaver in fact[:] am I bound to write

 [?]

I have rehearsed the Vtet with three sets (sets does not sound right) *suits* (sounds like a pack of cards) suits of players & have had to explain this—otherwise they play thus:—

played Va.

(?see Overture Don Giovanni for further ex.)

ⓒ another thing. In the last movement just before the 'return' the Viola has

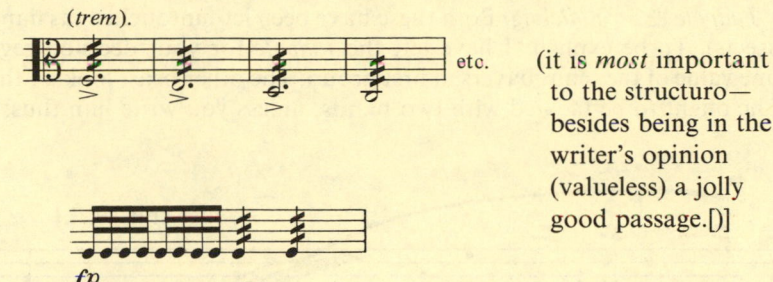

etc.   (it is *most* important
to the structuro—
besides being in the
writer's opinion
(valueless) a jolly
good passage.[)]

I want

now, is it worth while, *in the part only*, to put one poor crotchet's worth of
demisemiquavers or

to shew this? The players in each pack (suit or set) read it thus

which kills the effect & I have to enter into lengthy explanations, & although
one critic said it was the music of the spheres I don't want to be explan*e*tory!
which is a sort of paronomasia.

E.E.   June 21:1919

Brooke replied with further examples written out amid verbal notes.

Quintet *3rd movement*

Tadpole & Straddlebug. Both these have been left untouched (as dangerous insects). To be explicit, I have left the *tadpole* for your decision regarding time value of the semiquavers in first group. The other beast looks, I think, as if he ought to be tackled with two hands, unless you write him thus:—

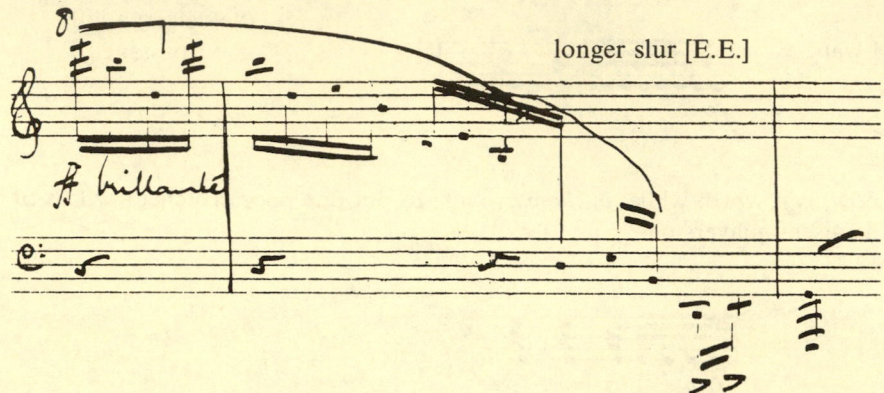

longer slur [E.E.]

tempts one (i.e. me) to start L[eft] H[and] where the stave is crossed [H.L.B.]

fpp etc. It seems to me that *fpp subito* should ensure the desired effect—at least I can't imagine any *musician* mis-understanding it. You have the instance you quote in proof. Will you settle it on that?

The viola passage 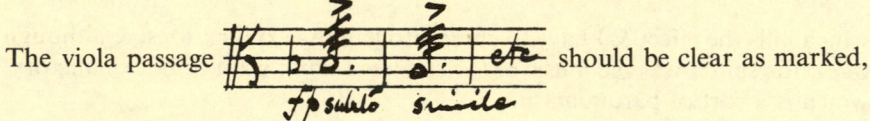 should be clear as marked,

but in case you do not think it sufficient I have written out part as

in part only—thus; ONE bar engraved out—then *simile*— [E.E]

Many accidentals crossed out of the strings in p[iano]f[orte] Score I have left in the parts.   [H.L.B.]
June 26.19

On the bottom of Brooke's manuscript Elgar wrote out the upper string notes with *fpp* on pages 32 and 40 of the printed score, but marked '*in parts only*'. Also:

pp 6.15,29.–mem:I have put a slur which will bring the bowing right

for ♪♪♪ .

With the Brooke suggestions there is also an undated sheet of music paper on which Elgar has written:

74 to two bars before 76 and at 83
this passage with strings to be bowed &c always thus

(The passage may be compared (generally) with the section at 83 .[)]

[E.E.]

Brinkwells, Fittleworth, Sussex.
June 27. I think [—] Friday, I am sure

My dear Brooke.

Here is the (your) m.s. of the IIIrd.movement [—] all questions answered & some small alterations affecting the strings mostly. All metronome marks must wait until the final proof as I have no machine here.

I also send the proof of IInd movemt. I am not sure of the ped.—you, being a pianist, might stick in a few where you yearn for them

I keep my original M S.—I suppose you do not want it

Yours sincerely
Edward Elgar

Early in July Elgar returned some proofs with comments on points in the Quintet first movement, together with a quotation from Schubert's *Wohin?* appropriate to the fishing life at Brinkwells—as Elgar was now for a fortnight, and rather unwillingly, back in town:

Severn House, 42, Netherhall Gardens, Hampstead, N.W.3
July 8 1919
My dear Brooke:

I return the proofs very quickly because

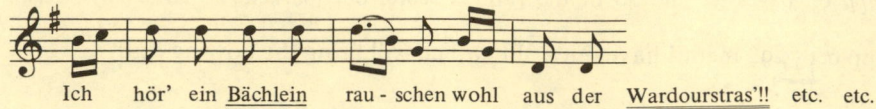

Ich   hör' ein <u>Bächlein</u>   rau - schen wohl   aus der   <u>Wardourstras'!!</u>   etc.   etc.

Note that I have copied the title [of the Quintet] from Schumann—which ought to satisfy you.

Knocking the first movement into 2/4 has made havoc of the *time words*—I have added the Met marks and it seems pretty clear to me now—except perhaps p 24;—at ⁻[23] do *you* feel you want a *time word*? after the *calando*?—I hope you do not as there is no room for it—I think that any person wd. feel they were in the same mood as at [9] without a hint: for the sake of uniformity I have put a few quaver legs, arms & eyes—if any of them (?e.g. the <u>a</u> first bar, 2nd system, p 27) mean <u>re</u>engraving DON'T DO IT

> Yours sincerely
> Edward Elgar

A later proof of the first movement was returned from Brinkwells a fortnight later. The passage which concerned Elgar now occurs before cue 21, together with the 'wireworm' arpeggiation signs.

Brinkwells, Fittleworth, Sussex.
Monday July 21 1919
My dear Brooke:

I recd the proofs this mg. & now return them all.

In the first movemt you will see—in *two* places some L.H. *crotchets* which looked rather *un*cared for—I have put

but (separate hooks) wd do quite well. The wire worm affair *is* already in the second passage. Some added bowings need not go in the score.

I like the look of the first movement now very much.

> Kind regards
> Yours sncy
> Edward Elgar

By the beginning of August the long process of correcting the Quintet was all but finished.

Brinkwells, Fittleworth, Sussex.

Augt 3 1919

My dear Brooke.

I do not want to see the 1st. & 2nd. movements again. I retd the last movemt. but am held up for want of a metronome[.] I hope to get one on Tuesday & will add the telephone numbers to the 3rd movement.

I am writing to the firm concerning the Cello Concerto

Yrs ever
EE[1]

Throughout the late spring and summer of 1919, side by side with correcting Quintet proofs, Elgar had been at work on his Violoncello Concerto. It was to be published by Novello, as was the chamber music, under the old 25 per cent royalty plan. But only a single letter appears to survive in reference to its preparation. This contained Elgar's answer to Harold Brooke's query as to whether the third movement half close might be altered to a full close for separate performances.

Brinkwells

Augt 12 1919

My dear Brooke:

Thanks for seeing to the erratum. I have *no* separate 'cello part.

I am sorry my remarks as to cues (in the solo pt) were illegible—please follow the example of the Violin concerto.

I fear I cannot think of anr. ending for the slow movement—it will do as it is if played separately.

I hope you will have a good holiday—it is very hot & I have been at work in the wood with serious detriment to my penmanship—as you see

Yours sny
Ed:Elgar

[1] In Percy Young's edition of Elgar's Letters, this letter's date was misread as 'September 3' (p. 253). Elgar's 'Augt' is however quite clear. On 3 Sept. 1919 Elgar was not at Brinkwells.

1920–1921

Although he was only sixty-two, the Cello Concerto proved to be Elgar's last major work. In the autumn his wife fell ill, and she died on 7 April 1920. The blow to his creative spirits seemed to be fatal. Among the flood of condoling letters from publishers, it was perhaps Henry Clayton who came nearest the mark.

160 Wardour Street W.
April 9th 1920.

My dear Elgar

You have all my sympathy.

Messages of this kind will be reaching you from every quarter, from the highest in the land downwards, & from all countries; but everyone had not the advantage & the privilege of knowing your wife, as I had: and it is because I knew her that my feeling for you is all the more intense, all the more heartfelt.

What you will do without her, & her help, it is impossible to imagine.

I only hope that your terrible misfortune will not overwhelm you.

Yours very sincerely
Henry R: Clayton[1]

The first correspondence after Lady Elgar's death now preserved in Novello archives is an exchange on 18 June to settle the format of the Cello Concerto full score. A week later Elgar received an offer to conduct the first concert of a new City of Birmingham Orchestra in November.

Brinkwells, Fittleworth, Sussex
June 28.1920

Dear Clayton:

In the good years before the war you were frequently so kind as to arrange terms for me with conductors etc:—this pleasant (for me) practice I think arose originally when there were works of mine to be performed carrying a performing fee.

Mr.Appleby Matthews, whose letters I enclose, is Director of the City of Bm.Orch:—to his first letter, I said in reply that I could manage the date: his second letter expresses joy but does not suggest any fee: also he names the 2nd Sym:—for this of course a fee wd. have to be paid. May I say to him that I have sent on the letters to you & that you will arrange terms? I do not want very much but, on principle, I will not go for nothing or expenses. If you wd.

[1] HWRO 705:445:539.

rather not undertake this & wd. prefer to deal with the Symphony only—if that question does arise—just let me know.

I am getting a good rest here & wish every worker I know cd. do the same.

> Kind regards
> Yours sincly
> Edward Elgar

[160, Wardour Street, London, W.]
June 29th. [192]0.

Dear Elgar

Thanks for your letter of the 28th.instt.

I am only too glad to act for you in the negotiations leading up to conducting contracts: & I will do my best to obtain good terms for you without risking loss of business.

I have already written to Appleby Matthews about Novr.10th: & I will write to you directly I hear from him. In the meantime I retain his two letters of June 2nd. & 25th.

I am glad you are having a good rest—you need it, I am sure. I only hope that Brinkwells, even under altered conditions, will completely restore you.

> Yours sincerely
> Henry R:Clayton.

Clayton's negotiations resulted in an offer of 50 guineas, which Elgar accepted. Yet his music was in noticeably less demand in these post-war years. When Elgar returned some marked orchestral parts to Novello's hire library, Clayton had to tell him: '. . . our hiring stock is already more than we require.'[2]

Much of Elgar's later correspondence with Novello was over arrangements from his works for smaller or different forces—arrangements suggested by Elgar, the publishers, or someone else. In one case it was H. Walford Davies, who wrote to Elgar suggesting an arrangement from *Gerontius* for a hymn-book he was editing. Elgar wrote to Clayton.

Severn House[,] Hampstead, N.W.
Nov 1 1920

My dear Clayton—

I have acknd. the receipt of the encl[ose]d letter.

What do you think? I am not sure if the arrgt could be made satisfactorily—

---

[2] 12 July 1920 (Novello archives).

I shd have said 'no' but I am reminded that 'Kyries' were made out of *Elijah* and it occurs to me that you, as pubrs., might like the notion.

You will see however that Dr.Walford Davies says something about pubn.—Please return his letter & I will reply

Yours siny
Edward Elgar

Clayton's reply showed his powers of repartee as formidable as ever, and his delight in whetting their edges on any adversary who presented himself:

160, Wardour Street, London, W.
November 2nd.1920.

Dear Elgar

Thanks for your letter enclosing Dr.Walford Davies's letter to you of the 22nd.ult, which I now return as requested.

By all means carry out the scheme as suggested, if you approve of it yourself. The only condition which we will ask you to make on our behalf is that you inform Dr.W.D. that we must retain the copyright, & see to its protection in the U.S.A., & that it must be in the Welsh Hymn Book by arrangement with us. We will of course see that you are suitably rewarded. In the old days Dr.W.D. would have approached us first in the matter; but since he took to lecturing us in the Press, warning us that our reputation as respectable Publishers was at stake, he naturally avoids us, & prefers to approach you, whose reputation as a respectable composer is not at stake!

So we want to have him recognize that he cannot, by avoiding us, ignore us.

Our experts here think that to do what Dr.W.D. wants will be a toughish job, if adherence to the original is a sine qua non.

But Dr.W.D. evidently has ideas of his own on the subject: so I should employ him as a literary hack, & ask him to submit an arrangement of his own for you to mould into shape, & finally approve.

No need, I suppose, to remind you of your engagement at Birmingham on the 10th instt.

Shall I collect the Fee for you: or will you gather it yourself?

Yours very sincerely
Henry R:Clayton.

This rhetoric was once more of considerable use to Elgar—especially in meeting proposals for engagements not likely to result in commensurate fees. One was an idea for a Royal Concert to include *With Proud Thanksgiving* (a shortened version of *For the Fallen* which Elgar had arranged and scored with band for performance at the dedication of Lutyens's Cenotaph in Whitehall in 1920). The other was an offer to conduct at Stoke-on-Trent, where the principal of Twyford's Sanitary Pottery at Hanley was patron.

Severn House[,] Hampstead, N.W.
Feb 18 1921

My dear Clayton:

Would it be troubling you too much to write to Stoke? Of course the occasion wd. be interesting but, as usual, the good people suggest no fee. Mr. Twyford is at the head of it & 'sees them through' (I understand) their exceeding activities at competitions & he *may* be (?) disposed to see them through this affair. You will see from the pencil sketch the sort of note my daughter has sent in acknowledgement—but do not give yourself more than the slightest trouble over it

Yours sincerely
Edward Elgar

And he enclosed a summary copy in Carice Elgar's hand:

Sent Feb:18th.1921

Dr M.James

Sir E.E. thanks letter

Would give him gt pleasure to come down to Hanley in Nov. if things cld be arrangd

Messrs Nov. usually arrange these things for him & they will probably write to you in a few days.

[160, Wardour Street, London, W.]
March 5th. [192]1.

Dear Elgar

Enclosed correspondence, re 'King Olaf' at Hanley next November, explains itself. I hope I acted in accordance with your views in *sitting on* the offer of Fifteen Guineas. There must be plenty of money in & around Stoke-on-Trent; & I look upon Lieutt. Wood's suggestions as distinctly mean, in spite of his protest that 'the *mercenary point of view*' is far from being the case with them!

On May 7th.Prox. there is to be a big Concert at the Albert Hall to celebrate the Jubilee of The Royal Albert Hall, & The Royal Choral Society. The Concert will be the joint Speculation of the two bodies, & the scheme is to include in the programme works of everyone who has taken part in the Conducting of the Concerts from start to finish. Gounod, Barnby, Mackenzie[,] Bridge, & Stainer as Organist. Other works are of course to be included. And you are to be represented by 'Land of Hope & Glory', with Clara Butt as Soloist (probably) & 'With proud Thanksgiving'.

The King & Queen have promised to be present & the occasion will be a really important one.

Gus:Littleton, who is on the Council of The Royal Choral Society, was instrumental in getting 'With proud Thanksgiving' included in the programme but he found that Lord Shaftesbury was equally keen on its being included. Lord Howe is endeavouring to secure the Services of Clara Butt— & Melba (Jewel Song from 'Faust' representing the Gounod epoch) on nominal terms & I believe they want you also to conduct things also on nominal terms!

But the point of all this preamble is to let you know that 'With Proud Thanksgiving' will have to be scored for an *ordinary Orchestra*[:] the Scheme obviously will not stand the [use] of a Military Band just for the 8 or 10 [minutes] occupied in the performance of that work. [Now] will you see to it? It will be a good [thing to be] done, as the work does not stand a [first] chance if its only accompaniment is a Military or a Brass Band.

Will you let me know whether I [can] send you any material to help you [put] together the Score—e.g. a Full Score, or [band] parts of 'For the Fallen'?

Yours very sincerely,
Henry R:Clayton[3]

Severn House[,] Hampstead, N.W.
March 8.1921

My dear Clayton:

Many thanks for the trouble you took over the Hanley people: I return the letters: you are quite right—all those presidents & people do nothing for the society except lend their names & think they are helping the cause by boring me to death by making me stay at their dreary houses!

As to the A.Hall on May 7th—I have made a note of the date & am looking into 'With proud thanksgiving'—I have the 8vo edn. & full sc. of the original work. Bridge wrote to me about it.

Kind regards
Yours sincerely
Edward Elgar

P.S. I don't know if you remember advising me & drafting letters about some U.S.A. trifles? I have just heard from *Canada* that it is desired to print my little things there & asking permission to do so as my '*original license covers the U.S.A. only*' So you see your advice was absolutely inclusive. Thanks.

The final reference in Elgar's letter seems to be about three brief songs for children which had been published by Silver, Burdett & Company in the United States. Back at home, he did the necessary reorchestration for *With Proud Thanksgiving* in early April, and conducted it at the Royal Concert in May.

The demand for Elgar's music, however, was nowhere near pre-war levels. Royalties now accruing on many small works and arrangements approached the vanishing point, and Elgar himself suggested that the publishers might care to

---

[3] The copy is defective at the right side. Words within square brackets in the final two paragraphs are conjectures based partly on beginnings of words faintly visible.

purchase these copyrights for a lump sum. Clayton accordingly made a list of these items, and added a second list of larger works which the firm considered similarly uncommercial.

[160, Wardour Street, London, W.]
June 10th.[192]1.

My dear Elgar

We are still busy preparing your annual Sales account. All the stock is counted, but it takes some time to make out the actual account; but we are pushing on with it.

In the meantime I have had prepared for your examination two accounts Marked A. & B. & now forwarded to you.

Each account covers a period of 5 years Sales.

Account A shows the revenue earned by those small things, all Octavo, published for a few pence, which you suggested that we might like to compound & get rid of.

Account B. shows the revenue earned by some more important & higher priced things, but which commercially are of no, or very little, annual value, & which we are prepared to deal with in precisely the same way as you have suggested that the things included in Account A might be dealt with.

The Sales in the 5 years total £256.9.7—viz:—

    Account A.   £218.3.3
    Account B.   38.6.4
              ————————
          £256.9.7

Of course the valuation to-day of these Royalties is a pure speculation—or a gamble—as owing to the varying fashions, tastes, & conditions, no one can say what their future is to be. But three of us have carefully gone into the matter, & we have formulated ideas as to what we can & ought to pay for the surrender of the Royalties in question, & without further explanations that sum is £500 for the lot!!

Please consider the matter, & if you would like any items extracted from either list, let me know what they are.

I must admit that I got a bit of a Shock when I saw the figures relating the [*sic*] 'The Variations' Pf.Solo £3.9.2 & Pf.duet £2.8.0 or £5.17.2 for both—in Five years!!!

Excuse the roughness of the enclosed accounts.

They were made out for my information, & were not written out with that care which would have been given to them if they had been originally intended to be put before you. But I want you to have the same information that we have.

                                Yours sincerely
                                Henry R:Clayton

Kindly return the accounts in due course. Th [*illegible*] so much work that I have had to register them.

The two lists comprised the following:

The Angelus, op 56

The Apostles, op 49: Introduction to Part 2 (arrgt for organ)

Ave Maria, op 2 no 2, and English version: 'Jesu, lord of life'

Ave Maris Stella, op 2 no 3, and English version: 'Jesu meek and lowly'

The Birthright (song for boys)

Cantique, op 3

A Child Asleep (song)

A Christmas Greeting, op 52

Coronation March, 1911, op 65: full score, arrgts for piano and organ

Death on the Hills, op 72

The Dream of Gerontius, op 38: Prelude and Angel's Farewell (arrgt for organ)

five separate vocal and choral extracts (arrgts by Elgar)

Elegy, op 58: full score and arrgt for organ

Evening Scene (part song)

Falstaff, op 68: Two Interludes: full score and arrgt for piano

Follow the Colours (Marching Song)

Go, Song of Mine, op 57

How Calmly the Evening (part song)

In the South Overture, op 50: arrgts for piano solo and duet

Canto popolare: arrgts for small orchestra, piano, organ, violin, viola, cello, and clarinet

Introduction and Allegro, op 47: full score and arrgt for piano duet

Lo! Christ the Lord is Born (carol)

Love, op 18 no 2

O Hearken Thou (Coronation Offertorium), op 64

Part Songs from the Greek Anthology, op 45: (*Yea, Cast Me from the Heights; Whether I Find Thee; After Many a Dusty Mile; It's Oh to be a Wild Wind; Feasting I Watch*)

Part Songs, op 53: (*There is Sweet Music; Deep in My Soul; O Wild West Wind; Owls*)

Part Songs, op 71: (*The Shower, The Fountain*)

Part Songs, op 73: (*Love's Tempest, Serenade*)

Psalm 29: 'Give unto the Lord', op 74

Psalm 48: 'Great is the Lord', op 67

The Reveille, op 54

Romance for Bassoon and Orchestra, op 62: full score, arrgts for piano and cello

Symphony no 1, op 55: Adagio: arrgt for organ

Themes arrgd for organ

They are at Rest (choral elegy)

Variations ('Enigma'), op 36: arrgts for piano solo and duet

'Dorabella' Intermezzo: arrgts for piano solo and duet.

Severn House[,] Hampstead, N.W.
June 12.1921   (Typewritten)

My dear Clayton,

Thank you for the "five years'" table of the royalties on the small things; it is, of course, sorry reading, but I have never permitted myself any illusions and have none now.

One point strikes me;—should not the account be tabulated until *this* June? You see there is apparently a slight rise in some of the part-song things, e.g. Angelus, Feasting I watch, Love's tempest, etc—you will easily see what I mean. Do these appreciations shew a revival of choral singing or merely that certain things have been used for, say, certain competitions? Are such advances sustained in the account ending in this present June?

You do not say if the sum offered is in lieu of the royalties, if any, accruing to date or if you propose to pay these to me and then give me £500.

I wish the firm could see it's [sic] way to buy me out entirely; I never really belonged to the musical world,—I detest my slightest necessary connection with it & should be glad to have done with it and get back to my (deceased) dogs & horses!

Do not trouble to write; I will come down one day this week, it will save much trouble.

> Yours sincerely,
> Edward Elgar

P.S.—I enclose an unimportant note about some errors.

[160, Wardour Street, London,W.]
June 15th, [192]1.

My dear Elgar,

I have now added, in red ink, the value of the sales for the year 1920–1921 of the items included in the accounts A. & B. returned herewith. The addition of these red ink figures leaves the matter practically in statu quo. In some cases there are increases, in others decreases. These are mainly due, I think, to the selection or the omission of the works concerned in or from Festival Competition Programmes. I know 'The Shower' has been included in several Competitions lately. Still that is to the credit of the work affected. You will notice that.—

On list A. the total for 1920–21 exceeds the total of 1919–20 by £9.13.4.
Thus   1920–1921 £78. 6. 2
     1919–1920   68.12.10
             ————
        £ 9.13. 2

of which sum 'The Shower' alone accounts for £8.1.9. This proves how the annual sales are affected by the inclusion of any particular item in this or that Festival Competition, which again is an item of pure speculation, in which I fear we are, in many cases, missing the powerful advocacy and influence of dear old McNaught.

On list B. the total for 1919–20 exceeds the total for 1920–1921 by £2.5.7.
Thus   1919–1920 £9.15. 2.

      1920–1921   7. 9. 7.

           2. 5. 7

So the gross difference between the two years on the total of both accounts is only £7.6.9.
Thus.   Increase   £9.13. 4.

             2. 5. 7.

        £7. 6. 9.

I can only repeat that we regard the deal, if you care to make a deal of it, as a pure speculation, but I think the chances of either party making a good thing out of it are fairly equal.

It is for you to decide. We have made up our minds that we cannot lay out more than £500 on the speculation. So if you are not quite satisfied with our valuation, no harm will be done in letting things run on in the old way. We shall of course pay you (in your 'Annual Sale Account') the sums earned by the Works included in accounts A & B during 1920–1921, over & above the £500.

I think early next week we shall have your annual sale account ready. As you will be in the country and as the cheque will be well over £600, would you like me to pay the cheque into your bank? If so, let me know which bank. Of course the accounts will be sent to you, and will be subject to adjustment as usual if anything is not correct. The point is not very material as I shall register the envelope anyhow: but it may save you trouble to have the money banked at once instead of subjecting it to two journeys through the post.

Hoping you will have a good time in Worcestershire.

                                 Yours sincerely
                                 Henry R:Clayton.

Two days later Elgar called at Novello's offices and they settled outstanding details. On the 23rd Clayton sent a contract for Elgar's signature covering all the works as from 8 June 1921. He wrote separately:

160, Wardour Street, London, W.
June 23rd, 1921

Dear Elgar,

I have to-day sent to your Bank—Messrs.Glyn & Co., 67 Lombard Street, E.C.3—by registered post—a cheque for £1185.12.7. made up as follows.—

                Annual Sales Account   £685.12.7.
                Purchase of Royalties   500. 0.0.

                                 £1185.12.7.

I enclose particulars of the sales referred to, and hope you will consider them satisfactory.

I also enclose a printed list of your works, published by us, on which we have struck out in red ink those works, the royalties payable in respect of which we have acquired.

I have compared the list with the two rough (and dirty) lists which were submitted to you for your information, and I find that the clean copy now enclosed correctly embodies the works dealt with in those two lists. I have, however, had them all set out in the Schedule to the Indenture of Surrender and Release which I am enclosing in duplicate. One copy we sealed at a Directors Meeting to-day, and that copy you will of course retain, the other copy is presented for the favour of your execution of it. Will you kindly sign it in the presence of a Witness and return it to us at your convenience.

I hope everything will prove to be in order.

With best wishes,

> Yours sincerely,
> [Henry R. Clayton]

Severn House[,] Hampstead, N.W.3
June 29:1921

Dear Clayton:

Your letter of the 23rd. enclosing the 'Indenture' & advising me that you had paid a cheque £1185.12.7 to Glyn reached me in the country;—I sent a word of acknowledgement being aware (alas!) that I had to return here for two days.

Many thanks for it all;—I keep the Inde. signed by the firm & the list of the works; with this I send the other Inde. signed & witnessed so the matter is now concluded—I hope we have both made good bargains,—sentimentally I am glad to be 'out of it'.

> Kindest rgrds
> Yours sincerely
> Edward Elgar

P.S.—We have always make our assignments etc in my *full* name but I do not think the omission of the *William* matters in the least

Yet that Spring had seen a return to music in a small way. In late April 1921 Elgar had orchestrated Bach's organ Fugue in C minor, BWV 537. This arose from a discussion with Richard Strauss about the lines on which such orchestrations should run. Strauss favoured a restrained approach, whereas Elgar thought it best to use the full forces of the modern orchestra. By making his own practical demonstration with the C minor Fugue, he hoped to tempt Strauss to orchestrate the matching Fantasia. A month later he prepared to send it to Novello, on the eve of departure for a final summer at Brinkwells.

Severn House[,] Hampstead, N.W.
May 22 1921

My dear Clayton:

I am sending the full score of an arrangement for large orch: of a Bach fugue—I will not go into the 'history' of the undertaking now, but I shd. be glad if you could get the score & orchl. parts printed as soon as may be— there are many performances in train.

Please (*particularly particular this*) do not let anyone outside see the score. You said that in the summer months there was less engraving going on—so perhaps this may be a convenient time for this piece. Anyhow go ahead if you can—& if the firm does not care to publish it the engraving can be my expense—but we will talk of terms etc another time.

I hoped I should have been able to see you about it but we have to take the opportunity to travel to the cottage (Brinkwells[,] Fittleworth[,] Sussex) tomorrow & you know how difficult it is to make a journey now so we seize on the car going down

> Kind rgrds
> Yrs sly
> Edward Elgar

The Fugue arrangement was engraved in full score before it was decided whether it should remain Elgar's property. He wrote to the music editor John E. West about the proof.

Brinkwells   Fittleworth   Sussex
Augt 9:1921

Dear West:

Many thanks for your note pinned to the proof. The differences in the phrasing of the subject were (mostly) intentional. I have gone carefully into these.

A few *bow* marks (Π V) have been added which need not go into the score.

For the sake of perfection will you look at ☐25☐ (bar after) Trombe. & see my suggestion?—if you have any rule in use to cover such a 'direction' for the Trombe—*the which are feminine*—pray use it. It looks odd—in the *part* for IIIrd to put *SOLO*—doesn't it? and yet we want to call attention to the importance of the situation.

There are one or two places (e.g. Fl.I.II—p 1) where the brackets are marked *divisi*—I thought this was done only in the strings—leave it as engd. if according to rule.

Fl I–II p.3.—the I° & [II°] have got muddled—I think it can be made clear.

In all the parts (bar before ☐23☐])] *poco allarg.* will do—we need not disturb anything to get in the whole word?

We are in a plague of wasps—so I can scarcely say I hope you are enjoying the country as much as we are.

> Kind rgrds
> Yours sincy
> Edward Elgar[4]

Several weeks later came Novello's offer for the copyright. Elgar responded:

Severn House[,] Hampstead, N.W.
Sep 22. 1921
Dear Sirs:

I write to accept the offer made by Mr.Augustus Littleton, viz: one hundred guineas, for the arrgt. of the Bach fugue. I mentioned that I wish Mr.Eugène Goossens to have the first performance on Oct 27th. & that any charge made shd. be small:
I return two title proofs

> Yrs v scly
> Edward Elgar

1922

Early in 1922 Elgar arranged the *Part-songs from the Greek Anthology*, Op. 45, for mixed voices. Novello paid him 50 guineas. But when he submitted a transcription of the Bach C minor Fantasia to match the Fugue, the firm jibbed at the composer's suggestion of a further hundred guineas. They pointed out that the Fantasia as it stood could not be performed alone since, following Bach, Elgar had made its ending a half close before *attacca* into the Fugue. They asked whether the Fantasia ending could be extended to a full close. Elgar replied from the flat he had taken after Severn House was closed for auction.

37, St.James's Place, S.W.1.
June 16 1922
Dear Sirs:

I cannot add anything to the Bach Fantasia—I have orchestrated it as it stands & an *ending* wd. be out of place. I really think I ought to receive the same fee as for the fugue.

> Yrs vy try
> Edward Elgar

[4] MS in possession of Raymond Monk.

[160, Wardour Street, London, W.]
June 17th [192]2
Dear Elgar,

Your letter of yesterday's date has been brought to me.

All right—We will pay you for the Fantasia the same fee as was paid for the Fugue.

Our idea was that the Fantasia cannot possibly be as successful *commercially* as the Fugue, because it cannot be performed by itself, as it has no ending other than the Fugue which follows it—consequently we cannot make any use of the Fantasia except as the Preface to the Fugue.

The Fugue on the other hand can stand, and has stood, by itself and we are very much more likely to get performances of the Fugue than of the Fugue plus Fantasia.

I can quite understand that you are not concerned about such trifles, but we have to be: and we realise that to a certain extent we have queered the pitch of the Fantasia by having issued the Fugue by itself.

That is the explanation which we want you to have. The cheque shall follow the explanation in a post or two.

[Yours sincerely
Henry R.Clayton]

37, St. James's Place, S.W.1.
June 20.1922
Dear Clayton:

I had no chance to write in answer to your letter of the 17th before your second letter, kindly enclosing the cheque, arrived.

Now I want the firm to be satisfied: I began the fantasia before I 'did' the fugue—but dropped it. Your Mr.West(?) & some one else (Harold Brooke *I think*) said 'Why not "do" the fantasia?' I am not trying in the least to shift the responsibility (if there's any) on to anyone else. I cannot ask you for a fee which you cannot see your way to recover from the public. As I said before, the actual work was more arduous than that required by the fugue;—then our position is rather like Charles Lamb, who—when his directors complained of his arriving frequently very late at the office—said 'But then I go away very early!'

Here is my proposition: let sufficient M.S. copies be made, entirely at my expense, for Dr.Brewer's Gloucester festival performance (which is announced) & after that I will 'scrap' the whole thing & we will say no more about it. How will that do?

Yours sincerely
Edward Elgar

[160, Wardour Street, London, W.]
June 21st. [192]2.

Dear Elgar

Many thanks for your letter.

I am sending back the cheque, as we are only too glad to pay you your fee for the Fantasia at the same figure as the fee for the Fugue. My long explanation was sent because I wanted you not to entertain the idea that, in proposing a less fee, we were 'trying it on': we thought the Fantasia would be less useful than the Fugue—We may be wrong. In any event we shall probably see our money back some day; even if the Fantasia pays its expenses at a slower rate than the Fugue does.

Moreover it is such a small matter that it need not be considered: and as for suppressing the scheme after Gloucester—well we cannot listen to it. So please Bank the money, & make yourself quite at ease about it. We are quite satisfied.

We shall start the engraving at once, unless a possible printers' strike comes off.!!

Yours sincerely
Henry R:Clayton.

37, St.James's Place, S.W.1.
June 22 1922

Dear Clayton:

All right: many thanks. here's the formal receipt & the agreement shall follow.

I am, of course, hard up (more or less) but I didn't want my memory to be cursed by generations of impoverished shareholders

Yours sicy
Edward Elgar

Next day he replied to questions written in the proof by the music editor.

37, St.James's Place, S.W.1.
June 23,1922

Dear West: I see your handwriting on the proof of the fantasia & note your queries.

I suggest a metro[nome]-mark: *but* if there is one (or a *tempo* WORD) in Novello's edition [of Bach's Organ Music] I think they shd. correspond: let me know if there are any directions in Novello's edition

In the theme

& its ramifications I want to *cut* the crot[chet]s[x] *off* from the minim—not violently but just enough to keep them well apart ♫ that sort of thing. I have put ♪ (wh: can be easily dropped in by the engraver): do *you* think that is clear? I do *not* want ♩ which will be played *staccato*—(wdn't it?) I *think* the dash with the dot over is right—but what does it convey to most people & how do you 'feel' it?

for the Introductory page, you might add
'For convenience in [performance] the original time-signature 6/4 has been altered to 3/4.'

It really saves ½ the time & trouble in rehearsing

> Kind rgrds
> Yrs siny
> Edward Elgar[1]

The word omitted in the performing direction was supplied by West, and the sentence was printed on the page facing the first page of score. Elgar's marks for cutting off the crotchet before the minim were also adopted.

On the same day he sent back proofs of Herbert Brewer's arrangement for organ of *The Kingdom* Prelude.

37, St.James's Place, S.W.1.
June 23 1922

Dear Sirs:

With this I return Dr Brewer's arrangemt [—] Most excellent.
I have corrected the two 'queried' chords on the last page

> Yours very try
> Edward Elgar

Little more in the shape of new music or arrangements emerged from the remainder of 1922.

---

[1] MS in possession of John Carol Case.

On 5 March 1923, W. W. Elkin wrote about the Organ Grinder's Songs which Charles Mott had sung in the original production of *The Starlight Express*. In 1918 Mott had been killed in France. But Elkin had hopes that the songs might become more popular. Only the following extract from his letter survives in Novello archives:

We should like to try whether we could get a better result by bringing them out in album form, in which shape we should propose to pay you a royalty of 4½d. per copy on sales in Great Britain and the Colonies, 13 copies counted as 12, and 3d. on sales in the United States of America.

Elkin also asked for a photograph of Mott as the Organ Grinder.

37, St.James's Place, S.W.1.
March 6th,1923.

Dear Elkin:

By all means do as you suggest about the 'Organ grinder's Songs' on the terms you name.

I have no picture of the character and I do not remember one being made; some photos of dear Mott were taken I think and appeared in the illustrated papers—perhaps one of these would form a good basis for a sketch?

Kind regards
Yours sincerely,
Edward Elgar

P.S. I saw Blackwood a week or two back and there is again a talk of reviving the play. U.S.N.A.

But it proved a false dawn, as did every attempt to revive *The Starlight Express* in Elgar's lifetime.

During 1923 Elgar orchestrated three works with a view to performances at the Worcester Festival in September. One was the Overture to Handel's Second Chandos Anthem. The others were anthems—Samuel Sebastian Wesley's *Let Us Lift Up Our Heart* and (at Ivor Atkins's special request) Jonathan Battishill's *O Lord, Look Down From Heaven*. In the case of the anthems, Elgar suggested that Novello should make copy parts and lend them, together with his manuscript full score, for the Worcester Festival performance. He wrote from the comfortable old house near Worcester he had now taken on a lease.

Napleton Grange, Kempsey, Worcs
May 27:1923

My dear Clayton—

I am sending the score of the Battishill Anthem & the Handel Overture as promised.

The Wesley Anthem is ready &, on hearing from you, that shall follow

It is marvellously *cold* today alas!

Yrs siny
Edward Elgar

[160, Wardour Street, London, W.]
May 28th [192]3

Dear Elgar,

Many thanks for your letter of yesterday's date.

The scores you refer to have not yet arrived.

We will do all that you suggested about the Battishill Anthem 'O Lord, look down', that is to say that, as you are presenting us with the manuscript of your orchestral accompaniment, we will copy the parts and lend them to the Worcester Festival Committee for nothing.

I am sorry however that we cannot make a similar arrangement about the big Wesley Anthem 'Let us lift up our heart'. Since you were here we have ascertained that we have a folio copy of the Anthem, already revised and edited for modern organ by J.E.West for publishing in cheap octavo form, but that we abandoned the enterprise when Messrs.Bayley & Ferguson issued their edition by Bairstow.

There is not room for two such editions, and as Messrs.Bayley & Ferguson were first in the field, and Sir Ivor Atkins has decided to use their edition, our edition would have to take a back seat! And we of course could not undertake the expense of providing the Worcester Festival Committee with band parts of a work of which we do not publish the vocal scores in available form.

I will drop you a line directly the two scores arrive.

[Yours sincerely,
Henry R. Clayton]

So Elgar sent his orchestration of the Wesley anthem to Bayley & Ferguson. There in later years it seems to have perished in a fire.

When the Handel Overture arrived at Novello, West's report was generally favourable:

Overture in D minor.

This is *very good Handel*, & doubtless Elgar's scoring, which is quite faithful in *texture*, would make it still more interesting to the hearer at any modern orchestral concert or one where orchestra is used. Perhaps it is not quite so interesting—either as music or orchestrally—as the Bach Fantasia &

Fugue, but it is more in character with the original (very likely the arranger felt that it required less of the *Elgarian fancy* in the details of its orchestration than the Bach movements), & Handel enthusiasts & others would probably *welcome* it.

Possibly such instruments as the Cor Anglais, Bass Clarinet, Contra Fagotto, &c, *could* be dispensed with on *some* occasions, if necessary? I don't know if the composer has hinted at this?

J.W.

[160, Wardour Street, London, W.]
June 13th [192]3.

Dear Elgar,

We have duly digested your orchestral version of the Handel Overture in D. minor.

It will suit us well enough, but we do not think that it will achieve the popularity that has declared itself with reference to the Bach Fugue. Bach is always in demand; but Handel only occasionally. If you think that Sixty Guineas is a fair offer for the Handel Overture we shall be glad to take it over on those terms. We will engrave the score and parts, and will publish the score only, reserving the parts for lending only for the present.

Yours faithfully,
[Henry R. Clayton]

Kempsey, Worcester.
June 15 1923

My dear Clayton:

Many thanks: I accept the firm's offer for the Handel arrgt.

You will remember that it is wanted for the Worcester festival & that I promised it 'free' for that charitable occasion. If 'this freedom' came not into the scope of your offer you must deduct something from the amount you offer me to make it straight

Kind rgrds
Yrs sicy
Edward Elgar

On 20 June the firm's cheque was sent to Elgar for the full amount.

Elgar wrote twice to West about the editing of the Handel arrangement:

Kempsey, Worcester.
July 10 1923

Dear West: Thank you for your note about the Handel Overture: I think '*arranged by Edward Elgar*' will cover my delinquencies: I cannot quite follow your reference to 'last bar but one of p.13'—all this is in the old score; the whole modern-looking passage 19–21 is Handel from his other version of the fugue.

> Kind regards
> Yours sincy
> Edward Elgar[1]

Kempsey, Worcester.
July 16.1923
Dear West:

I am delighted to find that you are interested in the Handel 'overture': I have looked at my own transcript from the old English scores with wh: the German edn. corresponds *generally*;—I have cut out *four* bars (the excision occurs halfway through the fifth bar of p.13)—this does away with a weak repetition of the modulation into the dom. & a wandering excursion into treble regions:—the pedal passage (on A here) is from the enlarged version of the fugue in F# minor.

I think I have ansd. all the queries. I have known the overture from the old two stave organ arrangement since I was a little boy and always wanted it to be heard in a large form—the weighty structure is (to me) so grand—epic.

I have suggested a new 'form' for the heading
OVERTURE in D minor
HANDEL.
arranged by E.E.
but please adopt whatever style you think best.

> Kind regards,
> Yours sincerely,
> Edward Elgar[2]

Meanwhile Elgar had been composing a little. He had not been able to respond to a suggestion sent to him by Clayton for a setting from Longfellow. But he answered a request from Robin Legge for male-voice part-songs to be sung by the 'American Quartet' (pupils of Jean de Reszke) with two settings from other sources. One was entitled *The Wanderer*. The last four stanzas were quoted from Isaac D'Israeli's *Curiosities of Literature*.[3] In choosing these four and writing an introductory stanza of his own, Elgar created a poem which reflected astonishingly his own mood since his wife's death.

---

[1] MS in possession of Raymond Monk.
[2] MS in possession of Raymond Monk.
[3] Vol. II, pp. 315–17. Elgar's copy was the 'new' edition (Frederick Warne, n.d., the 'Memoir' by Benjamin Disraeli dated 1848). Isaac D'Israeli found the poem in a Restoration anthology of 'Wit and Drollery'. The identification of the D'Israeli source I owe to Roger Savage.

The Wanderer

I wander through the woodlands,
Peace to you,—day's a-dying;
I tune a song
The trees among,
But oft-times comes a crying.
I know more than Apollo;
For, oft when he lies sleeping,
I see the stars
At mortal wars,
And the rounded welkin weeping.

The morn's my constant mistress,
The lovely owl my morrow;
The flaming drake
And the night-crow make
Me music, to my sorrow.

With a heart of furious fancies,
Whereof I am commander:
With a burning spear
And a horse of air
To the wilderness I wander.

With a knight of ghosts and shadows,
I summoned am to tourney:
Ten leagues beyond
The wide world's end;
Methinks it is no journey.

Kempsey, Worcester.
July 17 1923
My dear Clayton:

Here is a T.T.B.B.; *not* the words by Longfellow which you suggested;—I had tried to do something with those long ago but, as no repetition of the words was possible, failed to make a satisfactory thing of them.

You wanted something primarily for competition purposes: I do not suppose you will think the piece sent with this will do,—the words are strange & weird. In any case I should like it printed at once & if the firm does not want it, it may remain my property.

Yours sincerely
Edward Elgar

But West's report this time was less favourable:

This is smooth & singable—if at times rather *ordinary* in character; but it is not what I shd. of [*sic*] thought the composer *could* have done with the poem. There were opportunities of *contrast* & more independence of part-writing.

However, the setting is as brief as it *could* be, & is fairly *easy*.

J.W.

Accordingly, Clayton made the firm's offer modest:

20/7/23

My dear Elgar

The M.S. of the Partsong for Men's Voices (T.T.B.B.) 'The Wanderer' came duly to hand. It will answer our purposes very well, they tell me, & we should like to add it to our Orpheus Series.

May we have it for a lump sum of Twenty-five Guineas, you retaining the Mechanical Instrument Rights as usual

[Yours sincerely,
Henry R. Clayton]

Elgar was hurt by this offer. His reply was to send the other male-voice part-song, by which he set more store. This was a setting of a poem beginning with the repeated rhythmic syllable 'Zut! zut! zut!', and with the telling subtitle, 'Remember?' The words, he said, were by 'Richard Mardon'—whose address turned out to be that of Elgar's sister Pollie Grafton in Bromsgrove.

> *Zut! zut! zut! zut! &c*
> Come! give it a lift, our old-time march-song,
>   Sing with a will,
>   Sing with a thrill!
> Come! give it a leg, our old-time march-tune,
>   Grind up the hill;
>   Lads, 'twas a grill!
>   How we worked and drilled together,
>   And laughed and camped in foulest weather,
>   And fought where arms were brightly flashing,
>   Across the hail of bullets dashing:—
> Gloried in danger, our sinews tight'ning,
> A firm front shewed in the cannons' lightning.
>   Hurrah!
>
> *Zut! zut! zut! zut! &c*
> Come! shall we forget our old-time march-song?
>   The lads sang it so,
>   Long, long ago;
> No! never forget their old-time march-tune,
>   Sung with a go!
>   Straight on the foe.

How they fiercely fought for freedom,
And only this our land could breed 'em,
And how they nobly died, and wondrous
Was the battle, grim and thunderous:—
Glory to them and a fame transcending
The heroes of old in time unending.
     Hurrah!
Zut! zut! zut! zut! &c

Kempsey, Worcester.
24 JUL 1923
My dear Clayton:

Many thanks for your letter about the T T.B B 'The Wanderer'—I do not
think your offer is quite good enough. With this I send anr. TT.B.B. which
shd. be very popular: could you give me one hundred guineas for the two?
Failing that wd. you publish them for me as 'author's property' on the usual
terms?

Yours sincly
Edward Elgar

160, Wardour Street, W.-I.
July 26th 1923.
Dear Elgar

Thanks for your letter of the 24th instt. with the manuscript of the second
part-song for Men's voices. 'Zut, Zut, Zut'. This shall have prompt attention,
& I hope to write definitely tomorrow or on Monday.

I am sorry that our offer for 'The Wanderer' was so inadequate as to
amount to only half of your price for it. We of course had to keep before us
the fact that music of any kind written for Male voices appeals to a very
restricted market—at all events very restricted as compared with the circulation which one looks for hopefully in the case of music for mixed voice
choirs.

Yours sincerely
Henry R:Clayton.

West's report on the Marching Song—perhaps influenced by the words—was worse:

I am sorry to say this is rather *cheap* for Elgar—*cheap* without being
sufficiently *interesting*. Is it my judgment that's at fault, or is the composer
falling off in the value of his ideas?

J.W.

It was a question at the back of many minds then, though to anyone close to Elgar and his thoughts, this music would be haunting enough. Clayton could only follow the music editor's lead:

160, Wardour Street, W.-I.
July 31st. [192]3.
My dear Elgar,

Your two part-songs for men's voices have been very carefully considered and I am sorry to say that we cannot take them over from you on your terms, which are more than we can give for partsongs for men's voices—all 'male voice' things necessarily have a rather limited sale, which is the deciding factor in the case.

We will therefore put the two partsongs in hand and will publish them for you as your own property, as suggested in your letter of the 24th inst.

Yours faithfully,
[Henry R. Clayton]

Thus, after more than thirty years' association, and spectacular profits on all sides, they were back to the basis of a composer paying for the publication of his own work. Ten days later a note from the publishing manager C. J. May confirmed the position.

160, Wardour Street, W.-I.
Aug 9 1923
Dear Sir,

We shall be in a position to start on your two Partsongs very soon, & we shall be glad to know whether you wish us to *engrave* them or set them up in *type*.

Awaiting the favour of your reply

We are,
Yours faithfully,
Novello & Co. Ltd.
CJM

Elgar realized he was unwilling to revert to this state of things.

Kempsey, Worcester.
Augt 11:1923
My dear Clayton:

I am too old to begin altering the method of publication I have been accustomed to &, after due thought, will not ask you to print the PtSongs as 'author's property'. Just tear up the M.S.S.— or return them to me & I can do so.

I hope you are having or about to have a good change & rest—it is lovely in the country just now

Yours sincly
Edward Elgar

P.S. Perhaps you will kindly deal with the enclosed enquiry—which really made me think!

[160 Wardour Street, W.I.]
August 14th [192]3

My dear Elgar,

Many thanks for your letter.

Neither I nor anyone else here would wantonly destroy an Elgar MS., so if that is to be the fate of your two partsongs for men's voices, you must apply the finishing touch yourself. I am returning them to you; not for that purpose, but in the hope that you will reconsider your judgment, and that you will at all events grant a reprieve.

To my mind it seems absurd to destroy two properties which are worth 50 Guineas to us; and, unless you do it as a protest, you had better consider whether there is any good reason for throwing away that sum.

We will gladly publish both of the Partsongs at our own expense and, in the usual way, and [sic] will pay you 50 Guineas for the two—so why sacrifice everything? You view can only be explained by a feeling of annoyance that we are either underrating your property, or are not willing to pay a proper price for it. We cannot plead guilty to either proposition.

The whole difficulty about these two compositions is, that we never do, and never can, sell partsongs for men's voices in large quantities. Send us something effective for mixed voices, or for women's voices, and the whole situation will be changed at once.

[Yours
Henry R. Clayton]

Kempsey, Worcester.
Augt 15 1923

My dear Clayton:

Many thanks for your letter: the pt songs are not bad & had better appear so I leave it to you to bring them out & you give me fifty guineas.

There was no thought of the firm undervaluing the things. Perpend! If you give me 26.5.0 for a thing, that means I receive about £16—I invest this &

receive 10/- per ann.—I *may* live another three years & the prospective personal benefit to me is 30/-: such is the result of taxes but this is nothing to do with anybody.

> Kind rgrds
> Yours sncly
> Edward Elgar

Clayton's firmness and tact had saved the situation again. But it was not to be without some lingering bitterness on Elgar's part.

[160, Wardour Street, W.I.]
August 16th [192]3

Dear Elgar,

Many thanks for your letter. I am glad you have revoked you[r] edict about the two partsongs.

I enclose cheque and assignment.

Will you let us know who Richard Mardon is, and if he still exists, where he is to be found. We must make some arrangement with him about the use of his words 'Remember'.

Of course my sympathies are with you when you point out that £26.5.0 is only worth £16. to you. That is because the Inland Revenue choose to regard lump sums paid for copyrights as *being Income*, and they tax you accordingly for Income-tax and Super-tax. So if you invest the £16. it represents income derived from income, not income derived from capital: although of course you capitalize the income the moment you invest it. We are all hit in the same boat—at least those of us who are $\dfrac{\text{unfortunate}}{\text{fortunate}}$ enough to be liable for Supertax.

> [Yours
> Henry R. Clayton]

Kempsey, Worcester.
Aug 17:1923

My dear Clayton:

Many thanks: here are a receipt & assignment.

I forgot about Mardon's words: he will want something. I will get a letter from him & let you hear

The other words ('The Wanderer') are free

> Yours sincly
> Edward Elgar

Kempsey, Worcester.
Augt 23.1923
My dear Clayton:

Here is a letter from the *American Quartet*—they made a great success last season: do you think it wd. be worth while to let them do *The Wanderer* for the first time? You see the date Nov.13th—I do not suppose they wd. prefer '*Zut!*' but if you decide that they might have the first performance of either or both let me know: I dare say they cd. have four 'advance' copies somewhat early. Let me have the letter back with your views & I will reply—they are a 'nice' lot of men & sing well

Yrs sincly
Edward Elgar

[160, Wardour Street, W.-I.]
August 24th [192]3
Dear Elgar,

Thanks for your letter of the 23rd inst.

I have read the letter of the 20th inst. addressed to you by Mr.J.Erwyn Mutch of 'The American Quartette', and return it herewith.

The two partsongs will be in proof long before November 13th. and by that day we will have taken out the American Copyright, which means that everything will be ready for publication.—assuming that there will be no difficulty about the words of 'Zut'. In any case 'The Wanderer' will be ready.

I presume that the performance at 'Wigmore, November 13th' means *Wigmore Hall in London*. If so, we will reserve the first performance of either or both of the partsongs for the occasion referred to.

If, however, Wigmore is some place in the *United States* we cannot give the Quartette the right of first performance, because, according to our Law, as America is not a party to the Berne or Berlin Conventions, a first performance in America would destroy the British and International Performing Right.

I will send you four clean sets of proofs of both partsongs directly you have passed them as correct.

Please let us hear about the words of 'Zut' directly you have any news.

[Yours
Henry R. Clayton]

Kempsey, Worcester.
Augt 25 1923
My dear Clayton:

Thanks for yours about the first performance of the Pt Songs TTBB—the *U.S.A.tians* mean Wigmore Hall. I am placing your views before them.

Mardon wants a guinea for the use of his words or three guineas for the copyright—they are unpublished: if you will decide I will get a letter from him. I have got him to alter *one* line which might stand in the way of performance in U.S.A. I write it out 'fair' on the other side: one of your editors cd. alter the M.S. I think without sending it to me. I shall be at St James's Place on Monday till Thursday for festl rehearsals

Ever yours
Edward Elgar

Alter *in 2nd. Verse*
> for
>> And only this our land could breed 'em,
>
> *substitute*
>> And glad our land and proud to breed 'em,

EE

The following letter was then produced from Pollie Grafton's house, typewritten but signed with a hand suspiciously like Elgar's own:

at
Perryfield House,
BROMSGROVE.
September 10th 1923.

Dear Sir Edward,

I have been away. I am very grateful to you and feel the honor you have done my words very much.

Thanks for telling me Novello & Co. will pass me Three Guineas for the copyright of the Marching Song, I shall be glad to assign it to them. The words have not been printed.

Yours faithfully

Richard Mardon.

P.S. I should be glad to submit some other poems to you.

Elgar enclosed this in a letter to Clayton:

Kempsey, Worcester
14 SEP 1923

My dear Clayton:

Here is a letter about the words: the poet is staying at my sister's & may come on to me here, so when you write it does not matter which address you send to.

Yours ever
Edward Elgar

In addition to extensive drafts of the poem in Elgar's hand preserved at the Elgar Birthplace, the Elgar archives in the Hereford and Worcester County Record Office also contain Novello's letter of 22 September 1923 enclosing a cheque for three guineas for the copyright of the words.[4]

Elgar relapsed into silence. He went for a cruise to South America and a thousand miles up the Amazon at the end of 1923.

1924

In the new year, he was back in his flat in St James's, rather in need of money as his old royalties attenuated and no new ones came to take their place. Looking over old assignments, Elgar thought he found a lacuna in the payments for *The Apostles* contracted twenty years earlier. On 18 February he went to see Clayton about it. Clayton was astonished, but promised to investigate. He wrote next day:

160, Wardour Street, W.
February 19th 1924

Dear Elgar,

Since I had my talk with you yesterday I have looked into the documents and accounts relating to 'The Apostles'. When you spoke to me about it yesterday it occurred to me that it must have been an extraordinary blunder on our part if we had commenced, and continued, to pay you the agreed royalties all these years without having paid you the large (?small) capital sums which the contract declares were to be paid before the royalties were to commence to run.

I am glad for our sakes, and sorry for yours, that no blunder has been made.

I have before me your receipts for the following amounts, viz:—

October 19th,1903.	£250
„ 27th „	250
September 23rd,1904	150
January 5th,1905	100
February 21st,1906	250
	£1000

The account was made up to February 1906, when we found that, including English vocal scores, German vocal scores, and Tonic Sol-fa copies, but without claiming the benefit of the 13th copy for each dozen, we had disposed of 10,000 copies. We commenced paying you royalties as from that date, and the first royalty account for the work taken on May 17th,1906. showed £14.15.0 to be due to you for copies sold between February 15th and May 17th, 1906.

Yours sincerely
Henry R:Clayton.

[4] HWRO Bulk Accession 5664.

Brooks's, St.James's Street, S.W.1
Feb.21.1924

Dear Clayton:

All right: the royalty (as arrgd or reported to be arrgd by G H.J[ohnstone]) was to be payable at once, irrespective of the sum down—but I see it is written otherwise. So there's an end.

Yrs sincy
Edward Elgar

He had accepted a commission to write music for a huge Empire Exhibition to open at Wembley in April. There is no record of his approaching Novello over these works. Instead, on 27 February 1924, he signed a contract with Enoch for the publication of *The British Empire March*. The terms were £100 advance against a ten per cent royalty. The *March* was hardly a shadow of Elgar's earlier marches, and the advance was never covered. There were also eight solo and choral songs for the 'Pageant of Empire', the copyrights of which he sold to Enoch on 10 September 1924 for one shilling and a small royalty. They hardly sold, and more than half a century later Enoch's successor Messrs Edwin Ashdown still held extensive stocks of almost all the 'Pageant of Empire' songs in the original edition.

Times were changing, and what had been popular twenty years earlier now invited rearrangement. The lines on which such arrangements might run were suggested in a letter from Novello's American agent H. W. Gray, who had done much to arrange Elgar's American tours in pre-war days:

159 East 48th Street, New York
March 8. 24

Dear Sir Edward

I am sure you will be glad to know that you have at last been recognised as a composer. On Feb 12. Paul Whiteman and his Jazz Band performed 'Pomp & Circumstances'. I enclose the programme—it was immense. The saxophones were lovely, the Brass mostly had tin cans or old hats tied to them, for colour I presume. note one man plays *nine* instruments not all at once! the Tuba & Bass Viol interchange, & you ought to see the man drop one & grab the other, great juggling.

Awfully sorry not to see you last summer but somehow I could not find you anywhere, it seems a long time since we met but my memory of the good times I had when you were here, is very strong. Hope you are enjoying yourself but suppose you will not be coming this way at present:

Yours sincerely
H W Gray[1]

In April, following the death of Sir Walter Parratt, Elgar let it be known that he would accept the Mastership of the King's Music, so as to preserve the old office from extinction, and it was given to him.

[1] HWRO 705:445:5900.

Yet in the world of practical music-making everything seemed to go against Elgar. When he wrote new music, publishers were less than keen to publish it; and when they did, the returns were not a shadow of those in former days. Loyal old friends like Henry Embleton continued to devise performances of Elgar's great works from former years: in June he took the Leeds Choral Union to Paris for a performance of *Gerontius* conducted by the composer. But when he arrived, Elgar found that Novello had sent no vocal scores or notes of any kind for sale to the audience.

Early in July came a letter from Landon Ronald's nephew, Sheridan Russell, a cellist in the Monte Carlo Orchestra, wanting to play the Cello Concerto for the first time in France, but complaining that Novello demanded a hire fee of £8 for the parts and a guarantee of £12. Despite the fact that these terms arose directly from the business arrangements he himself had made with the publishers in former years, Elgar was incensed. No doubt it was less with the arrangements themselves than with widespread lack of enthusiasm for his music, of which so many examples had recently come to hand, and which was emphasized so unhappily by the wide gulf opened between the high fees echoing former expectations and the badly reduced circumstances of the present. Elgar's anger burned for several days. Then he wrote a note of illogical but deeply felt complaint to his old publishers of the good years.

37, St.James's Place, S.W.1.
July 18th, 1924.

Gentlemen,

I enclose a letter from Mr Sheridan Russell: I suppose there is nothing to be done and that you are not disposed to help matters any more than you did for Mr Embleton's Concert in Paris?

Yours faithfully,
Edward Elgar:

This drew a stinging reply from Augustus Littleton, who had continued as chairman during the decade since his brother Alfred's death.

[160, Wardour Street, W.1.]
July 21. 24

Dear Sir Edward Elgar

Your letter of the 18th has been laid before me. I am quite unable to understand the insinuation contained therein that Novellos were not disposed to help Mr.Embleton's Concert in Paris. No suggestion that Mr.Embleton was in need of assistance has ever reached me and I can only conclude that you must be in possession of facts which have been withheld from me or that you have discussed the matter with Mr.Embleton and that he has made some complaint to you. It is quite impossible for me to allow your letter to pass without further and most careful enquiry: so I hope you will send me all the explanation you possibly can

Yours faithfully
Augustus Littleton

37, St.James's Place, S.W.1.
July 23.1924

Dear Mr.Augustus Littleton:

There was no question of assisting Mr.Embleton but Mr.Embleton's Concert. I did not see a single copy of the French edn of Gerontius or the libretto—these were published years ago and I thought the Publishers shd see that the things are on sale —that is all.

Yours truly
Edward Elgar

160, Wardour Street, W.-I.
July 25.24

Dear Sir Edward Elgar

With your letter of July 18 you sent us a communication from Mr.Sheridan Russell in which he pointed out to you that in his opinion the fees for your Cello Concerto were prohibitive, and you say in this letter 'I suppose there is nothing to be done and that you are not disposed to help matters any more than you did for Mr.Embleton's Concert in Paris.' I concluded, not unnaturally I think, that your suggestion was that we had charged Mr.Embleton too much for the use of material and that we had refused to help matters by reducing the amount. Your letter of July 18 as I read it placed Mr.Embleton's concert & Mr.Russell's proposition in the same category. Now by your letter of July 23 I note that your suggestion really means that we had not helped matters by sending copies of your works to Paris and Dieppe for sale at the Concerts. I think I can show that we made every possible effort in this direction. On May 28 we wrote to Mr.Embleton (see enclosure A[)] and on June 3 we received his reply [(]enclosure B[)]. On receipt of this latter we wrote to three French publishers, Durand & Co[,] Durdilly & Co of Paris and L.Gaillard of Dieppe. With these letters we forwarded gratis copies of most of the items in the programmes of our publication including of course yours, and offered to send further copies on sale or return. One of these publishers acknowledged our letter[;] the other two were silent[.] I consider that every possible effort was made to 'see that the things were on sale', but in the face of the evident wane of interest on the part of the French public in British Music our efforts did not have the desired result.

Yours faithfully
Augustus Littleton

37, St.James's Place, S.W.1.
July 26th,1924.

Dear Mr.Littleton,

Many thanks for your letter and for the two enclosures which I return. I am sorry that the firm's efforts were futile; knowing the feeling of the French publishers I quite understand that they would not receive music on sale. I think there might have been half a dozen copies of the work and the libretto in the theatre—but that was probably impossible to arrange,

> Yours very truly,
> Edward Elgar

1925–1927

If these letters make sad reading, sadder still was to come. There came a major parting of the ways with the last of the old guard at Novello, Henry Clayton. In 1925 Clayton omitted to take the steps necessary to renew the American copyright of the *'Enigma'* *Variations*. Whether this was a cause or an effect of the rift, henceforth all communications to Elgar drafted by Clayton[1] were 'Dear Sir' letters sent over a 'Novello & Co.' signature.

Correspondence with Novello trickled on. In May 1925 Elgar made an arrangement for female voices of his old part-song *How Calmly the Evening*, for which the firm paid 20 guineas. Then he sent another male-voice part-song.

Napleton Grange, Kempsey, Worcester.
3rd July 1925.
Gentlemen,

With this I send the M.S. of a partsong (The Herald) for T.T.B.B. I shall be obliged if you will let me know if you are willing to publish it for me, and if so, on what terms.

> Believe me to be,
> Yours faithfully,
> Edward Elgar

Novello offered perhaps £40 for the copyright.

Napleton Grange, Kempsey, Worcester.
July 7th 1925
Gentlemen:

I am obliged to you for your letter of the 6th—I had thought of 50 guis for the Part Song—but am willing to take 40. which will almost meet your offer

The words are by the Victorian Scotsman Alexander Smith. I 'invented' the title which I think is apt but it could be altered if you think of anything better

> Believe me to be
> Yours faithfy
> Edward Elgar

---

[1] Some of the file copies retained are in Clayton's hand. The typewritten file copies are designated 'X', which was Clayton's code. (Information from the late Harry Fowle, who began at Novello during Clayton's time there.)

Whatever the cause, Elgar's next part-song, a setting of Walter de la Mare's *The Prince of Sleep* for mixed voices, was published by Elkin. The terms were 20 guineas, and a further 20 after the sale of ten thousand copies: but such expectations were as distant as the moon in these post-war days. Elgar signed the copyright assignment on 3 August, and later in the month received this note from Elkin:

20, Kingly Street, Regent Street, London, W.1.
21st August 1925.

My dear Elgar,

We returned a few days ago all the better for our experiment in the shape of a 'nature cure'.

I am sending you by this post first proof of 'THE PRINCE OF SLEEP'. It seems to me very beautiful, and I hope it may be often heard.

With kindest regards,

Yours sincerely,
W.W.A.Elkin[2]

Elkin knew as well as anyone what Elgar was feeling during these years. On 19 November 1925 Elgar conducted a concert of his works for the Philharmonic Society, and during the evening was presented with the Society's gold medal. Elkin wrote next day:

20, Kingly Street, Regent Street, W.1
20.11.25

My dear Elgar,

I have a feeling—in which I must indulge myself—to send you a line of congratulation on last night. The gold medal is only part (& perhaps the smaller part) of the reason why you may look upon the evening with pride & pleasure. It seems to me that the appreciation of the audience in the whole programme is more important than the conferring of the medal. But what I thought more important still was the character of the applause, in which one could easily feel a personal desire in everyone present to pay you *personally* almost affectionate homage. I hope that note reached you, for I am sure it was there.

Yours very sincerely
W.W.A.Elkin[3]

A month later Elgar had to undergo an operation for haemorrhoids, and he was ill for some time. Elkin tried to encourage further composition.

[2] HWRO 705:445:5611.   [3] HWRO 705:445:5717.

20, Kingly Street, Regent Street, London, W.1.
16th February 1926

My dear Elgar,

I was very sorry to see some little while back that you had evidently been rather seriously ill. I hope by now you have quite got over the trouble.

I was wondering whether you would feel inclined to write something of a fairly light character for us, either for violin and piano, or piano solo. While it is true, of course, that neither 'CARISSIMA' nor 'ROSEMARY' quite did what we all hoped, still the former at any rate was not far from it, and I shall be very glad to have another shot, if you feel inclined.

I have been more or less on the sick list myself for a couple of months, but am now much better.

With kindest regards,

> Yours very sincerely,
> W.W.A.Elkin[4]

Elgar's reply is missing, but no new music emerged. So in April 1926 Elkin acquired the *May Song* of 1901 from W. H. Broome.[5]

Meanwhile, in the Autumn of 1925 Elgar had taken up correspondence again with Harold Brooke at Novello. Brooke's letters are missing, but the tone of Elgar's reply shows how he welcomed it.

Napleton Grange, Kempsey, Worcester.
Nov 10th 1925

My dear Brooke.

I am so sorry your letter has remained unacknowledged for so long a time I have been ill with bronchitis & my correspondence is all behindhand It is GOOD of you to write & later I will see what can be done

> In great haste
> Yrs v.siny
> Edward Elgar

On the heels of this came an enquiry from a competition festival organizer about the pronunciation of the rhythmic syllable 'zut' in the part song *Zut! zut! zut!* which Novello had published in 1923. Elgar wrote again to Brooke, this time from his flat in London.

---

[4] HWRO 705:445:5483.
[5] Contract dated 22 Apr. 1926 (Novello archives).

St James's Place
Nov 14

My dear Brooke:

You know I never will communicate with competitors—will you see to the enclosed letter: Of course the pronunciation is as 'soot' but quite short. If you are ever reprinting cd not a note be added & save these questionings

> Best rgrds
> Yrs sincy
> Edward Elgar

Brooke suggested using 'wood' as a touchstone.

Brooks's. St. James's Street, S.W.1.
Novr.17th 1925

My dear Brooke:

Your thought is genius;—'*wood*' by all means for the note in the Pt-Song

> Yours very sincerely
> Edward Elgar

Then came the illness, operation, and slow recovery. In mid-February Elgar received a cheque from Novello on account of royalties. His personal regard was kept for the younger directors, A. J. B. Littleton and Harold Brooke.

Napleton Grange, Kempsey, Worcester.
Feb 16th 1926

My dear Brooke:

Thank you for sending the cheque; a receipt is enclosed.

My kind regards to Jack & to you. I am better but the weather is too dreadful & I cannot get out. I went up to London a fortnight back & intended to call but a cold seized me & I had to return. However things are going on well.

I want to ask sometime what attitude the firm takes regarding Broadcasting fees: some pubrs send me a good percentage but I do not know how the land lies

> Yours very sincy
> Edward Elgar

Life was expensive in the post-war world.

Napleton Grange, Kempsey, Worcester.
Feb 17th 1926

My dear Brooke:

If my acct. promises fairly well might I have say £100 now, instead of waiting till June? This has been done on a previous occasion—belike more than once—if it dislocates anything or anybody I can quite well do without. I have been laid up for some time now—too long to bear thinking of but am getting all right again

> Best regards
> Yours sincly
> Edward Elgar

The firm accommodated him in this way whenever possible.

A week later he raised with Novello the question of broadcasting fees.

Napleton Grange, Kempsey, Worcestershire.
24th February 1926.

Dear Sirs,

There seems to be no settled system as to composers receiving a share of broadcasting fees. I hold the opinion that these should be divided equitably; this is done by at least one firm and I shall be glad to know your views on the subject.

> Believe me to be
> Yours faithfully,
> Edward Elgar

160, Wardour Street, W. 1
February 25th 1926

Dear Sir,

We are favoured with your letter of the 24th.instant.

We imagine that the reason why there is no settled system as to Composers receiving a share of broadcasting fees is that different Publishers, who own the rights, are acting according to their own individual views of the matter.

At present we have not formulated any views of our own; and it is possible that we may throw the consideration of the matter upon other shoulders by joining a Society, possibly the Performing Right Society, which is in the habit of receiving revenue from such sources, and apportioning it in accordance with its rules.

It must, however, be recognized that in nearly every case it is the Publisher who would be asked to bring the right into Hotch Pot, and it is he who has to do all the work of investigating titles, dates of publication, conducting correspondence, keeping accounts and so on; and those facts must not be overlooked in any consideration of the question of equitable division.

May we ask whether your suggestion of an equitable division applies equally to fees derived from mechanical instruments rights, which would generally be brought into Hotch Pot by the Composer?

> Yours faithfully
> Novello & Co Ltd[6]

[6] Elgar Birthplace parcel 238. The copy in Novello archives is signed 'X/EH', signifying the authorship of Henry Clayton.

Napleton Grange, Kempsey, Worcestershire.
3rd March 1926.

Dear Sirs,

I am obliged to you for your letter of the 25th ult.; I asked for your views on the apportionment of Broadcasting fees and you say you have none.

As to mechanical rights, I am in favour of *equitable* division; when such rights have been reserved by me, such reservation has been allowed for in fixing the fees paid, and royalties to be paid to me by the publishers.

Yours faithfully,
Edward Elgar.

160, Wardour Street, W. I.
March 9th 1926

Dear Sir,

We are much obliged by your letter of the 3rd. instant.

We still are negotiating with the Performing Right Society with a view to ascertaining whether it would be possible for us to join that Society under modified conditions, and we hope to come to a definite decision in the matter during this week.

In any event, whether we join that Society or not, we shall very shortly be in a position to enter into some arrangement with you whereby you will receive a portion of the Fees payable to us in respect of broadcasting performances of your works published by us.

Yours faithfully,
Novello & Co. Ltd.[7]

Later Elgar himself joined the Performing Rights Society.

Yet the contrast of neglect for his few new works with the successes of the past made for continual unhappiness. Suggestions were received by both composer and publishers about making new arrangements of old works. A proposal from Wales for a male-voice arrangement of 'The Challenge of Thor' from *King Olaf* was declined by Novello on commercial grounds.[8] A proposal from Lancashire for a mixed-voice arrangement of *The Reveille* was put to Elgar on 9 August 1926. But in the midst of these possibilities came something less happy.

At the Coliseum, the dancer Anton Dolin announced to the press that he was choreographing *Chanson de nuit* and *Chanson de matin*. The press reported that this was new music, and on 5 August Clayton wrote an official letter on behalf of Novello asking how Elgar could use old titles (published by the firm) for new music. Elgar telegraphed that it was not new music: Dolin was merely dancing to the old music just as it stood. Clayton officially apologized,[9] and Elgar responded:

---

[7] Elgar Birthplace parcel 238. The copy in Novello archives is signed 'X/EH', signifying the authorship of Henry Clayton.

[8] HWRO 705:445:3971–2.

[9] Elgar Birthplace parcel 238; copy in Clayton's hand in Novello archives.

Napleton Grange, Kempsey, Worcestershire.
10th August 1926.
Dear Sirs,

I have to acknowledge the receipt of your three letters, one dated August 5th and two dated the 9th.

Immediately on the arrival of the first letter I sent you a telegram explaining my position in the matter. I now express my regret that you allowed yourselves to assume that I could be capable of publishing new music under names already in your catalogue; I have never heard of such a thing being done. As to the second letter about the ballet, the only point which concerned me is cleared up by the new annoncements [*sic*] in the press that the music is not specially composed; so the incident closes.

Your letter as to a possible arrangement of 'The Reveille' for S.A.T.B. I hold over until I have considered the practical side of the question, but you might let me hear in the meantime what fee you would consider right and fair for such an arrangement.

Yours faithfully,
Edward Elgar.

August 12th, 1926
Dear Sir,

We are much obliged by your letter of the 10th. instant.

We are sorry that our letter of the 5th. instant about the Coliseum Ballet announcement appears to you to contain an innuendo which you resent. The announcement was made in so many Newspapers, as one of considerable importance, that we were left no ground for doubting its accuracy; and the fact that we gave credence to the announcement hardly puts us in the position of allowing ourselves 'to assume' what for the time we believed. We hope that the matter is now disposed of to your satisfaction. The only real offenders in the matter are apparently the Press or their Agents.

Should you decide to arrange your 'The Reveille' for mixed voices we suggest a fee of 25 Guineas.

Yours faithfully,
(X/EH)

Elgar in these later years of the 1920s was an unhappy man, and matters reflecting backward to his years of success made him difficult to deal with. When the secretary of the Leeds Festival, Charles Haigh, enquired whether Sir Edward could honour the Leeds Festival in October 1928 with his presence to conduct a concert, Elgar replied to Novello:

Napleton
16 DEC. 1926

Dear Sirs: Leeds Festival 1928

I am much obliged to you for your letter of the 16th enclosing a copy of
one from the Secretary of the festival. I shall be further obliged if you will tell
Mr.Haigh that to conduct such a concert as he proposes and the rehearsals
my fee would be two hundred guineas

> Believe me to be
> Yours faithfy.[10]

These terms were impossible, and the Leeds Festival of 1928 was to take place without
Elgar's participation.

His answers to proposals for new composition were likely to be similarly unpromis-
ing. For years he had had requests from Herbert Whiteley (1873–1953), music editor
for the brass band publishers R. Smith & Co., to write something for brass band.
Early in 1927 Whiteley sent another request, together with several brass band scores
of existing works in the hope of tempting Elgar. Elgar replied:

2 FEB 1927

Dear Sir:

Many thanks for your letter and the scores of the Brass Band pieces. I fear
I am too much occupied to be able to find time for a composition; I regret
this as the Brass Band is a most interesting combination

> Believe me to be
> Yours faithfully
> [Edward Elgar][11]

Yet he would sometimes turn his hand to remaking former things. When Elkin
wanted a children's arrangement of 'The Blue-Eyes Fairy' from *The Starlight
Express*, Elgar replied:

By all means use the 'Blue Eyes Fairy' as you wish. I have suggested (*only
suggested*) some further simplifications,—it remains rather awkward for little
hands.[12]

And in reply to Novello's request for a female-voice arrangement of 'As torrents in
summer' from *King Olaf*:

[10] Letter book (Elgar Birthplace). These notebooks contain Elgar's handwritten drafts for
letters to be typewritten by his secretary Mary Clifford for his signature.

[11] Letter book.

[12] 4 Nov. 1926. This portion alone of Elgar's letter survives in a transcript now in Novello
archives.

Napleton Grange, Kempsey, Worcester.
8 MAR.1927

Dear Sirs: *As torrents arrgd. S.S.C.*

I send an arrgt as suggested: it has to be looked at from quite a different point of view; I have adapted a suggestion for the accompaniment from the cantata. It will make an effective little piece—but it may not be what you require from the practical side

> Yours faithfully
> Edward Elgar

Then Novello asked whether he would consider making a unison arrangement for schools of 'It comes from the misty ages' from *The Banner of St George*. Elgar replied:

Napleton Grange, Kempsey, Worcester.
22nd April 1927.

Dear Sirs,

I am obliged to you for your letter enquiring as to a possible arrangement of 'It comes from the misty ages'. I find it is possible to make such an arrangement; the accompaniment should be extremely simple and two verses of the poem omitted. I hope to send a sketch of this next week.

> Believe me to be,
> Yours faithfully,
> Edward Elgar.

Napleton Grange, Kempsey, Worcester.
April 24th 1927

Dear Sirs: 'It comes from the misty ages', *Unison*

With this I send an arrgt for children. The accompt. is *very* simple; this, of course, cd. be made fuller (& more difficult) but I think it is better as it is for the purpose indicated

> Yours faithfully
> Edward Elgar

This arrangement met with considerable success when it appeared.

Birthdays and anniversaries had always upset Elgar, and the approach of his seventieth birthday in June 1927 was anticipated with special misgiving. The inevitable congratulations must sound hollow to their recipient. Yet they came. Elkin's was as game a shot as any:

20, Kingly Street, Regent Street, W.1
1.6.27

My dear Elgar,

I do not quite know why one's 70th birthday should be particularly singled out for celebration, but I suppose the Psalmist is responsible for it. In age it is nothing now-a-days, & I am too near it myself to consider it otherwise than middle life! Anyhow I should like to take part in the full chorus of good wishes & congratulations which are certain to reach you to-morrow. Like so many others I owe to you many hours of musical happiness, & from a thoroughly selfish point of view (not to mention others) I most sincerely wish you a further harvest of good years, to the satisfaction of yourself, & to the advantage of the world. I will only add a word to express the great pleasure with which I look back on our association in the past.

Yours very sincerely
W.W.A.Elkin.

Thanks for letter received yesterday.[13]

What Elgar could feel at the worst was shown in response to a letter from old Charles Volkert of Schott, whose firm had joined the Performing Rights Society, and who wanted Elgar to join. Volkert's letter contained a first cheque in respect of broadcasting fees.

London
May 30.

Dear Mr.Volkert:

Thank you for the cheque £3.14.0 for the *B.B.C.* affairs which I do not understand but conclude the am[oun]t is due to me as you offer it.

I am not sure as to the possibility of the performing rights society but I shall be glad to know more of it & its working.

It is fifty years since you, in Regent Street, purveyed five violin pieces to a 'prescription' by Pollitzer for me. I remember the pride & pleasure I had in presenting the 'order'. Much has happened since then—I have had some satisfaction & even pleasure in my life but have no pleasant memories connected with music.

Yours very truly
Edward Elgar.[14]

This letter contradicted itself. When Volkert wrote again about the Performing Rights Society, Elgar joined it, but sent Volkert a bitter letter (whose location is now unknown) apparently complaining about his treatment even from Schott. Volkert responded:

---

[13] HWRO 705:445:5942. [14] *Letters of Edward Elgar*, p. 297.

48 Gt.Marlborough Street, W.1.
June 20 1927
Dear Sir Edward

I think your bitter remarks are justified, but it is really our Laws that are at fault. 'Salut d'amour' was a great success, therefore 10 or 12 American firms reproduced [*i.e.*, pirated] it. I cannot trace a single sale there and for this reason alone I have transferred USA rights to A P Schmidt & Co for Twenty Guineas in 1902.

The American right expires next year, but it can be extended for a further 28 years, though neither you nor I will gain a Penny.

The 'Sursum Corda' was a very moderate success, you would have had less, if a royalty bargain had been entered: I never had performing fees on any of your works until last year, when I considered it my duty to share them with you and I will do so in future.

Mechanical right belongs to you, I never had a penny [in respect of] it. Unfortunately *our* Laws practically disallow all fees on works produced before 1912. I am glad you have joined the P.R.S. now.

> With kind regards
> Yours sincerely
> Chas Volkert[15]

The biggest scheme which came to any fruition in these years was a proposal from a cinema man, S. W. Smith, that Elgar should write music to a film to be called *Land of Hope and Glory*. As films were still silent, the music would be played by an actual orchestra. Smith had it in mind that Elgar himself might conduct. He had made his approach in October 1926 through Leslie Boosey, whose firm controlled *Land of Hope and Glory* both in the song version and as *Pomp and Circumstance* March No. 1. Elgar replied:

Napleton Grange, Kempsey, Worcestershire.
23rd October 1926.
Dear Leslie,

Many thanks for your letter about the suggested film production of 'Land of Hope and Glory'. I am quite prepared to consider the question of writing incidental music; my consent would depend upon the general 'scenario' and, of course, the terms.

> Kindest regards,
> Yours sincerely,
> Edward Elgar

Boosey replied with Smith's offer of £100. Elgar responded:

[15] HWRO 705:445:3988.

Napleton Grange, Kempsey, Worcestershire.
27th October 1926.

My dear Leslie,

Many thanks for your letter of yesterday's date.

I think Mr Smith's offer is entirely inadequate,—i.e. if you have any copyright in the title 'Land of Hope & Glory'. It is a *first-class* title for a film and the offer of one hundred pounds, if the film goes forward, is, to my mind, ludicrous.

I quite understand the process of film-building and that all kinds of emendations and additions are made; for that sort of thing we are prepared. If Mr Smith is ready to pay something reasonable for the *Title* the question as to my personal connection with the arrangement, or composition of more music, can be considered on a royalty basis.

Let me know what you think.

> Kindest regards,
> Yours sincerely,
> Edward Elgar

Unfortunately Boosey had to tell him that the title itself was not copyright.

Napleton Grange, Kempsey, Worcester.
29th October 1926.

My dear Leslie,

Many thanks; the question of non-copyright settles the matter and I leave it to you to do the best you can; at the same time you might look into our original contract—I do not think your firm paid me any sum down for the song, or the Coronation Ode; I believe it has been a mere royalty arrangement; if that is so I think any sum paid for the use of the song should come to me and not you.

I find an old circular letter from the firm which has been overlooked; I cannot agree to the 'asterisked' paragraph as it appears to give away my existing rights.

> Yours sincerely,
> Edward Elgar.

Boosey thereupon looked up the old contracts and quoted the sums paid nearly a quarter century ago. It was the problem Clayton had encountered at Novello: the old composer, his income severely reduced, allowed himself to hope that somehow, somewhere had been a loophole in the contracts covering his greatest successes; and that such loopholes, if found, would now produce a new fount of income to match his continuing feelings for these inspirations of former years. Boosey's reply is missing from the files, but he was clearly hurt by Elgar's suggestion that his firm could have been negligent. Elgar responded from Eastbourne, where he had to conduct a concert.

Grand Hotel, Eastbourne.
Nov 9th 1926

My dear Leslie,

Thank you for your letter—I fear mine must have struck you—judging from your reply—as somewhat crude—

I am too much occupied here just now but I will try to call on you on my way through town to my home. In the meantime, if anything further shd. occur, do exactly whatever you like & think best. As you say I have no *rights* in the matter you cannot expect me to accept charity so I think I am out of it

> Kind rgrds
> Yours sncy
> Edward Elgar[16]

Preparations for the film went forward on the basis of arrangements from earlier works. In late July 1927 Boosey forwarded Smith's payment on account, together with the suggestion that Sir Edward should conduct the first performance.

Napleton Grange, Kempsey, Worcester.
July 28th 1927

My dear Leslie:

Thank you for the cheque on acct of the 'Land of Hope' film production; I had quite forgotten the proposal & am glad to hear that it is proceeding.

I shall be glad to consider Mr.Smith's suggestion as to conducting either the 'overture' or, possibly, the whole first 'show'—this wd. be a matter of terms which had better be proposed by Mr.Smith. I will gladly look through the arrangement of the music—I should think that the *whole* of the music shd. be mine as I feel 'Land of Hope' should not be used to advertise other authors: 'Cockaigne', for instance might furnish many themes &, if I had a sort of free hand, wd. be glad to suggest their use & wd. go so far as to write some original music, if this wd. call attention to the Film. I am anxious that British Films shd. be put forward as much as possible

> Kind regards
> Yours sincy
> Edward Elgar

P.S. I could make a rare 'pasticcio' out of the four marches, the Coronation Ode, Cockaigne, & if necessary, for quiet effects the Songs—

Boosey enquired what further fee Elgar would want for conducting, or for actual new composition. Elgar replied from his daughter's house, where he was paying a short visit.

---

[16] MS in possession of John Franca.

Hoes, Petworth, Sussex. address Kempsey Worcs.
Augt 7th 1927

My dear Leslie:

Many thanks for your letter about the Film[.] I am glad to hear that you think it is shaping well.

As a separate 'event' I should have fifty guineas to conduct the 'overture'—but, if I am to receive 'possible fee for composing(?) music & overlooking arrts etc['] I shd. not stand in Mr Smith's way—the whole thing might go together.

I only hope my music will be used as, if that shd be so, we might print the whole of the music in a sort of Album, don't you think?

> Kindest regards
> Yours sincerely
> Edward Elgar

Boosey transmitted Smith's proposal to Elgar, who replied:

Napleton Grange, Kempsey, Worcester.
Augt 16th 1927

My dear Leslie:

Thank you for yours of the 12th:—looking at Mr.Smith's proposal *generally* the fee is not what I usually receive, but of course the possibilities of royalties on a (possible) copyrightable edn with new music makes it more acceptable: can it wait until I see (roughly) how much & what sort of new music will be required? Of course I shall not stand in the way by insisting on anything unreasonable

> In haste
> Kind regards
> Yours sincerely
> Edward Elgar

The film was to open on 11 November. Elgar was already engaged to conduct *For the Fallen* in a BBC broadcast that evening. It meant he could not do the third of the proposed film showings.

Napleton Grange, Kempsey, Worcester.
Oct 28th 1927

My dear Leslie:

Film

I have this moment heard from the *B.B.C.* that I am wanted at 8.0 till 9.30 on the Armistice day so that knocks out the proposed 9.0'c show: I *could* manage 3. and *6*—if I could get off in time for 8.15 (Queen's Hall)

I am sorry you are troubled over this & the terms! Strauss was paid £700 to come over & conduct one (whole) performance of his film!

> Yours ever
> Edward Elgar

(That was for a silent film of *Der Rosenkavalier*, for which Strauss had arranged much of the vocal music for orchestra and written some new sections of music.)

S. W. Smith invited Elgar to a press luncheon before the film première on 11 November,[17] and afterwards Elgar conducted one performance. The only new music he had actually written in 1927 was a small *Civic Fanfare* for the Opening Service of the Hereford Festival.

1928–1929

Inducements to work were constantly made. One came from Leslie Boosey, who sent words for a possible patriotic song to fit the Trio tune of *Pomp and Circumstance March No.4.* Elgar responded from the house he now rented at Stratford:

Tiddington House, Stratford-upon-Avon.
10 June 1928

My dear Leslie:

I have been having a long struggle with the enclosed words, I cannot by any help of Providence, or old Nick, make them fit. One other thing: I think the *pronounced* praise of England is not quite so popular as it was; the loyalty remains but the people seem to be more shy as to singing about it.
Is there no other *corporate* idea we could base a song upon?

> Kindest regards
> Yours sincly
> [Edward Elgar][1]

Boosey asked whether they might try Kipling, but after that poet's behaviour over *The Fringes of the Fleet,* Elgar would have none of it.

Tiddington House, Stratford-upon-Avon.
11 Sep.1928

My dear Leslie:

There's no chance of getting Kipling, who is an unmusical brute. Have you thought of Alfred Noyes? He has a *feeling* for music & wrote some excellent 'stuff', at a moment's notice, for the unfortunate Pageant at Wembley. You

---

[17] HWRO 705:445:5798.

[1] Letter book.

could easily find his address &, if you think well of the notion, I wd. write to him. He was a very pleasant & understanding person to work with.

> Kind rgrds
> Yours sny
> [Edward Elgar]²

He wrote to Alfred Noyes, reminding him of their collaboration for the Wembley Empire Exhibition. Ultimately the song was published as *Song of Victory*.

A provisional programme for the Gloucester Festival of 1928 had been drafted by Sir Herbert Brewer before his death in March. It had contained the *May Song*, and Elkin (who had purchased the work from W. H. Broome) wrote to enquire. Elgar replied with suggestions of his own.

Tidd[ington]
26 June 1928

My dear Elkin:

No,—the *May Song* was only a memorandum by the late Sir H. Brewer & got transcribed into the first ed[itio]n of the programme of the festival.

I am sorry for the error.

> Kindest rgrds
> Yours sincerely
> [Edward Elgar]

P.S. When I come up I shd like to talk to you about the 'Fan Ballet', Starlight Express, the music I wrote for Binyon's 'Arthur' & anr. trifle; wd a sort of short 'Suite' (Arthur) be worth considering?³

There were proposals to revive *The Starlight Express* as a radio production. But the 'Arthur' suite came to nothing. When Harold Brooke of Novello saw a paragraph in *The Daily Mail* about a new Elgar work and wrote to enquire, Elgar replied:

Tiddington House near Stratford-upon-Avon.
22nd Sep 1928

My dear Brooke:

I can say nothing about your paragraph—I have seen no pens or paper about this un(musically) desecrated abode. Tons of autumn manure are arriving and the D.Mail man probably mistook this for—what you adumbrate

> Yrs ever
> E.E.

Yet he had agreed in principle to write the music for Gerald Lawrence's production of Bertram Mathews's play *Beau Brummel*, to open in Birmingham on 5 November. Elgar conducted the première, and a few days later sent to Elkin the *Minuet* which formed the centre of the incidental music. Elkin proposed to issue this immediately in

---

² Letter book.   ³ Letter book.

a piano arrangement by Ernest Austin (1874–1947). Elgar raised questions over terms, and ultimately over the publication itself: he wanted to make an orchestral suite of the incidental music. Elkin responded:

20, Kingly Street, Regent Street, London, W.1.
15th November, 1928.

My dear Elgar,

Thanks for your letter of yesterday.

I am of course in your hands, but I would very much prefer to go ahead with the Minuet. Thinking that the matter was settled when I saw you, I wrote to Lawrence and asked him to put a note in his programme that the Minuet was published by us. He has also had a photo taken for reproduction on the title page.

These are comparatively small points. What influences me much more, is that it would be a pleasure to publish the Minuet and to push it in every way, in the hope that the initial fee would not be so much a matter for your consideration, as the royalties which might accrue from the sale of the sheet music and from the Gramophone and Performing Rights.

In the hope that this aspect may appeal to you and that we can go ahead, I am enclosing our cheque for 25 guineas and an Assignment embodying the terms quoted at our interview.

Would you feel happier about it if we sent you 20 guineas on account of royalties. If so, this will be done with pleasure.

I hope later on you will let us have the Suite which you said you would make from the incidental music.

With kindest regards,

Yours sincerely,
W.W.A.Elkin[4]

It was still early enough in the play's Birmingham run to hope for a London production and much publicity. Unfortunately this was not to be. The plan for a published suite came to nothing, and even Elgar's manuscript full score has disappeared, perhaps with the rest of the production. Only the *Minuet* was published, and Elgar accepted Elkin's terms.

A suggestion came from The Gramophone Company to record the *Minuet*. Elgar relayed this to Elkin, and sent him the full score with the suggestion that it be engraved with orchestral parts in time for the recording on 20 December. But Elkin was guarded: 'It would be rather too risky to put this in the engraver's hands as we might not get the parts ready by the time you want them and therefore we will have them copied.'[5] Elgar suggested that the numbers of string parts be 4-4-3-3-3.

The recording was duly made—only to be issued after some delay as a 'coupling' for *The Wand of Youth*. Elkin ultimately issued several arrangements of the *Minuet*, but none made much impact. His other suggestions for performances and revivals of Elgar works he published[6] came to nothing.

Elgar's correspondence with Novello yielded better results. On 30 October 1928 he had sent them a setting of Ben Jonson's 'I sing the birth was born tonight'. The publishers offered 15 guineas for the copyright. Elgar replied:

[4] Elgar Birthplace parcel 241.   [5] Elgar Birthplace parcel 241.   [6] Elgar Birthplace parcel 241.

37 St James's Place
Nov 1st 1928

Dear Sirs:

I am obliged to you for yr letter as to the B.Jonson Carol. I accept your offer. I took the words from *Gifford's* edn which is authentic & I do not think has been superseded by any modern edition, but the spelling is modernised: if you prefer the original—which might *look* well—I can easily get the first version[.] But you are the best judges of the *utility* of quaint spelling

> Yrs very try
> Edward Elgar

The modern spelling was retained for Novello's edition.

Then, at the publisher's request,[7] Elgar made an arrangement for strings to accompany the unison version of 'It comes from the misty ages' which he had done eighteen months earlier. Novello paid him 20 guineas for this. As with everything he did with young people in mind, Elgar took a good deal of trouble over it.

Tiddington House near Stratford-upon-Avon.
Nov 8th 1928

Dear Sirs:

With this I send the String accpt to the 'Misty Ages'. I have made it as simple as possible.

I do not know if you will think it worth while to engrave the P.F. part as in the Score; of course that in the V[ocal] Sc. can be used but in the arrgt I have made it fuller in places.

It seems necessary that some rehearsal letters (or figures) shd be added: the *pages* of the v.sc. might be sufficient & I have added these to my M.S.;— naturally, if you reprint the v.sc. letters cd. be added in convenient places but for all practical purposes the 'paging' wd. be enough.

> Yours faithfully
> Edward Elgar

P.S. In case you are sending proofs of the Carol I shall be at the Grand Hotel[,] Eastbourne until *Monday*

The contrast with the great works of the past was pointed again when Novello, having failed to renew the American copyright of the *'Enigma' Variations*, reminded him that the American renewal of *Gerontius* was due. Elgar had replied on 28 June 1928 asking the firm to do what was necessary. But the matter dragged on, and at the end of the year he wrote again.

---

[7] 17 Oct. 1928 (Elgar Birthplace parcel 238).

Tiddington House near Stratford-upon-Avon.
14th December 1928.

Dear Sirs,

The Dream of Gerontius: (U.S.A.)

I regret that your letter of 18th October has been overlooked so long. I am greatly obliged to you for the trouble you have been put to in the matter of registration in the U.S.A.

As to the export of copies,—I do not know what is the usual procedure in these cases. I presume that the work is worthless, or as nearly valueless to me in the U.S.A. as it is in England. I shall be glad of your counsel.

> Believe me to be,
> Yours very truly,
> Edward Elgar

Clayton responded officially with a year-by-year tabulation of *Gerontius* vocal sales in the United States since 1919, showing that the demand there was now less than during the war period:

... Judging from the position as it exists to-day, we are afraid that we must agree with your description of the property as being worthless; in the sense that, having regard to the present demand for the work in America, it would not be worth while for anyone to incur the expense of engraving a new set of plates for the purpose of supplying the American demand. ...[8]

The American copyright was renewed for Elgar by the firm, who continued to supply any orders from their own printed stock.

On 13 February 1929 Clayton wrote about an Australian plan, undertaken by Mrs Louise Dyer for the British Music Society in Melbourne, to acquire copies of every work Elgar had ever published:

... We hope the scheme is one which you will favour. We may add that the Patrons of the Australian Branch of The British Music Society are prepared to spend large sums of money in giving effect to it.[9]

Elgar gave what help he could.[10]

Clayton was almost the only survivor from Elgar's great days with Novello. At the end of February 1929 came the sudden death of John E. West, only just retired as Novello's music editor. West had initially been a doubter, and he had also passed severe judgments on Elgar's later works. But there was no doubt of respect on both sides, arising from skilful editorial advice over piano arrangements, some of which were West's own work. His widow wrote:

[8] 14 Dec. 1928 (Novello archives).
[9] Elgar Birthplace parcel 238.
[10] Elgar's draft reply, dated 20 Feb. 1929 and merely giving the names of his publishers, is contained in the Letter Book.

50, Lauderdale Mansions, Maida Vale, W.9.
March 11th: 1929

Dear Sir Edward,

Perhaps you have been out of England during this most terrible weather, and have not heard of the passing of my dear husband John E.West—He loved your music which often brought tears to his eyes, and he always spoke of you as our greatest British composer. He also cherished the memory of the first production of your 'Dream of Gerontius', when he told me he sat with Lady Elgar and rejoiced in the beautiful reception of your great work—

Your lovely Song 'Pleading' which he tried to teach me will be a pleasant memory.

Yours very sincerely
Marion West[11]

13 MAR 1929

Dear Mrs.West:

It was very kind of you to write; I read of the death of your husband with very deep regret & send you all sympathy in your loss.

Our friendship dates from long ago & during the active part of my life your husband's care of my compositions was of very great value to me.

Believe me to be

Yours sincerely
[Edward Elgar][12]

In April he had a request forwarded from Leslie Boosey about the use of *Land of Hope and Glory*. In his reply, Elgar did not disguise his political feelings.

Lord Chamberlain's Office, St. James's Palace, S.W.1.
April 17th 1929

My dear Leslie:

I have been laid up & only seeing to things again to-day. Thanks for your letter of the 12th.—all right about Lady Rodd & the *conservatives*—don't let any blasted labour rogues or liberals use the tune!

Yrs sincerely
Edward Elgar[13]

In June the violist Lionel Tertis (1876–1975) brought to Elgar his arrangement of the solo part in the Cello Concerto for his own instrument. Elgar was impressed, and wrote to Novello:

[11] HWRO 705:445:2050.
[12] Letter book.
[13] MS in possession of John Franca.

Tiddington[,] S-on-A
20th June 1929
Dear Sirs:
Mr.Lionel Tertis has to-day played through to me a suggested arrangement
of the Cello Concerto for Viola: it is admirably done & is *fully* effective
on his inst.

I hope you will see your way to print the solo part;—the piano accpt & the
full score will require no alteration.

Mr.Tertis wd. propose to play the concerto in Rome etc: next winter: I
think he will write to you on the matter: this is only to say that I fully approve
of the arrgt.

> Yours faithfully
> Edward Elgar

Later that day he received a letter from Novello about an entirely different matter.

160, Wardour Street, London, W.1.
June 19th, 1929
Dear Sir,

We have an enquiry from Mr.Edwin Fleisher of Philadelphia for a Full
Score and set of parts of the 'Toccata in F' orchestrated by Esser, with Coda
by yourself written for a Worcester Festival.

The score and parts are not intended for public performance but for
inclusion in the Philadelphia Reference Library and for private use by
Mr.Fleisher's orchestra.

We shall be obliged if you will kindly let us know whether we may supply
this material including your Coda?

> Yours faithfully,
> Novello & Co Ltd.[14]

For the Worcester Festival in September 1929, Ivor Atkins wanted to play the
orchestral arrangement of Bach's Toccata in F (BWV 540) by Heinrich Esser (1818–
72). But Esser had substituted an ending of his own. Atkins persuaded Elgar to
provide a new orchestration of Bach's final bars, to restore the original ending.

Elgar marked Novello's letter 'Yes', and replied to it in that sense on 20 June. In his
letter he made some observations about critics. Fleisher saw this letter, and begged for
the original. Novello wrote to Elgar again:

---

[14] Elgar Birthplace parcel 238. This and the remaining Novello letters of 1929 to Elgar bear no
sign of Clayton's authorship.

160, Wardour Street, London, W.1.
June 22nd, 1929
Dear Sir,

Bach—Esser Toccata.

We are obliged by your letter of the 20th.instant.

There is no memorandum in the only score we have in our possession and, if you are willing, we should like to attach your autograph letter in the copy which we are making for Mr.Fleisher. Mr.Fleisher was in our office when your letter arrived and he expressed a very keen desire to have the information about the work in your own writing, for the Library in which the copy would be placed.

Yours faithfully,
Novello & Co. Ltd.[15]

Tiddington House, Stratford-upon-Avon.
24 JUN 1929
Dear Sirs

Bach-Esser Toccata

I do not wish my letter of the 20th to go out of your possession, or a copy of it made, as it contains some remarks about English critics. It shd. be sufficient for Mr.Fleisher's purpose if a short memo:—e.g. 'Bach's ending is reinstated in this arrangement' is added by the copyist

Yours faithfully
[Edward Elgar][16]

160, Wardour Street, London, W.1.
26th June 1929.

Dear Sir,

We thank you for your letter of the 20th inst. regarding the arrangement of your 'Cello Concerto for Viola, which we shall be happy to engrave if you will kindly ask Mr.Lionel Tertis to forward the arrangement to us.

With regard to the Bach-Esser 'Toccata', we will add the note to the score as you suggest. We quite appreciate your reasons for not wishing your letter to be passed on.

Yours faithfully,
Novello & Co. Ltd.,
W.C.H.[17]

Harold Brooke wrote about some points in the solo part of the Concerto, and Elgar replied:

---

[15] Elgar Birthplace parcel 238.   [16] Letter book.   [17] HWRO 705:445:2774.

S-on-A
22nd July 1929
My dear Brooke:

Alas! I have no copy! I think the 'Cello *Solo* part is mostly correct regarding the small details—I seem to remember that Felix Salmond evolved some little improvements—I will *try & call* this week

> Best regards
> Yrs sny
> E E

The details were settled during Elgar's visit to London commencing next day.

King George V had recently recovered from a very serious illness, and a commemorative book was talked about, with contributions from leading figures of the day. There were newspaper reports of an Elgar-Kipling collaboration, and this brought a fresh enquiry from Leslie Boosey.

295, Regent Street, London, W.1.
26th June 1929
Dear Sir Edward,

I saw in the Papers on Monday evening that you were co-operating with Mr.Rudyard Kipling in a March to commemorate His Majesty's recovery. Is there any chance of our being the publishers of this? You will remember you promised some time ago that you would endeavour to make up the complete set of [six *Pomp and Circumstance*] Marches you originally set out to write for us.

We should very much appreciate the chance of publishing something of yours again.

> I am,
> Yours sincerely
> Leslie Boosey[18]

Tiddington House, Stratford-upon-Avon.
27 JUN 1929
My dear Leslie: Alas! the announcement in the press is the first (and last) I have heard of 'it';—in other words the whole thing is an invention of the D[aily] M[ail]—I know nothing of it

> Kind regards
> Yours sncly
> Edward Elgar[19]

[18] HWRO 705:445:1317.   [19] MS in possession of John Franca.

295, Regent Street, London, W.1.
28th June 1929

My dear Sir Edward,

Thank you for your letter. The newspapers are certainly the very devil! However, if you ever do feel like writing another March I hope you won't forget us.

> Yours sincerely,
> Leslie Boosey[20]

Then a letter came from the editor of the commemorative book:

The King's Book. Commemorative of HIS MAJESTY'S Restoration to Health. Tendered by Artists, Authors and Advertisers of the Empire. Administration Offices: 18, Charing Cross Road, London, W.C.2.
9th July 1929.

Sir,

... It has been suggested and it seems to be the general consensus of opinion that a musical composition on the lines of a 'March of Praise' would be of tremendous Empire interest, and I have been instructed by my Committee to invite your co-operation towards making this item the outstanding feature of 'The King's Book'.

Several distinguished lyrical writers including Mr.Rudyard Kipling and Dr.Robert Bridges have been communicated with and subject to appropriate verses being inspired, my Committee would be honoured by your setting the same to music.

I sincerely trust that you will view with sympathetic consideration the invitation that I have the honour to extend to you.

I am, Sir,

> Your Obedient Servant,
> D.Mackenzie
> Honorary Editor.

On the verso Elgar made some notes:

Questions   *Alfred Noyes*

1).About separate publication as in the case of '*King Albert's Book*' (Carillon)
2).Album can only produce vocal (score) with *pianoforte* acct.
3).The work wd. be designed for public performance with *orchestral* (or military band) accompt.
4).The copyright should remain with the composer whose (*music*) publisher wd. be the only person capable of dealing with orchl. work.

[20] HWRO 705:445:2041.

5) There wd. be nothing to interfere with people desirous of performing the work (piano version) as printed in the Album.

6) Mr Kipling is entirely ignorant of music & has no sense of rhythm (apart from verse)   Dr. Bridges has a knowledge but does not seem to care to be rhythmical.

7) Mr. Alfred Noyes is a far-better poet for such an occasion (and, perhaps, any other).

Elgar sent the editor's letter with his own notes to Leslie Boosey on 11 July. Boosey was naturally encouraging, and on 26 August Elgar informed the firm that he had seen Noyes, who was 'considering the possibilities of a poem'. But the proposed collaboration went no farther.

Elgar then decided to celebrate the King's recovery in a different way. Walford Davies asked for a carol to be sung by the choristers of St George's Chapel, Windsor, for their annual concert in December. Elgar thereupon looked out an old tune of his youth, and set it to verses of the Tudor poet George Gascoigne entitled *Good Morrow*. He offered it to Novello, in a letter written from his London flat.

37 St James's Place SW1   5214 Gerrard
6th Nov 1929
Dear Sirs:

I have a *Partsong Carol* sort of thing
          'A simple Carol for His Majesty's happy recovery.'
& it has struck me that you might care to issue it in the Decr. *Musical Times*. Sir Walford Davies will perform it for the first time on *Decr 9th*. at the St.G's Choir Concert in *Windsor* which I conduct & which will be broadcast.

> Yrs vy try
> Edward Elgar

P.S. On the slender chance that Mr. Harold Brooke might be disengaged & cd. come down here (where I am engaged all the morning) & see me about the 'Carol' I send my telephone number   Gerrard 5214

Apparently Brooke did visit Elgar's flat, and two days later Novello offered ten guineas down and a royalty of 15 per cent. After some hesitation, Elgar accepted the terms.

At the end of the year a new musical copyright bill appeared in Parliament, the effect of which would have been to reduce to virtually nothing the composer's performing royalty. Leslie Boosey's cousin William, writing about this proposal a year later, summarized it thus:

At the present moment, composers are enormously dependent upon the fees collected for them by the Performing Right Society. Naturally, the society has had to contend with a huge combination of vested interests, who are always out to fight and see if they can obtain something of value for nothing. Fortunately, our position has been made so strong that even such an inane Bill as the Bill seeking to amend performing rights in the last session of the

House of Commons has been laughed out of court. This Bill was god-fathered principally by a collection of wealthy hotel and restaurant proprietors. The repertoire of the Performing Right Society includes the works of all the most popular composers in this country and on the Continent. In the season, some of these hotels would pay from £500 a week to £1,000 a week to their orchestras, and they grudged and fought against a paltry £3 or £4 a week to the composers, British and Continental, without whose music they could have had no orchestras at all ...

I foresee the day when composers will depend almost entirely for their income upon the fees obtained for them by the Performing Right Society, more particularly as the broadcasting authorities have had to recognise that they are powerless to reproduce music for public performance except by treaty with those who hold the copyright.[21]

Fifty years later, these truths are self-evident. But if the Bill before Parliament in 1929 had succeeded, the story might have been very different. Elgar saw this clearly, and drafted a letter which he sent to all the leading papers.

Draft:
>   To the Editor of Times
>   Mg Post
>   D.Tel
>   D.Mail
>   D.News
>   E.Standard

Sir:

Musical Copyright Bill

The most serious blow ever aimed at the unfortunate art of English music is proposed to be dealt by some of the very persons to whom creative artists might not unreasonably have looked for sympathy and assistance. A situation such as that now existing could not have arisen in any artistically civilised community. At this moment I do not enter into details concerning the monstrous proposals contained in the bill; but I will record my strong protest against it, adding that the passing of such a measure would mean the extinction of creative musical.art in this country and the ruin of the majority of native composers.

>   Your obedient Servant
>   [Edward Elgar][22]

Its publication drew an immediate response from Leslie Boosey.

---

[21] *Fifty Years of Music*, pp. 175–6.   [22] HWRO 705:445:1337.

295, Regent Street, London, W.1.
Dec 18 1929

Dear Sir Edward

May I congratulate you on your excellent letter on the new Copyright bill[.] I am sure it will do a great deal of good[.] They made me Chairman of the Performing Rights Society in June and I can assure you it was an honour which I did not seek but I accepted because I am convinced the composers have got to look to this source of revenue in the future if they are going to get anything at all out of writing music[.] Now when I see such a monstrous bill as the present one passing its second reading I begin to wonder whether there is any justice in the old Country any more.

The musical people on the continent treat it as a rash joke [—] they simply cannot believe that a civilized community could put such an act on their Statute book[;] but alas nothing is impossible in these days.

With all good wishes for Christmas and the New Year

Yours sincerely
Leslie Boosey[23]

Bernard Shaw and other influential people joined the composers, and at last the Bill failed. But it had been a near thing.

1930

With Novello, things trickled on as before. Early in 1930 Elgar received a letter from a schoolmistress in Oxfordshire, a Miss Henman, suggesting a female voice arrangement of *Jesu, Word of God Incarnate* (the English version of *Ave Verum*): she enclosed her own suggestions. Elgar sent this on to Novello from the house he had recently purchased.

Marl Bank, Rainbow Hill, Worcester.
25 FEB 1930

Dear Sirs:

Jesu, word of God.

Enclosed is a letter which please return. I think the idea is a good one & if you approve I wd. make the arrgt. $\left(\begin{array}{l}\text{in } A^b \\ \text{or A better}\end{array}\right)$ for S.S.C.; some other things might be done in the same way for school services

Yours faithfully
Edward Elgar

P.S. The suggested alterations by Miss Henman will *not* do.

[23] HWRO 705:445:1336.

[160, Wardour Street, London, W.1.]
February 26th, 1930.

Dear Sir,

We are much obliged by your letter of the 25th.inst., enclosing Miss Henman's letter, and the copy of your '*Jesu, Word of God Incarnate*' as marked by her, both of which we return herewith.

We should like to act upon your suggestion that we publish an arrangement of that Anthem for three women's voices, which you kindly offer to prepare.

We enclose a clean copy; also a list of similar things, published by us, in which we propose to include 'Jesu Word of God Incarnate' when arranged as suggested.

Will a fee of Five Guineas for the arrangement meet your views?

Yours faithfully,
(X/EH)

Marl Bank, Rainbow Hill, Worcester.
8th March 1930

Dear Sirs:

Thank you for your letter of 26th Feby
I now enclose the arrgt (S.S.C.) of the Motet.
I think the fee should be seven guineas but you will know best

Yours faithfy
Edward Elgar

Two days later Novello sent the agreement for seven guineas.

A small sign of American interest came from Novello's agent in New York, H. W. Gray. One of the American radio networks was beginning to broadcast music with their own orchestra and chorus, in this case under the baritone Reinald Werrenrath (1883–1953). Gray wrote:

159 East 48th Street, New York
April 9 1930

My dear Sir Edward,

Acting on the instructions received from Novello & Company I am enclosing herewith a draft for £13-7-9, the equal of $67.50 representing the fee we received from the National Broadcasting Company of $75.00 less 10%, for their performance of the 'Dream of Gerontius', under Reginald [*sic*] Werrenrath. I should like to add that it was a most admirable performance given with a small but competent professional choir and presumably the tone was amplified when broadcasted.

It seems a very long time ago since you and I joined the Potato Club after the celebrated trip to Cincinnati. I only wish you would pay us another visit.

Trusting that you are in the best of health.

Yours truly,
H.W.Gray[1]

Elgar had last visited Cincinnati with Gray in 1911, and the ancient high spirits of the Potato Club are now too distant for anyone to remember.

Yet the early months of 1930 saw the beginnings of a reviving creative interest long dormant. Herbert Whiteley, the brass band editor, had never ceased his appeals for a piece to use as test material for the competition festival held at the Crystal Palace. 1930 would see the twenty-fifth of these festivals. Elgar had at last seemed to promise a short score (to be fully scored for brass band by an expert, Henry Geehl)—and then after all said he could not. Whiteley replied:

31st January 1930.

Dear Sir Edward Elgar

Your last letter was a very keen disappointment to me, especially after your promise to send a short score. It is over 20 years since I first received your first letter on this subject & all along through the time I have been encouraged in the hope that one day you would write the music. The next Festival is the 25th, & I declined other works on the strength of your promise—(with the understanding that the fee should be reconsidered).

£60 was the largest fee paid previously; I suggested £100 in your case & half gramophone rights or £150 inclusive. What more can I add?—except to ask you to name your terms.

Please do not let me down.

I shall not—nor ever have done in the past—benefit one penny piece by supporting British composers. Not that your work requires the slightest support from me, but *I have* in the past (when living in the Manchester district) upheld & supported *your music* & your photograph (and the only one) was hung in the old farmhouse where, on the Yorkshire and Lancashire border, many musicians used to meet and discuss native music at a time when almost every British composer was ignored. But even *then* your music spoke for itself and required no mans [sic] word to add to its appeal. Those days were long before Richter came to Manchester

So I again appeal to you—for the sake of the brass band—to write the next work. It will be quite in time if I get the score within the next six weeks & in the meantime I could—if you desire it—call to see you, either in London or Worcester.

Believe me to remain, Sir Edward

Yours faithfully
Herbert Whiteley.[2]

---

[1] Elgar Birthplace parcel 238.   [2] HWRO 705:445:2084.

Such a request, couched in this way, was at last impossible to ignore. So Elgar agreed to venture on medium-scale composition for the first time since the *Arthur* music of 1923 and *Beau Brummel*. It was to be a *Severn Suite*, with the ideas coming mainly from old sketchbooks. On 14 March Elgar received Whiteley's cheque, and signed this receipt:

Received from Herbert Whiteley, on behalf of R. Smith & Co., Ltd., 210 Strand[,] London, the sum of One hundred and Fifty Pounds, for the copyright and all other rights for brass band, of my new work, entitled, 'The Severn Suite'

It is understood that the composer retains *all rights* in the above work apart from the brass band rights.[3]

In April it was finished. Soon it would lead Elgar to write further music.

Within a few weeks he scored and sent to Boosey a new *Pomp and Circumstance* March—No. 5 in C major. He asked what Leslie Boosey would offer.

295, Regent Street, London, W.1.
2nd May 1930

My dear Sir Edward,

I am delighted to receive 'Pomp and Circumstance No 5'.

I feel sure that the terms we arranged were Fifty Guineas on account of Royalties for each [previous *Pomp and Circumstance*] March; but if by any chance this was not your understanding perhaps you will kindly let me know, as we did not put anything down in writing. On having your confirmation of this I will have an Agreement sent to you for your approval.

By the way, I thought you might be interested to hear that the Select Committee on the new Copyright Bill had what I understand was its last public sitting yesterday, at which we were called to give evidence again. Of course I don't know what the result will be, but I did have it from one of the Committee that the evidence of the Performing Right Society had completely altered his views on the subject of the Bill, and he told me he thought that at the very least there would be a minority report against any fresh legislation, and he did not think there was any chance of a Bill becoming law. Of course the Bill in its old form is, to use the words of a Board of Trade Representative, 'as dead as mutton'.

Kind regards,

Yours sincerely,
Leslie Boosey[4]

Elgar was undoubtedly glad to hear this news of the Copyright Bill. On the question of payment for *Pomp and Circumstance* No. 5, he thought he ought to have £75 advance on royalties.

---

[3] R. Smith & Co. archives.   [4] Elgar Birthplace parcel 235.

[295, Regent Street, London, W.1.]
7th May 1930

My dear Sir Edward,

I have no desire to dispute terms for 'Pomp and Circumstance' No 5, with you, especially as you always seem to think that Boosey & Company do not treat you properly. I certainly thought that £50 was the figure mentioned, but if you want £75 it must be £75.

The only point I have to suggest is that we should have 50%, not only of the Mechanical Royalties, but of the Broadcasting & Performing Fees, and all other Fees of this character.

You admitted on your own account that things are not what they were in the days when you wrote 'Pomp' No 1, and as a matter of fact you are mistaken in thinking that you received £100 for these Marches. It was never more than £50, and for some reason or other only Twenty Five Guineas for 'Pomp' No 2.; so actually 'Pomp' No 5 will be costing us £25 more than any of the others did, added to which is the immense increase in the cost of engraving and printing and the very serious falling off in the sale of the sheet copy.

I have drawn up an Agreement embodying these terms; also making an allowance of half royalties for the sale of copies in the United States of America and the British Dominions, and if you will let me know that it meets with your approval I will have the necessary cheque sent.

I notice on referring to the old Marches that the transcription for Piano was made by Adolf Schmid, but it is so long ago that we do not seem to be in touch with him now, in fact I don't know whether he is still alive. I would therefore suggest that we employ Mr Hely Hutchinson of the B.B.C., who has done some very useful work of this character for us lately; but before approaching him I should like to know that this meets with your approval.

Do you think we ought to have another Score made for small orchestra, or could the present one be cued in satisfactorily?

I am,
Yours sincerely,
[Leslie A. Boosey]

Both Boosey and Novello (with the exception of Augustus Littleton) had been extremely tactful in their dealings with the old composer. Yet he, embittered by personal loss, changing times, and a muse largely fallen silent over many years, could be difficult over small points. It must have seemed at times as if he was dusting off the year of legal training he had undergone sixty years earlier as a teenager. Elgar's reply to Boosey's letter of 7 May is missing, but Boosey's response shows renewed tact at renewed difficulties.

295, Regent Street, London, W.1.
15th May 1930

My dear Sir Edward,

It is our intention to bring out the new 'Pomp' March in the same form as the previous ones, and if you require any undertaking of this kind I am quite willing to incorporate it in the Agreement, though it wont really be necessary because I intend to give the Work out [to be engraved] at once.

The general lines of the Agreement are exactly the same as before, with the exception of the reduction of one penny in the royalty payable for sales in the British Dominions and in the United States, a point to which I drew your attention in the previous letter.

We have never paid any royalty on the Piano Conductor copies of the other Marches, and as we are paying £75 in the first place, and our expenses are likely to far exceed any money we receive for the sale of sheet music, I presumed you would not be asking for it in this case.

I don't quite see what you mean when you say that you might receive nothing after the initial £75. I suppose you mean that if we never publish the Work, it could never be performed &c., in which case your contention is logical; but we certainly should not spend £75 on a Work from you above all people, and then be foolish enough to keep it on the shelves; but as I say, if you tell us the clause you want, It shall be put in. I suggest one as follows:— 'It is understood that the Publishers shall publish the Work in the following forms———— within————of the signing of this Agreement'

Yours sincerely
Leslie A. Boosey[5]

Marl Bank, Rainbow Hill, Worcester.
16th May 1930

My dear Leslie:

I do not want to quibble, *but* if the assignment was to be interpreted by mere legal experts the publisher might suppress my original score, make any arrangements of any part (I mean a few bars or, in fact any arrgt. or mutilation)—for two ukeleles or any absurd, merely commonplace combination—on which the composer wd. receive nothing as expressly covenanted in the last par:

Between you and me there could not possibly be any misunderstanding but I can only say that what I suggest above has really happened to me.

Later agreements usually say that when the expense of Mil[itar]y & Brass [Band versions] have been covered the composer shares: but that does not matter. I think your suggestion is just what is wanted—i.e. 'It is understood. etc'

Yours sincerely
Edward Elgar

[5] Elgar Birthplace parcel 235.

19th May 1930

My dear Sir Edward,

I quite follow your point and I have endeavoured to cover it in the last paragraph.

We are going to put the Work in hand right away; but would you let me know what you feel about the Piano Arrangement. I asked you whether you thought Hely Hutchinson would be a suitable person to make it.

Kindest regards,
Yours sincerely,
[Leslie A. Boosey]

Marl Bank, Rainbow Hill, Worcester.
20 MAY 1930

My dear Leslie:

Here is the Assignment duly signed; I retain the duplicate.

As to an arranger: I have heard nothing of Adolf Schmid since *1914*. I shall be satisfied with anyone you think usefully good enough for the task. You will, of course, not employ anyone to *fantasticate* the piano arrgts. etc—we must be practical

Kind rgrds
Yrs sincerely
Edward Elgar

On 4 June Novello sent news that no fewer than sixty copies of the Cello Concerto (with piano accompaniment) had been ordered in Paris. On investigation it proved that the Concerto had been chosen as the test piece for advanced students at the Conservatoire.[6] One of the students that year was to become perhaps the most distinguished interpreter of the Concerto in his generation—Paul Tortelier (b. 1914).

In the same month, Elgar was negotiating with a firm which had never published any of his music, Keith Prowse & Company. The introduction to this old firm had been made by Sir Landon Ronald, whose compositions they published. At the end of May Elgar had lunched with the firm's managing director, Herbert Smith, and the publishing manager, Simon van Lier. The terms they discussed were in some ways reminiscent of the exclusive contract with Novello in the great days of 1904 to 1911. The Keith Prowse agreement would provide for an annual payment to the composer of £250, together with royalties and a considerable proportion of broadcasting and mechanical (e.g., gramophone recording) rights. In return, 'the Composer will in each year during the period of this agreement compose and submit to the Publisher manuscripts of not less than three songs or pieces'. The main point was the contract's exclusivity: Keith Prowse wanted control of everthing Elgar should publish henceforth.

Elgar replied that he intended to write one more *Pomp and Circumstance* March to complete the set, and that should go to Boosey. Choral works he felt should also be excluded: was he even now thinking of a third oratorio to complete the trilogy whose first two parts were published by Novello? In any case, Keith Prowse were glad to agree to these conditions, and the Managing Director wrote:

[6] HWRO 705:445:1272.

159, New Bond Street, London, W.1.
3rd June. 1930

Dear Sir Edward Elgar,

It was a very great pleasure to me to be afforded the opportunity of having such a pleasant lunch and chat with you last week through the kind introduction of our mutual friend, Sir Landon Ronald. I feel that as a result of our talk we shall, in the future, be associated with I hope, many happy and successful Compositions by your goodself.

I have been talking the matter over, further, with Mr. Van Lier, who is naturally most interested and he already has I believe, in his mind some ideas and suggestions to make to you in due course.

I have prepared and enclose herewith the suggested outline of the Agreement which we discussed. I think that I have covered the necessary essentials, but the various points would, of course, be set out more completely in a draft Agreement for your consideration and acceptance.

I might say that on the enclosed notes I have followed the idea of the Agreement which I have made with Sir Landon Ronald.

I would be pleased if you would be good enough to let me hear if you approve the suggestions I have made. If you do I will proceed to have a draft Agreement drawn up embodying the conditions. On the other hand you would, of course, let me know if there is anything which you would like added or altered.

With kindest personal regards,

Yours sincerely,
Herbert Smith[7]

Elgar's early letters to Keith Prowse are missing from the files, but it is clear that he signified general acceptance. The agreement was to run for three years in the first instance. No such hopeful sign for Elgar's future music had emerged since the Novello agreement had ceased almost twenty years earlier. But Elgar himself was now seventy-three.

A fortnight later the new contract was ready. It was sent by Van Lier, who was keen to pursue several ideas for new Elgar works.

42 & 43, Poland Street, London, W.1.
June 20th, 1930.

Dear Sir Edward,

I have pleasure in now enclosing agreements. Will you please sign both copies and return one to me.

In order to save you trouble, I have been thinking that it would, perhaps, be a good idea if I were to come to Worcester for a few days. I could then discuss fully with you the matter of future compositions, and it is possible that you may already have some manuscripts which may interest us. I could

---

[7] Elgar Birthplace parcel 234.

go over them with you and it would save you the bother of coming up to town or sending on any such works.

As I shall be leaving for my holiday about July 15th, any time prior to this date or after the beginning of August would be quite convenient for me. I think a week-end would be preferable. Will you kindly suggest a date?

I trust this may be the beginning of a very happy and successful business relationship between us.

> Yours very truly,
> KEITH, PROWSE & Co. LTD.
> S. Van Lier.
> Gen.Manager, Publishing Dept.[8]

Elgar, not in the best of health, did not immediately arrange a date for Van Lier to visit. But he did return the agreement, and on 28 June Van Lier sent a cheque for £125—the first six months' retaining fee.

That summer he assigned to Keith Prowse his remaining rights in the *Severn Suite*—all but the brass band rights owned by R. Smith & Co. Then, during the second half of the year, he produced three fresh works for his new publisher. By an assignment dated 15 December 1930, Elgar conveyed to Keith Prowse a new version of a very old but never previously published piano Sonatina, a Scottish song entitled *It isnae me*, and a *Nursery Suite* for orchestra. The last-named had been suggested by one of the men at 'His Master's Voice', on hearing that Elgar had recently come upon a trunk full of early manuscripts. The idea was passed to Van Lier, as a commemoration of the recent birth of Princess Margaret Rose to the Duke and Duchess of York. By December the new score was virtually finished.

1931

The completion of the *Nursery Suite* was announced in the press early in the new year. On 9 January Fred Gaisberg wrote on behalf of The Gramophone Company to ask about recording it. Elgar sent his letter on to Van Lier next day.

42 & 43, Poland Street, London, W.1.
Jan.14th, 1931.

Dear Sir Edward,

Many thanks for your letter of the 10th inst., with communication enclosed from the Gramophone Company which I now return.

I have this morning received the MS copy which I had made of your score of the 'Nursery Suite' and have passed this on at once for the parts to be engraved from it. You will understand that it took some little time getting the score copied but now it is in the engravers' hands we shall soon be having proofs, which I will let you have for recording and correction as you suggest.

[8] Elgar Birthplace parcel 234.

I was very interested to read that you are endeavouring to get H.R.H. to be present at the recording, and possibly arrange for a photograph to be taken on the occasion. This would be excellent.

With kind regards.

Yours sincerely,
KEITH PROWSE & Co. LTD.
S.vanLier
Gen.Manager, Publishing Dept.[1]

The recording was made in two sessions, 23 May and 4 June, which constituted the première of the *Nursery Suite*. The Duke and Duchess of York (later HM King George VI and Queen Elizabeth) attended the second session with Princess Elizabeth (now HM The Queen).

Compared with these events, Elgar's contacts with his earlier publishers were of small importance. Elkin pursued possibilities of reviving *The Starlight Express* in a broadcast performance and *Polonia*.[2] Boosey still wondered about a collaboration with Kipling,[3] and secured Elgar's assent to distribute free copies of *Pomp and Circumstance* to French orchestras in the hope of encouraging performances.[4] Novello renewed American copyrights of *The Apostles* and the *Greek Anthology* part-songs.[5]

Novello also suggested a female-voice arrangement of his part-song for More-cambe, *Weary Wind of the West*.

Worcester
31st Decr 1930

Dear Sirs:

In reply to your enquiry I think a satisfactory arrangement of 'Weary wind' could be made for *S.S.C.* with free P.F accpt.

I shall be glad to hear if you think twenty-five guineas a proper fee for this.

I shd. propose to put the piece into 6/8 time—but your advisers will please tell me which time signature (6/8 or 3/4) is the more *useful*: it *looks* a little lighter in style in 6/8—see enclosed which do not return

Yrs faithfully
Edward Elgar

Novello's reply is missing, but a note in the files reads: 'H.R.C[layton] says Yes, & send him a cheque at once. We shd: also prefer 6/8.'

When it came to making the adaptation, Elgar found it far from easy.

---

[1] HWRO 705:445:1631.
[2] 2 Jan. 1931 (HWRO 705:445:1243).
[3] Elgar's renewed refusal was written on 9 Jan. 1931 (MS in possession of John Franca).
[4] 22 and 23 Jan. 1931 (Boosey & Hawkes archives).
[5] 2 Feb. 1931 (Elgar Birthplace parcel 238).

Marl Bank, Rainbow Hill, Worcester.
21st January 1931
Dear Sirs:

Weary wind

I find some difficulty in 'reducing' the middle section of this for S.S.A: if it falls in with your view I propose to rewrite this section presuming you do not want to follow the original quite closely. . . .

Yours very truly
Edward Elgar.

The firm agreed, but when they heard nothing further for several weeks, they enquired again.

Marl Bank, Rainbow Hill, Worcester.
3rd March 1931
Dear Sirs:

Weary wind S.S.C

I am extremely sorry for the delay: I have found the arrgt. the most intractable affair: I hope to send a version tomorrow for your consideration

Yrs Very ty
Edward Elgar

Three days later he finished and dated the manuscript,[6] and sent it to the publisher, who responded:

160, Wardour Street, London, W.1.
March 10th, 1931
Dear Sir,

We have now examined the S.S.C. version of 'Weary Wind of the West', and we should like to take this opportunity of thanking you for the transcription and of telling you how immensely pleased we are with it.

Yours faithfully
Novello & Co. Ltd.[7]

In the Birthday Honours in June Elgar was created Baronet. He received letters and telegrams of congratulation from Harold Brooke of Novello,[8] Elkin,[9] and the men at Keith Prowse,[10] among many others.

Van Lier wrote from Keith Prowse about sending Elgar's portrait to the Duchess of York in connection with the *Nursery Suite* recording, proposals for the first public performance of that work, and whether a performing fee should be charged. Elgar replied:

[6] Now incorporated in BL Add MS 57987.
[7] HWRO 705:445:1245.
[8] HWRO 705:445:4862.
[9] HWRO 705:445:4864.
[10] HWRO 705:445:4878 and 4909.

Marl Bank, Worcester.
June 14th 1931.

Dear Mr. van Lier,

Many thanks for your letter of June 11th. Regarding the performing fee of the NURSERY SUITE, I do not think it necessary to charge any special performing fee and will be guided by you entirely in the matter.

It is put down for the Gloucester Festival—the Evening [secular] Concert. The conductor, Mr.Sumsion[,] is anxious to know if that will be the first performance. I am telling him that I cannot assure him of this. Mrs.Cortauld has also written wishing to put the Suite down next year [for the Cortauld-Sargent Concerts]. I have been away and have got behind with my letters and I can now tell her that she is too late. I think the best thing would be to ignore all requests for first performances and let the work take its chance, unless you hear from the B.B.C. [who had asked about broadcasting the *Nursery Suite* as part of a Promenade Concert in August] very quickly. The Gloucester Festival is the first week in September or thereabouts.

I will let you hear about the portrait directly I hear from the Duchess. If it could [be] possible to put in small type in the first movement over the little section beginning in E^b (x see below) HYMN, it would be advisable to do so but I expect it is too late.

> Kind regards,
> Yours sincerely,
> Edwd. Elgar

Thus

in piano arrgt only[11]

In the event the first public performance took place in Queen's Hall at the Promenade Concert on 20 August, conducted by Sir Henry Wood. Van Lier wrote:

42 & 43, Poland Street, London, W.1.
August 25th, 1931.

Dear Sir Edward,

Many thanks for your letter. I am more than delighted with the splendid photograph you so kindly sent me.

I was at the Queen's Hall last Thursday and very much enjoyed the performance of 'THE NURSERY SUITE.' It certainly had an excellent reception. I have a large collection of press cuttings about it and all the critics

---

[11] This and all following letters from Elgar to Keith Prowse are in the firm's archives unless otherwise noted.

are unanimous in their praise of this exquisite Suite. I am sure that no other orchestral work of recent years has received such enormous publicity.

With kind regards.

> Yours sincerely,
> Keith Prowse & Co. Ltd.
> S.van Lier
> Gen.Manager, Publishing Dept.[12]

Anton Dolin now proposed to make a ballet of the *Nursery Suite* (to be given at the Old Vic in March 1932). Elgar's next surviving letter to van Lier dealt with this, a request for a new work from Sir Dan Godfrey, and an account of a visit of the Union of Graduates in Music to Worcester, during which Ivor Atkins had played the Fugue in the *Severn Suite* on the organ. Fred Gaisberg of 'His Master's Voice' had seen the account of this, and had written to ask whether it could be recorded.[13] Accordingly, Elgar wrote to Van Lier:

5 OCT.1931

Dear Mr.vanLier:

Unfortunately while in London for the concert last week I had a bad cold or I should have called.

The enclosed letter (HMV) refers to the occasion of the visit of the Union of Graduates in Music to Worcester in July. Sir Ivor Atkins played the fugue in the Cathedral—it is from the 'Severn Suite'; if you think it worth while to issue it as an organ solo,(or any other portions of the suite for organ) I suggest that Sir Ivor Atkins should be asked to make the arrgts: he played it from my original sketch for brass band

I also enclose a letter from Mr Anton Dolin: he used two little pieces (Novello) of mine for a short divertissement two or three years ago which I understand had some success: in acknowledging the receipt of his book I asked him what he thought of The Nursery Suite as a possible foundation for a Ballet: here is his reply. I shall be glad to know what you think of the matter.

The third affair is the letter & enclosure from Sir Dan Godfrey: of course I cannot undertake to write a composition for the U.S.A. people: but wd. it be possible to suggest to them the 'Severn Suite' of which you hold all rights except Brass Band?

> Kind rgds
> Yrs sncly
> [Edward Elgar][14]

Nothing further emerged from the American proposal. But as a result of this letter, each of the new Suites was to be transfigured in a new medium—Dolin's ballet of 1932, and an Elgar-Atkins 'Organ Sonata No. 2' founded on most of the *Severn Suite* movements, to be published by Keith Prowse in 1933.

---

[12] HWRO 705:445:1635.   [13] See *Elgar on Record*, p. 142.   [14] Letter book.

Novello sent for Elgar's inspection an organ arrangement of the 'Nimrod' Variation by William Henry Harris (1883–1973), organist of St George's Chapel, Windsor. Elgar responded:

Marl Bank, Rainbow Hill, Worcester.
12th Augt 1931
Dear Sirs:
Organ arrgt. 'Nimrod'
I am obliged to you for sending this for inspection: it seems to be very well done: perhaps a few more 'ties' might be added, but I hesitate to suggest these as they might interfere with Dr Harris's 'design'.

> Believe me to be
> Yours very try
> Edward Elgar

Some months later, when Elgar received printed copies of the arrangement, he responded:

Marl Bank, Rainbow Hill, Worcester.
25 MAR. 1932
Dear Sir:

Thank you for the copies of the organ arrangement of 'Nimrod' which seems to be very well done.
I venture to suggest that the title might read
'Adagio (elegiaco)'?
(or simply 'Adagio')
from the Variations on an original theme (No.9 Nimrod).
I fear the title 'Nimrod' may prevent the inclusion of the piece in church programmes, unless, indeed, the connection of N. with Holy Writ is more favourably thought of than I imagine it to be.

> Believe me to be
> Yours very try
> [Edward Elgar][15]

Despite Elgar's fears, 'Nimrod' made its way equally in sacred and secular settings.
Leslie Boosey made another proposal on behalf of his firm, now merged with Messrs Hawkes.

1st September 1931
Dear Sir Edward,

You may remember that some years ago I approached you with a view to making a small Orchestral Suite founded on the 'Sea Pictures'. At the time you decided against it because you did not think you would have the time to do it yourself.

[15] Letter book.

As however, the advisors to the Hawkes side of the catalogue, who have I suppose as wide an experience of orchestral music as anyone in the country, have now approached me with exactly the same suggestion, I feel justified in bringing it up with you again.

Mr Charles Woodhouse, who is their chief advisor, is very enthusiastic about the possibilities and quite willing to undertake the work. I therefore suggest that he should be given permission to go ahead, on the understanding of course, that the work should be submitted to you when finished, and it would not of course be published without your sanction.

The 'Sea Pictures', are quite one of my greatest favourites in the whole of our catalogue, and I feel sure that the better known they become the more they will be appreciated.

Kindest regards,
Yours sincerely
L.A.B.

Langham Hotel, Portland Place, London W.I.
Thursday [3 Sept. 1931]

My dear Leslie:

I am just passing thro' & have no time to call. Thank you for your letter: by all means, do anything you like about the 'Sea Pictures'. I only demurred on acct. of the trouble entailed in writing for small orch.: the *full* orch: is no trouble at all. Mr.Woodhouse is just the man.

Kindest regards
Yrs sincy
Edward Elgar.

Charles Woodhouse (1879–1937) was a well-known orchestral leader and string quartet player, and he also had extensive experience as pianist in small orchestras. His projected arrangement of *Sea Pictures*, embracing the second, fourth, and third songs, appeared only in 1935, after Elgar's death.

The revival-idea which caught Elgar's greatest interest then was for one of his least-known works, *The Sanguine Fan* ballet published by Elkin. In the summer of 1931 Elgar had a letter from the ballet's originator, Mrs Lowther, now married to Lord George Cholmondely. She hoped to take *The Sanguine Fan*, with other short ballets which she had commissioned or choreographed, on a foreign tour to be conducted by Constant Lambert (1905–51). Elkin gave this idea every encouragement,[16] and Elgar wrote to Lambert:

Marl Bank
21 OCT 1931

Dear Mr Constant Lambert:

Mr.Elkin has sent me your letter regarding the score of the little ballet which Lady George Cholmondely proposes to revive. I am very much honoured by your undertaking the care of it. The thing was written in the

[16] HWRO 705:445:1639.

greatest haste; it would have been no worse & no better if I had taken longer over it, but I mention this to account for the too great length of some of the *dances*—there was no opportunity to discuss these so I wrote a great deal too much with many repeats so that cuts cd. be made in an instant at the two rehearsals we had. Please deal with it unmercifully.

May I take this opportunity to say how much I have enjoyed your 'Rio Grande' & how highly I think of it.

> Believe me to be
> Yours very truly
> [Edward Elgar][17]

Nothing came of the plan to revive *The Sanguine Fan*, nor of another effort to have *The Starlight Express* broadcast.[18]

Music everywhere was depressed by bad economic conditions. A letter from Novello's American agent H. W. Gray reflected this.

The H.W.Gray Company, 159 East 48th Street, New York
8 Dec.1931.

Dear Sir Edward,

I am sending you herewith a draft for $27.00 the fee of $30.00 less our commission of 10%, which we finally obtained from the National Broadcasting Company, for relaying the first half of 'Gerontius' back in last June. I am sorry for the delay but we could not get payment before this day.

The complications in this business grow deeper every day. A short time ago I had a request from this Company by phone stating that a certain work would be on the air in three minutes, could they relay without payment. I had to say no, not that I knew anything about it. I hope that there are no radios in Heaven.

Hoping you are enjoying the best of health and with Compliments of the Season.

> Yours truly,
> H W Gray[19]

Only with Keith Prowse could affairs be said to be moving forward. A week after opening the new Gramophone Studios at Abbey Road, Elgar wrote to Van Lier about a film made of the occasion, which included 'The Waggon Passes' from the *Nursery Suite*.

---

[17] Letter book.
[18] Letters from Elkin and the BBC Light Music adviser Joseph Lewis (HWRO 705:445:1632–4) and a reply from Elgar (23 Oct. 1931 in the Letter book).
[19] HWRO 705:445:1235.

19 NOV.1931

Dear Mr.vanLier:

Many thanks for your letter of the 12th; I am glad you are safely back in England. Thank you also for the list of performances of the Suite: at the opening of the new premises of the H.M.V. I took part in a little Pathe Gazette sound film & conducted (besides 'Land of Hope') 'The Waggon Passes': I hear it is a passable film & may be sold.

I am interested in the Italian journal: & will return it soon.

> Kind regards
> Yours sincerely
> [Edward Elgar][20]

There was talk of Elgar writing something for the opening of the new Shakespeare Memorial Theatre at Stratford-upon-Avon. The director, W. Bridges-Adams, was a friend from the time of Elgar's residence at Stratford: he was very keen for music from Elgar. Van Lier was equally keen for an Elgar overture, and he took up this idea at the end of his reply to Elgar's letter.

42 & 43, Poland Street, London, W.1.
November 23rd, 1931.

Dear Sir Edward,

Many thanks for your letter of the 19th inst.

I was very interested to hear that you had recorded 'THE WAGGON PASSES' in the Pathé Sound Film. Mr.Watts, of the Pathé Company told me that it had come out beautifully and is going to let me hear a private performance this week.

You will be pleased to know that during my visit to New York I arranged with Messrs.G.Schirmer, Inc., to take over the sole selling agency of the 'Nursery Suite' for America for a period of three years. They gave us quite a nice initial order.

I wonder if I may take this opportunity of venturing to ask what you think of the suggestion of your writing an overture. I know you appreciated the suggestion I passed on for the 'Nursery Suite'. Perhaps you will kindly let me know what you feel about this at your convenience.

With kind regards.

> Yours sincerely,
> KEITH PROWSE & Co. LTD.
> S. Van Lier.
> Gen.Manager, Publishing Dept.[21]

[20] Letter book.   [21] Elgar Birthplace parcel 234.

Marl Bank, Rainbow Hill, Worcester.

25 NOV.1931

Dear Mr.vanLier:

I am glad to hear that you have arranged with Messrs.Schirmer & Co. about the Suite in U.S.A.

I will think over the question of an overture; this would, of course, have to be on the 'facile' side.

I shall be glad to know how the Pathé film comes out

> Kind regards
> Yours sincerely
> [Edward Elgar][22]

1932

Van Lier suggested that an attractive record of *It isnae me* might be made by the soprano Flora Woodman. On 6 January Elgar replied, offering to go through the song with her.[1] He also wrote to Fred Gaisberg at 'His Master's Voice', but Miss Woodman's voice was not thought suitable to the recording microphone.[2]

Elgar's next letter concerned the production of the *Nursery Suite* as a ballet:

Marl Bank.

15/1/32

Dear Mr van Lier,

I enclose a letter from Miss Baylis of The Old Vic. and my reply. Will you decide what is best to be done: it struck me that these few performances might possibly lead to something more definite in the future but as you see from my letter to Miss Baylis, the matter rests with you and I will be guided by your decision.

I am sorry I am not able to get to town just now. I have been indulging in influenza.

> With kind regards
> Yours Sincerely
> [Edward Elgar][3]

Van Lier then proposed a group of simple pieces for school ensembles, and reminded Elgar of a suggestion to write some simple piano pieces. The publisher was probably aware that the Overture for Stratford was not going to materialize. Many reasons were adduced, including Elgar's personal dislike of the very modern style of the new Shakespeare Memorial Theatre.

[22] Letter book.

[1] Letter book (in the hand of Mary Clifford).

[2] See *Elgar on Record*, pp. 156–7. Flora Woodman had recorded for 'His Master's Voice' by the acoustic process, but the electric microphone (introduced to the recording studio in 1925) demanded different vocal skills.

[3] Letter book (in the hand of Mary Clifford).

Marl Bank, Rainbow Hill, Worcester.
2 MAR.1932

Dear Mr.vanLier:

Many thanks for your letter.

Private. I had some thought of your suggestion for an overture in connection with the opening of the new building in Stratford, but have had to give up my proposed connection with that affair: so the overture will not materialise—just yet anyhow.

I am glad the 'Nursery Suite' goes on seemingly well. I wonder if the records sell at all;—Enclosed I send a letter, a type of those I receive.

As to the proposal for some *ensemble* pieces, I think there wd. be no difficulty: wd. you propose an *ad lib*: cello or Viola or both?

I have not forgotten the piano pieces but I have been too unwell all this winter to do anything although I have just managed to get through several engagements, as you may have seen, without *coughing*,—which I do better than anything else just now

With kind rgds.
Yours sncy
[Edward Elgar]

P.S.—I duly suggested to H.M.V. that 'It is nae me' shd. be recorded by Miss Woodman & they were to let me hear if her voice is entirely suitable for recording.[4]

It was Elgar's way of suggesting the negative answer.

42 & 43, Poland Street, London, W.1.
March 3rd, 1932.

Dear Sir Edward,

Thank you for yours of the 2nd inst., and for enclosing letter from the Secretary of the Athenaeum for me to see. I am now returning this. Every music lover certainly seems to be enraptured with the 'NURSERY SUITE'.

With regard to the sale of the records, I understand this is satisfactory, for as you know, classic works do not have a very rapid sale.

I am very pleased that you will write some ensemble pieces as I suggested. The instrumentation I should like is as follows:—

Piano
Solo Violin
1st Violin
2nd Violin
2 Obbligati Violin parts
Viola
Cello

['C.B. ad lib' added by Elgar, who has also bracketed items 3–5]

[4] Letter book.

I am sorry you have been so unwell this winter, but trust that with the approach of spring and the brighter days you will soon recover your usual good health.

With kind regards.

> Yours sincerely,
> KEITH PROWSE & Co. LTD.
> S. Van Lier
> Gen.Manager, Publishing Dept.

P.S. I quite understand that the proposed overture will have to stand over for the present.[5]

In lieu of the Stratford overture, Bridges-Adams suggested that passages from *Falstaff* might be rearranged and rescored for the purpose. This occasioned correspondence with Novello. Elgar wrote to the firm:

[Marl Bank paper]
[24 Feb. 1932]

Dear Sirs:

I proposed to use excerpts from *Falstaff* for the performances of 'Henry IV' at the opening of the new theatre at Stratford upon Avon; I shall not be personally responsible for the actual performance but anything extracted wd. be well done & due acknowledgment made. Before anything is undertaken, I shall be glad to know if you will give your consent & what performing fees, if any, you would suggest.

> Yours very try
> [Edward Elgar][6]

160, Wardour Street, London, W.1.
February 26th, 1932

Dear Sir,

We are much obliged to you for your letter of yesterday, and are greatly interested to hear of the proposal to use excerpts from 'Falstaff' at the Stratford-on-Avon performance of 'Henry IV'.

We rather gather from your letter that you do not wish us to treat the use of 'Falstaff' for this occasion as an ordinary commercial transaction, and, if that is so, we shall of course agree and shall make a small charge for the hire of the necessary material, to cover wear and tear etc., but this we can arrange with the person who sends us particulars of the number of parts etc. that will be wanted.

> Yours faithfully,
> Novello & Co. Ltd.
> [A.]J[.B.]L[ittleton]/EH.[7]

---

[5] Elgar Birthplace parcel 234.   [6] Letter book.   [7] HWRO 705:445:4419.

Marl Bank, Rainbow Hill, Worcester.
27th February 1932.   Copy
Dear Sirs,

Stratford-upon-Avon.

I am obliged to you for your letter. The 'selected portions' from *Falstaff* would necessarily be used to accompany the scenes in which he appears (generally). A few bars here and there or a short passage would have to be extracted and *arranged* for the small orchestra to be employed; probably the two *Intermezzi* might be used intact: there are funds at the disposal of the management and there is I imagine, no reason why some sort of performing fee should not be asked for; this might be considered later. For the moment I only want to know your 'attitude' to the proposal. This, from your letter, I take to be sympathetic.

The orchestral parts would have to be copied (by the theatre) from the re-arrangement: it would be easy to stipulate that such arrangement (if any) is only to be used at *Stratford-upon-Avon.* etc.etc.

On hearing from you I will consult the musical director.

> Believe me to be
> Yours very truly,
> [Edward Elgar][8]

160, Wardour Street, London, W.1.
February 29th, 1932.

Dear Sir,

We thank you for your letter of the 27th. instant, and need hardly say that we shall be perfectly satisfied for any use to be made of the 'Falstaff' music that is quite satisfactory to you.

When we know fuller details, such as the amount of material that they will want us to lend them, we can then fix on a performing fee and credit the usual proportion of it to your account.

> Yours faithfully,
> Novello & Co Ltd.
> C[harles] B[rooke]/EH[9]

---

[8] HWRO 705:445:4418.
[9] HWRO 705:445:4417, drafted by Harold Brooke's brother Charles.

Marl Bank
2nd March 1932
Dear Sirs:

Stratford upon Avon

Many thanks for your letter of the 29th Feby.

I will let you know if anything happens but since I wrote to you I am informed that the musical director, with whom I was to consult, has been superseded. So the matter is in abeyance.

> Yours very try
> [Edward Elgar][10]

Fair as Novello's proposals over *Falstaff* had been, Elgar still found cause for complaint when the Irish conductor Sir Hamilton Harty wrote to the composer over the fees charged by Novello for performing Elgar works. In replying to Harty, Elgar's mind went on to the broader question of English names in music.

Marl Bank
18 APR.1932
My dear Harty:

Many thanks for your very kind letter: the question of fees is always in the way; I have taken the liberty of sending your letter to the publishers. The prejudice against anything *published* in England is still enormous; trifles published by Breitkopf are done without question: my name is old Saxon but it is not mispronounced by any nation & no foreigner can tell what nationality it is: the 'W' in Edward gives it away: if the name has a 'V' (Scandinavian) or a 'U' (German) there wd be no hesitation in at least *looking* at the music, but the 'W' settles it: my things in Germany had to be published by 'Ed:'—then they passed.

> Kindest regards
> Yours sincerely
> [Edward Elgar][11]

And he wrote to Novello:

Marl Bank
19 APR.1932
Dear Sirs:

With this I send a letter from Sir Hamilton Harty which explains itself; I do not think it necessary to say anything further as foreigners make every possible excuse to avoid English publishers: the things published by Breit-

---

[10] Letter book.   [11] Letter book.

kopf are played by everybody all over the world. I only send it so that you may know a conductor's view

> Believe me to be
> Yours faithfully
> [Edward Elgar][12]

The Novello performing fees were survivors from the antediluvian times before the World War, when the markets for serious music were different. Yet with his own income much reduced, Elgar must have opposed any attempt to reduce his proportion still further, and the Novello men knew this. To such protests, they could only send temporizing replies.

Since Keith Prowse had all the rights in the *Severn Suite* except in the original version for brass band, Elgar had made a new version for full orchestra in the autumn of 1930. On 17 March 1932 Fred Gaisberg of 'His Master's Voice' wrote to Elgar wishing to record this version of the music. Elgar passed the request to Keith Prowse:

18 MAR 1932

Dear Mr.vanLier:

In a letter from H.M.V;—to which company I am attached as I think you already know,—is the following:

'We should also be very pleased to hear if you are willing to record the *"SEVERN SUITE"* in its original form for orchestra. If you agree to do this recording we can fix a mutually convenient date.'

Have you done anything about the orchestral version of [the] Suite? I sent you the score for full orchestra last year.

> Kind regards
> Yrs sncy
> [Edward Elgar][13]

A proposed recording date of 7 April had to be postponed to give the publishers time to prepare the performing material for what would be the actual first performance of the orchestral version. The recording took place on 14 April in the new Abbey Road Studio No. 1

Elgar's seventy-fifth birthday on 2 June was followed six days later by the première of another new work. This was a choral ode in memory of Queen Alexandra with words by the Poet Laureate, John Masefield, beginning 'So many true Princesses who have gone . . .'. The occasion was the dedication of a statue of the late Queen by Sir Alfred Gilbert. Elgar conducted, and technically Keith Prowse were the publishers, though in fact the music was never printed. The firm produced vocal and military band parts, and was reimbursed by the Crown. A letter from Buckingham Palace, dated 10 June, conveyed a request from HM King George V for the original score of the Ode to be lodged at Windsor Castle.

---

[12] Letter book.   [13] Letter book.

42 & 43, Poland Street, London, W.1.
June 14th, 1932.

Dear Sir Edward,

Sometime ago I wrote you suggesting a selection of pieces for school orchestra. Do you think I shall be able to arrange my plans so that these works could be announced at the commencement of the Autumn term next September? Incidentally, this would be an opportune time to issue some compositions similar to 'CHANSON [DE] MATIN', 'CARISSIMA' etc. The press publicity accorded to the 'Ode' has been very considerable, so that we should also have this ready for next season. I should be glad, however, if Mr.Masefield could be induced to write alternative words for the second, third and fourth stanzas, as the original text would probably prevent choral societies from performing the work on any large scale. The original words, of course, would be printed together with any others that might be forthcoming, so that no objection could be made regarding such an arrangement. I think that this suggestion had, perhaps, better emanate from you, although if it is your wish, I will write direct to the Poet Laureate.

Kind regards.

> Yours sincerely,
> KEITH PROWSE & Co. LTD.
> S. Van Lier
> Gen. Manager, Publishing Dept.[14]

Worcester.
15th June, 1932.

Dear Mr. Van Lier,

I do not know how it will suit your plans but I should have six short pieces ready for you very soon for the school orchestra: these might be issued separately or as a suite—I think separately under separate titles.—but this you can settle when you see them. I mention this as you may like a preliminary notice to go out and can word it discreetly, non-comittally I mean.

I am sorry about the 'Ode'[.] I have been waiting for an answer to my letter which I wrote to Mr.Masefield quite a month ago but have heard nothing.

Would Mr.Herbert Smith and yourself lunch with me next Monday? I shall hope to be in town this day, arriving about 11-30—we could meet at my club or as you please. I hope I may have heard something by this time, Monday the 20th I mean.

I enclose a letter from the King, I shall have to send full score and the

---

¹⁴ Elgar Birthplace parcel 234.

piano arrangement—I have just acknowledged the letter saying the MSS shall be sent as soon as they can be spared. Please return the letter.

> Kind regards,
> Yours sincerely,
> E.E.[15]

The publishers accepted the luncheon date.

Marl Bank, Worcester.
17th [June 1932]
Dear van Lier:

Many thanks: I am glad Mr.Herbert Smith & yourself can lunch with me on Monday: unless anything interferes let us meet at Brooks's, St.James's Street at one o'clock.

I have recd. the enclosed letter from Mr.Masefield and send you a copy of my reply: it is, of course, impossible to think of the new stanza but we will talk this over on Monday.

> [Yours sincerely,
> Edward Elgar][16]

28th June, 1932.
Dear Sir Edward,

I am sending you to-day by registered post, the autograph score and our copy of the 'Queen Alexandra Memorial Ode'. Perhaps you will let me have the latter back after you have corrected it. Masefield has been written to with regard to the proposed alteration of the text, but up to date we have had no reply.

> Yours sincerely,
> p.p. KEITH PROWSE & Co. LTD.
> [L. Wane Daley]
> MANAGER. Educational Department.[17]

---

[15] This letter survives only in a typewritten transcript without paragraphing (Keith Prowse archives). The paragraphing here is editorial.

[16] Letter book.

[17] Letters such as this one, showing no address of origin and the signature in square brackets, have been taken from file copies in the firm's archives.

Marl Bank
5 JULY 1932
Dear van Lier:

I return the letter from the Society regarding Mr Masefield's ode: I think he might be asked to write an alternative version, not to *alter* it: of course the original ode wd. appear. It might be worthwhile to ask this

Kind rgds
Yours sincerely
[Edward Elgar][18]

If this request was made, Masefield remained obdurate. So the Queen Alexandra Ode remains to this day the least known of Elgar's mature works.

Correspondence with Novello continued, often with younger members of the firm. Alfred Littleton's son Alfred Joseph Brooke Littleton, known as Jack, had driven down to Worcester in a car loaded with Elgar's manuscript full scores, which had remained in the firm's archives for many years. In the bad economic climate of the early 1930s, Elgar had thought of selling some of them. (Fortunately these plans came to nothing, and the bulk of the Elgar manuscripts are now in the British Library.) Elgar sent Jack Littleton a signed photograph in gratitude, and the younger man sent effusive thanks.[19]

A week later Elgar acknowledged receipt of his latest royalty statement from Novello—£234.0.2 plus £114.9.0 in performing fees.

Marl Bank, Rainbow Hill, Worcester.
11 JUNE 1932
Dear Sirs:

I am obliged to you for the statement of acct. & the cheque: the amount of this is gratifying under present circumstances & I should like it to be understood that I am thankful to those concerned in the various departments. I quite understand the situation regarding L.Powell's affairs

Yours faithfy
Edward Elgar

The late Lionel Powell (1878–1932) had managed the London Symphony Orchestra among others, and the financial affairs of his firm were in temporary disarray owing to the difficult economic times. These affairs were shortly put right by Powell's successor Harold Holt.

On 14 and 15 July 1932 Elgar conducted a gramophone recording of the Violin Concerto with the sixteen-year-old Yehudi Menuhin as soloist. It was Menuhin's first performance of the work, and Elgar wrote to Novello about future plans and prospects:

[19] HWRO 705:445:4523.

Marl Bank, Worcester.
20th July 1932.
Dear Sirs,

Violin Concerto.

I have been rehearsing this work and have made records with the young artist Yehudi Menuhin who, as you will know, holds the most remarkable place amongst Violinists; he is desirous of playing the work a great deal, when possible with orchestra and, on his tour in U.S.A. etc. with piano. I assented to the suggested shortening of the '*tuttis*' for piano but naturally any question of permission to perform or fees did not arise. I conclude that his father or agent will communicate with you in due course if the idea is pursued. He is the most wonderful artist I have ever heard.

Yours faithfully,
Edward Elgar.

The reply, drafted by Henry Clayton, survives in a file copy at the firm's archives.

July 21st.1932
Dear Sir,

We are obliged by your letter of the 20th. instant and are much interested in reading your remarks about the young artist Yehudi Menuhin.

We have been in correspondence with his father with reference to placing at his disposal a full score and band parts of your *Violin Concerto.*

This has now been arranged on satisfactory terms, and he took the score and band parts with him to France at the end of last week. They will remain in his possession and will be available for his use wherever he may be.

Yours faithfully,
(X/EH.)

Throughout much of 1932 there was a protracted correspondence between Novello and the conductor of the Cape Town Orchestra, W. J. Pickerill, about a possible visit by Elgar to conduct in South Africa. This had arisen out of a suggestion from George Bernard Shaw when visiting Cape Town. Pickerill wrote direct to Elgar, who turned the matter over to Novello in the following letter:

Marl Bank, Rainbow Hill, Worcester.
1 JUNE 1932
Dear Sirs:

I received the enclosed letter to-day: you will see that the writer, whom I do not know, repeats what he said to Mr Bernard Shaw.

I wish you wd. write to this conductor: I am not sending any reply. You were kind enough to write, in years gone by, in answer to proposals such as those contained in the last paragraph: it wd. be very kind if you wd. say that I am prepared to consider the proposal of a visit

Yours very try
Edward Elgar

So Henry Clayton took up the matter on Elgar's behalf, writing Pickerill a long letter next day with the formidable acumen of earlier years, though Clayton was now seventy-seven. Pickerill had already written to Novello asking for the score and parts of Elgar's Symphonies 'on something like (to us at least) reasonable terms'. Clayton cited five earlier performances of the Elgar Symphonies in South Africa, running back to 1927, where no complaint had been made over fees. Then Clayton spelt matters out to Pickerill:

You should know that these great works could not earn anything in the nature of adequate remuneration for the Composer unless we were able to obtain substantial Fees for all performances of them. Consequently the bulk of all fees charged is handed over by us to Sir Edward Elgar.

In the earlier cases, out of seven and a half guineas a performance, Elgar had five.

Sir Edward Elgar asks us to say that he is prepared to consider a visit to South Africa, with a view to conducting performances of his works, if you will supply further particulars as to dates, and Towns. We presume Johannesburg and Durban, and the orchestras and conductors of those Towns, would participate in the scheme. That is an important item in the consideration; because Sir Edward would expect all his Travelling and Hotel Expenses to be paid, as well as a substantial fee for each Concert at which he would conduct his works. If it is desired that Sir Edward should conduct works other than his own, a list of those works should be supplied.

To sum up—Sir Edward is prepared to consider a visit to South Africa, but he cannot seriously entertain it unless a cut and dried scheme, giving the fullest possible details, is laid before him.

Yours faithfully
(X/EH)[20]

A copy of the letter to Pickerill was sent to Elgar, who replied to the firm:

---

[20] 2 June 1932 (copy in Novello archives).

Brooks's, St.James's Street, S.W.1.
3rd June 1932
Dear Sirs:

I am greatly obliged to you for writing to S.Africa about the symphonies & adding the excellent portion referring to a possible visit by me: this puts the matter in a business like way.

Yours very try
Edward Elgar

The result was a disagreeable letter from Pickerill to the firm. Later Elgar had another enquiry from Pretoria. He wrote to Novello:

Marl Bank, Worcester.
29th Sept 1932
Dear Sirs:

South Africa

I forget if you were kind enough to write to some enquirer about my going to S.A.

I have another long letter from *Pretoria* which I will not trouble you with: there are also newspaper articles & pars:—I think that it might save us all trouble if the matter was turned over to Ibbs & Tillett as it seems to be involved in complication

Yours very try
Edward Elgar

Novello thankfully agreed to the suggestion, and John Tillett took over the reins. Even he was unable to convince the South Africans that it would have to be done Elgar's way or not at all. And thus South Africa missed an opportunity that was not to come again.

Another proposal for Elgar to conduct came from Thomas Hammond, the secretary of the North Staffordshire Choral Society, which in 1896 had given the première performance of *King Olaf* under Elgar's baton. Thirty-six years later they wanted him to conduct them in *King Olaf* again—on 27 October 1932. Hammond approached Novello with the request, and Clayton sent the letter on to Elgar, who replied to the firm:

Royal Societies Club, St.James's Street, S.W.1.
31st Augt 1932   home to-day Worcester
Dear Sirs:

I am greatly obliged to you for your letter & shall be further obliged if you will be kind enough to write to the N.Staffs people: I am free on the 27th October, but the question of any possible fee is not mentioned: wd. you find out what the idea of the committee is?

Yours vy try
Edward Elgar

In answer to Clayton's enquiry, Hammond hinted at thirty to thirty-five guineas, citing hard economic times. Clayton replied that it would be inadvisable to submit any such offer to Elgar: the offer should be a hundred guineas, but he would submit seventy-five guineas, adding that the firm charged Elgar no commission for this service. Hammond replied that he would come and see Clayton, and Clayton made a note of the conversation for his files:

8.Sept:1932

I saw Mr.Hammond at 2.30 p.m. on Thursday the 8th.instant.

I had to listen to the usual tale of poverty in the Potteries, and the enthusiasm of the people for Elgar and his music, and a suggestion that Elgar should take into consideration all that Hanley had done for him.

I said that he must be approached with great tact and that it would probably annoy him to be told what anyone had done for him—and that I would prefer not to offer him less than 75 Guineas.

Mr.Hammond thought that his Committee might possibly offer 60 Guineas and he would tell the Committee who are meeting on Friday, September 9th. what I had said.

I replied that although, in my opinion, no offer less than 75 Guineas should be made, I would submit an offer of 60 Guineas, if the Committee insists.

H:R:C.

Hammond meanwhile approached Ibbs and Tillett as well, and induced John Tillett to take up their case. Tillett then wrote to Elgar saying that fifty guineas was 'the most they could go to.' Elgar wrote to Novello:

Marl Bank, Worcester.
10th Septr 1932

Dear Sirs:

I enclose a letter from Messrs. Ibbs & Tillett: you will see that the N.Staffs: people have written to that firm as well as to you.

I have written to Mr.Tillett saying that under the circumstances I wd. accept the low fee & that I was passing on the 'idea' to you. I shall be glad if *you* will conclude the matter—you see that Mr.Tillett suggests this course.

Yours vy try
Edward Elgar

And so it was arranged. It was the last booking in which Clayton was involved.

As always in these late years, the vital correspondence was with Keith Prowse. Their Educational Department manager Wane Daley had returned the score and parts of the orchestral *Severn Suite* for final correction. Then Elgar met him in London.

Worcester
10th June 1932
Dear Mr.Daley:

Many thanks for sending the score of The Severn Suite[.] I will see to the revision of the orch parts at once.

I was very glad to see you again & to have your views about the third Symphony.

> Kind regards
> Yours sincerely
> Edward Elgar[21]

Here was one of the very earliest references in Elgar's correspondence to the project which was to become the *cause célèbre* of his next and final year. The conversation presumably took place during Elgar's previous few days in London. And he himself must somehow have initiated the subject—unless the publisher's man had had the extraordinary forwardness to make such a suggestion to the Master of the King's Music. Whatever the course of the conversation, it is clear that Elgar was not annoyed.

His next project was more modest. Instead of Van Lier's suggestion for schools' orchestra pieces (which never appeared), Elgar took up a suggestion from a young Worcester schoolmaster, Stephen Moore, to write a unison song for children. Stephen Moore's father was vicar of Claines Church, where Elgar's grandparents were buried, and the young man had met the great composer through local connections. Elgar had written to him from Torquay on 9 April 1932: 'I will see about the Unison song when I return . . .'.[22] In due course he found two poems by the Victorian writer Charles Mackay, 'The Woodland Stream' and 'The Rapid Stream'. Stephen Moore recalled:

When I first asked Sir Edward if he would write a unison song for the Worcester City Schools' Music Festival, he agreed provided he could find suitable words. There was quite a gap until he let me know he had written two songs and would I come to his house and hear them. He played the two over and I selected [*The Woodland Stream*]. . . . At that time children left school at 14 so that part singing was more limited to secondary schools and this kind of unison writing was very acceptable.[23]

In the summer of 1932 Elgar sent both manuscripts to Keith Prowse, *The Woodland Stream* with a dedication to Stephen Moore. When the young man suggested making a simple arrangement for schools of 'It comes from the misty ages' from *The Banner of St George*, Elgar wrote to Novello to give approval.[24]

So far the prospect for a Third Symphony was a closely guarded secret. But at the Worcester Festival, during the first week in September 1932, Elgar himself referred to it in casual conversation. The newspapers got wind of it, and soon everyone was talking about the possibility. Another young man, Basil Maine, was writing Elgar's biography, and the two things came together in the mind of Wane Daley.

[21] Elgar Birthplace.
[22] MS in possession of Michael Toll.
[23] 2 Jan. 1971 to Sir Adrian Boult (photocopy in possession of the writer).
[24] 13 Sept. 1932 (Letter book).

13th September, 1932.

Dear Sir Edward,

As you are undoubtedly aware, Basil Maine is working on a new biography of your good self, which I understand will be published towards the end of the year. Naturally the author aims at making the book as informative and comprehensive as possible, so do you think we may pass on any information regarding the Third Symphony? I really believe it would be a pity to let the book be printed without some reference to this pending work, and any notes that we can let Maine have would be greatly valued.

Kind regards.

> Yours sincerely,
> p.p. KEITH PROWSE & CO. LTD.
> [L. Wane Daley]
> MANAGER. Educational Department.

Marl Bank, Worcester.
15th September 1932

Dear Mr Daley,

Thank you for your letter of the 13th; I am not aware of the date of the proposed publication and will communicate with Mr Basil Maine; if it is possible to say anything I will do so. All references to the symphony that I have seen are quite unwarranted.

> Kind regards
> Yours sincerely,
> Edward Elgar

P.S. Are you doing anything with the two small songs?[25]

The publishers had been investigating the copyright of Mackay's poems without definite result. On 27 September Van Lier came to lunch at Marl Bank, and next day he wrote that they would presume no copyright existed and go ahead with printing.[26] But Elgar had decided to make some revisions.

Marl Bank, Worcester.
29th Sept 1932

Dear van Lier: Here are the (slightly revised) unison songs: go ahead.

I also send two sketches: let me know *soon* if your experts can manage to decipher them & can make anything of them: they can be adapted to any 'arrgt.' you think fit.

Thank you for your letter: I was glad indeed to see you here.

> Yours sincerely
> Edward Elgar

---

[25] Elgar Birthplace.   [26] HWRO 705:445:4476.

The two sketches were entitled *Serenade* and *Adieu*. Elgar's remark about adapting them indicates a basic attitude about small 'popular' works. Even with such early works as *Salut d'amour* it is often difficult to determine which instrumentation was the original. This letter shows that, even in old age, Elgar retained the attitude of Bach, Handel, and Vivaldi for his small works—that they might be given almost any realization.

Elgar's letter was answered by Wane Daley:

30th September, 1932.

Dear Sir Edward,

In Mr. Van Lier's absence in Holland, I am acknowledging receipt of the two revised unison songs and the two little sketches. In addition to the piano version, we shall be issuing a violin and piano arrangement of the latter compositions which shall be put in hand as soon as possible. The songs we are going ahead with immediately.

Concerning 'The Severn Suite'.—Although Mr. Van Lier on his recent visit to you, mentioned that we had a piano arrangement in manuscript, he was under a misapprehension. Will it be of any use to Sir Ivor if I send along a Military Band conductor copy?

> Yours sincerely,
> p.p. KEITH PROWSE & CO. LTD.
> L. Wane Daley.
> MANAGER, Educational Department.[27]

The publishers were responding at last to Elgar's two-year-old suggestion that Atkins should arrange the *Severn Suite* for organ. Wane Daley posted the copy to Atkins on 3 October.

Elgar had been asked by Novello to make simple arrangements of *The Snow* and *Fly, Singing Bird* for two soprano voices and accompaniment. He wrote to the firm:

Marl Bank, Worcester.

13th Oct 1932

Dear Sirs:

With this I have the pleasure to send the arrgts for S.S. of the two part-songs. The second voice does not go below *C* except some *alternative* B's at the end of *The Snow*. In this form they will be quite effective

> Yours faithfy
> Edward Elgar

In an agreement dated the following day, Novello paid Elgar 30 guineas for the two arrangements.

Keith Prowse sent proofs of the unison songs, and a piano version of the *Serenade*.

---

[27] Elgar Birthplace.

Worcester
25th Oct 1932

Dear Mr.Daley: Here is the M.S. [of the piano *Serenade*] which I shd. think will do very well—I do not play the piano.

I sent back the 2nd proofs of the unison songs yesterday.

> Kind regards
> Yours sincerely
> Edward Elgar

26th October, 1932.

Dear Sir Edward,

Just a note to acknowledge receipt of the 'Serenade' and unison songs, and to enclose herewith the revised piano version of the 'Adieu'.

> Yours sincerely,
> p.p. KEITH PROWSE & CO. LTD.
> [L. Wane Daley]
> MANAGER. Educational Department.

In early December Elgar sent in another instrumental sketch entitled *Mina*, after his pet cairn.

5th December,1932.

Dear Sir Edward,

Just to acknowledge receipt of 'Mina' and to send you herewith the [orchestral] score of Henry Geehl's arrangement of the 'Serenade'.

> Yours sincerely,
> p.p. KEITH PROWSE & CO. LTD.
> [L. Wane Daley]
> MANAGER. Educational Department.

Worcester
9th Decr 1932

Dear Mr.Daley:

Here is the score which will do very well [—] thank Mr Geehl.

By the way there is an error which I hope is not in the P.F. etc arrgts: the last note on p.2. in the tune shd. be $\underline{\underline{D}}$ & also in corresponding places—pp 5, 10

> Kind regards
> Yours sincly
> Edward Elgar[28]

---

[28] Elgar Birthplace.

13th December, 1932.

Dear Sir Edward,

Many thanks for the score of the 'Serenade'. I have referred to the proof of the piano copy, and find that this coincides with your alterations in the score. I have also passed on to Mr.Geehl your appreciation of his good work. The orchestral arrangement is being put into the printer's hands straight away.

Kind regards.

> Yours sincerely,
> pp. KEITH PROWSE & CO. LTD.
> [L. Wane Daley]
> MANAGER. Educational Department.

That night the last of the old guard, Henry Clayton, died 'after a short & very trying illness' (as A. J. B. Littleton informed Elgar next day[29]). Yet Elgar himself was looking to the future. On the evening of 14 December, in the midst of BBC celebrations to mark Elgar's seventy-fifth birthday year, Sir Landon Ronald announced that the BBC had commissioned the Third Symphony. It would naturally be published by Keith Prowse. Next morning the papers were full of it, and Harold Brooke wrote from Novello—whose work for Elgar at that moment consisted of a separate reprint of the composer's programme note on *Falstaff*.

160 Wardour Street[,] W.1
Dec.15.'32

Dear Sir Edward,

Do you want to make any alteration in the wording of the Falstaff article? I send a copy for this purpose if you decide to do so. But I should think it might be printed exactly as it stands, with a line saying—Re-printed from the Musical Times of September 1913. Would a $\frac{1}{4}$ royalty satisfactorily represent your interest?

And so the 3rd Symphony is officially announced. I heard a good deal of talk about it at Worcester, but never a word from you! It is a bitter pill to swallow, that it will not appear here—or is there a chance that we are not finally excluded? How I hope that you may be able to give me the answer we all want!

> Yours sincerely
> Harold L.Brooke

We want to advertise the Falstaff essay in the January Musical Times. Time is very short—could you let me know the wording you would like for the title?[30]

At Keith Prowse all was jubilation. And the second instrumental piece, *Adieu*, had got as far as an orchestral version for submission to the composer. Wane Daley wrote:

[29] HWRO 705:445:4534.   [30] HWRO 705:445:4434.

15th December, 1932.

Dear Sir Edward,

Herewith the score of the 'Adieu' for your approval. The announcement in to-day's press regarding the coming appearance of the Third Symphony has whetted the appetites of the musical public to such a considerable extent, that we are being requested for more detailed information. If it is at all possible, for you to let me have a few particulars to pass on, such as the key, opus, movements etc., I shall be extremely grateful.

> Yours sincerely,
> pp. KEITH PROWSE & CO. LTD.
> [L. Wane Daley]
> MANAGER. Educational Department.

Elgar did not answer the question about the Symphony then, for all these matters were still under consideration.

Marl Bank, Worcester.
16 DEC.1932

Dear Mr Daley:

Can you send me a copy of the *Serenade* (PF Solo) with the DEDICATION on? any rough proof wd do. I am anxious to give it to Mr Austin on *Tuesday*

> Yrs ever
> Edward Elgar[31]

Elgar had dedicated the *Serenade* to his old helper with musical proof-reading, John Austin—'Friend and "Editor" for forty years'. A copy of the second proof was sent in time, and on 20 December, at one of the last meetings of the old Worcester Glee Club, Elgar presented it to Austin.

On the day after requesting the *Serenade* proof, Elgar sent to Keith Prowse a manuscript by one Descard-Delville. Was this a slyly chosen pseudonym to cover a fragment of early work?

Worcester
17th Decr 1932

Dear Mr Daley: It wd. [be] a merciful act if you wd very kindly deal with the enclosed M.S.—the writer of the letter lives here apparently & it wd. save much trouble if you wd return it (it looks worthless to me) with your firm's compliments & thanks & add that it was submitted to you by me. This wd. save endless letters etc.

> Kind regards
> Yrs sincy
> Edward Elgar

P.S. I enclose another of the children's unison songs[32]

This was a setting of Charles Mackay's *When Swallows Fly*.

[31] Elgar Birthplace.   [32] Elgar Birthplace.

20th December, 1932.

Dear Sir Edward,

Many thanks for the unison song 'When Swallows Fly'. I shall look after the MS by Descard-Delville, which is, as you remark, very poor stuff.

Your suggestions with regard to the scoring of the 'Adieu' are being carried out, and the orchestral arrangement of this and the 'Serenade' will I hope, be ready for issue early in the new year.

I am delighted to see that our good friends at the Old Vic are presenting the ballet version of the 'Nursery Suite' in their Christmas pantomime 'Hansel and Gretel'—it will add a most piquant flavour to Humperdinck. Personally I think this is one of Dolin's cleverest achievements, and indeed delicious entertainment.

Kind regards

> Yours sincerely,
> p.p. KEITH PROWSE & CO. LTD.
> [L. Wane Daley]
> MANAGER. Educational Department.

After Christmas, Daley wrote about *The Woodland Stream* and *The Rapid Stream*:

28th December, 1932.

Dear Sir Edward,

I must apologise for troubling you so soon after the holidays, but Messrs. G.Schirmer of New York have expressed an interest in your published Mackay settings, and suggest that these would be more readily accepted by American schools if second voice parts (optional) were added. This really means turning these into two-part songs, so if the proposal is agreeable to you, will you kindly see what can be done. I am enclosing copies of both songs in case you do not happen to have them by you.

> Yours sincerely
> p.p. KEITH PROWSE & CO. LTD.
> [L. Wane Daley]
> MANAGER. Educational Department.

Elgar made and sent the two-part arrangements, and they were given to the engravers.

28 DEC.1932

Dear van Lier:

When you did me the honour to lunch here you said something about lending me a short grand piano: Chappell's have done this for years & no doubt would continue to do so. The one of their make which I have now is worn & must be changed. Before writing to them I am asking what you feel about it: the instrument must be very small, the full length is about 4 ft. 8 in.—I don't see *why* you shd. lend me a piano but it wd. be very nice to have one.

Kindest regards
Yrs sincerely
[Edward Elgar][33]

1933–1934

Van Lier confirmed his offer, and Elgar replied:

Marl Bank, Rainbow Hill, Worcester.
9 JAN.1933
My dear Van Lier:

Thank you for your letter about the piano that I shall be very glad to have.

Bach's Toccata.

There has been an enquiry about recording this: I only wrote the *coda*—(still in MS. with Novello's)—the *coda* only is my property: I am not sure if the work will be recorded, if it is I shall naturally hear of it & will communicate with Keith Prowse: this is only to say that (in case it is mentioned [)] I have it in view 'that your firm will be interested'—nothing need be done now.

Kindest regards
Yours sincly
EE[1]

Sir Ivor Atkins had sent in his arrangement of the *Severn Suite* Op. 87 as Organ Sonata No. 2, and this was the subject of Wane Daley's first letter of the new year.

5th January, 1933.
Dear Sir Edward,

The 'Second Organ Sonata' is now in the engravers' hands. Subject to your approval, it is proposed to make this Op.87a, in place of Sir Ivor Atkins' designation 'after op.87'. Also, although the information 'edited by Ivor Atkins' will appear on the copy, I do not think it wise to state that it is

---

[33] Letter book.

[1] Letter book. The recording was made by 'His Master's Voice' with the London Symphony Orchestra under Albert Coates.

arranged by him. I am writing Sir Ivor by this post, who no doubt will appreciate our motive for the latter.

> Yours sincerely,
> p.p. KEITH PROWSE & CO. LTD.
> [L. Wane Daley]
> MANAGER. Educational Department.

Six days later a proof was available.

11th January, 193[3].

Dear Sir Edward,

I have sent you to-day under separate cover, first proofs of the 'Second Organ Sonata', as I presume you will wish to go through these with Sir Ivor Atkins. I have written to Sir Ivor advising him that this has been done.

When returning proofs, perhaps you will be good enough to include the autograph score of 'The Severn Suite' which, you will remember was sent you sometime ago for reference purposes.

Kind regards.

> Yours sincerely,
> pp. KEITH PROWSE & CO. LTD.
> L. Wane Daley
> MANAGER. Educational Department.[2]

Marl Bank
[16 or 17 Jan. 1933]

Dear Mr. Daley:

I will bring the M.S. Score 'Severn Suite' with me when I come up next week.

The proofs of the 'Organ Sonata' are here but Sir Ivor Atkins is away for a short time.

Thanks for the piano copies of the two little pieces.

> Kind rgrds
> Yours sincerely
> [Edward Elgar][3]

On 24 January Elgar was to go to London for a Musicians Company dinner. But in the event he posted the *Severn Suite* score to Daley, who replied:

26th January, 1933.

Dear Sir Edward,

Many thanks for the full score of the 'Severn Suite' received to-day. I had delayed sending you proofs of 'When Swallows Fly' and the two part

---

[2] Elgar Birthplace. The year was typewritten as '1932', a typical beginning-of-year error.
[3] Letter book.

versions of the streamlet songs, as I was under the impression that you were coming up to town. These are being despatched to-day.

The Second organ sonata is being advertised as ready for issue during February, as a number of enquiries have been made for this work.

Kind regards.

> Yours sincerely,
> p.p. KEITH PROWSE & CO. LTD.
> [L. Wane Daley]
> MANAGER. Educational Department.

There had been another letter from Elkin, still bravely trying to revive the larger Elgar works he published.

20, Kingly Street, Regent Street, London, W.1.
25th January, 1933.

My dear Elgar,

You may have seen that Stoll is about to start a season of Ballet at the Coliseum. I am wondering whether you would like me to communicate with him, suggesting your 'FAN BALLET'. If you think it is suitable for a place like the Coliseum, I will with pleasure, put the idea forward. In that case I shall be glad if you will please let me know about how long it plays, and if you have a copy of the scenario you might send me that also.

I am very glad indeed to read that before long we are to have a Third Symphony from you. I have often much enjoyed Numbers One and Two (especially, if I may say so, the latter) and I look forward with the greatest pleasure to hearing their successor.

> With kindest regards,
> Yours sincerely,
> W.W.A.Elkin[4]

No performance of *The Sanguine Fan* resulted then. In fact it was to be more than forty years before it could be seen again—among other places at The Coliseum.

Early in February the Second Organ Sonata seemed to be approaching publication.

7th February, 1933.

Dear Sir Edward,

I am enclosing herewith a 'pull' of the organ sonata title page. Will you kindly confirm the Opus, as we are anxious to get the work on the market. The additional enclosure is one received from Weingartner.

> Yours sincerely,
> p.p. KEITH PROWSE & CO. LTD.
> [L. Wane Daley]
> MANAGER. Educational Department.

Felix Weingartner was conducting the *Nursery Suite*.

[4] Elgar Birthplace parcel 241.

Marl Bank, Rainbow Hill, Worcester.
19th Feb 1933

Dear Mr. Wayn-Daley: [*sic*]

Sir Ivor Atkins is wondering what has happened to the proofs of the organ
sonata: he has gone to Ireland so perhaps you will let me know

☞ I shall be at the *Langham* Hotel on Tuesday until Friday & shd.
be glad to see you or Mr. van Lier.

I want to make a baritone song (with orch) of *Tarantella* poem so named
by Hilaire Belloc: Can you find out who publishes the poem; if we can get the
use of it for music & if it is already set.

Can you also find out if there is any copyright in Col.*John Hay*'s poems
(U.S.A. author)—my copy is 1876

> Kind regards
> Yrs sincy
> Edward Elgar[5]

As long ago as 1885 Elgar had set a poem by John Hay in the song *Through the Long
Days*. At that time he had obtained permission from the distinguished American
himself: Hay had been private secretary to Abraham Lincoln and his biographer, and
later United States Ambassador to Great Britain. He had died in 1905.

22nd February, 1933.

Dear Sir Edward,

I am enclosing herewith the piano solo arrangement of 'Mina', and a copy
of the Second Organ Sonata.

As mentioned over the telephone, I have been in communication with
Belloc's agent, who stated that the author would only allow us use of the
words provided all royalties were equally divided. This of course, is useless,
but we are negotiating further with a view to getting Belloc to accept a
nominal fee for the use of his poems.

Copyright still exists in the works of Col.John Hay, so if you will let me
know which poem you are setting to music, I shall be able to approach the
publishers.

> Yours very truly,
> p.p.KEITH PROWSE & CO. LTD.
> [L. Wane Daley]
> MANAGER, Educational Department.

Negotiations with Belloc's agent were unsatisfactory.

---

[5] Elgar Birthplace.

42 & 43, Poland Street, London, W.1.
February 24th, 1933.

Dear Sir Edward,

The following is a copy of the letter I have received this morning with regard to Belloc's 'Tarantella'—

'Thank you for your letter of yesterday's date with reference to Mr.Belloc's "Tarantella." I am sorry that Sir Edward Elgar cannot see his way to sharing his royalties with Mr.Belloc. I am afraid that I cannot agree to accept so small a fee as ten guineas for all rights in this proposed musical setting as Mr.Belloc's share and suggest that Sir Edward retains two-thirds of all monies that may accrue from the sale of the song and pay one-third to Mr.Belloc. I shall be glad to hear what he thinks of this proposal.'

The above is from A.D.Peters, Literary Agent for Mr.Belloc.

Will you kindly let me know if the suggested arrangement of royalties is acceptable to you.

With kind regards.

> Yours sincerely,
> pp. KEITH PROWSE & CO.,LTD.,
> S. Van Lier
> Gen.Manager, Publishing Dept.[6]

Marl Bank, Rainbow Hill, Worcester.
9th March 1933.

Dear Mr Daley,

I have been laid up with a cold and regret that your letter of the 22nd [*sic*] February has remained unanswered so long.

We will drop Belloc. As to Col.John Hay;—this can remain in abeyance for the time being—now I know we can get permission to use the words I can go on with the composition.

I think you ought to have sent a final proof to Sir Ivor: I have given him my copy of the Sonata: please send me another.

> Kind regards,
> Yours sincerely,
> Edward Elgar[7]

11th March, 1933.

Dear Sir Edward,

I am sorry to hear of your indisposition, and hope that you have now fully recovered. I called at the Langham Hotel on the Friday morning during your visit here, but unfortunately you had left for Worcester a short time before.

It is a pity that we have to discard the Belloc project, as this would have been a magnificent proposition for a singer like Keith Falkner.

With regard to the Organ Sonata, it was my impression that a second

---

[6] Elgar Birthplace parcel 234.   [7] Elgar Birthplace.

proof had been sent to Sir Ivor. However, I despatched a sale copy immediately the work was returned. I must get in touch with the postal authorities at this end, and see what has happened, as Sir Ivor must have thought us extremely discourteous.

Two copies of the Sonata have been addressed to you to-day so should any misprints exist, perhaps you would let me have the corrected copy back for when we reprint. The work is creating a great amount of interest, and in case you have not see[n] it, I am enclosing a copy of the 'Daily Telegraph' review.

Kind regards.

> Yours sincerely
> p.p. KEITH PROWSE & CO. LTD.
> L. Wane Daley
> MANAGER. Educational Department.[8]

The first edition of the Sonata, with green covers, was nearly sold out by May.

9th May, 1933.

Dear Sir Edward,

Would you kindly let me know [i]f any corrections are needed in the Organ Sonata, as this work is due for reprinting. Perhaps you will be good enough to go through the copy which is being sent you by this post.

Is it likely that the 'Third Symphony' will be included in this session's Promenade Concert Programme, or the B.B.C.'s Symphony Concerts? We have numerous enquiries from orchestral societies regarding the work, and wondered if it were possible to give them any definite information.

I understand that Herbert Dawson will be recording the Organ Sonata for His Master's Voice. The 'Serenade' has already been done by this company and Decca.

Kind regards.

> Yours sincerely,
> [L. Wane Daley]
> MANAGER. Educational Department.

Herbert Dawson (b. 1890) had given the Second Sonata its première for the Organ Music Society on 30 March.

The Rutland Arms Hotel, Newmarket   (Home tomorrow[)]
11th May 1933

Dear Mr Wane Daley: I will look at the Sonata as soon as I return

As to the Sym:—it is too big (or will be D.V.) for the Promenade

---

[8] Elgar Birthplace parcel 234.

Concerts—I think there will be a special 'introduction' of it.

I hope to begin to send portions of the full score &c very shortly

Kind regards
Yrs siny
Edward Elgar[9]

But when Elgar returned to Worcester, Atkins was away, so there was a little delay over the Second Organ Sonata.

Marl Bank, Rainbow Hill, Worcester.
22 MAY 1933

Dear Mr Wayne Daley [*sic*]:

Sir Ivor returned on Saty & we immediately looked at the Sonata[.] Here it is. There is nothing much to correct.

p 17 wd. look better if the Cadenza was small—but that wd mean a new plate

Kind regards
Yrs sny
Edward Elgar

Please send Sir Ivor an[othe]r copy when ready[10]

The Cadenza following the Fugue expanded the original transition to the work's Coda with inserted virtuoso arpeggios devised by Atkins. The page was re-engraved with these arpeggios printed in small notes, and a proof was sent to Elgar on 27 May.

That day Elgar flew to Paris to conduct the Violin Concerto for Yehudi Menuhin. He returned on 2 June to find congratulations from many (including Van Lier[11]) not only on his birthday but on receiving the GCVO. On 5 June Elgar returned the Cadenza proof. The second edition of the Sonata, with the re-engraved Cadenza, was issued in a buff cover.

On 14 June Wane Daley sent brass and military band arrangements of *Adieu* for Elgar's approval.

Worcester
15 JUNE 1933

Dear Mr Daley:

Many thanks: the arrgts *look* all right—I am not an expert in reading these wind-scores.

Kind regards
Yrs siny
· Edward Elgar[12]

On that day the managing director of Keith Prowse wrote to Elgar to remind him that their three-year agreement was nearing its end.

[9] Elgar Birthplace.
[10] Elgar Birthplace.
[11] HWRO 705:445:4264.
[12] Elgar Birthplace.

159, New Bond Street, London, W.1.
15th June, 1933.

My dear Sir Edward Elgar,

Mr. Van Lier reminded me some weeks ago that the arrangement between yourself and my Company was shortly expiring. Unfortunately since then I have been away for some weeks from business, being laid up after an operation for appendicitis. I am glad to say that I am fully recovered now and back in harness.

I sincerely hope that the agreement which I made with you in 1930 has been satisfactory from your point of view. As you are only too well aware, we have been passing through very difficult times and this has seriously affected the sale of music. I do feel that if conditions had been more normal the results would have been very much better.

I should be very glad to hear from you as to whether you are prepared to continue the arrangement on the same lines, and if you are I would suggest that the arrangement as set out in our agreement dated 24th June 1930 be extended for a further period of twelve months from the first day of July, 1933. Needless to say, I sincerely hope that we can continue on these lines and that the very happy relations which have existed during these last three years may be continued for many years to come.

Trusting that you are in the best of health and not overworking on your new great work, which I expect is now nearing completion,

> With kind regards,
> Yours very sincerely,
> Herbert Smith[13]

In the third paragraph, Elgar underlined Smith's words about extending the agreement for twelve months from 1 July 1933, and wrote in the margin 'yes'. He sent a letter of acceptance (now missing), and Smith responded:

159, New Bond Street, London, W.1.
19th June, 1933.

My dear Sir Edward Elgar,

Very many thanks for your nice letter of the 17th instant. It is very good to hear from you that you are so happy with us under existing conditions, also to receive your expression of appreciation of the various people in my Publishing Department.

With regard to the continuance of our arrangement, I will just have a word with my solicitor as to the best means of giving effect to this and I imagine

---

[13] Elgar Birthplace parcel 234.

that a few words by way of an endorsement added to the present agreement will meet the case.

> With kindest regards,
> Yours very sincerely,
> Herbert Smith[14]

Four days later Smith sent a draft of the words to be added. Elgar sketched the following reply:

Marl Bank, Worcester
24th June 1933
My dear Mr.Herbert Smith:

Thank you for the draft 'rider' to our existing agreement: I quite approve of it & return it with the original agreement. If you like to make the new arrangements for two years I am quite agreeable.

> Kind regards
> Yours sny
> Edward Elgar[15]

But on second thought he struck out the last sentence and returned the draft rider as it stood. On 28 June the new agreement was sent for Elgar's signature, and the following day Elgar signed and returned it.

Soon there was further publishing activity.

3rd July, 1933.
Dear Sir Edward,

I am troubling you once more with a Brass and Military Band arrangement, this time of the 'Serenade'.

The Gramophone Company has just issued records of the above and the 'Adieu', also Herbert Dawson's record of the Organ Sonata. The latter work is spendidly recorded, the 'Fugue' sounding particularly fine. If you do not already possess these discs, perhaps you will let me know if you would like them sent on.

It is a great pity that they have held up the 'Severn Suite' in its orchestral form for so long. However, we keep agitating them from this end so perhaps we may look forward to seeing it shortly.

Kind regards.

> Yours sincerely,
> p.p. KEITH PROWSE & CO. LTD.
> [L. Wane Daley]
> MANAGER. Educational Department.

The *Severn Suite*, recorded in April 1932 on five sides, was still awaiting a 'coupling' for the sixth side. In the event, it was not issued until 1934.

---

[14] Elgar Birthplace parcel 234.   [15] Elgar Birthplace parcel 234.

Marl Bank, Worcester:
4 JULY 1933
Dear Mr.Daley:

Many thanks. I return the wind scores: they look all right—very good [—]
but I am no judge of this sort of thing.

I should like to have the records you name in your letter

Kind rgrds
Yrs sny
Edward Elgar[16]

Novello again asked him to make simple arrangements of earlier works. On 12 July
they had requested a unison version of 'As torrents in summer' from *King Olaf*. Elgar
replied:

Worcester
15th July 1933
Dear Sirs:

Many thanks for your letter of the 12th: I think a satisfactory, simple
version of 'As torrents' can be made as a unison song. The key wd. be D. and
I propose to omit two bars, as indicated in the enclosed copy. If this is
agreeable to you I wd. let you have the MS. in a few days. I propose ten
guineas as a fee

Yours very try
Edward Elgar

Let me have the copy back

It was agreed, and on 19 July Elgar sent in his manuscript.

Then Novello asked for two-part arrangements of *My Love Dwelt in a Northern
Land, How Calmly the Evening*, and *Weary Wind of the West*. Elgar responded:

Worcester
29th July 1933
Dear Sirs:

With this I send the three suggested arrgts. for two voices. Naturally these
things are not easy to remodel satisfactorily in this combination. If they are
useful for your purpose I leave you to settle the fee. If they will not 'do'—
W[aste]—P[aper] B[asket].

Yours very truly
Edward Elgar

Novello paid him thirty guineas for the three. Returning the proofs in August, Elgar
sent a memorandum:

---

[16] Elgar Birthplace.

Mem: There are a few *alterations* in the 3 pt songs which will naturally affect the Sol-fa transcriptions

EE

With this courteous attention to minor detail, Elgar's correspondence of nearly half a century with his greatest publisher ended.

With Keith Prowse matters moved forward. For the Hereford Festival of 1927, Elgar had written his short *Civic Fanfare*. That was before his association with Keith Prowse. But when the manuscript of the unpublished *Fanfare* was wanted again for the 1933 Festival, Elgar thought it might have gone to the Keith Prowse files. On 3 August Wane Daley reported that it was not there. Thereupon Elgar rescored the *Fanfare*, using an unpublished gramophone record of the première performance as a guide. He sent the new score to Keith Prowse.

Marl Bank, Worcester
7th Augt. 1933
Dear Mr Daley:

Will you please have orchl. parts made (for the Hereford Festival) as soon as possible: the '*Fanfare*' is a prelude to the National Anthem: it was performed six years ago: I do not think it is worth publishing so you must charge *me* for copying the parts.

Kind rgrds
Yrs sincly
Edward Elgar

For *Hereford Festival*

No Violins
one each wind & percussion & organ
One each Viola
      ,,   Cello
      ,,   C.Basso
(I will let you know the number of duplicate Va., Cello & C.B. later)
['3' was later pencilled after each]

Number each bar as in score in red ink

EE

9th August, 1933.
Dear Sir Edward,

I expect to be able to send you early next week the required parts to the 'Civic Fanfare', together with a copy of the score. Although such a work, owing to its character, may not be a commercial proposition from a publishing viewpoint, it should be very useful in connection with films, where a particular situation calls for a fanfare. As the composition is intended as a prelude to the National Anthem, nothing of course, would be done in this matter without your sanction.

I do hope that the newspaper reports of your being indisposed are entirely without foundation.

Kind regards.

Yours sincerely,
p.p. KEITH PROWSE & CO. LTD.
[L. Wane Daley]
MANAGER. Educational Department.

The film suggestion was shortly to be taken further. Elgar was not feeling well, but it was put down to the extremely hot summer weather.

Three days later Daley sent the copy parts for the *Civic Fanfare*, which it had been decided Keith Prowse would officially 'publish'. Elgar invited Daley to the London rehearsals for the Festival, to be held at the Royal College of Music. Daley replied:

15th August, 1933.

Dear Sir Edward,

I shall certainly come along to the R.C.M. on the 30th.

If it is at all likely that you will be able to use the parts of 'Fanfare' on any future occasion, do not trouble to return them, for I am having an additional set copied.

The usual assignment will follow, and under separate cover I am having sent you a new record by Alfred Campoli of the 'Serenade'.

Kind regards.

Yours sincerely,
p.p. KEITH PROWSE & CO. LTD.
[L. Wane Daley]
MANAGER. Educational Department.

Ten days later the printed copies of the new band arrangements were available.

25th August, 1933.

Dear Sir Edward,

Herewith copies of the Military and Brass Band arrangements of 'Serenade' and 'Adieu'. Perhaps I may trouble you to sign and return the P[erforming] R[ight] S[ociety] letters enclosed.

Yours sincerely,
p.p. KEITH PROWSE & CO. LTD.
[L. Wane Daley]
MANAGER. Educational Department.

Worcester
26 AUG. 1933

Dear Mr. Daley:

Here are the *P.R.S.* letters duly signed.

'Mina'—(temporary title) was returned to me—I hope to send the full score with Solo *Celesta* (as I suggested to Mr van Lier) in a few days

Kind rgrds
Yrs sny
Edward Elgar

Wane Daley attended the RCM rehearsals on 30 August, and wrote next day:

31st August, 1933.

Dear Sir Edward,

I am sorry that we were only able to have a few fleeting words at the R.C.M. yesterday. I hesitated to intrude further as the three hours rehearsal must have been very taxing for you.

The 'Fanfare' is such a fitting prelude to the National Anthem, that I wondered if it would be possible to effect an arrangement with the powers that be, whereby the work should always precede the latter on official occasions. In the event of such a proposal achieving fruition, we could then go ahead with the Military Band version.

Kind regards.

Yours sincerely,
p.p. KEITH PROWSE & CO. LTD.
[L. Wane Daley]
MANAGER. Educational Department.

But Elgar's attention was elsewhere in the days before the Hereford Festival. Adrian Boult, as director of music for the BBC (who had commissioned the Third Symphony), had suggested the possibility of recording the new Symphony for the gramophone in advance of its public première, so as to have the records in the hands of critics for their prior study. Elgar had written about this to Van Lier, who replied:

42 & 43, Poland Street, London, W.1.
August 29th, 1933.

Dear Sir Edward Elgar,

Many thanks for your letter of the 19th inst., which I found awaiting me on my return from holiday. I had a very pleasant time in the South of France and we were burnt up there as well.

With regard to the suggestion of recording the 3rd Symphony before it is performed, Mr.Herbert Smith tells me that he has been in touch with Mr.Garvin Brown of the B.B.C. and he is of the opinion that it would be best to have the performance before the work is released for recording. However, there is a lot to be said for the suggestion of Dr.Boult and yourself, but I feel it will be a matter for you to really arrange with the B.B.C. I understand that the performance would be about May next year.

I would like to come and see you sometime next week as there are a few matters I wish to talk over with you. Any day that is convenient for you I can arrange to come.

With kind regards.

> Yours sincerely,
> pp. KEITH PROWSE & CO., LTD.,
> S. Van Lier
> Gen.Manager, Publishing Dept.[17]

The following week brought the Hereford Festival. Van Lier lunched at Marl Bank on 14 September. They discussed the possibility of writing or arranging music for the film *Colonel Blood*. The commission was announced in the papers, but only one letter survives in the files about it.

42 & 43, Poland Street, London, W.1.
Oct. 2nd, 1933.
Dear Sir Edward Elgar,

With further reference to the film production 'COLONEL BLOOD,' I am now enclosing draft agreement for your perusal.

Will you kindly return it to me at your early convenience with any suggestions and I will then submit it to the Film Company for their approval.

You will note that the Film Company will only have the exclusive right of the use of this music for this film and that the performing, mechanical and all other rights will be our property under the General Agreement existing between us.

I am pleased to be able to tell you that the Film Company have agreed to pay the additional £100 as this Company's commission, to which I referred in my previous letter.

With kind regards.

> Yours sincerely,
> pp. KEITH PROWSE & CO., LTD.,
> S. Van Lier
> Gen.Manager, Publishing Dept.[18]

None of this was to come about, for five days later Elgar entered a nursing home for an operation, and it was discovered that he had inoperable cancer. Towards the end of October there seemed to be some remission—just enough, it might be, to hope that the uncompleted Third Symphony might still be saved. Perhaps it was in hopes of such encouragement that Wane Daley wrote his last letter in the files.

[17] Elgar Birthplace parcel 234.   [18] Elgar Birthplace parcel 234.

31st October 1933.

Dear Sir Edward,

If you are still in the early stages of convalescing, please do not bother to reply to the matter out-lined below.

In brief, I have suggested to Mr. Van Lier that it would be a good plan to issue an autograph subscription edition of the full score of the Third Symphony. This would be bound in roan or morocco, limited to 250 copies, and be priced at £10.10.

Such a project, would I believe, be extremely successful.

Before going ahead with it however, I should like to know if the proposal is agreeable to you.

With best wishes for a rapid recovery, and kindest regards.

> Yours sincerely,
> p.p. KEITH PROWSE & CO. LTD.
> L. Wane Daley.
> MANAGER. Educational Department.[19]

It was a final throw of the dice in the brave game this old but small firm of publishers had played against time to bring the aged composer back to full creative activity. The plan for the limited edition shows the narrow margin by which the game was lost. It is true that the sketches Elgar left represent nothing like the amount of music he tried over again and again for friends through the earlier months of 1933. Much if not most of the basic thematic material was there—waiting for final insight as to patterns and relationships. Elgar had begun to score, suggesting that he was at least on the threshold of decision. After putting off proposals for a première in 1933, he had enthusiastically accepted the BBC proposal for a first performance in May 1934. If the illness had not gradually crept over him?—even if the summer of 1933 had not been so uncomfortably hot to distract and discomfort him? Never could the desire to rewrite history be more compelling.

Elgar lingered, without being able to complete the Symphony or even score the tiny *Mina*, until 23 February 1934. The last word belongs to one of the younger generation in the firm at the centre of this correspondence, Novello. Harold Brooke wrote to Elgar's daughter two days after her father's death.

5, Freeland Road, Ealing Common W.5.
Feb.25.'34

Dear Carice,

Among the many hundreds of letters you must have received, I hope you may perhaps find time to read this one—but I beg you not to answer it. It is rather more than an ordinary expression of sympathy that I would send. In music your father meant everything to me, and I shall always account it the highest privilege that I was admitted to his circle of acquaintances, and perhaps friends. Did he know, I wonder, how much at least two of us, besides Nimrod, who came to know him through commerce, venerated him for the

---

[19] Elgar Birthplace parcel 234.

beauty he made? I hope so. For Jack [Littleton] and I are of one mind in our admiration, and proud that we knew it earlier than many others, all thanks to Nimrod.

For me—le Roi est mort—and there is no answering cry of Vive le Roi! My wife joins me in sending you a message of sympathy, and

> I am
> Yours very sincerely
> Harold L.Brooke[20]

[20] HWRO 705:445:675.

INDEX

by Frederick Smyth

For obvious reasons, index entries for Elgar and his wife and daughter, Jaeger and his wife, Alfred Littleton, Clayton, and certain other persons are selective and generally omit references to purely domestic or routine events. Casual and unimportant references to Elgar's major works have also been restricted.

The firm of Novello is very frequently mentioned from about 1897. The principal entries relating to the firm up to 1925, when correspondence became formal and intermittent, will be found under the names of their directors and staff and, of course, under titles of the works with which they were concerned. The correspondence between Jaeger and Elgar (1897–1908) is between pages 48 and 717. Matters therein referred to are indexed under relevant headings.

Elgar's compositions are indexed alphabetically under his name, as are arrangements by him and unfulfilled projects and proposals.